AUTOBIOGRAPHICAL WRITINGS

SAMUEL LANGHORNE CLEMENS was born on November 30, 1835, in Florida, Missouri, a village about forty miles southwest of Hannibal, the Mississippi River town that he would later celebrate, writing as Mark Twain. In 1853 he left home to work as an itinerant printer and four years later became a steamboat pilot on the Mississippi. With his piloting career cut short by the outbreak of the Civil War in 1861, he went west and prospected and worked as a journalist in Nevada and California. In February 1863 he signed the pseudonym "Mark Twain" for the first time in an article for Virginia City's *Territorial Enterprise*. His trip to Europe and the Holy Land in 1867 became the basis of his first major book, *The Innocents Abroad* (1869), which made him famous. *Roughing It* (1872), his account of experiences in the Far West, was followed by a satirical novel, *The Gilded Age* (1873), *Sketches: New and Old* (1875), *The Adventures of Tom Sawyer* (1876), *A Tramp Abroad* (1880), *The Prince and the Pauper* (1881), *Life on the Mississippi* (1883), and his masterpiece, *Adventures of Huckleberry Finn* (1885). In 1891, he was compelled by mounting expenses to move his family abroad. In 1895–96, he undertook a round-the-world lecture tour to pay off creditors of his bankrupt publishing firm and then remained in Europe until 1900. His fortunes mended, he returned to America and found himself celebrated—not only for heroically pulling himself out of debt but also for his uncompromising stands against injustice and imperialism. He died in his final home in Redding, Connecticut, on April 21, 1910.

R. KENT RASMUSSEN has written and edited eight other books on Mark Twain, including the forthcoming *Dear Mark Twain: Letters from His Readers,* as well as many books on other subjects. He is best known for his award-winning *Mark Twain A to Z* (recently revised as the two-volume *Critical Companion to Mark Twain*) and *The Quotable Mark Twain*. He holds a doctorate in history from UCLA and recently retired from his job as a reference book editor in Southern California.

MARK TWAIN

Autobiographical Writings

Edited with an Introduction by
R. KENT RASMUSSEN

PENGUIN BOOKS

PENGUIN BOOKS

Published by the Penguin Group

Penguin Group (USA) Inc., 375 Hudson Street, New York, New York 10014, U.S.A.

Penguin Group (Canada), 90 Eglinton Avenue East, Suite 700, Toronto,
Ontario, Canada M4P 2Y3 (a division of Pearson Penguin Canada Inc.)

Penguin Books Ltd, 80 Strand, London WC2R 0RL, England

Penguin Ireland, 25 St Stephen's Green, Dublin 2, Ireland (a division of Penguin Books Ltd)

Penguin Group (Australia), 250 Camberwell Road, Camberwell,
Victoria 3124, Australia (a division of Pearson Australia Group Pty Ltd)

Penguin Books India Pvt Ltd, 11 Community Centre, Panchsheel Park, New Delhi - 110 017, India

Penguin Group (NZ), 67 Apollo Drive, Rosedale, Auckland 0632,
New Zealand (a division of Pearson New Zealand Ltd)

Penguin Books (South Africa) (Pty) Ltd, 24 Sturdee Avenue,
Rosebank, Johannesburg 2196, South Africa

Penguin Books Ltd, Registered Offices: 80 Strand, London WC2R 0RL, England

First published in Penguin Books 2012

1 3 5 7 9 10 8 6 4 2

Introduction and selection copyright © R. Kent Rasmussen, 2012
All rights reserved

LIBRARY OF CONGRESS CATALOGING-IN-PUBLICATION DATA
Twain, Mark, 1835-1910.
[Autobiography]
Autobiographical writings / Mark Twain ; edited with an introduction R. Kent Rasmussen.
p. cm.—(Penguin classics)
Includes bibliographical references.
ISBN 978-0-14-310667-8 (pbk.)
1. Twain, Mark, 1835-1910. 2. Authors, American—19th century—Biography.
I. Rasmussen, R. Kent. II. Title.
PS1331.A2 2012
818'.4'0924—dc23
2012003123

Printed in the United States of America
Set in Sabon

Contents

Introduction

Samuel Langhorne Clemens, the man best known to the world as Mark Twain, is one of the most autobiographical of American writers. His presence can be felt in almost everything he wrote. Overtly or through proxies, he placed himself in most of his essays and nonfiction books and built much of his fiction around his experiences. He was ever his own favorite subject and his thoughts often went back to his own past, so it should not be surprising that he eventually turned to composing autobiography—initially by hand and later by dictation. During the last years of his life, his daily autobiographical dictations* were becoming an obsession. According to his autobiography itself, he told his close friend William Dean Howells, "if I should talk to the stenographer two hours a day for a hundred years, I should still never be able to set down a tenth part of the things which have interested me in my lifetime." Moreover, his autobiography would not be a mere book but an entire library—and not a small one, either:

> if I should live long enough, the set of volumes could not be contained merely in a city, it would require a State, and . . . there would not be any multi-billionaire alive, perhaps, at any time during its existence who would be able to buy a full set, except on the instalment plan.

* In the present volume the term "autobiographical writings" is used in a broad sense to encompass Mark Twain's daily dictations, which actually made up the great bulk of his formal autobiography. After a stenographer typed up his dictations, he hand-corrected them on paper.

In all this, he was, of course, exaggerating. However, he was serious about composing a big autobiography. By the time he died in early 1910, the manuscripts constituting what he regarded as his *formal* autobiography had grown to nearly one-half million words. He led a long and complex life and had much to tell. Moreover, the history of his attempts to write his autobiography is a long and complex story in itself.

BACKGROUND

Mark Twain's career as a professional writer commenced during the early 1860s, when he worked as a reporter for Nevada and California newspapers and contributed stories and sketches to literary magazines. By the time he left the Far West at the end of 1866, he had built a modest reputation as a skillful humorist but was still several years away from thinking of himself as an author. That transformation began with the publication in 1869 of *The Innocents Abroad*, his best-selling account of his travels in Europe and the Holy Land with the *Quaker City* steamship excursion two years earlier. The travel letters he wrote for newspapers during that trip and the book that grew out of those letters earned him a national reputation. Publication of *Roughing It* (1872), about his experiences in the Far West during the early 1860s, completed his transformation from journalist to author. His reputation then grew steadily, as he published *The Gilded Age* (1873), *The Adventures of Tom Sawyer* (1876), *A Tramp Abroad* (1880), *The Prince and the Pauper* (1881), *Life on the Mississippi* (1883), *Adventures of Huckleberry Finn* (1884/1885), *A Connecticut Yankee in King Arthur's Court* (1889), and other books, along with a steady stream of magazine sketches, short stories, and essays. Meanwhile, he further enhanced his reputation by undertaking a number of extended lecture tours. Even before he reached the age of forty, he had an international reputation and was regarded as an important American author—albeit one who was best known as a humorist.

Mark Twain's interest in writing autobiography began relatively early. In 1870, for example, he wrote about the disastrous effect of the Tennessee land that his father had bequeathed to his family. It was a subject to which he would return several times more than thirty-five years later. In the meantime, he made fictional use of that part of his family's history in *The Gilded Age*, a partly autobiographical novel he coauthored with his Hartford, Connecticut, neighbor Charles Dudley Warner. In 1877, he wrote a brief memoir about the time he spent in Florida, Missouri, as a child. Through the next three decades, he made other attempts at starting an autobiography, but none of them succeeded in holding his interest. The first major breakthrough came in 1904, while he was staying in Florence, Italy, where he had taken his family for the sake of his wife's health. Using his secretary Isabel Lyon as a scribe, he discovered that he could efficiently dictate his autobiography. Lyon was not a proficient stenographer, but she was an appreciative listener who satisfied Mark Twain's need for an audience. Raised in a tradition of oral storytelling, he was a natural speaker.

On January 16, 1904, Mark Twain wrote excitedly from Florence to William Dean Howells:

I've struck it! And I will give it away—to you. You will never know how much enjoyment you have lost until you get to dictating your autobiography; then you will realize, with a pang, that you might have been doing it all your life if you had only had the luck to think of it. And you will be astonished (& charmed) to see how like talk it is, & how real it sounds, & how well & compactly & sequentially it constructs itself, & what a dewy & breezy & woodsy freshness it has, & what a darling & worshipful absence of the signs of starch, & flatiron, & labor & fuss & the other artificialities! . . .

Try it, & you will see. But with a long-hand scribe, not with a stenographer. At least not at first. Not until you get your hand in, I should say. There's a good deal of waiting, of course, but that is no matter; soon you do not mind it.

Miss Lyon does the scribing, & is an inspiration, because she takes so much interest in it. I dictate from 10.30 till noon. The

result is about 1500 words. Then I am a free man & can read &
smoke the rest of the day, for there's not a correction to be made. . . .

The death of Mark Twain's wife, Livy, the following June
deeply unsettled him and ended his experiments in composing
autobiography. However, after he returned to the United States
and had time to settle down, an unexpected development
brought him back to that work. In January 1906, free-lance
writer Albert Bigelow Paine approached him about becoming
his biographer. Mark Twain not only granted Paine's request
with some enthusiasm, he also quickly invited Paine to move
into his New York City home to allow Paine convenient access
to his papers. Soon Paine was interviewing him regularly to
gather information for his biography, and Mark Twain engaged
a professional stenographer, Josephine Hobby, to record their
interviews in shorthand and later make typescripts of them.
Paine's questions renewed his interest in creating his own autobiography, and the interview sessions were transformed into
autobiography dictation sessions, with Paine helping to provide focus and inspiration.

Over the next two years, Mark Twain conducted about 250
dictation sessions. Early on, he developed a technique that he
explains in the opening of the first installment of the *North
American Review* chapters:

a form and method whereby the past and the present are constantly brought face to face, resulting in contrasts which newly
fire up the interest all along, like contact of flint with steel. . . .

Howells was here yesterday afternoon, and I told him the
whole scheme of this autobiography and its apparently systemless system—only apparently systemless, for it is not really that.
It is a deliberate system, and the law of the system is that I shall
talk about the matter which for the moment interests me, and
cast it aside and talk about something else the moment its interest for me is exhausted. It is a system which follows no charted
course and is not going to follow any such course. It is a system
which is a complete and purposed jumble—a course which

begins nowhere, follows no specified route, and can never reach
an end while I am alive . . .

The almost inevitable result of Mark Twain's free-form dictations is an enormous manuscript with almost no discernible
shape. When he suggested changing subjects the moment his
interest in what he is talking about fades, he was not exaggerating. His dictations switch subjects frequently, moving their
narratives about in space and back and forth in time. The
absence of a chronological framework is particularly noticeable. In 1906, he serialized a portion of his dictations in the
North American Review under the title "Chapters from My
Auobiography." The first installment opened with some discussion of Clemens family ancestors, but the series did not get
around to discussing Mark Twain's own birth until the thirteenth installment. When the first edition of the autobiography
in book form (edited by Paine) was published in 1924, a review
in the Dallas *Morning News* of October 19 called it

surely the most strangely put together of all memoirs. It is a
work of shreds and patches, a hodge-podge of miscellaneous
papers and dictations written in various parts of the world—
Vienna, Florence, New York City, Dublin (New Hampshire)—
and in as many different manners as could well be found in a
book not an anthology. Still worse, there is no sort of chronol-
ogy; each new chapter begins with whatever subject happens to
come into the muser's mind. When after a time, the book
becomes a combination of diary and autobiography, there is a
semblance of order and the author claims again and again he has
at last hit on the way to write this sort of thing. This is the best
way because most natural. Well, it is natural. But the vaunted
"method" is simply to have no method.

The "miscellaneous papers" to which the review alludes are
texts Paine added to the dictations and were not part of what
Mark Twain considered to be his formal autobiography.
However, the points the review makes accurately describe the

dictations. In any case, these eccentricities did not greatly vex the reviewer, who went on to say,

> This is in no sense a complaint, only the statement of fact—of a fact that must surprise the reader, at least mildly. What a life the man led. Mississippi pilot; in Nevada and California when the exploits of the Forty-Niners were recent history; newspaper correspondent in Hawaii; around the world on the Quaker City; long seasons of residence abroad . . . And what a succession of people he knew about whom one is curious . . .

Despite all the effort Mark Twain invested in composing "autobiography," little of what he recorded resembles what is generally regarded as true autobiography. Indeed, it might even be argued that this most autobiographical of American writers never actually wrote an autobiography. This is not to say that he did not write about his own life. He truly was his own favorite subject, and what he called his autobiography is filled with fascinating and often moving reminiscences of his past. What he did *not* record was an introspective narrative connecting events, finding patterns, or, more generally, seeking an understanding of how he came to be the person he was.

TRUTH

In September 1906, the fortnightly *North American Review* published the first in the series of twenty-five "Chapters" from Mark Twain's autobiography. The widely publicized event quickly attracted newspaper comments, which generally expressed eager anticipation. An editorial in the September 14 issue of California's San Jose *Mercury News* said of the developing autobiography, "This ought to be the best of his books. His life has had variety enough and adventure enough to make good reading when told in his own inimitable way." The paper's observation was accurate: Variety was never lacking in Mark Twain's life, and the autobiographical chapters that were eventually published would not disappoint readers. At the same time, however, cautious skepticism crept into some commentaries. By 1906, the name Mark Twain had become so closely associated with humor and hoaxes that many people were unsure how seriously to take *anything* he wrote. When the *Mercury News* expressed the hope that Mark Twain's forthcoming autobiography would reveal "how much of *Tom Sawyer, Huckleberry Finn* and the *Innocents Abroad* is founded upon his own history and how much is fiction," it also added,

Or it may be that, led astray by his picturesque imagination, he may add another book, a mixture of fact and fancy, to the old list. Unless he takes a solemn affidavit to the truth of all that he writes there will be some people suspicious of his autobiography.

There were reasons aplenty to be skeptical about the veracity of Mark Twain's autobiography. The grossly exaggerated estimate of how large his autobiography would become that he gave to Howells appears in the autobiography itself. Indeed, it opens the first chapter of "Chapters from My Autobiography." Furthermore, it not only contains a ludicrous exaggeration, it also leads into another statement obviously stretching the truth:

Howells applauded, and was full of praises and endorsement, which was wise in him and judicious. If he had manifested a different spirit, I would have thrown him out of the window. I like criticism, but it must be my way.

It is safe to assume that Mark Twain would not really have thrown Howells out a window. The remark is merely a bit of silly fun. Nevertheless, it alerts readers not to take Mark Twain at his word for all that follows. It is a timely warning, as the very next paragraph in that first chapter opens with an even more doubtful statement about the Clemens family ancestry: "Back of the Virginia Clemenses is a dim procession of ancestors stretching back to Noah's time. According to tradition, some of them were pirates and slavers in Elizabeth's time." No family can trace its ancestry back to Noah's time, and the business about pirates and slavers is pure poppy-cock. However, these remarks lead into a more concrete discussion about an ancestor named Geoffrey Clement, who helped sentence England's King Charles I to death in 1649 and consequently "made me vain." This story sounds more reasonable, especially when one knows that Clement really was a historical figure involved in King Charles's execution. Was he, however, an ancestor of Mark Twain's? Probably not, as no evidence of a family connection has yet been found.

The *Mercury News* editorial's suggestion that "some people" would be suspicious of Mark Twain's autobiography was an understatement. People were, indeed, suspicious of it in 1906. One such person was Mark Twain's biographer Paine. As a knowledgeable participant in most of the autobiographical dictation sessions, no one was better placed than he to judge the authenticity of what Mark Twain said. The monumental biography of Mark Twain he published in 1912 contains vivid first-hand descriptions of dictation sessions and recalls his growing suspicion that what he was hearing was not quite right:

> It was not for several weeks that I began to realize that these marvelous reminiscences bore only an atmospheric relation to history; that they were aspects of biography rather than its veritable narrative, and built largely—sometimes wholly—from an imagination that, with age, had dominated memory, creating details, even reversing them, yet with a perfect sincerity of purpose on the part of the narrator to set down the literal and unvarnished truth. It was his constant effort to be frank and faithful to fact, to record, to confess, and to condemn without stint. If you wanted to know the worst of Mark Twain you had only to ask him for it. He would give it, to the last syllable—worse than the worst, for his imagination would magnify it and adorn it with new iniquities, and if he gave it again, or a dozen times, he would improve upon it each time, until the thread of history was almost impossible to trace through the marvel of that fabric; and he would do the same for another person just as willingly. Those vividly real personalities that he marched and countermarched before us were the most convincing creatures

in the world, the most entertaining, the most excruciatingly humorous, or wicked, or tragic; but, alas, they were not always safe to include in a record that must bear a certain semblance to history. They often disagreed in their performance, and even in their characters, with the documents in the next room, as I learned by and by when those records, disentangled, began to rebuild the structure of the years.

His gift of dramatization had been exercised too long to be discarded now. The things he told of Mrs. Clemens and of Susy were true—marvelously and beautifully true, in spirit and in aspect—and the actual detail of these mattered little in such a record. The rest was history only as *Roughing It* is history, or the *Tramp Abroad*; that is to say, it was fictional history, with fact as a starting-point. In a prefatory note to these volumes I have quoted Mark Twain's own lovely and whimsical admission, made once when he realized his deviations:

"When I was younger I could remember anything, whether it happened or not; but I am getting old, and soon I shall remember only the latter." (chapter 239)

Paine went on to modify his remarks on the truthfulness of the autobiography:

I do not wish to say, by any means, that his so-called autobiography is a mere fairy tale. It is far from that. It is amazingly truthful in the character-picture it represents of the man himself. It is only not reliable—and it is sometimes even unjust—as detailed history. Yet, curiously enough, there were occasional chapters that were photographically exact, and fitted precisely with the more positive, if less picturesque, materials. It is also true that such chapters were likely to be episodes intrinsically so perfect as to not require the touch of art.

In the talks which we usually had, when the dictations were ended and Miss Hobby had gone, I gathered much that was of still greater value. Imagination was temporarily dispossessed, as it were, and, whether expounding some theory or summarizing some event, he cared little for literary effect, and only for the idea and the moment immediately present.

It was at such times that he allowed me to make those inquiries we had planned in the beginning, and which apparently had little place in the dictations themselves. Sometimes I led him to speak of the genesis of his various books, how he had come to write them, and I think there was not a single case where later I did not find his memory of these matters almost exactly in accord with the letters of the moment, written to Howells or [Joseph] Twichell, or to some member of his family. Such reminiscence was usually followed by some vigorous burst of human philosophy, often too vigorous for print, too human, but as dazzling as a search-light in its revelation.

Later biographers have shared Paine's suspicions. Justin Kaplan, for example, in his Pulitzer Prize–winning biography, *Mr. Clemens and Mark Twain* (1966), summed up Mark Twain's autobiography as "that piece of near-fiction." However, that harsh judgment did not lessen Kaplan's admiration for the work. "As a record of magnificent talk, magical, hilarious, savage, and tender," he added, "the autobiography is a major work, Mark Twain's last, a sprawling and shapeless masterpiece whose unity is in the accent and rhythm and attack of his voice." A still later biographer, Forrest Robinson, brings a different perspective. In *The Author-Cat: Clemens's Life in Fiction* (2007), he argues that Mark Twain is more truthful about his life in his fictional writings than he is in his autobiography.

One root of distrust in Mark Twain's truthfulness goes back to a characteristic trait of much of his writing—a cavalier disregard for fine distinctions among literary forms and genres. Stories, sketches, essays, and memoirs were often seemingly as one to him. Usually more interested in telling a good yarn than in sticking to the petrified truth, he was always willing to overlook inconvenient differences between fact and fiction. This tendency is most evident in his travel books, which were ostensibly factual descriptions of places he visited and the experiences he had during his travels. *Roughing It*, one of the books to which Paine alluded, is a prime example. In that lively volume about his Western adventures, lines between fact and fiction are often too thin to discern what Mark Twain himself actually did and what his anonymous narrator claims he merely did. Mark Twain wrote the book in the first person and clearly built it around his own experiences. However, from the book's opening paragraph it is apparent that its unnamed narrator is not quite Mark Twain himself:

> My brother had just been appointed Secretary of Nevada Territory . . . and the title of "Mr. Secretary" gave to the great position an air of wild and imposing grandeur. I was young and ignorant, and I envied my brother. I coveted his distinction and his financial splendor, but particularly and especially the long, strange journey he was going to make, and the curious new world he was going to explore. He was going to travel! I never had been away from home, and that word "travel" had a seductive charm for me.

Typical of Mark Twain's travel writings, *Roughing It* exaggerates its narrator's youthfulness and inexperience. In 1861, when he went to Nevada with his brother, he was twenty-five years old and was already impressively accomplished and well traveled. After spending several years working as a journeyman printer in midwestern and eastern cities, including St. Louis, Cincinnati, New York, and Philadelphia, he had spent four years piloting steamboats between St. Louis and New Orleans on the Mississippi. As a pilot, he had already earned a larger salary than his brother would ever receive. *Roughing It* sustains its narrator's youthful greenhorn pose throughout its early chapters, while embellishing Mark Twain's actual experiences with exaggerations, distortions, and outright inventions that make the narrative much livelier and more vivid than a straightforward account could possibly be. The result is a mixture that may justifiably be classified equally as both memoir and fiction. One thing it is not, however, is autobiography. The same may be said of *The Innocents Abroad*, *A Tramp Abroad*, and parts of *Life on the Mississippi*. Nonetheless, as extracts reprinted in the present volume show, each of those books contains patches of authentic autobiography.

Modern readers of Mark Twain generally know enough about him not to be greatly troubled by his mixing of fact and fiction in his books. His contemporary readers, though, were less comfortable with it. In December 1880, he received a letter from a New York cheese merchant named Charles W. Rhodes, who had read *The Innocents Abroad*, *Roughing It*, and other works and was just finishing *A Tramp Abroad*, Mark Twain's account of his most recent travels in western Europe. Rhodes wished to know

> by what rule a fellow can infallibly judge when you are lying and when you are telling the truth. I write this in case you intend to afflict an innocent and unoffending public with any more such works. I would suggest the next volume be published with the truth printed in italics.

Mark Twain evidently merely laughed at this letter, for on it he jotted, "Ha!—ha! captured another idiot." He did not, of course, adopt Rhodes's suggestion about using italics, so his readers were left wondering which passages in his writings to believe. Always fascinated with the concept of truth, Mark Twain was doubtless aware of his own reputation. In a discussion of lying in *Following the Equator* (1897), his book about his round-the-world lecture tour in 1895–1896, he ruefully remarked, "My own luck has been curious all my literary life; I never could tell a lie that anybody would doubt, nor a truth that anybody would believe." Is it, then, any wonder that readers approached his serialized autobiography with some skepticism in 1906?

EDITIONS OF THE AUTOBIOGRAPHY

In 2010, the University of California Press issued the first of three projected volumes of the superbly edited *Autobiography of Mark Twain*, prepared by the editors of Berkeley's Mark Twain Papers. This publication is accurately billed as the first "complete and authoritative" edition of the autobiography, that is, the first to include *every* manuscript and dictation that Mark Twain himself regarded as part of his formal autobiography. It is also the first edition to arrange the material strictly as he intended, which is essentially the order in which he created it.

Although Mark Twain directed that his autobiography not be published until one hundred years after he died, four different versions were published between 1906 and 1959. None was close to being complete or authoritative. Not long after Mark Twain recorded his intention of having his autobiography published posthumously, he succumbed to an attractive offer from George Harvey, the president of Harper and Brothers, to publish twenty-five installments, or "chapters," in the *North American Review*, beginning in September 1906. With an eye toward pleasing readers, Harvey selected about 110,000 words of material to go into the magazine, omitting a few possibly controversial passages with the recommendations and approval of Mark Twain, who stipulated that none of his autobiography would be published in book form during his lifetime. The *North American Review* chapters were later reprinted in several book editions, including *Mark Twain's Own Autobiography* (1990; rev. 2010), edited by Michael J. Kiskis. (The chapters also appear in the present volume.)

In 1924, Albert Bigelow Paine, Mark Twain's biographer and literary executor and the first editor of the Mark Twain Papers, published about 250,000 words of Mark Twain's autobiographical writings in two volumes as *Mark Twain's Autobiography*. Despite Paine's immense knowledge of Mark Twain and his intimate personal acquaintance with him, his edition is probably the least authoritative yet published. He tried to follow Mark Twain's wish by arranging the material in the order in which it was created, but he included material that Mark Twain did not intend to be part of his formal autobiography, while omitting portions he himself regarded as uninteresting and rewording some passages without revealing what he had changed.

Bernard DeVoto, Paine's successor as editor of the Mark Twain Papers, published what might be regarded as a supplement to

Paine's edition in 1940: *Mark Twain in Eruption: Hitherto Unpublished Pages About Men and Events*. Both DeVoto's and Paine's editions included material that had previously appeared in the *North American Review* in 1906–1907, but none of the approximately 120,000 words of material in DeVoto's edition is in Paine's edition. Much of this material contains scathing remarks about people that Paine was too timid to use. Like Paine, DeVoto selected the material that most interested him. When he was done, he declared that the approximately 120,000 words of still-unpublished material that remained would be of interest only to scholars. Meanwhile, in contrast to what Paine had done, DeVoto departed radically from Mark Twain's instructions by arranging the material topically, under nine subject headings: "Theodore Roosevelt," "Andrew Carnegie," "The Plutocracy," "Hannibal Days," "Two Halos," "In a Writer's Workshop," "Various Literary People," "The Last Visit to England," and "Miscellany."

The next edition of the autobiography had an even more radical rearrangement of the material. In 1959, Charles Neider published *The Autobiography of Mark Twain*, drawing material from all previous editions and adding about 30,000 words of previously unpublished material. Dissatisfied with how the previous editions had been organized and baffled by Mark Twain's preferred arrangement, Neider attempted to force the material into a traditional cradle-to-grave arrangement. The resulting book has the appearance of a traditional autobiography, but that appearance can be deceptive. Sequential passages are often drawn from different dictations and occasionally were not composed to mean what they appear to mean in their new settings.

Michael J. Kiskis's edition of *Mark Twain's Own Autobiography*, first published in 1990, is essentially a reprint of the original *North American Review* chapters. Apart from correcting minor errors in the magazine versions, Kiskis changed nothing. He did, however, add substantial annotations and a useful table summarizing the textual sources of each edition of Mark Twain's autobiography. In 2010, Kiskis published a revised edition of *Mark Twain's Own Autobiography* with expanded annotations and a new Introduction.

CONTENTS OF THE PRESENT VOLUME

If, indeed, an argument can be made that Mark Twain never wrote a true autobiography, then all the various autobiographical fragments and reminiscences scattered throughout his writings should have equal validity as pieces of his autobiography. This Penguin Classics volume is the first book to collect many of those fragments under one cover.

The materials in the present volume are loosely arranged among three sections. The first section, "Autobiographical Dictations," contains all twenty-five parts of "Chapters from My Autobiography," which originally appeared in the *North American Review* between September 1906 and December 1907 and were later serialized in Sunday newspaper supplements. The texts of these chapters are rendered here exactly as they appeared in the original magazine.

The second section, "Youthful Memories," includes several brief and self-contained memoirs, an extract from an early attempt at formal autobiography, and extracts from four of Mark Twain's travel books. Selections within this section are arranged chronologically by their composition dates. "My First Literary Venture" is a lighthearted but reasonably accurate account of Mark Twain's earliest journalistic work in Hannibal, a period in Mark Twain's youth not addressed directly in the *North American Review* articles. "Early Years in Florida, Missouri" is an important fragment of Mark Twain's attempt to construct a formal autobiography in 1877. It covers some of the same information presented in several *North American Review* chapters but perhaps because it was written nearly three decades earlier, it provides a richer and more intimate portrait of an early phase of Mark Twain's life that he also used in *Tom Sawyer* and *Huckleberry Finn*. Written around the same time he was dictating his autobiography, "Hunting the Deceitful Turkey" adds another dimension to Mark Twain's memories of his Florida days. "Jane Lampton Clemens"—which Mark Twain wrote after his mother died in 1890—is rich in his boyhood memories and is laced with observations on relatives, several of whom he used as models for fictional characters.

Mark Twain's five travel books constitute an important but enigmatic part of his autobiographical writings for reasons discussed above. None of these books is, strictly speaking, autobiography, but each covers, more or less accurately, a significant phase of his life. *The Innocents Abroad* (1869) traces his tour of Mediterranean Europe and the Middle East on the *Quaker City* excursion of 1867—an important turning point in his life that he barely mentions in his *North American Review* chapters. It offers a broadly accurate reconstruction of his itinerary and the high points of his trip, but it is so permeated with inventions and exaggerations that it is difficult not only to know which of its incidents actually happened but also to know which actions attributed to the book's unnamed narrator Mark Twain himself performed. *Roughing It* (1872), Mark Twain's account of his five years in Nevada, California, and Hawaii, is a very different kind of narrative, but as an autobiographical work it poses the same challenges as *The Innocents Abroad*. Nevertheless, one cannot possibly understand Mark Twain's experiences during the early 1860s without reading it.

As an account of Mark Twain's return to continental Europe during the late 1870s, *A Tramp Abroad* (1880) resembles *The Innocents Abroad* in many ways. However, as autobiography it is even less reliable than the earlier book. In contrast to *The Innocents Abroad*, which Mark Twain constructed around the actual itinerary of the *Quaker City* excursion, *A Tramp Abroad* uses a more artificial structure that only loosely followed Mark Twain's actual travels in 1878–1879, while inserting wholly imaginary episodes and characters and employing an anonymous narrator who often scarcely resembles Mark Twain himself.

Life on the Mississippi (1883), which followed only three

years later, is yet another kind of travel book and, as such, presents different challenges to readers seeking Mark Twain autobiography. Mark Twain wrote the book with the idea of creating a standard work on the Mississippi River. To that end, he opened the book with several chapters on the river's geomorphology and history. He then inserted eighteen chapters on steamboat piloting that he expanded from "Old Times on the Mississippi," which he had serialized in the *Atlantic Monthly* in 1875. All but four of the book's piloting chapters are a first-person account of Mark Twain's experiences as an apprentice pilot during the late 1850s. Although the chapters depict their unnamed narrator as younger and less experienced than Mark Twain actually was during his cub piloting days and contain some embellishments similar to those in his earlier travel books, they nevertheless constitute an important part of his autobiography. (They are reprinted in the present volume as "Cub Piloting Days.") The rest of *Life on the Mississippi*—more than half the entire book—is a relatively sober account of Mark Twain's return to the Mississippi in 1882, when he traveled by boat from St. Louis down to New Orleans and then back up the river as far as Minnesota. This part of the book has strong autobiographical elements, but they are diluted by Mark Twain's insertion of several tall tales unrelated to his own life and enough fictional embellishments to his narrative to make most of the chapters as unreliable as autobiography as the earlier travel books. However, chapters 53–56, recounting Mark Twain's visit to Hannibal, contain important reminiscences of his childhood there. They are reprinted here as "My Boyhood's Home."

Mark Twain's final travel book, *Following the Equator* (1897), is yet another kind of narrative. Written when Mark Twain was worn down by his travels and was grieving over the recent death of his daughter Susy (an event poignantly described in the third *North American Review* chapter), the book is a relatively straightforward narrative of the round-the-world lecture tour that Mark Twain undertook in 1895–1896. Indeed, much of it is taken directly from the journals he kept on his trip. As autobiography, the book is more reliable than his earlier travel

books and is particularly valuable for its expressions of Mark
Twain's critiques of European imperialism—particularly British imperialism—in the South Pacific, South Asia, and Southern Africa.

As has been shown, Mark Twain's travel books are generally
unreliable as autobiography—or at best difficult to interpret.
Nevertheless, they contain valuable autobiographical scraps
about his youth that pop up in unlikely passages and make one
wonder what Mark Twain's thought processes must have been
when he wrote them. Three such fragments are reprinted here.
The first, "An Unpleasant Adventure," appears in the middle
of *The Innocents Abroad*'s chapter on the great cathedral of
Milan, Italy. After describing a graphically realistic sculpture
of a man who had been skinned alive, Mark Twain makes a
remark about the difficulty of forgetting repulsive things that
seems suddenly to have evoked a memory of a dramatic incident that occurred during his Hannibal boyhood. "A Mississippi River Story" intrudes in a similarly unlikely passage of *A
Tramp Abroad* discussing German theater. Here a description
of an actor performing without the encouragement of his
audience's applause reminded Mark Twain of an incident during his first steamboat ride at the age of ten, when he awak-
ened from a nightmare late at night and burst into the ladies'
saloon. The third extract, "The Space-Annihilating Power of
Thought," comes from a chapter in *Following the Equator* on
Bombay, India. When Mark Twain saw a German hotel proprietor cuff an Indian servant, he instantly remembered his
father doing the same thing to slaves when he was a boy. In
contrast to the previous two memories, which Mark Twain
seemed to evoke during the act of writing, Mark Twain's boyhood memory of slavery appears to have entered his mind at
the very moment the Bombay incident happened. The anecdote is brief, but it admits to a harsher reality of Hannibal
slavery than his more formal autobiographical writings reveal.

The third section of writings, "Essays," contains three
pieces that Mark Twain consciously wrote as autobiographical
reflections but did not regard as part of his autobiography
proper. In 1900, he wrote "My Boyhood Dreams" for *McClure's*

Magazine while he was in Sweden. The largely facetious essay recalls an imaginary gathering of friends many years earlier, when each man revealed to the others his private hopes for his future. The essay might be read as a reflection of Mark Twain's own boyhood aspirations. Written in 1909 in response to an invitation from *Harper's Bazar* and published shortly before Mark Twain died in 1910, "The Turning-Point of My Life" is a more serious reflection on his past that takes a very deterministic view of the forces that directed his life. He actually conceived the idea of writing such an essay several years earlier, after he had written "What Is Man?" (1906), his masterwork on determinism. The essay's argument that his entire life was shaped by the case of measles he contracted as a boy might profitably be compared to Mark Twain's account of the measles in the twenty-third of the *North American Review* chapters.

Of the thirteen chapters in the last book Mark Twain published during his lifetime, *Is Shakespeare Dead? From My Autobiography* (1909), the two chapters reprinted here as "Is Shakespeare Dead?" have the strongest autobiographical content. The central argument of this little book is that William Shakespeare could not have written the plays attributed to him because no evidence exists showing he had the legal training that their actual author must have had. Mark Twain supports his case by drawing comparisons between what is publicly known about his own life and what was known about Shakespeare during his time.

MARK TWAIN A CENTURY LATER

Two months after Mark Twain's April 21, 1910, death, the New York literary magazine *Bookman* published several articles about him. In "Mark Twain a Century Hence," the magazine's first editor, Henry Thurston Peck, analyzed the juvenilian characteristics of Mark Twain's humor and speculated on how long his works would be remembered. While his appreciation of the humorous side of Mark Twain was generous, his prediction of how Mark Twain would be regarded in the year 2010 was dismal:

> Going over the entire list of the many volumes to which this author set his name, there are only four or five at the most that are likely to last for a great length of time. I am certain that not more than three of them [*The Jumping Frog*, *The Innocents Abroad*, and *Roughing It*] will be read a century from now. . . . *The Adventures of Tom Sawyer* (1876) and *Huckleberry Finn* (1885) will remain for perhaps two decades. All the rest of Mr. Clemens' books may perhaps be sold by subscription agents among his "complete works" for a certain time, but they will not be read. *A Tramp Abroad* marks the beginning of a first decline. *A Yankee at the Court of King Arthur* makes one feel sorry for its author. *Joan of Arc* is distinctly dull; and *The Autobiography of Mark Twain*, which has been dragging its slow way along for many months, is formless and in places without any meaning whatsoever. His best friends have regretted that he ever began to write it. It is to be hoped that his heirs and executors will suppress it.

In an anonymous *Bookman* editorial published nine years earlier, Peck had dismissed Mark Twain as "first and last and all the time, so far as he is anything, a humorist and nothing more." During the intervening years his opinion had evidently hardened, and the serialized publication of "Chapters from My Autobiography" had not changed his mind. His assessment of Mark Twain's future reputation probably did not reflect the majority view in 1910, but he was not alone in regarding Mark Twain as primarily a humorist. Time has shown that view to be wrong. Indeed, it is a shame that Peck did not live long enough to learn how spectacularly inaccurate his predictions were. Far from being mostly forgotten, virtually all Mark Twain's books were in print a century after he died. *Tom Sawyer* and *Huckleberry Finn*, of course, have lasted far longer than two decades. Moreover, neither has ever gone out of print, and the literary reputations of both *Huckleberry Finn* and *Connecticut Yankee* have grown stronger with each passing year. Most impressive of all, perhaps, is the increasing interest in Mark Twain's life. Every year sees the publication of at least a half-dozen major new studies of him, and biennial conferences focusing on his life and writings draw growing numbers of attendees. Yes, his autobiography may be formless; however, the 760-page portion published by the University of California Press in 2010 spent twenty-four weeks on the *New York Times* bestseller list. Reports of Mark Twain's death were, indeed, exaggerated.

R. KENT RASMUSSEN

Suggestions for Further Reading

Camfield, Gregg. *The Oxford Companion to Mark Twain*. New York: Oxford University Press, 2002.

Clemens, Susy. *Papa: An Intimate Biography of Mark Twain*. Edited by Charles Neider. Garden City, N.Y.: Doubleday, 1985.

Couser, G. Thomas. "Autobiography as Anti-Biography: The Case of Twain vs. Paine." *Auto/Biography Studies* 3, no. 3 (Fall 1987): 13–20.

Cox, James M. *Mark Twain: The Fate of Humor*. Princeton, N.J.: Princeton University Press, 1966.

———. *Recording Literature's Lost Ground: Essays in American Autobiography*. Baton Rouge: Louisiana State University Press, 1989.

Dawidziak, Mark. *Horton Foote's "The Shape of the River": The Lost Teleplay About Mark Twain with History and Analysis*. New York: Applause, 2003.

Eakin, Paul John, ed. *American Autobiography: Retrospect and Prospect*. Madison: University of Wisconsin Press, 1991.

Emerson, Everett. *Mark Twain: A Literary Life*. Philadelphia: University of Pennsylvania Press, 2000.

Fisher Fishkin, Shelley, ed. *The Mark Twain Anthology: Great Writers on His Life and Works*. New York: Library of America, 2010.

Hill, Hamlin. *Mark Twain: God's Fool*. New York: Harper & Row, 1973.

Kaplan, Justin. *Mr. Clemens and Mark Twain: A Biography*. New York: Simon & Schuster, 1966.

Kiskis, Michael J. "Coming Back to Humor: The Comic Voice in Mark Twain's Autobiography." In *Mark Twain's Humor: Critical Essays*. Edited by David E. E. Sloan. New York: Garland, 1993.

———. "Dead Man Talking: Mark Twain's Autobiographical Deception." *American Literary Realism* 40, no. 2 (Winter 2008): 95–113.

LeMaster, J. R., and James D. Wilson, eds. *The Mark Twain Encyclopedia*. New York: Garland, 1993.

Paine, Albert Bigelow. *Mark Twain, A Biography: The Personal and Literary Life of Samuel Langhorne Clemens*. 3 vols. New York: Harper & Brothers, 1912.

Powers, Ron. *Dangerous Water: A Biography of the Boy Who Became Mark Twain*. New York: Basic Books, 1999.

———. *Mark Twain: A Life*. New York: Random House, 2005.

Rasmussen, R. Kent. *Critical Companion to Mark Twain: A Literary Reference to His Life and Work*. 2 vols. New York: Facts on File, 2007.

Robinson, Forrest G. *The Author-Cat: Clemens's Life in Fiction*. New York: Fordham University Press, 2007.

———. "The Late Writing of Mark Twain." In *A Companion to Mark Twain*. Edited by Peter Messent and Louis J. Budd. Malden, Mass.: Blackwell, 2005.

———. "Mark Twain, 1835–1910: A Brief Biography." In *A Historical Guide to Mark Twain*. Edited by Shelley Fisher Fishkin. New York: Oxford University Press, 2002.

Scharnhorst, Gary, ed. *Mark Twain: The Complete Interviews*. Tuscaloosa: University of Alabama Press, 2006.

Shelden, Michael. *Mark Twain: Man in White—The Grand Adventure of His Final Years*. New York: Random House, 2010.

Smith, Henry Nash, and William M. Gibson, eds. *Mark Twain–Howells Letters: The Correspondence of Samuel L. Clemens and William D. Howells, 1872–1910*. 2 vols. Cambridge, Mass.: Harvard University Press, 1960.

Smith, Sidonie, and Julia Watson. *Reading Autobiography: A Guide for Interpreting Life Narratives.* 2d ed. Minneapolis: University of Minnesota Press, 2010.

Tenney, Thomas Asa. *Mark Twain: A Reference Guide.* Boston: G. K. Hall, 1977.

Twain, Mark. *Autobiography of Mark Twain.* Vol. 1. Edited by Harriet Elinor Smith et al. Berkeley: University of California Press, 2010.

———. *The Autobiography of Mark Twain: Including Chapters Now Published for the First Time.* Edited by Charles Neider. New York: Harper & Brothers, 1959.

———. *Chapters from My Autobiography.* Edited by Shelley Fisher Fishkin, with Introduction by Arthur Miller and Afterword by Michael J. Kiskis. New York: Oxford University Press, 1996.

———. *Mark Twain in Eruption: Hitherto Unpublished Pages About Men and Events.* Edited by Bernard DeVoto. New York: Capricorn Books, 1940.

———. *Mark Twain's Autobiography.* Edited by Albert Bigelow Paine. 2 vols. New York: Harper & Brothers, 1924.

———. *Mark Twain's Own Autobiography: The Chapters from the "North American Review."* Edited by Michael J. Kiskis. 2d ed. Madison: University of Wisconsin Press, 2010.

———. *My Autobiography: "Chapters" from the North American Review.* Introduction by Thomas Wortham. Mineola, N.Y.: Dover, 1999.

Zaccra, Jennifer L. "Mark Twain, Isabel Lyon, and the 'Talking Cure': Negotiating Nostalgia and Nihilism in the *Autobiography.*" In *Constructing Mark Twain: New Directions in Scholarship*, edited by Laura E. Skandera Trombley and Michael J. Kiskis. Columbia: University of Missouri Press, 2001.

A Note on the Texts

All texts in this volume are taken from their original publications, except as noted below. All footnotes are from the original texts, but their numbers have been changed to symbols, such as asterisks, to avoid confusion resulting from changing page breaks. Texts are unaltered, except for the closing of contractions, such as "don't" for "do n't."

The texts of "Chapters from My Autobiography" come directly from the twenty-five original articles of the same title appearing in *North American Review* between September 6, 1906, and December 1907. All original chapter numbers, headnotes, and footnotes are retained. The only omissions are the original copyright notices and the boldfaced years inserted within parentheses near the outside margins of pages beginning in chapter 8. (These insertions repeat dates provided in the text, of which they are not part.) The many ellipses throughout the articles are original to the texts.

"An Unpleasant Adventure" is extracted from chapter 18 of *The Innocents Abroad* (American Publishing Co.,1869). "My First Literary Venture" is reprinted from *Mark Twain's Sketches New & Old* (American Publishing Co., 1875).

"Cub Piloting Days" reprints chapters 4–13 and 18–21 of *Life on the Mississippi* (James R. Osgood & Co., 1883), whose original chapter titles are retained: (4) "The Boys' Ambition," (5) "I Want to Be a Cub-Pilot," (6) "A Cub-Pilot's Experience," (7) "A Daring Deed," (8) "Perplexing Lessons," (9) "Continued Perplexities," (10) "Completing My Education," (11) "The River Rises," (12) "Sounding," (13) "A Pilot's Needs," (18) "I Take a Few Extra Lessons," (19) "Brown and I Exchange Compliments," (20) "A Catastrophe," and (21) "A Section in My Biography." Chapters 4–13 appeared earlier in a slightly different form in seven articles titled "Old Times on the Mississippi" published in the *Atlantic Monthly* (January–June and August 1875). Chapters 14–17 of *Life on the Mississippi* are not included here because they contain almost no autobiographical content.

"Early Years in Florida, Missouri" and "Jane Lampton Clemens" are extracted from "Unpublished Chapters from the Autobiography of Mark Twain (Part I)," edited by Albert Bigelow Paine, in the February 1922 issue of *Harper's Monthly*. "A Mississippi River Story" is extracted from chapter 10 of *A Tramp Abroad* (American Publishing Co., 1880).

"My Boyhood's Home" comprises chapters 53–56 of *Life on the Mississippi* and retains the original chapter titles: (53) "My Boyhood's Home," (54) "Past and Present," (55) "A Vendetta and Other Things," and (56) "A Question of Law."

"The Space-Annihilating Power of Thought" is extracted from chapter 38 of *Following the Equator* (American Publishing Co., 1897). "Hunting the Deceitful Turkey" is reprinted from the December 1906 issue of *Harper's Monthly*.

"My Boyhood Dreams" is reprinted from the January 1900 issue of *McClure's Magazine*. "Is Shakespeare Dead?" comprises chapters 6–7 of the book of the same title published in 1909. "The Turning-Point of My Life" is reprinted from the February 1910 issue of *Harper's Bazar*.

Chronology

November 30, 1835: Samuel Langhorne Clemens—later better known as Mark Twain—is born in the northeastern Missouri village of Florida. The sixth of seven children of John Marshall and Jane Lampton Clemens, he will outlive all his siblings, his wife, and three of his own four children.

1839–1853: Lives in Missouri's Mississippi River town of Hannibal, on which he will later model the fictional St. Petersburg of *Tom Sawyer* and *Huckleberry Finn*. After leaving school at eleven, he does printing work for local newspapers, including his brother Orion's papers, and writes occasional sketches and essays.

March 24, 1847: John Marshall Clemens's death leaves his family impoverished.

1853–1856: Sam Clemens leaves Missouri to work as a printer in St. Louis, Philadelphia, and New York; after returning to the Midwest, he does similar work for Orion in southern Iowa.

May 1857–April 1861: Spends two years training as a steamboat pilot on the Lower Mississippi—mostly under Horace Bixby—and two more years as a licensed pilot.

June 13, 1858: Steamboat "Pennsylvania" blows up south of Memphis, severely injuring Clemens's younger brother, Henry, who dies eight days later.

April 12, 1861: Civil War begins when Confederates fire on Fort Sumter in Charleston, S.C. Clemens, who is in New Orleans, will soon end his piloting career when war stops steamboat traffic on the Lower Mississippi.

June 1861: Clemens drills for about two weeks with a Missouri militia unit called up by the state's pro-Confederate governor.

July 1861: Crosses the plains with his brother Orion, who has been appointed secretary to the government of the newly created Nevada Territory.

July 1861–September 1862: Prospects and collects mining claims in western Nevada.

September 1862–May 1864: Works as a reporter for the *Virginia City Territorial Enterprise*.

February 3, 1863: Uses the pen name "Mark Twain" for the first time in a report written in Carson City for the *Enterprise*.

June 1864–December 1866: After relocating to California, briefly reports for the *San Francisco Morning Call*, does some prospecting in the depleted gold fields of Tuolumne and Calaveras counties, and writes for a variety of publications.

November 18, 1865: Publication of his jumping frog story in New York's *Saturday Press* helps build his national reputation.

March–August 1866: Visits the Hawaiian (Sandwich) Islands as a correspondent for the *Sacramento Union*. After returning to San Francisco, he launches what will become a long and successful lecturing career by speaking on the islands in Northern California and western Nevada.

May 14, 1867: Publishes his first book, *The Celebrated Jumping Frog of Calaveras County and Other Sketches*.

June–November 1867: Tours Mediterranean Europe and the Holy Land with the *Quaker City* excursion; his travel letters to San Francisco and New York newspapers are widely reprinted, expanding his reputation. After he returns, Elisha Bliss of the American Publishing Co. (APC) of Hartford, Conn., invites him to write the book about his travels that will become *The Innocents Abroad*.

March–July 1868: Visits California for the last time to secure the rights to his *Quaker City* letters from the *San Francisco Alta California;* while there, he finishes writing his book with the help of Bret Harte.

July 20, 1869: APC publishes *The Innocents Abroad, Or, The New Pilgrim's Progress*, the first of Clemens's five travel books, which will be his best-selling book throughout his lifetime and the best-selling American travel book of the nineteenth century.

August 1869: Clemens buys an interest in the *Buffalo Express* and becomes one of the newspaper's editors. After settling in Buffalo, N.Y., he begins the first of several major eastern lecture tours.

February 2, 1870: Marries Olivia (Livy) Langdon, the daughter of a wealthy Elmira, N.Y., coal magnate. The newlyweds settle in a Buffalo house given to them by his father-in-law.

November 7, 1870: The couple's first child, a son named Langdon, is born; he will live only twenty-two months.

February 1871: Isaac Sheldon publishes *Mark Twain's Burlesque Autobiography and First Romance*, the first part of which is essentially a farce about imaginary ancestors that Clemens would later regret having published.

March 1871: After a year of family misfortunes, Clemens sells his Buffalo house and interest in the *Express* and relocates to

Elmira, where his family stays on the Quarry Farm of Livy's sister, Susan Crane. Over the next two decades, his family will spend most of its summers on the farm, where Clemens will do much of his most important writing.

October 1871: His family settles in Hartford, Conn., before he starts another long lecture tour. His first daughter, Susy, is born the following March. In September 1874, the family will move into a magnificent new house that will be their home until 1891.

February 29, 1872: APC publishes *Roughing It*, an embellished account of Clemens's years in the Far West and Hawaii.

August–November 1872: Clemens makes his first visit to England, to which he will soon return with his family.

December 1873: APC publishes *The Gilded Age*, a novel by Clemens and his Hartford neighbor Charles Dudley Warner. Clemens's portions of the novel revolve around events modeled on his own family's history.

June 1874: Clemens begins writing *Tom Sawyer* during the same month his second daughter, Clara, is born.

January–August 1875: Publishes "Old Times on the Mississippi," his first extended work about steamboating, in a seven-part series in the *Atlantic Monthly*.

July 21, 1875: APC publishes *Mark Twain's Sketches New & Old*, which includes "My First Literary Venture."

June 9, 1876: *The Adventures of Tom Sawyer* is published first in England. American publication is delayed until December.

December 17, 1877: Clemens delivers burlesque speech at a Boston birthday banquet for poet John Greenleaf Whittier that afterward causes him great embarrassment.

April 1878–August 1879: Travels in western Europe with his family.

November 12, 1879: Delivers triumphant speech honoring Gen. Ulysses S. Grant at a Union Army reunion in Chicago.

March 13, 1880: APC publishes *A Tramp Abroad*, a fictionalized account of episodes from Clemens's recent European travels.

July 7, 1880: His last daughter, Jean, is born at Quarry Farm in Elmira, N.Y.

December 12, 1881: James Osgood of Boston publishes *The Prince and the Pauper*, Clemens's novel about boys switching places in sixteenth-century England.

April–May 1882: Clemens travels by steamboat from St. Louis, Mo., to New Orleans, and then upriver to St. Paul, Minn., to gather material for the book to be called *Life on the Mississippi*.

May 17, 1883: Osgood publishes *Life on the Mississippi*, which expands Clemens's 1875 "Old Times on the Mississippi" articles and adds new material from his 1882 return to the river.

May 1, 1884: Clemens founds his own publishing house, Charles L. Webster & Co., with Webster, his nephew by marriage, as company president.

December 10, 1884: *Adventures of Huckleberry Finn* sees its first publication in England, by Chatto & Windus, which will become Clemens's only authorized English publisher.

February 18, 1885: *Huckleberry Finn* is belatedly released in America by Webster.

December 10, 1889: Webster publishes *A Connecticut Yankee in King Arthur's Court*, Clemens's novel about a contemporary American thrust back to sixth-century England.

October 27, 1890: Jane Lampton Clemens, Clemens's mother, dies at the age of eighty-seven.

June 1891–May 1895: Clemens family closes down the Hartford house—to which they will never return—and goes to Europe to live to cut down living expenses. As the family moves around in western Europe, Clemens makes numerous trips to the United States to look after his failing business interests.

May 1892: Webster publishes *The American Claimant*, Clemens's novel about an American who claims to be heir to an English earldom.

1893–1894: Clemens publishes *Tom Sawyer Abroad*, first as a serial in *St. Nicholas Magazine*, then as the last book issued by his firm, Webster & Co., which goes into bankruptcy in April 1894.

November 28, 1894: APC publishes *Pudd'nhead Wilson*, Clemens's novel about slavery and miscegenation set in another fictional Missouri town modeled on Hannibal.

April 1895–April 1896: *Harper's Monthly* serializes Clemens's novel *The Personal Recollections of Joan of Arc*, which afterward is issued in book form by Harper & Brothers, Clemens's new authorized American publisher. Harper will soon begin reissuing all his books in uniform editions.

May 1895–July 1896: Clemens leaves England with his family, beginning a round-the-world lecturing trip. After summering at Elmira, he, Livy, and daughter Clara travel cross-country to British Columbia, whence they cross the Pacific to Hawaii, Fiji, Australia, and New Zealand, and then cross the Indian Ocean to Ceylon, India, and South Africa, before returning to England. Meanwhile, daughters Susy and Jean remain behind in Elmira. Profits from the lecturing tour will pay off debts from Clemens's publishing firm's bankruptcy, and he returns to America hailed as a triumphant hero.

July 1896–October 1900: After being rejoined by daughter Jean, the family remains in Europe four more years.

August 18, 1896: Daughter Susy dies of spinal meningitis while Clemens is in England.

August–September 1896: Clemens publishes *Tom Sawyer, Detective* as a serial in *Harper's New Monthly Magazine*.

November 13, 1897: Harper and APC publish Clemens's fifth travel book, *Following the Equator*, a relatively sober account of his round-the-world trip.

December 11, 1897: Brother Orion Clemens dies.

January 1900: "My Boyhood Dreams" appears in *McClure's Magazine*.

October 15, 1900: After an unbroken absence of five years, Clemens returns to the United States with his family and rents a house in New York City.

April 10, 1902: Harper publishes Clemens's *A Double-Barrelled Detective Story*, a novella that includes Sherlock Holmes as a bumbling detective.

May 1902: Clemens pays his last visit to Hannibal and the Mississippi River during a trip to Columbia to accept an honorary degree from the University of Missouri.

November 1903–June 1904: Takes his family to Florence, Italy, hoping the mild climate will help his wife Livy's failing health.

January 14, 1904: Begins dictating his autobiography to his family secretary, Isabel Lyon.

June 5, 1904: Livy dies in Florence; the rest of the family soon returns to the United States.

August 31, 1904: Pamela Clemens Moffett, Clemens's last surviving sibling, dies.

September 1904–June 1908: Clemens takes up residence on Fifth Avenue in New York City, where he is lionized as a public speaker and banquet guest.

December 5, 1905: Col. George Harvey, president of Harper & Brothers and editor of *Harper's Weekly*, hosts a grand seventieth birthday banquet for Clemens at New York's Delmonico's restaurant.

January 1906: Albert Bigelow Paine moves into Clemens's home to begin work as Clemens's authorized biographer; Clemens soon begins dictating his autobiography to Paine and a professional stenographer, Josephine Hobby.

September 7, 1906–December 1907: Twenty-five installments of "Chapters from My Autobiography" appear in the fortnightly *North American Review*.

December 1906: "Hunting the Deceitful Turkey" appears in *Harper's Monthly*.

June–July 1907: Clemens makes last transatlantic voyage, to accept an honorary degree at Oxford University in England.

October 27, 1907–September 27, 1908: Illustrated reprints of "Chapters from My Autobiography" appear in the *Sunday Magazine* of the *New York Tribune* and at least nine other newspapers.

June 18, 1908: Clemens moves into his last home, a newly built house outside Redding, Conn., that he initially dubs "Autobiography House" because it has been built with income from "Chapters from My Autobiography"; he later renames the house "Stormfield."

April 8, 1909: Publishes *Is Shakespeare Dead?*, which is sub-titled "From My Autobiography."

December 24, 1909: His youngest daughter, Jean, dies of a heart attack suffered during a seizure. Clemens spends two days writing "The Death of Jean" as the "last chapter" of his autobiography. With his only remaining child, Clara, recently married to the Russian musician Ossip Gabrilowitsch and living in Europe, Clemens is alone for the first time since he married.

January–April 1910: Visits Bermuda on his last trip outside the United States. When his health seriously declines, Paine goes to Bermuda to bring him home.

February 1910: "The Turning-Point in My Life" appears in *Harper's Bazar.*

April 21, 1910: Samuel Langhorne Clemens dies of heart failure in his Stormfield home at the age of seventy-four. Three days later, he is buried in Elmira's Woodlawn Cemetery, where all members of his family will eventually be interred.

August 18, 1910: His only grandchild, Nina Gabrilowitsch, is born at Stormfield to this daughter Clara.

September 1910: William Dean Howells publishes *My Mark Twain*, a personal tribute to his close friend.

1911: Archibald Henderson publishes *Mark Twain.*

January 1911: "The Death of Jean" appears in *Harper's Monthly.*

August 1912: Now Clemens's literary executor, Paine publishes his three-volume *Mark Twain, A Biography*. Over the next quarter-century he will edit and publish numerous collections of Clemens's previously unpublished writings.

February–June 1922: Paine publishes "Unpublished Chapters from the Autobiography of Mark Twain" in *Harper's Monthly*.

October 1924: Harper publishes *Mark Twain's Autobiography*, edited by Paine, in two volumes.

April 9, 1937: Paine dies in New Smyrna, Fla.; Bernard DeVoto succeeds him as editor of the Mark Twain Papers.

April 16, 1940: Harper publishes *Mark Twain in Eruption: Hitherto Unpublished Pages About Men and Events*, edited by DeVoto.

January 1946: DeVoto resigns as editor of the Mark Twain Papers. His successor, Dixon Wecter, will move the collection to the University of California at Berkeley three years later.

1959: Harper publishes *The Autobiography of Mark Twain: Including Chapters Now Published for the First Time*, edited by Charles Neider.

November 19, 1962: Clara Clemens Samossoud, Clemens's longest surviving child, dies in San Diego, Calif.

January 16, 1966: Nina Gabrilowitsch, Clemens's only grandchild and last direct descendant, dies in Los Angeles.

1990: University of Wisconsin Press publishes *Mark Twain's Own Autobiography*, the first book edition of the *North American Review*'s "Chapters from My Autobiography," edited by Michael Kiskis.

1996: Oxford University Press's twenty-nine-volume Oxford Mark Twain edition, edited by Shelley Fisher Fishkin, includes *Chapters from My Autobiography*, a volume containing facsimile reproductions of the original magazine articles.

2010: University of California Press publishes the first of three projected volumes of the *Autobiography of Mark Twain*, edited by Harriet Elinor Smith and other editors of the Mark Twain Papers. The book will spend twenty-four weeks on the *New York Times* list of best-selling nonfiction.

Autobiographical Writings

AUTOBIOGRAPHICAL
DICTATIONS

CHAPTERS FROM MY AUTOBIOGRAPHY

North American Review

No. DXCVIII.

SEPTEMBER 7, 1906

CHAPTERS FROM MY AUTOBIOGRAPHY—I

BY MARK TWAIN

PREFATORY NOTE—Mr. Clemens began to write his autobiography many years ago, and he continues to add to it day by day. It was his original intention to permit no publication of his memoirs until after his death; but, after leaving "Pier No. 70," he concluded that a considerable portion might now suitably be given to the public. It is that portion, garnered from the quarter-million of words already written, which will appear in this REVIEW during the coming year. No part of the autobiography will be published in book form during the lifetime of the author.—EDITOR N. A. R.

INTRODUCTION

I intend that this autobiography shall become a model for all future autobiographies when it is published, after my death, and I also intend that it shall be read and admired a good many centuries because of its form and method—a form and method whereby the past and the present are constantly brought face to face, resulting in contrasts which newly fire up the interest all along, like contact of flint with steel. Moreover, this autobiography of mine does not select from my life its showy episodes, but deals mainly in the common experiences which go to make up the life of the average human being, because these episodes are of a sort which he is familiar with in his own life, and in which he sees his own life reflected and set down in print. The usual, conventional autobiographer seems to particularly hunt out those occasions in his career when he came into contact with celebrated persons, whereas his contacts with the uncelebrated were just as interesting to him, and would be to his reader, and were vastly more numerous than his collisions with the famous.

Howells was here yesterday afternoon, and I told him the whole scheme of this autobiography and its apparently systemless system—only apparently systemless, for it is not really that. It is a deliberate system, and the law of the system is that I shall talk about the matter which for the moment interests me, and cast it aside and talk about something else the moment its interest for me is exhausted. It is a system which follows no charted course and is not going to follow any such course. It is a system which is a complete and purposed jumble—a course which begins nowhere, follows no specified route, and can never reach an end while I am alive, for the reason that, if I should talk to the stenographer two hours a day for a hundred years, I should still never be able to set down a tenth part of the things which have interested me in my lifetime. I told Howells that this autobiography of mine would live a couple of thousand years, without any effort, and would then take a fresh start and live the rest of the time.

He said he believed it would, and asked me if I meant to make a library of it.

I said that that was my design; but that, if I should live long enough, the set of volumes could not be contained merely in a city, it would require a State, and that there would not be any multi-billionaire alive, perhaps, at any time during its existence who would be able to buy a full set, except on the instalment plan.

Howells applauded, and was full of praises and endorse-

ment, which was wise in him and judicious. If he had manifested a different spirit, I would have thrown him out of the
window. I like criticism, but it must be my way.

I

Back of the Virginia Clemenses is a dim procession of ancestors stretching back to Noah's time. According to tradition,
some of them were pirates and slavers in Elizabeth's time. But
this is no discredit to them, for so were Drake and Hawkins
and the others. It was a respectable trade, then, and monarchs
were partners in it. In my time I have had desires to be a pirate
myself. The reader—if he will look deep down in his secret
heart, will find—but never mind what he will find there; I am
not writing his Autobiography, but mine. Later, according to
tradition, one of the procession was Ambassador to Spain in the
time of James 1, or of Charles 1, and married there and sent
down a strain of Spanish blood to warm us up. Also, according
to tradition, this one or another—Geoffrey Clement, by name—
helped to sentence Charles to death.

I have not examined into these traditions myself, partly
because I was indolent, and partly because I was so busy polishing up this end of the line and trying to make it showy; but
the other Clemenses claim that they have made the examination and that it stood the test. Therefore I have always taken for
granted that I did help Charles out of his troubles, by ancestral
proxy. My instincts have persuaded me, too. Whenever we
have a strong and persistent and ineradicable instinct, we may
be sure that it is not original with us, but inherited—inherited
from away back, and hardened and perfected by the petrifying
influence of time. Now I have been always and unchangingly
bitter against Charles, and I am quite certain that this feeling
trickled down to me through the veins of my forebears from
the heart of that judge; for it is not my disposition to be bitter
against people on my own personal account. I am not bitter
against Jeffreys. I ought to be, but I am not. It indicates that
my ancestors of James II's time were indifferent to him; I do

not know why; I never could make it out; but that is what it indicates. And I have always felt friendly toward Satan. Of course that is ancestral; it must be in the blood, for I could not have originated it.

. . . . And so, by the testimony of instinct, backed by the assertions of Clemenses who said they had examined the records, I have always been obliged to believe that Geoffrey Clement the martyr-maker was an ancestor of mine, and to regard him with favor, and in fact pride. This has not had a good effect upon me, for it has made me vain, and that is a fault. It has made me set myself above people who were less fortunate in their ancestry than I, and has moved me to take them down a peg, upon occasion, and say things to them which hurt them before company.

A case of the kind happened in Berlin several years ago. William Walter Phelps was our Minister at the Emperor's Court, then, and one evening he had me to dinner to meet Count S., a cabinet minister. This nobleman was of long and illustrious descent. Of course I wanted to let out the fact that I had some ancestors, too; but I did not want to pull them out of their graves by the ears, and I never could seem to get the chance to work them in in a way that would look sufficiently casual. I suppose Phelps was in the same difficulty. In fact he looked distraught, now and then—just as a person looks who wants to uncover an ancestor purely by accident, and cannot think of a way that will seem accidental enough. But at last, after dinner, he made a try. He took us about his drawing-room, showing us the pictures, and finally stopped before a rude and ancient engraving. It was a picture of the court that tried Charles I. There was a pyramid of judges in Puritan slouch hats, and below them three bareheaded secretaries seated at a table. Mr. Phelps put his finger upon one of the three, and said with exulting indifference—

"An ancestor of mine."

I put my finger on a judge, and retorted with scathing languidness—

"Ancestor of mine. But it is a small matter. I have others."

It was not noble in me to do it. I have always regretted it since.

But it landed him. I wonder how he felt? However, it made no difference in our friendship, which shows that he was fine and high, notwithstanding the humbleness of his origin. And it was also creditable in me, too, that I could overlook it. I made no change in my bearing toward him, but always treated him as an equal.

But it was a hard night for me in one way. Mr. Phelps thought I was the guest of honor, and so did Count S.; but I didn't, for there was nothing in my invitation to indicate it. It was just a friendly offhand note, on a card. By the time dinner was announced Phelps was himself in a state of doubt. Something had to be done; and it was not a handy time for explanations. He tried to get me to go out with him, but I held back; then he tried S., and he also declined. There was another guest, but there was no trouble about him. We finally went out in a pile. There was a decorous plunge for seats, and I got the one at Mr. Phelps's left, the Count captured the one facing Phelps, and the other guest had to take the place of honor, since he could not help himself. We returned to the drawing-room in the original disorder. I had new shoes on, and they were tight. At eleven I was privately crying; I couldn't help it, the pain was so cruel. Conversation had been dead for an hour. S. had been due at the bedside of a dying official ever since half past nine. At last we all rose by one blessed impulse and went down to the street door without explanations—in a pile, and no precedence; and so, parted.

The evening had its defects; still, I got my ancestor in, and was satisfied.

Among the Virginian Clemenses were Jere. (already mentioned), and Sherrard. Jere. Clemens had a wide reputation as a good pistol-shot, and once it enabled him to get on the friendly side of some drummers when they wouldn't have paid any attention to mere smooth words and arguments. He was out stumping the State at the time. The drummers were grouped in front of the stand, and had been hired by the opposition to drum while he made his speech. When he was ready to begin, he got out his revolver and laid it before him, and said in his soft, silky way—

"I do not wish to hurt anybody, and shall try not to; but I

have got just a bullet apiece for those six drums, and if you should want to play on them, don't stand behind them."

Sherrard Clemens was a Republican Congressman from West Virginia in the war days, and then went out to St. Louis, where the James Clemens branch lived, and still lives, and there he became a warm rebel. This was after the war. At the time that he was a Republican I was a rebel; but by the time he had become a rebel I was become (temporarily) a Republican. The Clemenses have always done the best they could to keep the political balances level, no matter how much it might inconvenience them. I did not know what had become of Sherrard Clemens; but once I introduced Senator Hawley to a Republican mass meeting in New England, and then I got a bitter letter from Sherrard from St. Louis. He said that the Republicans of the North—no, the "mudsills of the North"—had swept away the old aristocracy of the South with fire and sword, and it ill became me, an aristocrat by blood, to train with that kind of swine. Did I forget that I was a Lambton?

That was a reference to my mother's side of the house. As I have already said, she was a Lambton—Lambton with a p, for some of the American Lamptons could not spell very well in early times, and so the name suffered at their hands. She was a native of Kentucky, and married my father in Lexington in 1823, when she was twenty years old and he twenty-four. Neither of them had an overplus of property. She brought him two or three negroes, but nothing else, I think. They removed to the remote and secluded village of Jamestown, in the mountain solitudes of east Tennessee. There their first crop of children was born, but as I was of a later vintage I do not remember anything about it. I was postponed—postponed to Missouri. Missouri was an unknown new State and needed attractions.

I think that my eldest brother, Orion, my sisters Pamela and Margaret, and my brother Benjamin were born in Jamestown. There may have been others, but as to that I am not sure. It was a great lift for that little village to have my parents come there. It was hoped that they would stay, so that it would become a city. It was supposed that they would stay. And so there was a boom; but by and by they went away, and prices went down, and it was many years before Jamestown got another start. I have written about Jamestown in the "Gilded Age," a book of mine, but it was from hearsay, not from personal knowledge. My father left a fine estate behind him in the region round about Jamestown—75,000 acres.* When he died in 1847 he had owned it about twenty years. The taxes were almost nothing (five dollars a year for the whole), and he had always paid them regularly and kept his title perfect. He had always said that the land would not become valuable in his time, but that it would be a commodious provision for his children some day. It contained coal, copper, iron and timber, and he said that in the course of time railways would pierce to that region, and then the property would be property in fact as well as in name. It also produced a wild grape of a promising sort. He had sent some samples to Nicholas Longworth, of Cincinnati, to get his judgment upon them, and Mr. Longworth had said that they would make as good wine as his Catawbas. The land contained all these riches; and also oil, but my father did not know that, and of course in those early days he would have cared nothing about it if he had known it. The oil was not discovered until about 1895. I wish I owned a couple of acres of the land now. In which case I would not be writing Autobiographies for a living. My father's dying charge was, "Cling to the land and wait; let nothing beguile it away from you." My mother's favorite cousin, James Lampton, who figures in the "Gilded Age" as "Colonel Sellers," always said of that land—and said it with blazing enthusiasm, too,— "There's millions in it—millions!" It is true that he always said that about everything—and was always mistaken, too; but this time he was right; which shows that a man who goes around with a prophecy-gun ought never to get discouraged; if he will keep up his heart and fire at everything he sees, he is bound to hit something by and by.

Many persons regarded "Colonel Sellers" as a fiction, an invention, an extravagant impossibility, and did me the honor to call him a "creation"; but they were mistaken. I merely put

* Correction. 1906: it was above 100,000, it appears.

him on paper as he was; he was not a person who could be exaggerated. The incidents which looked most extravagant, both in the book and on the stage, were not inventions of mine but were facts of his life; and I was present when they were developed. John T. Raymond's audiences used to come near to dying with laughter over the turnip-eating scene; but, extravagant as the scene was, it was faithful to the facts, in all its absurd details. The thing happened in Lampton's own house, and I was present. In fact I was myself the guest who ate the turnips. In the hands of a great actor that piteous scene would have dimmed any manly spectator's eyes with tears, and racked his ribs apart with laughter at the same time. But Raymond was great in humorous portrayal only. In that he was superb, he was wonderful—in a word, great; in all things else he was a pigmy of the pigmies.

The real Colonel Sellers, as I knew him in James Lampton, was a pathetic and beautiful spirit, a manly man, a straight and honorable man, a man with a big, foolish, unselfish heart in his bosom, a man born to be loved; and he was loved by all his friends, and by his family worshipped. It is the right word. To them he was but little less than a god. The real Colonel Sellers was never on the stage. Only half of him was there. Raymond could not play the other half of him; it was above his level. That half was made up of qualities of which Raymond was wholly destitute. For Raymond was not a manly man, he was not an honorable man nor an honest one, he was empty and selfish and vulgar and ignorant and silly, and there was a vacancy in him where his heart should have been. There was only one man who could have played the whole of Colonel Sellers, and that was Frank Mayo.*

It is a world of surprises. They fall, too, where one is least expecting them. When I introduced Sellers into the book, Charles Dudley Warner, who was writing the story with me, proposed a change of Sellers's Christian name. Ten years

---

* Raymond was playing "Colonel Sellers" in 1876 and along there. About twenty years later Mayo dramatized "Pudd'nhead Wilson" and played the title rôle delightfully.

before, in a remote corner of the West, he had come across a man named Eschol Sellers, and he thought that Eschol was just the right and fitting name for our Sellers, since it was odd and quaint and all that. I liked the idea, but I said that that man might turn up and object. But Warner said it couldn't happen; that he was doubtless dead by this time, a man with a name like that couldn't live long; and be he dead or alive we must have the name, it was exactly the right one and we couldn't do without it. So the change was made. Warner's man was a farmer in a cheap and humble way. When the book had been out a week, a college-bred gentleman of courtly manners and ducal upholstery arrived in Hartford in a sultry state of mind and with a libel suit in his eye, and *his* name was Eschol Sellers! He had never heard of the other one, and had never been within a thousand miles of him. This damaged aristocrat's programme was quite definite and businesslike: the American Publishing Company must suppress the edition as far as printed, and change the name in the plates, or stand a suit for $10,000. He carried away the Company's promise and many apologies, and we changed the name back to Colonel Mulberry Sellers, in the plates. Apparently there is nothing that cannot happen. Even the existence of two unrelated men wearing the impossible name of Eschol Sellers is a possible thing.

James Lampton floated, all his days, in a tinted mist of magnificent dreams, and died at last without seeing one of them realized. I saw him last in 1884, when it had been twenty-six years since I ate the basin of raw turnips and washed them down with a bucket of water in his house. He was become old and white-headed, but he entered to me in the same old breezy way of his earlier life, and he was all there, yet—not a detail wanting: the happy light in his eye, the abounding hope in his heart, the persuasive tongue, the miracle-breeding imagination—they were all there; and before I could turn around he was polishing up his Aladdin's lamp and flashing the secret riches of the world before me. I said to myself, "I did not overdraw him by a shade, I set him down as he was; and he is the same man today. Cable will recognize him." I asked him to excuse me a moment, and ran into the next room, which was

Cable's; Cable and I were stumping the Union on a reading tour. I said—

"I am going to leave your door open, so that you can listen. There is a man in there who is interesting."

I went back and asked Lampton what he was doing now. He began to tell me of a "small venture" he had begun in New Mexico through his son; "only a little thing—a mere trifle— partly to amuse my leisure, partly to keep my capital from lying idle, but mainly to develop the boy—develop the boy; fortune's wheel is ever revolving, he may have to work for his living some day—as strange things have happened in this world. But it's only a little thing—a mere trifle, as I said."

And so it was—as he began it. But under his deft hands it grew, and blossomed, and spread—oh, beyond imagination. At the end of half an hour he finished; finished with the remark, uttered in an adorably languid manner:

"Yes, it is but a trifle, as things go nowadays—a bagatelle— but amusing. It passes the time. The boy thinks great things of it, but he is young, you know, and imaginative; lacks the experience which comes of handling large affairs, and which tempers the fancy and perfects the judgment. I suppose there's a couple of millions in it, possibly three, but not more, I think; still, for a boy, you know, just starting in life, it is not bad. I should not want him to make a fortune—let that come later. It could turn his head, at his time of life, and in many ways be a damage to him."

Then he said something about his having left his pocketbook lying on the table in the main drawing-room at home, and about its being after banking hours, now, and—

I stopped him, there, and begged him to honor Cable and me by being our guest at the lecture—with as many friends as might be willing to do us the like honor. He accepted. And he thanked me as a prince might who had granted us a grace. The reason I stopped his speech about the tickets was because I saw that he was going to ask me to furnish them to him and let him pay next day; and I knew that if he made the debt he would pay it if he had to pawn his clothes. After a little further chat he shook hands heartily and affectionately, and took his leave. Cable put his head in at the door, and said—

"That was Colonel Sellers."

MARK TWAIN

(to be continued)

North American Review

No. DXCIX.

SEPTEMBER 21, 1906

CHAPTERS FROM MY AUTOBIOGRAPHY—II

BY MARK TWAIN

PREFATORY NOTE—Mr. Clemens began to write his autobiography many years ago, and he continues to add to it day by day. It was his original intention to permit no publication of his memoirs until after his death; but, after leaving "Pier No. 70," he concluded that a considerable portion might now suitably be given to the public. It is that portion, garnered from the quarter-million of words already written, which will appear in this REVIEW during the coming year. No part of the autobiography will be published in book form during the lifetime of the author.—EDITOR N. A. R.

II

My experiences as an author began early in 1867. I came to New York from San Francisco in the first month of that year and presently Charles H. Webb, whom I had known in San Francisco as a reporter on *The Bulletin*, and afterward editor of *The Californian*, suggested that I publish a volume of sketches. I had but a slender reputation to publish it on, but I was charmed and excited by the suggestion and quite willing to venture it if some industrious person would save me the trouble of gathering the sketches together. I was loath to do it myself, for from the beginning of my sojourn in this world there was a persistent vacancy in me where the industry ought to be. ("Ought to was" is better, perhaps, though the most of the authorities differ as to this.)

Webb said I had some reputation in the Atlantic States, but I knew quite well that it must be of a very attenuated sort. What there was of it rested upon the story of "The Jumping Frog." When Artemus Ward passed through California on a lecturing tour, in 1865 or '66, I told him the "Jumping Frog" story, in San Francisco, and he asked me to write it out and send it to his publisher, Carleton, in New York, to be used in padding out a small book which Artemus had prepared for the press and which needed some more stuffing to make it big enough for the price which was to be charged for it.

It reached Carleton in time, but he didn't think much of it, and was not willing to go to the typesetting expense of adding it to the book. He did not put it in the waste-basket, but made Henry Clapp a present of it, and Clapp used it to help out the funeral of his dying literary journal, *The Saturday Press*. "The Jumping Frog" appeared in the last number of that paper, was the most joyous feature of the obsequies, and was at once copied in the newspapers of America and England. It certainly had a wide celebrity, and it still had it at the time that I am speaking of—but I was aware that it was only the frog that was celebrated. It wasn't I. I was still an obscurity.

Webb undertook to collate the sketches. He performed this office, then handed the result to me, and I went to Carleton's establishment with it. I approached a clerk and he bent eagerly over the counter to inquire into my needs; but when he found that I had come to sell a book and not to buy one, his temperature fell sixty degrees, and the old-gold intrenchments in the roof of my mouth contracted three-quarters of an inch and my teeth fell out. I meekly asked the privilege of a word with Mr. Carleton, and was coldly informed that he was in his private office. Discouragements and difficulties followed, but after a while I got by the frontier and entered the holy of holies. Ah, now I remember how I managed it! Webb had made an appointment for me with Carleton; otherwise I never should have gotten over that frontier. Carleton rose and said brusquely and aggressively,

"Well, what can I do for you?"

I reminded him that I was there by appointment to offer him my book for publication. He began to swell, and went on swelling and swelling and swelling until he had reached the dimensions of a god of about the second or third degree. Then the fountains of his great deep were broken up, and for two or three minutes I couldn't see him for the rain. It was words, only words, but they fell so densely that they darkened the atmosphere. Finally he made an imposing sweep with his right hand, which comprehended the whole room and said,

"Books—look at those shelves! Every one of them is loaded with books that are waiting for publication. Do I want any more? Excuse me, I don't. Good morning."

Twenty-one years elapsed before I saw Carleton again. I was then sojourning with my family at the Schweitzerhof, in Luzerne. He called on me, shook hands cordially, and said at once, without any preliminaries,

"I am substantially an obscure person, but I have at least one distinction to my credit of such colossal dimensions that it entitles me to immortality—to wit: I refused a book of yours, and for this I stand without competitor as the prize ass of the nineteenth century."

It was a most handsome apology, and I told him so, and said it was a long-delayed revenge but was sweeter to me than any other that could be devised; that during the lapsed twenty-one years I had in fancy taken his life several times every year, and always in new and increasingly cruel and inhuman ways, but that now I was pacified, appeased, happy, even jubilant; and that thenceforth I should hold him my true and valued friend and never kill him again.

I reported my adventure to Webb, and he bravely said that not all the Carletons in the universe should defeat that book; he would publish it himself on a ten per cent. royalty. And so he did. He brought it out in blue and gold, and made a very pretty little book of it. I think he named it "The Celebrated Jumping Frog of Calaveras County, and Other Sketches," price $1.25. He made the plates and printed and bound the book through a job-printing house, and published it through the American News Company.

In June I sailed in the *Quaker City* Excursion. I returned in November, and in Washington found a letter from Elisha Bliss, of the American Publishing Company of Hartford, offering me five per cent. royalty on a book which should recount the adventures of the Excursion. In lieu of the royalty, I was offered the alternative of ten thousand dollars cash upon delivery of the manuscript. I consulted A. D. Richardson and he said "take the royalty." I followed his advice and closed with Bliss. By my contract I was to deliver the manuscript in July of 1868. I wrote the book in San Francisco and delivered the manuscript within contract time. Bliss provided a multitude of illustrations for the book, and then stopped work on it. The contract date for the issue went by, and there was no explanation of this. Time drifted along and still there was no explanation. I was lecturing all over the country; and about thirty times a day, on an average, I was trying to answer this conundrum:

"When is your book coming out?"

I got tired of inventing new answers to that question, and by and by I got horribly tired of the question itself. Whoever asked it became my enemy at once, and I was usually almost eager to make that appear.

As soon as I was free of the lecture-field I hastened to Hartford to make inquiries. Bliss said that the fault was not his; that he wanted to publish the book but the directors of his Company were staid old fossils and were afraid of it. They had examined the book, and the majority of them were of the opinion that there were places in it of a humorous character. Bliss said the house had never published a book that had a suspicion like that attaching to it, and that the directors were afraid that a departure of this kind would seriously injure the house's reputation; that he was tied hand and foot, and was not permitted to carry out his contract. One of the directors, a Mr. Drake—at least he was the remains of what had once been a Mr. Drake—invited me to take a ride with him in his buggy, and I went along. He was a pathetic old relic, and his

ways and his talk were also pathetic. He had a delicate purpose
in view and it took him some time to hearten himself sufficiently
to carry it out, but at last he accomplished it. He explained the
house's difficulty and distress, as Bliss had already explained
it. Then he frankly threw himself and the house upon my
mercy and begged me to take away "The Innocents Abroad"
and release the concern from the contract. I said I wouldn't—
and so ended the interview and the buggy excursion. Then I
warned Bliss that he must get to work or I should make trouble.
He acted upon the warning, and set up the book and I read the
proofs. Then there was another long wait and no explanation.
At last toward the end of July (1896, I think), I lost patience
and telegraphed Bliss that if the book was not on sale in twenty-
four hours I should bring suit for damages.

That ended the trouble. Half a dozen copies were bound
and placed on sale within the required time. Then the canvass-
ing began, and went briskly forward. In nine months the book
took the publishing house out of debt, advanced its stock from
twenty-five to two hundred, and left seventy thousand dollars
profit to the good. It was Bliss that told me this—but if it was
true, it was the first time that he had told the truth in sixty-five
years. He was born in 1804.

III

. . . This was in 1849. I was fourteen years old, then. We were
still living in Hannibal, Missouri, on the banks of the Mississippi, in the new "frame" house built by my father five years
before. That is, some of us lived in the new part, the rest in the
old part back of it—the "L." In the autumn my sister gave a
party, and invited all the marriageable young people of the village. I was too young for this society, and was too bashful to
mingle with young ladies, anyway, therefore I was not invited—
at least not for the whole evening. Ten minutes of it was to be
my whole share. I was to do the part of a bear in a small fairy
play. I was to be disguised all over in a close-fitting brown
hairy stuff proper for a bear. About half past ten I was told to

go to my room and put on this disguise, and be ready in half an hour. I started, but changed my mind; for I wanted to prac- tise a little, and that room was very small. I crossed over to the large unoccupied house on the corner of Main and Hill streets,* unaware that a dozen of the young people were also going there to dress for their parts. I took the little black slave boy, Sandy, with me, and we selected a roomy and empty chamber on the second floor. We entered it talking, and this gave a cou- ple of half-dressed young ladies an opportunity to take refuge behind a screen undiscovered. Their gowns and things were hanging on hooks behind the door, but I did not see them; it was Sandy that shut the door, but all his heart was in the the- atricals, and he was as unlikely to notice them as I was myself.

That was a rickety screen, with many holes in it, but as I did not know there were girls behind it, I was not disturbed by that detail. If I had known, I could not have undressed in the flood of cruel moonlight that was pouring in at the curtainless windows; I should have died of shame. Untroubled by appre- hensions, I stripped to the skin and began my practice. I was full of ambition; I was determined to make a hit; I was burn- ing to establish a reputation as a bear and get further engage- ments; so I threw myself into my work with an abandon that promised great things. I capered back and forth from one end of the room to the other on all fours, Sandy applauding with enthusiasm; I walked upright and growled and snapped and snarled; I stood on my head, I flung handsprings, I danced a lubberly dance with my paws bent and my imaginary snout sniffing from side to side; I did everything a bear could do, and many things which no bear could ever do and no bear with any dignity would want to do, anyway; and of course I never suspected that I was making a spectacle of myself to any one but Sandy. At last, standing on my head, I paused in that atti- tude to take a minute's rest. There was a moment's silence, then Sandy spoke up with excited interest and said—

"Marse Sam, has you ever seen a smoked herring?"

"No. What is that?"

* That house still stands.

"It's a fish."

"Well, what of it? Anything peculiar about it?"

"Yes, suh, you bet you dey is. *Dey eats 'em guts and all!*"

There was a smothered burst of feminine snickers from behind the screen! All the strength went out of me and I toppled forward like an undermined tower and brought the screen down with my weight, burying the young ladies under it. In their fright they discharged a couple of piercing screams—and possibly others, but I did not wait to count. I snatched my clothes and fled to the dark hall below, Sandy following. I was dressed in half a minute, and out the back way. I swore Sandy to eternal silence, then we went away and hid until the party was over. The ambition was all out of me. I could not have faced that giddy company after my adventure, for there would be two performers there who knew my secret, and would be privately laughing at me all the time. I was searched for but not found, and the bear had to be played by a young gentleman in his civilized clothes. The house was still and everybody asleep when I finally ventured home. I was very heavy-hearted, and full of a sense of disgrace. Pinned to my pillow I found a slip of paper which bore a line that did not lighten my heart, but only made my face burn. It was written in a laboriously disguised hand, and these were its mocking terms:

"You probably couldn't have played *bear*, but you played *bare* very well—oh, very very well!"

We think boys are rude, unsensitive animals, but it is not so in all cases. Each boy has one or two sensitive spots, and if you can find out where they are located you have only to touch them and you can scorch him as with fire. I suffered miserably over that episode. I expected that the facts would be all over the village in the morning, but it was not so. The secret remained confined to the two girls and Sandy and me. That was some appeasement of my pain, but it was far from sufficient—the main trouble remained: I was under four mocking eyes, and it might as well have been a thousand, for I suspected all girls' eyes of being the ones I so dreaded. During several weeks I could not look any young lady in the face; I dropped my eyes in confusion when any one of them smiled upon me and gave me greeting; and I said to myself, "*That is one of them*," and got quickly away. Of course I was meeting the right girls everywhere, but if they ever let slip any betraying sign I was not bright enough to catch it. When I left Hannibal four years later, the secret was still a secret; I had never guessed those girls out, and was no longer expecting to do it. Nor wanting to, either.

One of the dearest and prettiest girls in the village at the time of my mishap was one whom I will call Mary Wilson, because that was not her name. She was twenty years old; she was dainty and sweet, peach-bloomy and exquisite, gracious and lovely in character, and I stood in awe of her, for she seemed to me to be made out of angel-clay and rightfully unapproachable by an unholy ordinary kind of a boy like me. I probably never suspected her. But—

The scene changes. To Calcutta—forty-seven years later. It was in 1896. I arrived there on my lecturing trip. As I entered the hotel a divine vision passed out of it, clothed in the glory of the Indian sunshine—the Mary Wilson of my long-vanished boyhood! It was a startling thing. Before I could recover from the bewildering shock and speak to her she was gone. I thought maybe I had seen an apparition, but it was not so, she was flesh. She was the granddaughter of the other Mary, the original Mary. That Mary, now a widow, was up-stairs, and presently sent for me. She was old and gray-haired, but she looked young and was very handsome. We sat down and talked. We steeped our thirsty souls in the reviving wine of the past, the beautiful past, the dear and lamented past; we uttered the names that had been silent upon our lips for fifty years, and it was as if they were made of music; with reverent hands we unburied our dead, the mates of our youth, and caressed them with our speech; we searched the dusty chambers of our memories and dragged forth incident after incident, episode after episode, folly after folly, and laughed such good laughs over them, with the tears running down; and finally Mary said suddenly, and without any leading up—

"Tell me! What is the special peculiarity of smoked herrings?"

It seemed a strange question at such a hallowed time as this. And so inconsequential, too. I was a little shocked. And yet I was aware of a stir of some kind away back in the deeps of my memory somewhere. It set me to musing—thinking—searching. Smoked herrings. Smoked herrings. The peculiarity of smo. . . . I glanced up. Her face was grave, but there was a dim and shadowy twinkle in her eye which— All of a sudden I knew! and far away down in the hoary past I heard a remembered voice murmur, "Dey eats 'em guts and all!"

"At—last! I've found one of you, anyway! Who was the other girl?"

But she drew the line there. She wouldn't tell me.

IV

. . . But it was on a bench in Washington Square that I saw the most of Louis Stevenson. It was an outing that lasted an hour or more, and was very pleasant and sociable. I had come with him from his house, where I had been paying my respects to his family. His business in the Square was to absorb the sunshine. He was most scantily furnished with flesh, his clothes seemed to fall into hollows as if there might be nothing inside but the frame for a sculptor's statue. His long face and lank hair and dark complexion and musing and melancholy expression seemed to fit these details justly and harmoniously, and the altogether of it seemed especially planned to gather the rays of your observation and focalize them upon Stevenson's special distinction and commanding feature, his splendid eyes. They burned with a smouldering rich fire under the penthouse of his brows, and they made him beautiful.

I said I thought he was right about the others, but mistaken as to Bret Harte; in substance I said that Harte was good company and a thin but pleasant talker; that he was always bright, but never brilliant; that in this matter he must not be classed with Thomas Bailey Aldrich, nor must any other man, ancient or modern; that Aldrich was always witty, always brilliant, if there was anybody present capable of striking his flint at the right angle; that Aldrich was as sure and prompt and unfailing as the red-hot iron on the blacksmith's anvil—you had only to hit it competently to make it deliver an explosion of sparks. I added—

"Aldrich has never had his peer for prompt and pithy and witty and humorous sayings. None has equalled him, certainly none has surpassed him, in the felicity of phrasing with which he clothed these children of his fancy. Aldrich was always brilliant, he couldn't help it, he is a fire-opal set round with rose diamonds; when he is not speaking, you know that his dainty fancies are twinkling and glimmering around in him; when he speaks the diamonds flash. Yes, he was always brilliant, he will always be brilliant; he will be brilliant in hell—you will see."

Stevenson, smiling a chuckly smile, "I hope not."

"Well, you will, and he will dim even those ruddy fires and look like a transfigured Adonis backed against a pink sunset."

There on that bench we struck out a new phrase—one or the other of us, I don't remember which — "submerged renown." Variations were discussed: "submerged fame," "submerged reputation," and so on, and a choice was made; "submerged renown" was elected, I believe. This important matter rose out of an incident which had been happening to Stevenson in Albany. While in a book-shop or book-stall there he had noticed a long rank of small books, cheaply but neatly gotten up, and bearing such titles as "Davis's Selected Speeches," "Davis's Selected Poetry," Davis's this and Davis's that and Davis's the other thing; compilations, every one of them, each with a brief, compact, intelligent and useful introductory chapter by this same Davis, whose first name I have forgotten. Stevenson had begun the matter with this question:

"Can you name the American author whose fame and acceptance stretch widest in the States?"

I thought I could, but it did not seem to me that it would be modest to speak out, in the circumstances. So I diffidently said nothing. Stevenson noticed, and said—

"Save your delicacy for another time—you are not the one. For a shilling you can't name the American author of widest note and popularity in the States. But I can."

Then he went on and told about that Albany incident. He had inquired of the shopman—

"Who is this Davis?"

The answer was—

"An author whose books have to have freight-trains to carry them, not baskets. Apparently you have not heard of him?"

Stevenson said no, this was the first time. The man said—

"Nobody has heard of Davis: you may ask all around and you will see. You never see his name mentioned in print, not even in advertisement; these things are of no use to Davis, not any more than they are to the wind and the sea. You never see one of Davis's books floating on top of the United States, but put on your diving armor and get yourself lowered away down and down and down till you strike the dense region, the sunless region of eternal drudgery and starvation wages—there you'll find them by the million. The man that gets that market, his fortune is made, his bread and butter are safe, for those people will never go back on him. An author may have a reputation which is confined to the surface, and lose it and become pitied, then despised, then forgotten, entirely forgotten—the frequent steps in a surface reputation. A surface reputation, however great, is always mortal, and always killable if you go at it right—with pins and needles, and quiet slow poison, not with the club and tomahawk. But it is a different matter with the submerged reputation—down in the deep water; once a favorite there, always a favorite; once beloved, always beloved; once respected, always respected, honored, and believed in. For, what the reviewer says never finds its way down into those placid deeps; nor the newspaper sneers, nor any breath of the winds of slander blowing above. Down there they never hear of these things. Their idol may be painted clay, up there at the surface, and fade and waste and crumble and blow away, there being much weather there; but down below he is gold and adamant and indestructible."

V

This is from this morning's paper:

MARK TWAIN LETTER SOLD
Written to Thomas Nast, it Proposed a Joint Tour.

A Mark Twain autograph letter brought $43 yesterday at the auction by the Merwin-Clayton Company of the library and correspondence of the late Thomas Nast, cartoonist. The letter is nine pages note-paper, is dated Hartford, Nov. 12, 1877, and is addressed to Nast. It reads in part as follows:

HARTFORD, *Nov. 12.*

MY DEAR NAST: I did not think I should ever stand on a platform again until the time was come for me to say I die innocent. But the same old offers keep arriving that have arriven every year, and been every year declined—$500 for Louisville, $500 for St. Louis, $1,000 gold for two nights in Toronto, half gross proceeds for New York, Boston, Brooklyn, &c. I have declined them all just as usual, though sorely tempted as usual.

Now, I do not decline because I mind talking to an audience, but because (1) travelling alone is so heart-breakingly dreary, and (2) shouldering the whole show is such cheer-killing responsibility.

Therefore I now propose to you what you proposed to me in November, 1867—ten years ago, (when I was unknown,) viz.; That you should stand on the platform and make pictures, and I stand by you and blackguard the audience. I should enormously enjoy meandering around (to big towns—don't want to go to little ones) with you for company.

The letter includes a schedule of cities and the number of appearances planned for each.

This is as it should be. This is worthy of all praise. I say it myself lest other competent persons should forget to do it. It appears that four of my ancient letters were sold at auction, three of them at twenty-seven dollars, twenty-eight dollars, and twenty-nine dollars respectively, and the one above mentioned at forty-three dollars. There is one very gratifying circumstance about this, to wit: that my literature has more than held its own as regards money value through this stretch of thirty-six years. I judge that the forty-three-dollar letter must have gone at about ten cents a word, whereas if I had written it to-day its market rate would be thirty cents—so I have increased in value two or three hundred per cent. I note another gratifying circumstance—that a letter of General Grant's sold at something short of eighteen dollars. I can't rise to General Grant's lofty place in the estimation of this nation, but it is a deep happiness to me to know that when it comes to epistolary literature he can't sit in the front seat along with me.

This reminds me—nine years ago, when we were living in Tedworth Square, London, a report was cabled to the American journals that I was dying. I was not the one. It was another Clemens, a cousin of mine,—Dr. J. Ross Clemens, now of St. Louis—who was due to die but presently escaped, by some chicanery or other characteristic of the tribe of Clemens. The London representatives of the American papers began to flock in, with American cables in their hands, to inquire into my condition. There was nothing the matter with me, and each in his turn was astonished, and disappointed, to find me reading and smoking in my study and worth next to nothing as a text for transatlantic news. One of these men was a gentle and kindly and grave and sympathetic Irishman, who hid his sorrow the best he could, and tried to look glad, and told me that his paper, the *Evening Sun*, had cabled him that it was reported in New York that I was dead. What should he cable in reply? I said—

"Say the report is greatly exaggerated."

He never smiled, but went solemnly away and sent the cable in those words. The remark hit the world pleasantly, and to this day it keeps turning up, now and then, in the newspapers when people have occasion to discount exaggerations.

The next man was also an Irishman. He had his New York cablegram in his hand—from the New York *World*—and he was so evidently trying to get around that cable with invented softnesses and palliations that my curiosity was aroused and I wanted to see what it did really say. So when occasion offered I slipped it out of his hand. It said,

"If Mark Twain dying send five hundred words. If dead send a thousand."

Now that old letter of mine sold yesterday for forty-three dollars. When I am dead it will be worth eighty-six.

MARK TWAIN

(to be continued)

North American Review

No. DC.

OCTOBER 5, 1906

CHAPTERS FROM MY AUTOBIOGRAPHY—III

BY MARK TWAIN

PREFATORY NOTE—Mr. Clemens began to write his autobiography many years ago, and he continues to add to it day by day. It was his original intention to permit no publication of his memoirs until after his death; but, after leaving "Pier No. 70," he concluded that a considerable portion might now suitably be given to the public. It is that portion, garnered from the quarter-million of words already written, which will appear in this REVIEW during the coming year. No part of the autobiography will be published in book form during the lifetime of the author. —EDITOR N. A. R.

VI

To-morrow will be the thirty-sixth anniversary of our marriage. My wife passed from this life one year and eight months ago, in Florence, Italy, after an unbroken illness of twenty-two months' duration.

I saw her first in the form of an ivory miniature in her brother Charley's stateroom in the steamer "Quaker City," in the Bay of Smyrna, in the summer of 1867, when she was in her twenty-second year. I saw her in the flesh for the first time in New York in the following December. She was slender and beautiful and girlish—and she was both girl and woman. She remained both girl and woman to the last day of her life.

Under a grave and gentle exterior burned inextinguishable fires of sympathy, energy, devotion, enthusiasm, and absolutely limitless affection. She was *always* frail in body, and she lived upon her spirit, whose hopefulness and courage were indestructible. Perfect truth, perfect honesty, perfect candor, were qualities of her character which were born with her. Her judgments of people and things were sure and accurate. Her intuitions almost never deceived her. In her judgments of the characters and acts of both friends and strangers, there was always room for charity, and this charity never failed. I have compared and contrasted her with hundreds of persons, and my conviction remains that hers was the most perfect character I have ever met. And I may add that she was the most winningly dignified person I have ever known. Her character and disposition were of the sort that not only invites worship, but commands it. No servant ever left her service who deserved to remain in it. And, as she could choose with a glance of her eye, the servants she selected did in almost all cases deserve to remain, and they *did* remain. She was always cheerful; and she was always able to communicate her cheerfulness to others. During the nine years that we spent in poverty and debt, she was always able to reason me out of my despairs, and find a bright side to the clouds, and make me see it. In all that time, I never knew her to utter a word of regret concerning our altered circumstances, nor did I ever know her children to do the like. For she had taught them, and they drew their fortitude from her. The love which she bestowed upon those whom she loved took the form of worship, and in that form it was returned—returned by relatives, friends and the servants of her household. It was a strange combination which wrought into one individual, so to speak, by marriage—her disposition and character and mine. She poured out her prodigal affections in kisses and caresses, and in a vocabulary of endearments whose profusion was always an astonishment to me. I was born *reserved* as to endearments of speech and caresses, and hers broke upon me as the summer waves break upon Gibraltar. I was reared in that atmosphere of reserve. As I have already said, in another chapter, I never knew a member of my father's family to kiss another member of it except once, and that at a death-bed. And our village was not a kissing community. The kissing and caressing ended with courtship—along with the deadly piano-playing of that day.

She had the heart-free laugh of a girl. It came seldom, but when it broke upon the ear it was as inspiring as music. I heard it for the last time when she had been occupying her sickbed for more than a year, and I made a written note of it at the time—a note not to be repeated.

To-morrow will be the thirty-sixth anniversary. We were married in her father's house in Elmira, New York, and went next day, by special train, to Buffalo, along with the whole Langdon family, and with the Beechers and the Twichells, who had solemnized the marriage. We were to live in Buffalo, where I was to be one of the editors of the Buffalo "Express," and a part owner of the paper. I knew nothing about Buffalo, but I had made my household arrangements there through a friend, by letter. I had instructed him to find a boarding-house of as respectable a character as my light salary as editor would command. We were received at about nine o'clock at the station in Buffalo, and were put into several sleighs and driven all over America, as it seemed to me—for, apparently, we turned all the corners in the town and followed all the streets there were—I scolding freely, and characterizing that friend of mine in very uncomplimentary words for securing a boarding-house that apparently had no definite locality. But there was a conspiracy—and my bride knew of it, but I was in ignorance. Her father, Jervis Langdon, had bought and furnished a new house for us in the fashionable street, Delaware Avenue, and had laid in a cook and housemaids, and a brisk and electric young coachman, an Irishman, Patrick McAleer—and we were being driven all over that city in order that one sleighful of those people could have time to go to the house, and see that the gas was lighted all over it, and a hot supper prepared for the crowd. We arrived at last, and when I entered that fairy place my indignation reached high-water mark, and without any reserve I delivered my opinion to that friend of mine for being so stupid as to put us into a boarding-house whose terms would be far out of my reach. Then Mr. Langdon brought forward a very pretty box and opened it, and took from it a deed of the house. So the comedy ended very pleasantly, and we sat down to supper.

The company departed about midnight, and left us alone in our new quarters. Then Ellen, the cook, came in to get orders for the morning's marketing—and neither of us knew whether beefsteak was sold by the barrel or by the yard. We exposed our ignorance, and Ellen was full of Irish delight over it. Patrick McAleer, that brisk young Irishman, came in to get his orders for next day—and that was our first glimpse of him. . . .

Our first child, Langdon Clemens, was born the 7th of November, 1870, and lived twenty-two months. Susy was born the 19th of March, 1872, and passed from life in the Hartford home, the 18th of August, 1896. With her, when the end came, were Jean and Katy Leary, and John and Ellen (the gardener and his wife). Clara and her mother and I arrived in England from around the world on the 31st of July, and took a house in Guildford. A week later, when Susy, Katy and Jean should have been arriving from America, we got a letter instead.

It explained that Susy was slightly ill—nothing of consequence. But we were disquieted, and began to cable for later news. This was Friday. All day no answer—and the ship to leave Southampton next day, at noon. Clara and her mother began packing, to be ready in case the news should be bad. Finally came a cablegram saying, "Wait for cablegram in the morning." This was not satisfactory—not reassuring. I cabled again, asking that the answer be sent to Southampton, for the day was now closing. I waited in the post-office that night till the doors were closed, toward midnight, in the hope that good news might still come, but there was no message. We sat silent at home till one in the morning, waiting—waiting for we knew not what. Then we took the earliest morning train, and when we reached Southampton the message was there. It said the recovery would be long, but certain. This was a great relief to me, but not to my wife. She was frightened. She and Clara went aboard the steamer at once and sailed for America, to nurse Susy. I remained behind to search for a larger house in Guildford.

That was the 15th of August, 1896. Three days later, when my wife and Clara were about half-way across the ocean, I was standing in our dining-room thinking of nothing in particular, when a cablegram was put into my hand. It said, "Susy was peacefully released to-day."

It is one of the mysteries of our nature that a man, all unprepared, can receive a thunder-stroke like that and live. There is but one reasonable explanation of it. The intellect is stunned by the shock, and but gropingly gathers the meaning of the words. The power to realize their full import is mercifully wanting. The mind has a dumb sense of vast loss—that is all. It will take mind and memory months, and possibly years, to gather together the details, and thus learn and know the whole extent of the loss. A man's house burns down. The smoking wreckage represents only a ruined home that was dear through years of use and pleasant associations. By and by, as the days and weeks go on, first he misses this, then that, then the other thing. And, when he casts about for it, he finds that it was in that house. Always it is an *essential*—there was but one of its kind. It cannot be replaced. It was in that house. It is irrevocably lost. He did not realize that it was an essential when he had it; he only discovers it now when he finds himself balked, hampered, by its absence. It will be years before the tale of lost essentials is complete, and not till then can he truly know the magnitude of his disaster.

The 18th of August brought me the awful tidings. The mother and the sister were out there in mid-Atlantic, ignorant of what was happening; flying to meet this incredible calamity. All that could be done to protect them from the full force of the shock was done by relatives and good friends. They went down the Bay and met the ship at night, but did not show themselves until morning, and then only to Clara. When she returned to the stateroom she did not speak, and did not need to. Her mother looked at her and said:

"Susy is dead."

At half past ten o'clock that night, Clara and her mother

completed their circuit of the globe, and drew up at Elmira by the same train and in the same car which had borne them and me Westward from it one year, one month, and one week before. And again Susy was there—not waving her welcome in the glare of the lights, as she had waved her farewell to us thirteen months before, but lying white and fair in her coffin, in the house where she was born.

The last thirteen days of Susy's life were spent in our own house in Hartford, the home of her childhood, and always the dearest place in the earth to her. About her she had faithful old friends—her pastor, Mr. Twichell, who had known her from the cradle, and who had come a long journey to be with her; her uncle and aunt, Mr. and Mrs. Theodore Crane; Patrick, the coachman; Katy, who had begun to serve us when Susy was a child of eight years; John and Ellen, who had been with us many years. Also Jean was there.

At the hour when my wife and Clara set sail for America, Susy was in no danger. Three hours later there came a sudden change for the worse. Meningitis set in, and it was immediately apparent that she was death-struck. That was Saturday, the 15th of August.

"That evening she took food for the last time," (Jean's letter to me). The next morning the brain-fever was raging. She walked the floor a little in her pain and delirium, then succumbed to weakness and returned to her bed. Previously she had found hanging in a closet a gown which she had seen her mother wear. She thought it was her mother, dead, and she kissed it, and cried. About noon she became blind (an effect of the disease) and bewailed it to her uncle.

From Jean's letter I take this sentence, which needs no comment:

"About one in the afternoon Susy spoke for the last time."

It was only one word that she said when she spoke that last time, and it told of her longing. She groped with her hands and found Katy, and caressed her face, and said "Mamma."

How gracious it was that, in that forlorn hour of wreck and ruin, with the night of death closing around her, she should have been granted that beautiful illusion—that the latest vision which rested upon the clouded mirror of her mind should have been the vision of her mother, and the latest emotion she should know in life the joy and peace of that dear imagined presence.

About two o'clock she composed herself as if for sleep, and never moved again. She fell into unconsciousness and so remained two days and five hours, until Tuesday evening at seven minutes past seven, when the release came. She was twenty-four years and five months old.

On the 23d, her mother and her sisters saw her laid to rest—she that had been our wonder and our worship.

In one of her own books I find some verses which I will copy here. Apparently, she always put borrowed matter in quotation marks. These verses lack those marks, and therefore I take them to be her own:

> Love came at dawn, when all the world was fair,
> When crimson glories' bloom and sun were rife;
> Love came at dawn, when hope's wings fanned the air,
> And murmured, "I am life."
>
> Love came at eve, and when the day was done,
> When heart and brain were tired, and slumber pressed;
> Love came at eve, shut out the sinking sun,
> And whispered, "I am rest."

The summer seasons of Susy's childhood were spent at Quarry Farm, on the hills east of Elmira, New York; the other seasons of the year at the home in Hartford. Like other children, she was blithe and happy, fond of play; *un*like the average of children, she was at times much given to retiring within herself, and trying to search out the hidden meanings of the deep things that make the puzzle and pathos of human existence, and in all the ages have baffled the inquirer and mocked him. As a little child aged seven, she was oppressed and perplexed by the maddening repetition of the stock incidents of our race's fleeting sojourn here, just as the same thing has oppressed and perplexed maturer minds from the beginning of time. A myriad of men are born; they labor and sweat and struggle for bread; they squabble and scold and fight; they scramble for little mean advantages over each other; age creeps upon them; infirmities follow; shames and humiliations bring down their prides and their vanities; those they love are taken from them, and the joy of life is turned to aching grief. The burden of pain, care, misery, grows heavier year by year; at length, ambition is dead, pride is dead; vanity is dead; longing for release is in their place. It comes at last—the only unpoisoned gift earth ever had for them—and they vanish from a world where they were of no consequence; where they achieved nothing; where they were a mistake and a failure and a foolishness; there they have left no sign that they have existed—a world which will lament them a day and forget them forever. Then another myriad takes their place, and copies all they did, and goes along the same profitless road, and vanishes as they vanished—to make room for another, and another, and a million other myriads, to follow the same arid path through the same desert, and accomplish what the first myriad, and all the myriads that came after it, accomplished—nothing!

"Mamma, what is it all for?" asked Susy, preliminarily stating the above details in her own halting language, after long brooding over them alone in the privacy of the nursery.

A year later, she was groping her way alone through another sunless bog, but this time she reached a rest for her feet. For a week, her mother had not been able to go to the nursery, evenings, at the child's prayer hour. She spoke of it—was sorry for it, and said she would come to-night, and hoped she could continue to come every night and hear Susy pray, as before. Noticing that the child wished to respond, but was evidently troubled as to how to word her answer, she asked what the difficulty was. Susy explained that Miss Foote (the governess) had been teaching her about the Indians and their religious beliefs, whereby it appeared that they had not only a God, but several. This had set Susy to thinking. As a result of this thinking, she had stopped praying. She qualified this statement— that is, she modified it—saying she did not now pray "in the same way" as she had formerly done. Her mother said:

"Tell me about it, dear."

"Well, mamma, the Indians believed they knew, but now we know they were wrong. By and by, it can turn out that we are wrong. So now I only pray that there may be a God and a Heaven—or something better."

I wrote down this pathetic prayer in its precise wording, at the time, in a record which we kept of the children's sayings, and my reverence for it has grown with the years that have passed over my head since then. Its untaught grace and simplicity are a child's, but the wisdom and the pathos of it are of all the ages that have come and gone since the race of man has lived, and longed, and hoped, and feared, and doubted.

To go back a year—Susy aged seven. Several times her mother said to her:

"There, there, Susy, you mustn't cry over little things."

This furnished Susy a text for thought. She had been breaking her heart over what had seemed vast disasters—a broken toy; a picnic cancelled by thunder and lightning and rain; the mouse that was growing tame and friendly in the nursery caught and killed by the cat—and now came this strange revelation. For some unaccountable reason, these were not vast calamities. Why? How is the size of calamities measured? What is the rule? There must be some way to tell the great ones from the small ones; what is the law of these proportions? She examined the problem earnestly and long. She gave it her best thought from time to time, for two or three days—but it baffled her—defeated her. And at last she gave up and went to her mother for help.

"Mamma, what is 'little things'?"

It seemed a simple question—at first. And yet, before the answer could be put into words, unsuspected and unforeseen difficulties began to appear. They increased; they multiplied; they brought about another defeat. The effort to explain came to a standstill. Then Susy tried to help her mother out—with an instance, an example, an illustration. The mother was getting ready to go down-town, and one of her errands was to buy a long-promised toy-watch for Susy.

"If you forgot the watch, mamma, would that be a little thing?"

She was not concerned about the watch, for she knew it would not be forgotten. What she was hoping for was that the answer would unriddle the riddle, and bring rest and peace to her perplexed little mind.

The hope was disappointed, of course—for the reason that the size of a misfortune is not determinable by an outsider's measurement of it, but only by the measurements applied to it by the person specially affected by it. The king's lost crown is a vast matter to the king, but of no consequence to the child. The lost toy is a great matter to the child, but in the king's eyes it is not a thing to break the heart about. A verdict was reached, but it was based upon the above model, and Susy was granted leave to measure her disasters thereafter with her own tape-line.

As a child, Susy had a passionate temper; and it cost her much remorse and many tears before she learned to govern it, but after that it was a wholesome salt, and her character was the stronger and healthier for its presence. It enabled her to be good with dignity; it preserved her not only from being good for vanity's sake, but from even the appearance of it. In looking back over the long vanished years, it seems but natural and excusable that I should dwell with longing affection and preference upon incidents of her young life which made it beautiful to us, and that I should let its few small offences go unsummoned and unreproached.

In the summer of 1880, when Susy was just eight years of age, the family were at Quarry Farm, as usual at that season of the year. Hay-cutting time was approaching, and Susy and Clara were counting the hours, for the time was big with a great event for them; they had been promised that they might mount the wagon and ride home from the fields on the summit of the hay mountain. This perilous privilege, so dear to their age and species, had never been granted them before. Their excitement had no bounds. They could talk of nothing but this epoch-making adventure, now. But misfortune overtook Susy on the very morning of the important day. In a sudden outbreak of passion, she corrected Clara—with a shovel, or stick, or something of the sort. At any rate, the offence committed was of a gravity clearly beyond the limit allowed in the nursery. In accordance with the rule and custom of the house, Susy went to her mother to confess, and to help decide upon the size and character of the punishment due. It was quite understood that, as a punishment could have but one rational object and function—to act as a reminder, and warn the transgressor against transgressing in the same way again—the children would know about as well as any how to choose a penalty which would be rememberable and effective. Susy and her mother discussed various punishments, but none of them seemed adequate. This fault was an unusually serious one, and required the setting up of a danger-signal in the memory that would not blow out nor burn out, but remain a fixture there and furnish its saving warning indefinitely. Among the punishments mentioned was deprivation of the hay-wagon ride. It was noticeable that this one hit Susy hard. Finally, in the summing up, the mother named over the list and asked:

"Which one do you think it ought to be, Susy?"

Susy studied, shrank from her duty, and asked:

"Which do you think, mamma?"

"Well, Susy, I would rather leave it to you. *You* make the choice yourself."

It cost Susy a struggle, and much and deep thinking and weighing—but she came out where any one who knew her could have foretold she would.

"Well, mamma, I'll make it the hay-wagon, because you know the other things might not make me remember not to do it again, but if I don't get to ride on the hay-wagon I can remember it easily."

In this world the real penalty, the sharp one, the lasting one, never falls otherwise than on the wrong person. It was not *I* that corrected Clara, but the remembrance of poor Susy's lost hayride still brings *me* a pang—after twenty-six years.

Apparently, Susy was born with humane feelings for the animals, and compassion for their troubles. This enabled her to see a new point in an old story, once, when she was only six years old—a point which had been overlooked by older, and perhaps duller, people for many ages. Her mother told her the moving story of the sale of Joseph by his brethren, the staining of his coat with the blood of the slaughtered kid, and the rest of it. She dwelt upon the inhumanity of the brothers; their cruelty toward their helpless young brother; and the unbrotherly treachery which they practised upon him; for she hoped to teach the child a lesson in gentle pity and mercifulness which she would remember. Apparently, her desire was accomplished, for the tears came into Susy's eyes and she was deeply moved. Then she said:

"Poor little kid!"

A child's frank envy of the privileges and distinctions of its elders is often a delicately flattering attention and the reverse of unwelcome, but sometimes the envy is not placed where the beneficiary is expecting it to be placed. Once, when Susy was seven, she sat breathlessly absorbed in watching a guest of ours adorn herself for a ball. The lady was charmed by this homage; this mute and gentle admiration; and was happy in it. And when her pretty labors were finished, and she stood at last perfect, unimprovable, clothed like Solomon in all his glory, she paused, confident and expectant, to receive from Susy's tongue the tribute that was burning in her eyes. Susy drew an envious little sigh and said:

"I wish *I* could have crooked teeth and spectacles!"

Once, when Susy was six months along in her eighth year, she did something one day in the presence of company, which subjected her to criticism and reproof. Afterward, when she was alone with her mother, as was her custom she reflected a little while over the matter. Then she set up what I think—and what the shade of Burns would think—was a quite good philosophical defence.

"Well, mamma, you know I didn't see myself, and so I couldn't know how it looked."

In homes where the near friends and visitors are mainly literary people—lawyers, judges, professors and clergymen—the children's ears become early familiarized with wide vocabularies. It is natural for them to pick up any words that fall in their way; it is natural for them to pick up big and little ones indiscriminately; it is natural for them to use without fear any word that comes to their net, no matter how formidable it may be as to size. As a result, their talk is a curious and funny musketry clatter of little words, interrupted at intervals by the heavy artillery crash of a word of such imposing sound and size that it seems to shake the ground and rattle the windows. Sometimes the child gets a wrong idea of a word which it has picked up by chance, and attaches to it a meaning which impairs its usefulness—but this does not happen as often as one might expect it would. Indeed, it happens with an infrequency which may be regarded as remarkable. As a child, Susy had good fortune with her large words, and she employed many of them. She made no more than her fair share of mistakes. Once when she thought something very funny was going to happen (but it didn't), she was racked and torn with laughter, by anticipation. But, apparently, she still felt sure of her position, for she said, "If it had happened, I should have been transformed [transported] with glee."

And earlier, when she was a little maid of five years, she informed a visitor that she had been in a church only once, and that was the time when Clara was "crucified" [christened]. . . .

In Heidelberg, when Susy was six, she noticed that the Schloss gardens were populous with snails creeping all about everywhere. One day she found a new dish on her table and inquired concerning it, and learned that it was made of snails. She was awed and impressed, and said:

"Wild ones, mamma?"

She was thoughtful and considerate of others—an acquired quality, no doubt. No one seems to be born with it. One hot day, at home in Hartford, when she was a little child, her mother borrowed her fan several times (a Japanese one, value five cents), refreshed herself with it a moment or two, then handed it back with a word of thanks. Susy knew her mother would use the fan all the time if she could do it without putting a deprivation upon its owner. She also knew that her mother could not be persuaded to do that. A relief must be devised somehow; Susy devised it. She got five cents out of her money-box and carried it to Patrick, and asked him to take it down-town (a mile and a half) and buy a Japanese fan and bring it home. He did it—and thus thoughtfully and delicately was the exigency met and the mother's comfort secured. It is to the child's credit that she did not save herself expense by bringing down another and more costly kind of fan from up-stairs, but was content to act upon the impression that her mother desired the Japanese kind—content to accomplish the desire and stop with that, without troubling about the wisdom or unwisdom of it.

Sometimes, while she was still a child, her speech fell into quaint and strikingly expressive forms. Once—aged nine or ten—she came to her mother's room, when her sister Jean was a baby, and said Jean was crying in the nursery, and asked if she might ring for the nurse. Her mother asked:

"Is she crying hard?"—meaning cross, ugly.

"Well, no, mamma. It is a weary, lonesome cry."

It is a pleasure to me to recall various incidents which reveal the delicacies of feeling that were so considerable a part of her budding character. Such a revelation came once in a way which, while creditable to her heart, was defective in another direction. She was in her eleventh year then. Her mother had been making the Christmas purchases, and she allowed Susy to see the presents which were for Patrick's children. Among these was a handsome sled for Jimmy, on which a stag was painted; also, in gilt capitals, the word "Deer." Susy was excited and joyous over everything, until she came to this sled. Then she became sober and silent—yet the sled was the choicest of all the gifts. Her mother was surprised, and also disappointed, and said:

"Why, Susy, doesn't it please you? Isn't it fine?"

Susy hesitated, and it was plain that she did not want to say the thing that was in her mind. However, being urged, she brought it haltingly out:

"Well, mamma, it *is* fine, and of course it *did* cost a good deal—but—but—why should that be mentioned?"

Seeing that she was not understood, she reluctantly pointed to that word "Deer." It was her orthography that was at fault, not her heart. She had inherited both from her mother.

MARK TWAIN

(to be continued)

North American Review

No. DCI.

OCTOBER 19, 1906

CHAPTERS FROM MY AUTOBIOGRAPHY—IV

BY MARK TWAIN

PREFATORY NOTE—Mr. Clemens began to write his autobiography many years ago, and he continues to add to it day by day. It was his original intention to permit no publication of his memoirs until after his death; but, after leaving "Pier No. 70," he concluded that a considerable portion might now suitably be given to the public. It is that portion, garnered from the quarter-million of words already written, which will appear in this REVIEW during the coming year. No part of the autobiography will be published in book form during the lifetime of the author.—EDITOR N. A. R.

When Susy was thirteen, and was a slender little maid with plaited tails of copper-tinged brown hair down her back, and was perhaps the busiest bee in the household hive, by reason of the manifold studies, health exercises and recreations she had to attend to, she secretly, and of her own motion, and out of love, added another task to her labors—the writing of a biography of me. She did this work in her bedroom at night, and kept her record hidden. After a little, the mother discovered it and filched it, and let me see it; then told Susy what she had done, and how pleased I was, and how proud. I remember that time with a deep pleasure. I had had compliments before, but none that touched me like this; none that could approach it for value in my eyes. It has kept that place always since. I have had no compliment, no praise, no tribute from any source, that was so precious to me as this one was and still is. As I read it *now*, after all these many years, it is still a king's message to me, and brings me the same dear surprise it brought me then—with the pathos added, of the thought that the eager and hasty hand that sketched it and scrawled it will not touch mine again—and I feel as the humble and unexpectant must feel when their eyes fall upon the edict that raises them to the ranks of the noble.

Yesterday while I was rummaging in a pile of ancient note-books of mine which I had not seen for years, I came across a reference to that biography. It is quite evident that several times, at breakfast and dinner, in those long-past days, I was posing for the biography. In fact, I clearly remember that I *was* doing that—and I also remember that Susy detected it. I remember saying a very smart thing, with a good deal of an air, at the breakfast-table one morning, and that Susy observed to her mother privately, a little later, that papa was doing that for the biography.

I cannot bring myself to change any line or word in Susy's sketch of me, but will introduce passages from it now and then just as they came in their quaint simplicity out of her honest heart, which was the beautiful heart of a child. What comes from that source has a charm and grace of its own which may transgress all the recognized laws of literature, if it choose, and yet be literature still, and worthy of hospitality. I shall print the whole of this little biography, before I have done with it—every word, every sentence.

The spelling is frequently desperate, but it was Susy's, and it shall stand. I love it, and cannot profane it. To me, it is gold. To correct it would alloy it, not refine it. It would spoil it. It would take from it its freedom and flexibility and make it stiff and formal. Even when it is most extravagant I am not shocked. It is Susy's spelling, and she was doing the best she could—and nothing could better it for me. . . .

Susy began the biography in 1885, when I was in the fiftieth year of my age, and she just entering the fourteenth of hers. She begins in this way:

We are a very happy family. We consist of Papa, Mamma, Jean, Clara and me. It is papa I am writing about, and I shall have no trouble in not knowing what to say about him, as he is a *very* striking character.

But wait a minute—I will return to Susy presently.

In the matter of slavish imitation, man is the monkey's superior all the time. The average man is destitute of independence of opinion. He is not interested in contriving an opinion of his own, by study and reflection, but is only anxious to find out what his neighbor's opinion is and slavishly adopt it. A generation ago, I found out that the latest review of a book was pretty sure to be just a reflection of the *earliest* review of it; that whatever the first reviewer found to praise or censure in the book would be repeated in the latest reviewer's report, with nothing fresh added. Therefore more than once I took the precaution of sending my book, in manuscript, to Mr. Howells, when he was editor of the "Atlantic Monthly," so that he could prepare a review of it at leisure. I knew he would say the truth about the book—I also knew that he would find more merit than demerit in it, because I already knew that that was the condition of the book. I allowed no copy of it to go out to the press until after Mr. Howells's notice of it had appeared. That book was always safe. There wasn't a man behind a pen in all America that had the courage to find anything in the book which Mr. Howells had not found—there wasn't a man behind a pen in America that had spirit enough to say a brave and original thing about the book on his own responsibility.

I believe that the trade of critic, in literature, music, and the drama, is the most degraded of all trades, and that it has no real value—certainly no large value. When Charles Dudley Warner and I were about to bring out "The Gilded Age," the editor of the "Daily Graphic" persuaded me to let him have an advance copy, he giving me his word of honor that no notice of it would appear in his paper until after the "Atlantic Monthly" notice should have appeared. This reptile published a review of the book within three days afterward. I could not really complain, because he had only given me his word of honor as security; I ought to have required of him something substantial. I believe his notice did not deal mainly with the merit of the book, or the lack of it, but with my moral attitude toward the public. It was charged that I had used my reputation to play a swindle upon the public; that Mr. Warner had written as much as half of the book, and that I had used my name to float it and give it currency; a currency—so the critic averred—which it could not have acquired without my name, and that this conduct of mine was a grave fraud upon the people. The "Graphic" was not an authority upon any subject whatever. It had a sort of distinction, in that it was the first and only illustrated daily newspaper that the world had seen; but it was without character; it was poorly and cheaply edited; its opinion of a book or of any other work of art was of no consequence. Everybody knew this, yet all the critics in America, one after the other, copied the "Graphic's" criticism, merely changing the phraseology, and left me under that charge of dishonest conduct. Even the great Chicago "Tribune," the most important journal in the Middle West, was not able to invent anything fresh, but adopted the view of the humble "Daily Graphic," dishonesty-charge and all.

However, let it go. It is the will of God that we must have critics, and missionaries, and Congressmen, and humorists, and we must bear the burden. Meantime, I seem to have been drifting into criticism myself. But that is nothing. At the worst, criticism is nothing more than a crime, and I am not unused to that.

What I have been travelling toward all this time is this: the first critic that ever had occasion to describe my personal appearance littered his description with foolish and inexcusable errors whose aggregate furnished the result that I was distinctly and distressingly unhandsome. That description floated around the country in the papers, and was in constant use and wear for a quarter of a century. It seems strange to me that apparently no critic in the country could be found who could look at me and have the courage to take up his pen and destroy that lie. That lie began its course on the Pacific coast, in 1864, and it likened me in personal appearance to Petroleum V. Nasby, who had been out there lecturing. For twenty-five years afterward, no critic could furnish a description of me without fetching in Nasby to help out my portrait. I knew Nasby well, and he was a good fellow, but in my life I have not felt malignant enough about any more than three persons to charge those persons with resembling Nasby. It hurts me to the heart. I was always handsome. Anybody but a critic could have seen it. And it had long been a distress to my family—including Susy—that the critics should go on making this wearisome mistake, year after year, when there was no foundation for it. Even when a critic wanted to be particularly friendly and complimentary to me, he didn't dare to go beyond my clothes. He never ventured beyond that old safe frontier. When he had finished with my clothes he had said all the kind things, the pleasant things, the complimentary things he could risk. Then he dropped back on Nasby.

Yesterday I found this clipping in the pocket of one of those ancient memorandum-books of mine. It is of the date of thirty-nine years ago, and both the paper and the ink are yellow with the bitterness that I felt in that old day when I clipped it out to preserve it and brood over it, and grieve about it. I will copy it here, to wit:

A correspondent of the Philadelphia "Press," writing of one of Schuyler Colfax's receptions, says of our Washington correspondent: "Mark Twain, the delicate humorist, was present; quite a lion, as he deserves to be. Mark is a bachelor, faultless in taste, whose snowy vest is suggestive of endless quarrels with Washington washerwomen; but the heroism of Mark is settled for all time, for such purity and smoothness were never seen before. His lavender gloves might have been stolen from some Turkish harem, so delicate were they in size; but more likely—anything else were more likely than that. In form and feature he bears some resemblance to the immortal Nasby; but whilst Petroleum is brunette to the core, Twain is golden, amber-hued, melting, blonde."

Let us return to Susy's biography now, and get the opinion of one who is unbiassed:

FROM SUSY'S BIOGRAPHY

Papa's appearance has been described many times, but very incorrectly. He has beautiful gray hair, not any too thick or any too long, but just right; a Roman nose, which greatly improves the beauty of his features; kind blue eyes and a small mustache. He has a wonderfully shaped head and profile. He has a very good figure—in short, he is an extrodinarily fine looking man. All his features are perfect, except that he hasn't extrodinary teeth. His complexion is very fair, and he doesn't ware a beard. He is a very good man and a very funny one. He *has* got a temper, but we all of us have in this family. He is the loveliest man I ever saw or ever hope to see—and oh, so absentminded. He does tell perfectly delightful stories. Clara and I used to sit on each arm of his chair and listen while he told us stories about the pictures on the wall.

I remember the story-telling days vividly. They were a difficult and exacting audience—those little creatures.

Along one side of the library, in the Hartford home, the bookshelves joined the mantelpiece—in fact there were shelves on both sides of the mantelpiece. On these shelves, and on the mantelpiece, stood various ornaments. At one end of the procession was a framed oil-painting of a cat's head, at the other end was a head of a beautiful young girl, life-size—called Emmeline, because she looked just about like that—an impressionist watercolor. Between the one picture and the other there were twelve or fifteen of the bric-à-brac things already mentioned; also an oil-painting by Elihu Vedder, "The Young Medusa." Every now and then the children required me to construct a romance—always impromptu—not a moment's preparation permitted—and into that romance I had to get all that bric-à-brac and the three pictures. I had to start always with the cat and finish with Emmeline. I was never allowed the refreshment of a change, end-for-end. It was not permissible to introduce a bric-à-brac ornament into the story out of its place in the procession.

These bric-à-bracs were never allowed a peaceful day, a reposeful day, a restful Sabbath. In their lives there was no Sabbath, in their lives there was no peace; they knew no existence but a monotonous career of violence and bloodshed. In the course of time, the bric-à-brac and the pictures showed wear. It was because they had had so many and such tumultuous adventures in their romantic careers.

As romancer to the children I had a hard time, even from the beginning. If they brought me a picture, in a magazine, and required me to build a story to it, they would cover the rest of the page with their pudgy hands to keep me from stealing an idea from it. The stories had to come hot from the bat, always. They had to be absolutely original and fresh. Sometimes the children furnished me simply a character or two, or a dozen, and required me to start out at once on that slim basis and deliver those characters up to a vigorous and entertaining life of crime. If they heard of a new trade, or an unfamiliar animal, or anything like that, I was pretty sure to have to deal with those things in the next romance. Once Clara required me to build a sudden tale out of a plumber and a "bawgunstrictor," and I had to do it. She didn't know what a boa-constrictor was, until he developed in the tale—then she was better satisfied with it than ever.

FROM SUSY'S BIOGRAPHY

Papa's favorite game is billiards, and when he is tired and wishes to rest himself he stays up all night and plays billiards, it seems to rest his head. He smokes a great deal almost incessantly. He has the mind of an author exactly, some of the simplest things he cant understand. Our burglar-alarm is often out of order, and papa had been obliged to take the mahogany-room off from the alarm altogether for a time, because the burglar-alarm had been in the habit of ringing even when the mahogany-room was closed. At length he thought that perhaps the burglar-alarm might be in order, and he decided to try and see; accordingly he put it on and then went down and opened the window; consequently the alarm bell rang, it would even if the alarm had been in order. Papa went despairingly upstairs and said to mamma, "Livy the mahogany-room won't go on. I have just opened the window to see."

"Why, Youth," mamma replied "if you've opened the window, why of coarse the alarm will ring!"

"That's what I've opened it for, why I just went down to see if it would ring!"

Mamma tried to explain to papa that when he wanted to go and see whether the alarm would ring while the window was closed he *mustn't* go and open the window—but in vain, papa couldn't understand, and got very impatient with mamma for trying to make him believe an impossible thing true.

This is a frank biographer, and an honest one; she uses no sandpaper on me. I have, to this day, the same dull head in the matter of conundrums and perplexities which Susy had discovered in those long-gone days. Complexities annoy me; they irritate me; then this progressive feeling presently warms into anger. I cannot get far in the reading of the commonest and simplest contract—with its "parties of the first part," and "parties of the second part," and "parties of the third part,"— before my temper is all gone. Ashcroft comes up here every day and pathetically tries to make me understand the points of the lawsuit which we are conducting against Henry Butters, Harold Wheeler, and the rest of those Plasmon buccaneers, but daily he has to give it up. It is pitiful to see, when he bends his earnest and appealing eyes upon me and says, after one of his efforts, "Now you *do* understand *that*, don't you?"

I am always obliged to say, "I *don't*, Ashcroft. I wish I could understand it, but I don't. Send for the cat."

In the days which Susy is talking about, a perplexity fell to my lot one day. F. G. Whitmore was my business agent, and he brought me out from town in his buggy. We drove by the *porte-cochère* and toward the stable. Now this was a *single* road, and was like a spoon whose handle stretched from the gate to a great round flower-bed in the neighborhood of the stable. At the approach to the flower-bed the road divided and

circumnavigated it, making a loop, which I have likened to the
bowl of the spoon. As we neared the loop, I saw that Whitmore was laying his course to port, (I was sitting on the starboard side—the side the house was on), and was going to start
around that spoon-bowl on that left-hand side. I said,

"Don't do that, Whitmore; take the right-hand side. Then I
shall be next to the house when we get to the door."

He said, "*That* will not happen in *any case*, it doesn't make
any difference which way I go around this flower-bed."

I explained to him that he was an ass, but he stuck to his
proposition, and I said,

"Go on and try it, and see."

He went on and tried it, and sure enough he fetched me up
at the door on the very side that he had said I would be. I was
not able to believe it then, and I don't believe it yet.

I said, "Whitmore, that is merely an accident. You can't do
it again."

He said he could—and he drove down into the street,
fetched around, came back, and actually did it again. I was
stupefied, paralyzed, petrified, with these strange results, but
they did not convince me. I didn't believe he could do it another
time, but he did. He said he could do it all day, and fetch up
the same way every time. By that time my temper was gone,
and I asked him to go home and apply to the Asylum and I
would pay the expenses; I didn't want to see him any more for
a week.

I went up-stairs in a rage and started to tell Livy about it,
expecting to get her sympathy for me and to breed aversion in
her for Whitmore; but she merely burst into peal after peal of
laughter, as the tale of my adventure went on, for her head was
like Susy's: riddles and complexities had no terrors for it. Her
mind and Susy's were analytical; I have tried to make it appear
that mine was different. Many and many a time I have told
that buggy experiment, hoping against hope that I would some
time or other find somebody who would be on my side, but it
has never happened. And I am never able to go glibly forward
and state the circumstances of that buggy's progress without
having to halt and consider, and call up in my mind the spoon-

handle, the bowl of the spoon, the buggy and the horse, and my position in the buggy: and the minute I have got that far and try to turn it to the left it goes to ruin; I can't see how it is ever going to fetch me out right when we get to the door. Susy is right in her estimate. I can't understand things.

That burglar-alarm which Susy mentions led a gay and careless life, and had no principles. It was generally out of order at one point or another; and there was plenty of opportunity, because all the windows and doors in the house, from the cellar up to the top floor, were connected with it. However, in its seasons of being out of order it could trouble us for only a very little while: we quickly found out that it was fooling us, and that it was buzzing its blood-curdling alarm merely for its own amusement. Then we would shut it off, and send to New York for the electrician—there not being one in all Hartford in those days. When the repairs were finished we would set the alarm again and reestablish our confidence in it. It never did any real business except upon one single occasion. All the rest of its expensive career was frivolous and without purpose. Just that one time it performed its duty, and its whole duty—gravely, seriously, admirably. It let fly about two o'clock one black and dreary March morning, and I turned out promptly, because I knew that it was not fooling, this time. The bath-room door was on my side of the bed. I stepped in there, turned up the gas, looked at the annunciator, and turned off the alarm—so far as the door indicated was concerned—thus stopping the racket. Then I came back to bed. Mrs. Clemens opened the debate:

"What was it?"

"It was the cellar door."

"Was it a burglar, do you think?"

"Yes," I said, "of course it was. Did you suppose it was a Sunday-school superintendent?"

"No. What do you suppose he wants?"

"I suppose he wants jewelry, but he is not acquainted with the house and he thinks it is in the cellar. I don't like to disappoint a burglar whom I am not acquainted with, and who has done me no harm, but if he had had common sagacity enough to inquire, I could have told him we kept nothing down there but coal and vegetables. Still it may be that he *is* acquainted with the place, and that what he really wants is coal and vegetables. On the whole, I think it is vegetables he is after."

"Are you going down to see?"

"No; I could not be of any assistance. Let him select for himself; I don't know where the things are."

Then she said, "But suppose he comes up to the ground floor!"

"That's all right. We shall know it the minute he opens a door on that floor. It will set off the alarm."

Just then the terrific buzzing broke out again. I said, "He has arrived. I told you he would. I know all about burglars and their ways. They are systematic people."

I went into the bath-room to see if I was right, and I was. I shut off the dining-room and stopped the buzzing, and came back to bed. My wife said,

"What do you suppose he is after now?"

I said, "I think he has got all the vegetables he wants and is coming up for napkin-rings and odds and ends for the wife and children. They all have families—burglars have—and they are always thoughtful of them, always take a few necessaries of life for themselves, and fill out with tokens of remembrance for the family. In taking them they do not forget us: those very things represent tokens of his remembrance of us, and also of our remembrance of him. We never get them again; the memory of the attention remains embalmed in our hearts."

"Are you going down to see what it is he wants now?"

"No," I said, "I am no more interested than I was before. They are experienced people,—burglars; *they* know what they want; I should be no help to him. I *think* he is after ceramics and bric-à-brac and such things. If he knows the house he knows that that is all that he can find on the dining-room floor."

She said, with a strong interest perceptible in her tone, "Suppose he comes up here!"

I said, "It is all right. He will give us notice."

"What shall we do then?"

"Climb out of the window."

She said, a little restively, "Well, what is the use of a burglar-alarm for us?"

"You have seen, dear heart, that it has been useful up to the present moment, and I have explained to you how it will be continuously useful after he gets up here."

That was the end of it. He didn't ring any more alarms. Presently I said,

"He is disappointed, I think. He has gone off with the vegetables and the bric-à-brac, and I think he is dissatisfied."

We went to sleep, and at a quarter before eight in the morning I was out, and hurrying, for I was to take the 8.29 train for New York. I found the gas burning brightly—full head—all over the first floor. My new overcoat was gone; my old umbrella was gone; my new patent-leather shoes, which I had never worn, were gone. The large window which opened into the *ombra* at the rear of the house was standing wide. I passed out through it and tracked the burglar down the hill through the trees; tracked him without difficulty, because he had blazed his progress with imitation silver napkin-rings, and my umbrella, and various other things which he had disapproved of; and I went back in triumph and proved to my wife that he *was* a disappointed burglar. I had suspected he would be, from the start, and from his not coming up to our floor to get human beings.

Things happened to me that day in New York. I will tell about them another time.

FROM SUSY'S BIOGRAPHY

Papa has a peculiar gait we like, it seems just to sute him, but most people do not; he always walks up and down the room while thinking and between each coarse at meals.

A lady distantly related to us came to visit us once in those days. She came to stay a week, but all our efforts to make her happy failed, we could not imagine why, and she got up her anchor and sailed the next morning. We did much guessing, but could not solve the mystery. Later we found out what the trouble was. It was my tramping up and down between the courses. She conceived the idea that I could not stand her society.

That word "Youth," as the reader has perhaps already guessed, was my wife's pet name for me. It was gently satirical, but also affectionate. I had certain mental and material peculiarities and customs proper to a much younger person than I was.

FROM SUSY'S BIOGRAPHY

Papa is very fond of animals particularly of cats, we had a dear little gray kitten once that he named "Lazy" (papa always wears gray to match his hair and eyes) and he would carry him around on his shoulder, it was a mighty pretty sight! the gray cat sound asleep against papa's gray coat and hair. The names that he has given our different cats, are realy remarkably funny, they are namely Stray Kit, Abner, Motley, Fraeulein, Lazy, Buffalo Bill, Cleveland, Sour Mash, and Pestilence and Famine.

At one time when the children were small, we had a very black mother-cat named Satan, and Satan had a small black offspring named Sin. Pronouns were a difficulty for the children. Little Clara came in one day, her black eyes snapping with indignation, and said,

"Papa, Satan ought to be punished. She is out there at the greenhouse and there she stays and stays, and his kitten is downstairs crying."

FROM SUSY'S BIOGRAPHY

Papa uses very strong language, but I have an idea not nearly so strong as when he first maried mamma. A lady acquaintance of his is rather apt to interupt what one is saying, and papa told mamma that he thought he should say to the lady's husband "I am glad your wife wasn't present when the Deity said 'Let there be light.' "

It is as I have said before. This is a frank historian. She doesn't cover up one's deficiencies, but gives them an equal showing with one's handsomer qualities. Of course I made the remark which she has quoted—and even at this distant day I am still as much as half persuaded that if that lady had been present when the Creator said, "Let there be light," she would have interrupted Him and we shouldn't ever have got it.

FROM SUSY'S BIOGRAPHY

Papa said the other day, "I am a mugwump and a mugwump is pure from the marrow out. (Papa knows that I am writing this biography of him, and he said this for it.) He doesn't like to go to church at all, why I never understood, until just now, he told us the other day that he couldn't bear to hear any one talk but himself, but that he could listen to himself talk for hours without getting tired, of course he said this in joke, but I've no dought it was founded on truth.

MARK TWAIN

(to be continued)

North American Review

No. DCII.

NOVEMBER 2, 1906

CHAPTERS FROM MY AUTOBIOGRAPHY—V

BY MARK TWAIN

PREFATORY NOTE—Mr. Clemens began to write his autobiography many years ago, and he continues to add to it day by day. It was his original intention to permit no publication of his memoirs until after his death; but, after leaving "Pier No. 70," he concluded that a considerable portion might now suitably be given to the public. It is that portion, garnered from the quarter-million of words already written, which will appear in this REVIEW during the coming year. No part of the autobiography will be published in book form during the lifetime of the author.—EDITOR N. A. R.

Susy's remark about my strong language troubles me, and I must go back to it. All through the first ten years of my married life I kept a constant and discreet watch upon my tongue while in the house, and went outside and to a distance when circumstances were too much for me and I was obliged to seek relief. I prized my wife's respect and approval above all the rest of the human race's respect and approval. I dreaded the day when she should discover that I was but a whited sepulchre partly freighted with suppressed language. I was so careful, during ten years, that I had not a doubt that my suppressions had been successful. Therefore I was quite as happy in my guilt as I could have been if I had been innocent.

But at last an accident exposed me. I went into the bath-room one morning to make my toilet, and carelessly left the door two or three inches ajar. It was the first time that I had ever failed to take the precaution of closing it tightly. I knew the necessity of being particular about this, because shaving was always a trying ordeal for me, and I could seldom carry it through to a finish without verbal helps. Now this time I was unprotected, but did not suspect it. I had no extraordinary trouble with my razor on this occasion, and was able to worry through with mere mutterings and growlings of an improper sort, but with nothing noisy or emphatic about them—no snapping and barking. Then I put on a shirt. My shirts are an invention of my own. They open in the back, and are buttoned there—when there are buttons. This time the button was missing. My temper jumped up several degrees in a moment, and my remarks rose accordingly, both in loudness and vigor of expression. But I was not troubled, for the bath-room door was a solid one and I supposed it was firmly closed. I flung up the window and threw the shirt out. It fell upon the shrubbery where the people on their way to church could admire it if they wanted to; there was merely fifty feet of grass between the shirt and the passerby. Still rumbling and thundering distantly, I put on another shirt. Again the button was absent. I augmented my language to meet the emergency, and threw that shirt out of the window. I was too angry—too insane—to examine the third shirt, but put it furiously on. Again the button was absent, and that shirt followed its comrades out of the window. Then I straightened up, gathered my reserves, and let myself go like a cavalry charge. In the midst of that great assault, my eye fell upon that gaping door, and I was paralyzed.

It took me a good while to finish my toilet. I extended the time unnecessarily in trying to make up my mind as to what I would best do in the circumstances. I tried to hope that Mrs. Clemens was asleep, but I knew better. I could not escape by the window. It was narrow, and suited only to shirts. At last I made up my mind to boldly loaf through the bedroom with the air of a person who had not been doing anything. I made half the journey successfully. I did not turn my eyes in her direction, because that would not be safe. It is very difficult to look as if you have not been doing anything when the facts are the other way, and my confidence in my performance oozed steadily out of me as I went along. I was aiming for the left-hand door because it was furthest from my wife. It had never been opened from the day that the house was built, but it seemed a blessed refuge for me now. The bed was this one, wherein I am lying now, and dictating these histories morning after morning with so much serenity. It was this same old elaborately carved black Venetian bedstead—the most comfortable bedstead that ever was, with space enough in it for a family, and carved angels enough surmounting its twisted columns and its headboard and footboard to bring peace to the sleepers, and pleasant dreams. I had to stop in the middle of the room. I hadn't the strength to go on. I believed that I was under accusing eyes—that even the carved angels were inspecting me with an unfriendly gaze. You know how it is when you are convinced that somebody behind you is looking steadily at you. You *have* to turn your face—you can't help it. I turned mine. The bed was placed as it is now, with the foot where the head ought to be. If it had been placed as it should have been, the high headboard would have sheltered me. But the footboard was no sufficient protection, for I could be seen over it. I was exposed. I was wholly without protection. I turned, because I couldn't help it—and my memory of what I saw is still vivid, after all these years.

Against the white pillows I saw the black head—I saw that young and beautiful face; and I saw the gracious eyes with a something in them which I had never seen there before. They were snapping and flashing with indignation. I felt myself crumbling; I felt myself shrinking away to nothing under that accusing gaze. I stood silent under that desolating fire for as much as a minute, I should say—it seemed a very, very long time. Then my wife's lips parted, and from them issued—*my latest bath-room remark*. The language perfect, but the expression velvety, unpractical, apprenticelike, ignorant, inexperienced, comically inadequate, absurdly weak and unsuited to the great language. In my lifetime I had never heard anything so out of tune, so inharmonious, so incongruous, so ill-suited to each other as were those mighty words set to that feeble music. I tried to keep from laughing, for I was a guilty person in deep need of charity and mercy. I tried to keep from bursting, and I succeeded—until she gravely said, "There, now you know how it sounds."

Then I exploded; the air was filled with my fragments, and you could hear them whiz. I said, "Oh Livy, if it sounds like *that* I will never do it again!"

Then she had to laugh herself. Both of us broke into convulsions, and went on laughing until we were physically exhausted and spiritually reconciled.

The children were present at breakfast—Clara aged six and Susy eight—and the mother made a guarded remark about strong language; guarded because she did not wish the children to suspect anything—a guarded remark which censured strong language. Both children broke out in one voice with this comment, "Why, mamma, papa uses it!"

I was astonished. I had supposed that that secret was safe in my own breast, and that its presence had never been suspected. I asked,

"How did you know, you little rascals?"

"Oh," they said, "we often listen over the balusters when you are in the hall explaining things to George."

FROM SUSY'S BIOGRAPHY

One of papa's latest books is "The Prince and the Pauper" and it is unquestionably the best book he has ever written, some people want him to keep to his old style, some gentleman wrote him, "I enjoyed Huckleberry Finn immensely and am glad to see that you have returned to your old style." That enoyed me that enoyed me greatly, because it trobles me [Susy was troubled by that word, and uncertain; she wrote a *u* above it in the proper place, but reconsidered the matter and struck it out] to have so few people know papa, I mean realy know him, they think of Mark Twain as a humorist joking at everything; "And with a mop of reddish brown hair which sorely needs the barbars brush a roman nose, short stubby mustache, a sad careworn face, with maney crow's feet" etc. That is the way people picture papa, I have wanted papa to write a book that would reveal something of his kind sympathetic nature, and "The Prince and the Pauper" partly does it. The book is full of lovely charming ideas, and oh the language! It is *perfect*. I think that one of the most touching scenes in it, is where the pauper is riding on horseback with his nobles in the "recognition procession" and he sees his mother oh and then what followed! How she runs to his side, when she sees him throw up his hand palm outward, and is rudely pushed off by one of the King's officers, and then how the little pauper's consceince troubles him when he remembers the shameful words that were falling from his lips, when she was turned from his side "I know you not woman" and how his grandeurs were stricken valueless, and his pride consumed to ashes. It is a wonderfully beautiful and touching little scene, and papa has described it so wonderfully. I never saw a man with so much variety of feeling as papa has; now the "Prince and the Pauper" is full of touching places; but there is most always a streak of humor in them somewhere. Now in the coronation— in the stirring coronation, just after the little king has got his crown back again papa brings that in about the Seal, where the pauper says he used the Seal "to crack nuts with." Oh it is so funny and nice! Papa very seldom writes a passage without some humor in it somewhere, and I dont think he ever will.

The children always helped their mother to edit my books in manuscript. She would sit on the porch at the farm and read aloud, with her pencil in her hand, and the children would keep an alert and suspicious eye upon her right along, for the belief was well grounded in them that whenever she came across a particularly satisfactory passage she would strike it out. Their suspicions were well founded. The passages which were so satisfactory to them always had an element of strength in them which sorely needed modification or expurgation, and were always sure to get it at their mother's hand. For my own entertainment, and to enjoy the protests of the children, I often abused my editor's innocent confidence. I often interlarded remarks of a studied and felicitously atrocious character purposely to achieve the children's brief delight, and then see the

remorseless pencil do its fatal work. I often joined my supplications to the children's for mercy, and strung the argument
out and pretended to be in earnest. They were deceived, and so
was their mother. It was three against one, and most unfair.
But it was very delightful, and I could not resist the temptation. Now and then we gained the victory and there was much
rejoicing. Then I privately struck the passage out myself. It had
served its purpose. It had furnished three of us with good
entertainment, and in being removed from the book by me it
was only suffering the fate originally intended for it.

FROM SUSY'S BIOGRAPHY

Papa was born in Missouri. His mother is Grandma Clemens
(Jane Lampton Clemens) of Kentucky. Grandpa Clemens was of
the F.F.V's of Virginia.

Without doubt it was I that gave Susy that impression. I cannot imagine why, because I was never in my life much impressed
by grandeurs which proceed from the accident of birth. I did
not get this indifference from my mother. She was always
strongly interested in the ancestry of the house. She traced her
own line back to the Lambtons of Durham, England—a family which had been occupying broad lands there since Saxon
times. I am not sure, but I think that those Lambtons got along
without titles of nobility for eight or nine hundred years, then
produced a great man, three-quarters of a century ago, and
broke into the peerage. My mother knew all about the Clemenses of Virginia, and loved to aggrandize them to me, but she
has long been dead. There has been no one to keep those
details fresh in my memory, and they have grown dim.

There was a Jere. Clemens who was a United States Senator,
and in his day enjoyed the usual Senatorial fame—a fame
which perishes whether it spring from four years' service or
forty. After Jere. Clemens's fame as a Senator passed away, he
was still remembered for many years on account of another
service which he performed. He shot old John Brown's Governor Wise in the hind leg in a duel. However, I am not very
clear about this. It may be that Governor Wise shot *him* in the

hind leg. However, I don't think it is important. I think that the only thing that is really important is that one of them got shot in the hind leg. It would have been better and nobler and more historical and satisfactory if both of them had got shot in the hind leg—but it is of no use for me to try to recollect history. I never had a historical mind. Let it go. Whichever way it happened I am glad of it, and that is as much enthusiasm as I can get up for a person bearing my name. But I am forgetting the first Clemens—the one that stands furthest back toward the really original *first* Clemens, which was Adam.

FROM SUSY'S BIOGRAPHY

Clara and I are sure that papa played the trick on Grandma, about the whipping, that is related in "The Adventures of Tom Sayer"; "Hand me that switch." The switch hovered in the air, the peril was desperate—"My, look behind you Aunt!" The old lady whirled around and snatched her skirts out of danger. The lad fled on the instant, scrambling up the high board fence and dissapeared over it.

Susy and Clara were quite right about that.
Then Susy says:

And we know papa played "Hookey" all the time. And how readily would papa pretend to be dying so as not to have to go to school!

These revelations and exposures are searching, but they are just. If I am as transparent to other people as I was to Susy, I have wasted much effort in this life.

Grandma couldn't make papa go to school, so she let him go into a printing-office to learn the trade. He did so, and gradually picked up enough education to enable him to do about as well as those who were more studious in early life.

It is noticeable that Susy does not get overheated when she is complimenting me, but maintains a proper judicial and biographical calm. It is noticeable, also, and it is to her credit as a biographer, that she distributes compliment and criticism with a fair and even hand.

My mother had a good deal of trouble with me, but I think she enjoyed it. She had none at all with my brother Henry, who was two years younger than I, and I think that the unbroken monotony of his goodness and truthfulness and obedience would have been a burden to her but for the relief and variety which I furnished in the other direction. I was a tonic. I was valuable to her. I never thought of it before, but now I see it. I never knew Henry to do a vicious thing toward me, or toward any one else—but he frequently did righteous ones that cost me as heavily. It was his duty to report me, when I needed reporting and neglected to do it myself, and he was very faithful in discharging that duty. He is "Sid" in "Tom Sawyer." But Sid was not Henry. Henry was a very much finer and better boy than ever Sid was.

It was Henry who called my mother's attention to the fact that the thread with which she had sewed my collar together to keep me from going in swimming, had changed color. My mother would not have discovered it but for that, and she was manifestly piqued when she recognized that that prominent bit of circumstantial evidence had escaped her sharp eye. That detail probably added a detail to my punishment. It is human. We generally visit our shortcomings on somebody else when there is a possible excuse for it—but no matter, I took it out of Henry. There is always compensation for such as are unjustly used. I often took it out of him—sometimes as an advance payment for something which I hadn't yet done. These were occasions when the opportunity was too strong a temptation, and I had to draw on the future. I did not need to copy this idea from my mother, and probably didn't. Still she wrought upon that principle upon occasion.

If the incident of the broken sugar-bowl is in "Tom Sawyer"—I don't remember whether it is or not—that is an example of it. Henry never stole sugar. He took it openly from the bowl. His mother knew he wouldn't take sugar when she wasn't looking, but she had her doubts about me. Not exactly doubts, either. She knew very well I *would*. One day when she was not present, Henry took sugar from her prized and precious old English sugar-bowl, which was an heirloom in the family—and he managed to break the bowl. It was the first time I had ever had a chance to tell anything on him, and I was inexpressibly glad. I told him I was going to tell on him, but he was not disturbed. When my mother came in and saw the bowl lying on the floor in fragments, she was speechless for a minute. I allowed that silence to work; I judged it would increase the effect. I was waiting for her to ask "Who did that?"—so that I could fetch out my news. But it was an error of calculation. When she got through with her silence she didn't ask anything about it—she merely gave me a crack on the skull with her thimble that I felt all the way down to my heels. Then I broke out with my injured innocence, expecting to make her very sorry that she had punished the wrong one. I expected her to do something remorseful and pathetic. I told her that I was not the one—it was Henry. But there was no upheaval. She said, without emotion, "It's all right. It isn't any matter. You deserve it for something you've done that I didn't know about; and if you haven't done it, why then you deserve it for something that you are going to do, that I sha'n't hear about."

There was a stairway outside the house, which led up to the rear part of the second story. One day Henry was sent on an errand, and he took a tin bucket along. I knew he would have to ascend those stairs, so I went up and locked the door on the inside, and came down into the garden, which had been newly ploughed and was rich in choice firm clods of black mold. I gathered a generous equipment of these, and ambushed him. I waited till he had climbed the stairs and was near the landing and couldn't escape. Then I bombarded him with clods, which he warded off with his tin bucket the best he could, but without much success, for I was a good marksman. The clods smashing against the weather-boarding fetched my mother out to see what was the matter, and I tried to explain that I was amusing Henry. Both of them were after me in a minute, but I knew the way over that high board fence and escaped for that time. After an hour or two, when I ventured back, there was no one around and I thought the incident was closed. But it was not. Henry was ambushing me. With an unusually competent aim for him, he landed a stone on the side of my head which raised a bump there that felt like the Matterhorn. I carried it to my mother straightway for sympathy, but she was not strongly moved. It seemed to be her idea that incidents like this would eventually reform me if I harvested enough of them. So the matter was only educational. I had had a sterner view of it than that, before.

It was not right to give the cat the "Pain-Killer"; I realize it now. I would not repeat it in these days. But in those "Tom Sawyer" days it was a great and sincere satisfaction to me to see Peter perform under its influence—and if actions *do* speak as loud as words, he took as much interest in it as I did. It was a most detestable medicine, Perry Davis's Pain-Killer. Mr. Pavey's negro man, who was a person of good judgment and considerable curiosity, wanted to sample it, and I let him. It was his opinion that it was made of hell-fire.

Those were the cholera days of '49. The people along the Mississippi were paralyzed with fright. Those who could run away, did it. And many died of fright in the flight. Fright killed three persons where the cholera killed one. Those who couldn't flee kept themselves drenched with cholera preventives, and my mother chose Perry Davis's Pain-Killer for me. She was not distressed about herself. She avoided that kind of preventive. But she made me promise to take a teaspoonful of Pain-Killer every day. Originally it was my intention to keep the promise, but at that time I didn't know as much about Pain-Killer as I knew after my first experiment with it. She didn't watch Henry's bottle—she could trust Henry. But she marked my bottle with a pencil, on the label, every day, and examined it to see if the teaspoonful had been removed. The floor was not carpeted. It had cracks in it, and I fed the Pain-Killer to the cracks with very good results—no cholera occurred down below.

It was upon one of these occasions that that friendly cat came waving his tail and supplicating for Pain-Killer—which he got—and then went into those hysterics which ended with his colliding with all the furniture in the room and finally going out of the open window and carrying the flower-pots with him, just in time for my mother to arrive and look over her glasses in petrified astonishment and say, "What in the world is the matter with Peter?"

I don't remember what my explanation was, but if it is recorded in that book it may not be the right one.

Whenever my conduct was of such exaggerated impropriety that my mother's extemporary punishments were inadequate, she saved the matter up for Sunday, and made me go to church Sunday night—which was a penalty sometimes bearable, perhaps, but as a rule it was not, and I avoided it for the sake of my constitution. She would never believe that I had been to church until she had applied her test: she made me tell her what the text was. That was a simple matter, and caused me no trouble. I didn't have to go to church to get a text. I selected one for myself. This worked very well until one time when my text and the one furnished by a neighbor, who had been to church, didn't tally. After that my mother took other methods. I don't know what they were now.

In those days men and boys wore rather long cloaks in the winter-time. They were black, and were lined with very bright and showy Scotch plaids. One winter's night when I was starting to church to square a crime of some kind committed during the week, I hid my cloak near the gate and went off and played with the other boys until church was over. Then I returned home. But in the dark I put the cloak on wrong side out, entered the room, threw the cloak aside, and then stood the usual examination. I got along very well until the temperature of the church was mentioned. My mother said,

"It must have been impossible to keep warm there on such a night."

I didn't see the art of that remark, and was foolish enough to explain that I wore my cloak all the time that I was in church. She asked if I kept it on from church home, too. I didn't see the bearing of that remark. I said that that was what I had done. She said,

"You wore it in church with that red Scotch plaid outside and glaring? Didn't that attract any attention?"

Of course to continue such a dialogue would have been tedious and unprofitable, and I let it go, and took the consequences.

That was about 1849. Tom Nash was a boy of my own age—the postmaster's son. The Mississippi was frozen across, and he and I went skating one night, probably without permission. I cannot see why we should go skating in the night unless without permission, for there could be no considerable amusement to be gotten out of skating at night if nobody was going to object to it. About midnight, when we were more than half a mile out toward the Illinois shore, we heard some ominous rumbling and grinding and crashing going on between us and the home side of the river, and we knew what it meant—the ice was breaking up. We started for home, pretty badly scared. We flew along at full speed whenever the moonlight sifting down between the clouds enabled us to tell which was ice and which was water. In the pauses we waited; started again whenever there was a good bridge of ice; paused again when we came to naked water and waited in distress until a floating vast cake should bridge that place. It took us an hour to make the trip—a trip which we made in a misery of apprehension all the time. But at last we arrived within a very brief distance of the shore. We waited again; there was another place that needed bridging. All about us the ice was plunging and grinding along and piling itself up in mountains on the shore, and the dangers were increasing, not diminishing. We grew very impatient to get to solid ground, so we started too early and went springing from cake to cake. Tom made a miscalculation, and fell short. He got a bitter bath, but he was so close to shore that he only had to swim a stroke or two—then his feet struck hard bottom and he crawled out. I arrived a little later, without accident. We had been in a drenching perspiration, and Tom's bath was a disaster for him. He took to his bed sick, and had a procession of diseases. The closing one was scarlet-fever, and he came out of it stone deaf. Within a year or two speech departed, of course. But some years later he was taught to talk, after a fashion—one couldn't always make out what it was he was trying to say. Of course he could not modulate his voice, since he couldn't hear himself talk. When he supposed he was talking low and confidentially, you could hear him in Illinois.

Four years ago (1902) I was invited by the University of Missouri to come out there and receive the honorary degree of LL.D. I took that opportunity to spend a week in Hannibal—a city now, a village in my day. It had been fifty-three years since Tom Nash and I had had that adventure. When I was at the railway station ready to leave Hannibal, there was a crowd of citizens there. I saw Tom Nash approaching me across a vacant space, and I walked toward him, for I recognized him at once. He was old and white-headed, but the boy of fifteen was still visible in him. He came up to me, made a trumpet of his hands at my ear, nodded his head toward the citizens and said confidentially—in a yell like a fog-horn—

"Same damned fools, Sam!"

FROM SUSY'S BIOGRAPHY

Papa was about twenty years old when he went on the Mississippi as a pilot. Just before he started on his tripp Grandma Clemens asked him to promise her on the Bible not to touch intoxicating liquors or swear, and he said "Yes, mother, I will," and he kept that promise seven years when Grandma released him from it.

Under the inspiring influence of that remark, what a garden of forgotten reforms rises upon my sight!

MARK TWAIN

(to be continued)

North American Review

No. DCIII.

NOVEMBER 16, 1906

CHAPTERS FROM MY AUTOBIOGRAPHY—VI

BY MARK TWAIN

PREFATORY NOTE—Mr. Clemens began to write his autobiography many years ago, and he continues to add to it day by day. It was his original intention to permit no publication of his memoirs until after his death; but, after leaving "Pier No. 70," he concluded that a considerable portion might now suitably be given to the public. It is that portion, garnered from the quarter-million of words already written, which will appear in this REVIEW during the coming year. No part of the autobiography will be published in book form during the lifetime of the author. —EDITOR N. A. R.

FROM SUSY'S BIOGRAPHY

Papa made arrangements to read at Vassar College the 1st of May, and I went with him. We went by way of New York City. Mamma went with us to New York and stayed two days to do some shopping. We started Tuesday, at ½ past two o'clock in the afternoon, and reached New York about ¼ past six. Papa went right up to General Grants from the station and mamma and I went to the Everett House. Aunt Clara came to supper with us up in our room. . . .

We and Aunt Clara were going were going to the theatre right after supper, and we expected papa to take us there and to come home as early as he could. But we got through dinner and he didn't come, and didn't come, and mamma got more perplexed and worried, but at last we thought we would have to go without

him. So we put on our things and started down stairs but before
we'd goten half down we met papa coming up with a great bunch
of roses in his hand. He explained that the reason he was so late
was that his watch stopped and he didn't notice and kept thinking
it an hour earlier than it really was. The roses he carried were
some Col. Fred Grant sent to mamma. We went to the theatre and
enjoyed "Adonis" [word illegible] acted very much. We reached
home about ½ past eleven o'clock and went right to bed. Wednes-
day morning we got up rather late and had breakfast about ½
past nine o'clock. After breakfast mamma went out shopping and
papa and I went to see papa's agent about some business matters.
After papa had gotten through talking to Cousin Charlie, [Web-
ster] papa's agent, we went to get a friend of papa's, Major Pond,
to go and see a Dog Show with us. Then we went to see the dogs
with Major Pond and we had a delightful time seeing so many
dogs together; when we got through seeing the dogs papa thought
he would go and see General Grant and I went with him—this
was April 29, 1885. Papa went up into General Grant's room and
he took me with him, I felt greatly honored and delighted when
papa took me into General Grant's room and let me see the General and Col. Grant, for General Grant is a man I shall be glad all
my life that I have seen. Papa and General Grant had a long talk
together and papa has written an account of his talk and visit
with General Grant for me to put into this biography.

Susy has inserted in this place that account of mine—as
follows:

April 29, 1885.

I called on General Grant and took Susy with me. The General
was looking and feeling far better than he had looked or felt for
some months. He had ventured to work again on his book that
morning—the first time he had done any work for perhaps a
month. This morning's work was his first attempt at dictating,
and it was a thorough success, to his great delight. He had always
said that it would be impossible for him to dictate anything, but
I had said that he was noted for clearness of statement, and as a
narrative was simply a statement of consecutive facts, he was
consequently peculiarly qualified and equipped for dictation.

This turned out to be true. For he had dictated two hours that morning to a shorthand writer, had never hesitated for words, had not repeated himself, and the manuscript when finished needed no revision. The two hours' work was an account of Appomattox—and this was such an extremely important feature that his book would necessarily have been severely lame without it. Therefore I had taken a shorthand writer there before, to see if I could not get him to write at least a few lines about Appomattox.* But he was at that time not well enough to undertake it. I was aware that of all the hundred versions of Appomattox, not one was really correct. Therefore I was extremely anxious that he should leave behind him the truth. His throat was not distressing him, and his voice was much better and stronger than usual. He was so delighted to have gotten Appomattox accomplished once more in his life—to have gotten the matter off his mind—that he was as talkative as his old self. He received Susy very pleasantly, and then fell to talking about certain matters which he hoped to be able to dictate next day; and he said in substance that, among other things, he wanted to settle once for all a question that had been bandied about from mouth to mouth and from newspaper to newspaper. That question was, "With whom originated the idea of the march to the sea? Was it Grant's, or was it Sherman's idea?" Whether I, or some one else (being anxious to get the important fact settled) asked him with whom the idea originated, I don't remember. But I remember his answer. I shall always remember his answer. General Grant said:

"Neither of us originated the idea of Sherman's march to the sea. The enemy did it."

He went on to say that the enemy, however, necessarily originated a great many of the plans that the general on the opposite side gets the credit for; at the same time that the enemy is doing that, he is laying open other moves which the opposing general sees and takes advantage of. In this case, Sherman had a plan all thought out, of course. He meant to destroy the two remaining railroads in that part of the country, and that would finish up

---

* I was his publisher. I was putting his "Personal Memoirs" to press at the time.—S. L. C.

that region. But General Hood did not play the military part that he was expected to play. On the contrary, General Hood made a dive at Chattanooga. This left the march to the sea open to Sherman, and so after sending part of his army to defend and hold what he had acquired in the Chattanooga region, he was perfectly free to proceed, with the rest of it, through Georgia. He saw the opportunity, and he would not have been fit for his place if he had not seized it.

"He wrote me" (the General is speaking) "what his plan was, and I sent him word to go ahead. My staff were opposed to the movement." (I think the General said they tried to persuade him to stop Sherman. The chief of his staff, the General said, even went so far as to go to Washington without the General's knowledge and get the ear of the authorities, and he succeeded in arousing their fears to such an extent that they telegraphed General Grant to stop Sherman.)

Then General Grant said, "Out of deference to the Government, I telegraphed Sherman and stopped him twenty-four hours; and then considering that that was deference enough to the Government, I telegraphed him to go ahead again."

I have not tried to give the General's language, but only the general idea of what he said. The thing that mainly struck me was his terse remark that the enemy originated the idea of the march to the sea. It struck me because it was so suggestive of the General's epigrammatic fashion—saying a great deal in a single crisp sentence. (This is my account, and signed "Mark Twain.")

SUSY RESUMES

After papa and General Grant had had their talk, we went back to the hotel where mamma was, and papa told mamma all about his interview with General Grant. Mamma and I had a nice quiet afternoon together.

That pair of devoted comrades were always shutting themselves up together when there was opportunity to have what Susy called "a cozy time." From Susy's nursery days to the end of her life, she and her mother were close friends; intimate friends, passionate adorers of each other. Susy's was a beautiful mind, and it made her an interesting comrade. And with the fine mind she had a heart like her mother's. Susy never had an interest or an occupation which she was not glad to put aside for that something which was in all cases more precious to her—a visit with her mother. Susy died at the right time, the fortunate time of life; the happy age—twenty-four years. At twenty-four, such a girl has seen the best of life—life as a happy dream. After that age the risks begin; responsibility comes, and with it the cares, the sorrows, and the inevitable tragedy. For her mother's sake I would have brought her back from the grave if I could, but I would not have done it for my own.

FROM SUSY'S BIOGRAPHY

Then papa went to read in public; there were a great many authors that read, that Thursday afternoon, beside papa; I would have liked to have gone and heard papa read, but papa said he was going to read in Vassar just what he was planning to read in New York, so I stayed at home with mamma.

The next day mamma planned to take the four o'clock car back to Hartford. We rose quite early that morning and went to the Vienna Bakery and took breakfast there. From there we went to a German bookstore and bought some German books for Clara's birthday.

Dear me, the power of association to snatch mouldy dead memories out of their graves and make them walk! That remark about buying foreign books throws a sudden white glare upon the distant past; and I see the long stretch of a New York street with an unearthly vividness, and John Hay walking down it, grave and remorseful. I was walking down it too, that morning, and I overtook Hay and asked him what the trouble was. He turned a lustreless eye upon me and said:

"My case is beyond cure. In the most innocent way in the world I have committed a crime which will never be forgiven by the sufferers, for they will never believe—oh, well, no, I was going to say they would never believe that I did the thing innocently. The truth is they will know that I acted innocently, because they are rational people; but what of that? I never can look them in the face again—nor they me, perhaps."

Hay was a young bachelor, and at that time was on the "Tribune" staff. He explained his trouble in these words, substantially:

"When I was passing along here yesterday morning on my way down-town to the office, I stepped into a bookstore where I am acquainted, and asked if they had anything new from the other side. They handed me a French novel, in the usual yellow paper cover, and I carried it away. I didn't even look at the title of it. It was for recreation reading, and I was on my way to my work. I went mooning and dreaming along, and I think I hadn't gone more than fifty yards when I heard my name called. I stopped, and a private carriage drew up at the sidewalk and I shook hands with the inmates—mother and young daughter, excellent people. They were on their way to the steamer to sail for Paris. The mother said,

"'I saw that book in your hand and I judged by the look of it that it was a French novel. Is it?'

"I said it was.

"She said, 'Do let me have it, so that my daughter can practise her French on it on the way over.'

"Of course I handed her the book, and we parted. Ten minutes ago I was passing that bookstore again, and I stepped in and fetched away another copy of that book. Here it is. Read the first page of it. That is enough. You will know what the rest is like. I think it must be the foulest book in the French language—one of the foulest, anyway. I would be ashamed to offer it to a harlot—but, oh dear, I gave it to that sweet young girl without shame. Take my advice; don't give away a book until you have examined it."

FROM SUSY'S BIOGRAPHY

Then mamma and I went to do some shopping and papa went to see General Grant. After we had finnished doing our shopping we went home to the hotel together. When we entered our rooms in the hotel we saw on the table a vase full of exquisett red roses. Mamma who is very fond of flowers exclaimed "Oh I wonder who could have sent them." We both looked at the card in the midst of the roses and saw that it was written on in papa's handwriting, it was written in German. 'Liebes Geshchenk on die mamma.' [I am sure I didn't say "on"—that is Susy's spelling, not mine; also I am sure I didn't spell Geschenk so liberally as all that.—S. L. C.] Mamma was delighted. Papa came home and gave mamma her ticket; and after visiting a while with her went to see Major Pond and mamma and I sat down to our lunch. After lunch most of our time was taken up with packing, and at about three o'clock we went to escort mamma to the train. We got on board the train with her and stayed with her about five minutes and then we said good-bye to her and the train started for Hartford. It was the first time I had ever beene away from home without mamma in my life, although I was 13 yrs. old. Papa and I drove back to the hotel and got Major Pond and then went to see the Brooklyn Bridge we went across it to Brooklyn on the cars and then walked back across it from Brooklyn to New York. We enjoyed looking at the beautiful scenery and we could see the bridge moove under the intense heat of the sun. We had a perfectly delightful time, but weer pretty tired when we got back to the hotel.

The next morning we rose early, took our breakfast and took an early train to Poughkeepsie. We had a very pleasant journey to Poughkeepsie. The Hudson was magnificent—shrouded with beautiful mist. When we arived at Poughkeepsie it was raining quite hard; which fact greatly dissapointed me because I very much wanted to see the outside of the buildings of Vassar College and as it rained that would be impossible. It was quite a long drive from the station to Vassar College and papa and I had a nice long time to discuss and laugh over German profanity. One of the German phrases papa particularly enjoys is "O heilige maria Mutter Jesus!" Jean has a German nurse, and this was one of her phrases, there was a time when Jean exclaimed "Ach Gott!" to every trifle, but when mamma found it out she was shocked and instantly put a stop to it.

It brings that pretty little German girl vividly before me—a sweet and innocent and plump little creature with peachy cheeks; a clear-souled little maiden and without offence, notwithstanding her profanities, and she was loaded to the eyebrows with them. She was a mere child. She was not fifteen yet. She was just from Germany, and knew no English. She was always scattering her profanities around, and they were such a satisfaction to me that I never dreamed of such a thing as modifying her. For my own sake, I had no disposition to tell on her. Indeed I took pains to keep her from being found out. I told her to confine her religious exercises to the children's quarters, and urged her to remember that Mrs. Clemens was prejudiced against pieties on week-days. To the children, the little maid's profanities sounded natural and proper and right, because they had been used to that kind of talk in Germany, and they attached no evil importance to it. It grieves me that I have forgotten those vigorous remarks. I long hoarded them in my memory as a treasure. But I remember one of them still, because I heard it so many times. The trial of that little creature's life was the children's hair. She would tug and strain with her comb, accompanying her work with her misplaced pieties. And when finally she was through with her triple job she always fired up and exploded her thanks toward the sky, where they belonged, in this form: *"Gott sei Dank ich bin fertig mit'm Gott verdammtes Haar!"* (I believe I am not quite brave enough to translate it.)

FROM SUSY'S BIOGRAPHY

We at length reached Vassar College and she looked very finely, her buildings and her grounds being very beautiful. We went to the front doore and range the bell. The young girl who came to the doore wished to know who we wanted to see. Evidently we were not expected. Papa told her who we wanted to see and she showed us to the parlor. We waited, no one came; and waited, no one came, still no one came. It was beginning to seem pretty awkward, "Oh well this is a pretty piece of business," papa exclaimed. At length we heard footsteps coming down the long corridor and Miss C, (the lady who had invited papa) came into the room. She greeted papa very pleasantly and they had a nice little chatt together. Soon the lady principal also entered and she was very pleasant and agreable. She showed us to our rooms and said she would send for us when dinner was ready. We went into our rooms, but we had nothing to do for half an hour exept to watch the rain drops as they fell upon the window panes. At last we were called to dinner, and I went down without papa as he never eats anything in the middle of the day. I sat at the table with the lady principal and enjoyed very much seeing all the young girls trooping into the dining-room. After dinner I went around the College with the young ladies and papa stayed in his room and smoked. When it was supper time papa went down and ate supper with us and we had a very delightful supper. After supper the young ladies went to their rooms to dress for the evening. Papa went to his room and I went with the lady principal. At length the guests began to arrive, but papa still remained in his room until called for. Papa read in the chapell. It was the first time I had ever heard him read in my life—that is in public. When he came out on to the stage I remember the people behind me exclaimed "Oh how queer he is! Isn't he funny!" I thought papa was very funny, although I did not think him queer. He read "A Trying Situation" and "The Golden Arm," a ghost story that he heard down South when he was a little boy. "The Golden Arm" papa had told me before, but he had startled me so that I did not much wish to hear it again. But I had resolved this time to be prepared and not to let myself be startled, but still papa did, and very very much; he startled the whole roomful of people and they jumped as one man. The other story was also very funny and interesting and I enjoyed the evening inexpressibly much. After papa had finished reading we all went down to the collation in the dining-room and after that there was dancing and singing. Then the guests went away and papa and I went to bed. The next morning we rose early, took an early train for Hartford and reached Hartford at ½ past 2 o'clock. We were very glad to get back.

How charitably she treats that ghastly experience! It is a dear and lovely disposition, and a most valuable one, that can brush away indignities and discourtesies and seek and find the pleasanter features of an experience. Susy had that disposition, and it was one of the jewels of her character that had come to her straight from her mother. It is a feature that was left out of me at birth. And, at seventy, I have not yet acquired it. I did not go to Vassar College professionally, but as a guest—as a guest, and gratis. Aunt Clara (now Mrs. John B. Stanchfield) was a graduate of Vassar and it was to please her that I inflicted that journey upon Susy and myself. The invitation had come to me from both the lady mentioned by Susy and the President of the College—a sour old saint who has probably been gathered to his fathers long ago; and I hope they enjoy him; I hope they value his society. I think I can get along without it, in either end of the next world.

We arrived at the College in that soaking rain, and Susy has described, with just a suggestion of dissatisfaction, the sort of reception we got. Susy had to sit in her damp clothes half an hour while we waited in the parlor; then she was taken to a fireless room and left to wait there again, as she has stated. I do not remember that President's name, and I am sorry. He did not put in an appearance until it was time for me to step upon the platform in front of that great garden of young and lovely blossoms. He caught up with me and advanced upon the platform with me and was going to introduce me. I said in substance:

"You have allowed me to get along without your help thus far, and if you will retire from the platform I will try to do the rest without it."

I did not see him any more, but I detest his memory. Of course my resentment did not extend to the students, and so I had an unforgettable good time talking to them. And I think they had a good time too, for they responded "as one man," to use Susy's unimprovable phrase.

Girls are charming creatures. I shall have to be twice seventy years old before I change my mind as to that. I am to talk to a crowd of them this afternoon, students of Barnard College (the sex's annex to Columbia University), and I think I shall have as pleasant a time with those lasses as I had with the Vassar girls twenty-one years ago.

FROM SUSY'S BIOGRAPHY

I stopped in the middle of mamma's early history to tell about our tripp to Vassar because I was afraid I would forget about it, now I will go on where I left off. Some time after Miss Emma Nigh died papa took mamma and little Langdon to Elmira for the summer. When in Elmira Langdon began to fail but I think mamma did not know just what was the matter with him.

I was the cause of the child's illness. His mother trusted him to my care and I took him a long drive in an open barouche for an airing. It was a raw, cold morning, but he was well wrapped about with furs and, in the hands of a careful person, no harm would have come to him. But I soon dropped into a reverie and forgot all about my charge. The furs fell away and exposed his bare legs. By and by the coachman noticed this, and I arranged the wraps again, but it was too late. The child was almost frozen. I hurried home with him. I was aghast at what I had done, and I feared the consequences. I have always felt shame for that treacherous morning's work and have not allowed myself to think of it when I could help it. I doubt if I had the courage to make confession at that time. I think it most likely that I have never confessed until now.

FROM SUSY'S BIOGRAPHY

At last it was time for papa to return to Hartford, and Langdon was real sick at that time, but still mamma decided to go with him, thinking the journey might do him good. But after they reached Hartford he became very sick, and his trouble prooved to be diptheeria. He died about a week after mamma and papa reached Hartford. He was burried by the side of grandpa at Elmira, New York. [Susy rests there with them.—S. L. C.] After that, mamma became very very ill, so ill that there seemed great danger of death, but with a great deal of good care she recovered. Some months afterward mamma and papa [and Susy, who was perhaps fourteen or fifteen months old at the time.—S. L. C.] went to Europe and stayed for a time in Scotland and England. In Scotland mamma and papa became very well equanted with Dr. John Brown, the author of "Rab and His Friends," and he mett, but was not so well equanted with, Mr. Charles Kingsley, Mr. Henry M. Stanley, Sir Thomas Hardy grandson of the Captain Hardy to whom Nellson said "Kiss me Hardy," when dying on shipboard, Mr. Henry Irving, Robert Browning, Sir Charles Dilke, Mr. Charles Reade, Mr. William Black, Lord Houghton, Frank Buckland, Mr. Tom Hughes, Anthony Trollope, Tom Hood, son of the poet—and mamma and papa were quite well equanted with Dr. Macdonald and family, and papa met Harrison Ainsworth.

I remember all these men very well indeed, except the last one. I do not recall Ainsworth. By my count, Susy mentions fourteen men. They are all dead except Sir Charles Dilke.

We met a great many other interesting people, among them Lewis Carroll, author of the immortal "Alice"—but he was only interesting to look at, for he was the stillest and shyest full-grown man I have ever met except "Uncle Remus." Dr. Macdonald and several other lively talkers were present, and the talk went briskly on for a couple of hours, but Carroll sat still all the while except that now and then he answered a question. His answers were brief. I do not remember that he elaborated any of them.

At a dinner at Smalley's we met Herbert Spencer. At a large luncheon party at Lord Houghton's we met Sir Arthur Helps, who was a celebrity of world-wide fame at the time, but is quite forgotten now. Lord Elcho, a large vigorous man, sat at some distance down the table. He was talking earnestly about Godalming. It was a deep and flowing and unarticulated rumble, but I got the Godalming pretty clearly every time it broke free of the rumble, and as all the strength was on the first end of the word it startled me every time, because it sounded so like swearing. In the middle of the luncheon Lady Houghton rose, remarked to the guests on her right and on her left in a matter-of-fact way, "Excuse me, I have an engagement," and without further ceremony she went off to meet it. This would have been doubtful etiquette in America. Lord Houghton told a number of delightful stories. He told them in French, and I lost nothing of them but the nubs.

MARK TWAIN

(to be continued)

North American Review

No. DCIV.

DECEMBER 7, 1906

CHAPTERS FROM MY AUTOBIOGRAPHY—VII

BY MARK TWAIN

PREFATORY NOTE—Mr. Clemens began to write his autobiography many years ago, and he continues to add to it day by day. It was his original intention to permit no publication of his memoirs until after his death; but, after leaving "Pier No. 70," he concluded that a considerable portion might now suitably be given to the public. It is that portion, garnered from the quarter-million of words already written, which will appear in this REVIEW during the coming year. No part of the autobiography will be published in book form during the lifetime of the author.—EDITOR N. A. R.

I was always heedless. I was born heedless; and therefore I was constantly, and quite unconsciously, committing breaches of the minor proprieties, which brought upon me humiliations which ought to have humiliated me but didn't, because I didn't know anything had happened. But Livy knew; and so the humiliations fell to her share, poor child, who had not earned them and did not deserve them. She always said I was the most difficult child she had. She was very sensitive about me. It distressed her to see me do heedless things which could bring me under criticism, and so she was always watchful and alert to protect me from the kind of transgressions which I have been speaking of.

When I was leaving Hartford for Washington, upon the occasion referred to, she said: "I have written a small warning and put it in a pocket of your dress-vest. When you are dressing to go to the Authors' Reception at the White House you will naturally put your fingers in your vest pockets, according to your custom, and you will find that little note there. Read it carefully, and do as it tells you. I cannot be with you, and so I delegate my sentry duties to this little note. If I should give you the warning by word of mouth, now, it would pass from your head and be forgotten in a few minutes."

It was President Cleveland's first term. I had never seen his wife—the young, the beautiful, the good-hearted, the sympathetic, the fascinating. Sure enough, just as I had finished dressing to go to the White House I found that little note, which I had long ago forgotten. It was a grave little note, a serious little note, like its writer, but it made me laugh. Livy's gentle gravities often produced that effect upon me, where the expert humorist's best joke would have failed, for I do not laugh easily.

When we reached the White House and I was shaking hands with the President, he started to say something, but I interrupted him and said:

"If your Excellency will excuse me, I will come back in a moment; but now I have a very important matter to attend to, and it must be attended to at once."

I turned to Mrs. Cleveland, the young, the beautiful, the fascinating, and gave her my card, on the back of which I had written *"He didn't"*—and I asked her to sign her name below those words.

She said: "He didn't? He didn't what?"

"Oh," I said, "never mind. We cannot stop to discuss that now. This is urgent. Won't you please sign your name?" (I handed her a fountain-pen.)

"Why," she said, "I cannot commit myself in that way. Who is it that didn't?—and what is it that he didn't?"

"Oh," I said, "time is flying, flying, flying. Won't you take me out of my distress and sign your name to it? It's all right. I give you my word it's all right."

She looked nonplussed; but hesitatingly and mechanically she took the pen and said:

"I will sign it. I will take the risk. But you must tell me all about it, right afterward, so that you can be arrested before you get out of the house in case there should be anything criminal about this."

Then she signed; and I handed her Mrs. Clemens's note, which was very brief, very simple, and to the point. It said: "*Don't wear your arctics in the White House.*" It made her shout; and at my request she summoned a messenger and we sent that card at once to the mail on its way to Mrs. Clemens in Hartford.

When the little Ruth was about a year or a year and a half old, Mason, an old and valued friend of mine, was consul-general at Frankfort-on-the-Main. I had known him well in 1867, '68 and '69, in America, and I and mine had spent a good deal of time with him and his family in Frankfort in '78. He was a thoroughly competent, diligent, and conscientious official. Indeed he possessed these qualities in so large a degree that among American consuls he might fairly be said to be monumental, for at that time our consular service was largely—and I think I may say mainly—in the hands of igno-rant, vulgar, and incapable men who had been political heelers in America, and had been taken care of by transference to con-sulates where they could be supported at the Government's expense instead of being transferred to the poor house, which would have been cheaper and more patriotic. Mason, in '78, had been consul-general in Frankfort several years—four, I think. He had come from Marseilles with a great record. He had been consul there during thirteen years, and one part of his record was heroic. There had been a desolating cholera epi-demic, and Mason was the only representative of any foreign country who stayed at his post and saw it through. And during that time he not only represented his own country, but he rep-resented all the other countries in Christendom and did their work, and did it well and was praised for it by them in words of no uncertain sound. This great record of Mason's had saved him from official decapitation straight along while Republican

Presidents occupied the chair, but now it was occupied by a Democrat. Mr. Cleveland was not seated in it—he was not yet inaugurated—before he was deluged with applications from Democratic politicians desiring the appointment of a thousand or so politically useful Democrats to Mason's place. A year or two later Mason wrote me and asked me if I couldn't do something to save him from destruction.

I was very anxious to keep him in his place, but at first I could not think of any way to help him, for I was a mugwump. We, the mugwumps, a little company made up of the unenslaved of both parties, the very best men to be found in the two great parties—that was our idea of it—voted sixty thousand strong for Mr. Cleveland in New York and elected him. Our principles were high, and very definite. We were not a party; we had no candidates; we had no axes to grind. Our vote laid upon the man we cast it for no obligation of any kind. By our rule we could not ask for office; we could not accept office. When voting, it was our duty to vote for the best man, regardless of his party name. We had no other creed. Vote for the best man—that was creed enough.

Such being my situation, I was puzzled to know how to try to help Mason, and, at the same time, save my mugwump purity undefiled. It was a delicate place. But presently, out of the ruck of confusions in my mind, rose a sane thought, clear and bright—to wit: since it was a mugwump's duty to do his best to put the best man in office, necessarily it must be a mugwump's duty to try to *keep* the best man in when he was already there. My course was easy now. It might not be quite delicate for a mugwump to approach the President directly, but I could approach him indirectly, with all delicacy, since in that case not even courtesy would require him to take notice of an application which no one could prove had ever reached him.

Yes, it was easy and simple sailing now. I could lay the matter before Ruth, in her cradle, and wait for results. I wrote the little child, and said to her all that I have just been saying about mugwump principles and the limitations which they put upon me. I explained that it would not be proper for me to apply to her father in Mr. Mason's behalf, but I detailed to her

Mr. Mason's high and honorable record and suggested that she take the matter in her own hands and do a patriotic work which I felt some delicacy about venturing upon myself. I asked her to forget that her father was only President of the United States, and her subject and servant; I asked her not to put her application in the form of a command, but to modify it, and give it the fictitious and pleasanter form of a mere request—that it would be no harm to let him gratify himself with the superstition that he was independent and could do as he pleased in the matter. I begged her to put stress, and plenty of it, upon the proposition that to keep Mason in his place would be a benefaction to the nation; to enlarge upon that, and keep still about all other considerations.

In due time I received a letter from the President, written with his own hand, signed by his own hand, acknowledging Ruth's intervention and thanking me for enabling him to save to the country the services of so good and well - tried a servant as Mason, and thanking me, also, for the detailed fulness of Mason's record, which could leave no doubt in any one's mind that Mason was in his right place and ought to be kept there. Mason has remained in the service ever since, and is now consul-general at Paris.

During the time that we were living in Buffalo in '70-'71, Mr. Cleveland was sheriff, but I never happened to make his acquaintance, or even see him. In fact, I suppose I was not even aware of his existence. Fourteen years later, he was become the greatest man in the State. I was not living in the State at the time. He was Governor, and was about to step into the post of President of the United States. At that time I was on the public highway in company with another bandit, George W. Cable. We were robbing the public with readings from our works during four months—and in the course of time we went to Albany to levy tribute, and I said, "We ought to go and pay our respects to the Governor."

So Cable and I went to that majestic Capitol building and stated our errand. We were shown into the Governor's private office, and I saw Mr. Cleveland for the first time. We three stood chatting together. I was born lazy, and I comforted myself by turning the corner of a table into a sort of seat. Presently the Governor said:

"Mr. Clemens, I was a fellow citizen of yours in Buffalo a good many months, a good while ago, and during those months you burst suddenly into a mighty fame, out of a previous long-continued and no doubt proper obscurity—but I was a nobody, and you wouldn't notice me nor have anything to do with me. But now that I have become somebody, you have changed your style, and you come here to shake hands with me and be sociable. How do you explain this kind of conduct?"

"Oh," I said, "it is very simple, your Excellency. In Buffalo you were nothing but a sheriff. I was in society. I couldn't afford to associate with sheriffs. But you are a Governor now, and you are on your way to the Presidency. It is a great difference, and it makes you worth while."

There appeared to be about sixteen doors to that spacious room. From each door a young man now emerged, and the sixteen lined up and moved forward and stood in front of the Governor with an aspect of respectful expectancy in their attitude. No one spoke for a moment. Then the Governor said:

"You are dismissed, gentlemen. Your services are not required. Mr. Clemens is sitting on the bells."

There was a cluster of sixteen bell buttons on the corner of the table; my proportions at that end of me were just right to enable me to cover the whole of that nest, and that is how I came to hatch out those sixteen clerks.

In accordance with the suggestion made in Gilder's letter recently received I have written the following note to ex-President Cleveland upon his sixty-ninth birthday:

HONORED SIR:—

Your patriotic virtues have won for you the homage of half the nation and the enmity of the other half. This places your character as a citizen upon a summit as high as Washington's. The verdict is unanimous and unassailable. The votes of both sides are necessary in cases like these, and the votes of the one side are quite as valuable as are the votes of the other. Where the votes are all in a man's favor the verdict is against him. It is sand, and history will wash it away. But the verdict for you is rock, and will stand.

S. L. CLEMENS.

As of date March 18, 1906. . . .

In a diary which Mrs. Clemens kept for a little while, a great many years ago, I find various mentions of Mrs. Harriet Beecher Stowe, who was a near neighbor of ours in Hartford, with no fences between. And in those days she made as much use of our grounds as of her own, in pleasant weather. Her mind had decayed, and she was a pathetic figure. She wandered about all the day long in the care of a muscular Irishwoman. Among the colonists of our neighborhood the doors always stood open in pleasant weather. Mrs. Stowe entered them at her own free will, and as she was always softly slippered and generally full of animal spirits, she was able to deal in surprises, and she liked to do it. She would slip up behind a person who was deep in dreams and musings and fetch a warwhoop that would jump that person out of his clothes. And she had other moods. Sometimes we would hear gentle music in the drawing-room and would find her there at the piano singing ancient and melancholy songs with infinitely touching effect.

Her husband, old Professor Stowe, was a picturesque figure. He wore a broad slouch hat. He was a large man, and solemn. His beard was white and thick and hung far down on his breast. The first time our little Susy ever saw him she encountered him on the street near our house and came flying wide-eyed to her mother and said, "Santa Claus has got loose!"

Which reminds me of Rev. Charley Stowe's little boy—a little boy of seven years. I met Rev. Charley crossing his mother's grounds one morning and he told me this little tale. He had been out to Chicago to attend a Convention of Congregational clergymen, and had taken his little boy with him. During the trip he reminded the little chap, every now and then, that he must be on his very best behavior there in Chicago. He said: "We shall be the guests of a clergyman, there will be other guests—clergymen and their wives—and you must be careful to let those people see by your walk and conversation that you are of a godly household. Be very careful about this." The admonition bore fruit. At the first breakfast which they ate in the Chicago clergyman's house he heard his little son say in the meekest and most reverent way to the lady opposite him, "Please, won't you, for Christ's sake, pass the butter?"

MARK TWAIN

(to be continued)

North American Review

No. DCV.

DECEMBER 21, 1906

CHAPTERS FROM MY AUTOBIOGRAPHY—VIII

BY MARK TWAIN

PREFATORY NOTE—Mr. Clemens began to write his autobiography many years ago, and he continues to add to it day by day. It was his original intention to permit no publication of his memoirs until after his death; but, after leaving "Pier No. 70," he concluded that a considerable portion might now suitably be given to the public. It is that portion, garnered from the quarter-million of words already written, which will appear in this REVIEW during the coming year. No part of the autobiography will be published in book form during the lifetime of the author.—EDITOR N. A. R.

[*Dictated in* 1906.] In those early days duelling suddenly became a fashion in the new Territory of Nevada, and by 1864 everybody was anxious to have a chance in the new sport, mainly for the reason that he was not able to thoroughly respect himself so long as he had not killed or crippled somebody in a duel or been killed or crippled in one himself.

At that time I had been serving as city editor on Mr. Goodman's Virginia City "Enterprise" for a matter of two years. I was twenty-nine years old. I was ambitious in several ways, but I had entirely escaped the seductions of that particular craze. I had had no desire to fight a duel; I had no intention of provoking one. I did not feel respectable, but I got a certain amount of satisfaction out of feeling safe. I was ashamed of myself; the rest of the staff were ashamed of me—but I got along well enough. I had always been accustomed to feeling ashamed of myself, for one thing or another, so there was no novelty for me in the situation. I bore it very well. Plunkett was on the staff; R. M. Daggett was on the staff. These had tried to get into duels, but for the present had failed, and were waiting. Goodman was the only one of us who had done anything to shed credit upon the paper. The rival paper was the Virginia "Union." Its editor for a little while was Tom Fitch, called the "silver-tongued orator of Wisconsin"—that was where he came from. He tuned up his oratory in the editorial columns of the "Union," and Mr. Goodman invited him out and modified him with a bullet. I remember the joy of the staff when Goodman's challenge was accepted by Fitch. We ran late that night, and made much of Joe Goodman. He was only twenty-four years old; he lacked the wisdom which a person has at twenty-nine, and he was as glad of being *it* as I was that I wasn't. He chose Major Graves for his second (that name is not right, but it's close enough; I don't remember the Major's name). Graves came over to instruct Joe in the duelling art. He had been a Major under Walker, the "gray-eyed man of destiny," and had fought all through that remarkable man's filibustering campaign in Central America. That fact gauges the Major. To say that a man was a Major under Walker, and came out of that struggle ennobled by Walker's praise, is to say that the Major was not merely a brave man but that he was brave to the very utmost limit of that word. All of Walker's men were like that. I knew the Gillis family intimately. The father made the campaign under Walker, and with him one son. They were in the memorable Plaza fight, and stood it out to the last against overwhelming odds, as did also all of the Walker men. The son was killed at the father's side. The father received a bullet through the eye. The old man—for he was an old man at the time—wore spectacles, and the bullet and one of the glasses went into his skull and remained there. There were some other sons: Steve, George, and Jim, very young chaps—the merest lads—who wanted to be in the Walker expedition, for they had their father's dauntless spirit. But Walker wouldn't have them; he said it was a serious expedition, and no place for children.

The Major was a majestic creature, with a most stately and dignified and impressive military bearing, and he was by nature and training courteous, polite, graceful, winning; and he had that quality which I think I have encountered in only one other man—Bob Howland—a mysterious quality which resides in the eye; and when that eye is turned upon an individual or a squad, in warning, that is enough. The man that has that eye doesn't need to go armed; he can move upon an armed desperado and quell him and take him prisoner without saying a single word. I saw Bob Howland do that, once—a slender, good-natured, amiable, gentle, kindly little skeleton of a man, with a sweet blue eye that would win your heart when it smiled upon you, or turn cold and freeze it, according to the nature of the occasion.

The Major stood Joe up straight; stood Steve Gillis up fifteen paces away; made Joe turn right side towards Steve, cock his navy six-shooter—that prodigious weapon—and hold it straight down against his leg; told him that *that* was the correct position for the gun—that the position ordinarily in use at Virginia City (that is to say, the gun straight up in the air, then brought slowly down to your man) was all wrong. At the word "*One*," you must raise the gun slowly and steadily to the place on the other man's body that you desire to convince. Then, after a pause, "*two, three—fire—Stop!*" At the word "stop," you may fire—but not earlier. You may give yourself as much time as you please *after* that word. Then, when you fire, you may advance and go on firing at your leisure and pleasure, if you can get any pleasure out of it. And, in the meantime, the other man, if he has been properly instructed and is alive to his privileges, is advancing on *you*, and firing—and it is always likely that more or less trouble will result.

Naturally, when Joe's revolver had risen to a level it was pointing at Steve's breast, but the Major said "No, that is not wise. Take all the risks of getting murdered yourself, but don't run any risk of murdering the other man. If you survive a duel you want to survive it in such a way that the memory of it will not linger along with you through the rest of your life and interfere with your sleep. Aim at your man's leg; not at the knee, not above the knee; for those are dangerous spots. Aim below the knee; cripple him, but leave the rest of him to his mother."

By grace of these truly wise and excellent instructions, Joe tumbled Fitch down next morning with a bullet through his lower leg, which furnished him a permanent limp. And Joe lost nothing but a lock of hair, which he could spare better then than he could now. For when I saw him here in New York a year ago, his crop was gone; he had nothing much left but a fringe, with a dome rising above.

About a year later I got *my* chance. But I was not hunting for it. Goodman went off to San Francisco for a week's holiday, and left me to be chief editor. I had supposed that that was an easy berth, there being nothing to do but write one editorial per day; but I was disappointed in that superstition. I couldn't find anything to write an article about, the first day. Then it occurred to me that inasmuch as it was the 22nd of April, 1864, the next morning would be the three-hundredth anniversary of Shakespeare's birthday—and what better theme could I want than that? I got the Cyclopædia and examined it, and found out who Shakespeare was and what he had done, and I borrowed all that and laid it before a community that couldn't have been better prepared for instruction about Shakespeare than if they had been prepared by art. There wasn't enough of what Shakespeare had done to make an editorial of the necessary length, but I filled it out with what he hadn't done—which in many respects was more important and striking and readable than the handsomest things he had really accomplished. But next day I was in trouble again. There were no more Shakespeares to work up. There was nothing in past history, or in the world's future possibilities, to make an editorial out of, suitable to that community; so there was but one theme left. That theme was Mr. Laird, proprietor of the Virginia "Union." *His* editor had gone off to San Francisco too, and Laird was trying his hand at editing. I woke up Mr. Laird with some courtesies of the kind that were fashionable among newspaper editors in that region, and he came back at me the next day in a most vitriolic way. He was hurt by something I had said about him—some little thing—I don't remember what it was now—probably called him a horse-thief, or one of those little phrases customarily used to describe another editor. They were no doubt just, and accurate, but Laird was a very sensitive creature and he didn't like it. So we expected a challenge from Mr. Laird, because according to the rules—according to the etiquette of duelling as reconstructed and reorganized and improved by the duellists of that region—whenever you said a thing about another person that he didn't like, it wasn't sufficient for him to talk back in the same offensive spirit: etiquette required him to send a challenge; so we waited for a challenge—waited all day. It didn't come. And as the day wore along, hour after hour, and no challenge came, the boys grew depressed. They lost heart. But I was cheerful; I felt better and better all the time. They couldn't understand it, but *I* could understand it. It was my *make* that enabled me to be cheerful when other people were despondent. So then it became necessary for us to waive etiquette and challenge Mr. Laird. When we reached that decision, they began to cheer up, but I began to lose some of my animation. However, in enterprises of this kind you are in the hands of your friends; there is nothing for you to do but to abide by what they consider to be the best course. Daggett wrote a challenge for me, for Daggett had the language—the right language—the convincing language—and I lacked it. Daggett poured out a stream of unsavory epithets upon Mr. Laird, charged with a vigor and venom of a strength calculated to persuade him; and Steve Gillis, my second, carried the challenge and came back to wait for the return. It didn't come. The boys were exasperated, but I kept my temper. Steve carried another challenge, hotter than the other, and we waited again. Nothing came of it. I began to feel quite comfortable. I began to take an interest in the challenges myself. I had not felt any before; but it seemed to me that I was accumulating a great and valuable reputation at no expense, and my delight in this grew and grew, as challenge after challenge was declined, until by midnight I was beginning to think that there was nothing in the world so much to be desired as a chance to fight a duel. So I hurried Daggett up;

made him keep on sending challenge after challenge. Oh, well, I over-did it; Laird accepted. I might have known that that would happen—Laird was a man you couldn't depend on.

The boys were jubilant beyond expression. They helped me make my will, which was another discomfort—and I already had enough. Then they took me home. I didn't sleep any—didn't want to sleep. I had plenty of things to think about, and less than four hours to do it in—because five o'clock was the hour appointed for the tragedy, and I should have to use up one hour—beginning at four—in practising with the revolver and finding out which end of it to level at the adversary. At four we went down into a little gorge, about a mile from town, and borrowed a barn door for a mark—borrowed it of a man who was over in California on a visit—and we set the barn door up and stood a fence-rail up against the middle of it, to represent Mr. Laird. But the rail was no proper representative of him, for he was longer than a rail and thinner. Nothing would ever fetch him but a line shot, and then as like as not he would split the bullet—the worst material for duelling purposes that could be imagined. I began on the rail. I couldn't hit the rail; then I tried the barn door; but I couldn't hit the barn door. There was nobody in danger except stragglers around on the flanks of that mark. I was thoroughly discouraged, and I didn't cheer up any when we presently heard pistol-shots over in the next little ravine. I knew what that was—that was Laird's gang out practising him. They would hear my shots, and of course they would come up over the ridge to see what kind of a record I was making—see what their chances were against me. Well, I hadn't any record; and I knew that if Laird came over that ridge and saw my barn door without a scratch on it, he would be as anxious to fight as I was—or as I had been at midnight, before that disastrous acceptance came.

Now just at this moment, a little bird, no bigger than a sparrow, flew along by and lit on a sage-bush about thirty yards away. Steve whipped out his revolver and shot its head off. Oh, he was a marksman—much better than I was. We ran down there to pick up the bird, and just then, sure enough, Mr. Laird and his people came over the ridge, and they joined us. And when Laird's second saw that bird, with its head shot off, he lost color, he faded, and you could see that he was interested. He said:

"Who did that?"

Before I could answer, Steve spoke up and said quite calmly, and in a matter-of-fact way,

"Clemens did it."

The second said, "Why, that is wonderful. How far off was that bird?"

Steve said, "Oh, not far—about thirty yards."

The second said, "Well, that is astonishing shooting. How often can he do that?"

Steve said languidly, "Oh, about four times out of five."

I knew the little rascal was lying, but I didn't say anything. The second said, "Why, that is *amazing* shooting; I supposed he couldn't hit a church."

He was supposing very sagaciously, but I didn't say anything. Well, they said good morning. The second took Mr. Laird home, a little tottery on his legs, and Laird sent back a note in his own hand declining to fight a duel with me on any terms whatever.

Well, my life was saved—saved by that accident. I don't know what the bird thought about that interposition of Providence, but I felt very, very comfortable over it—satisfied and content. Now, we found out, later, that Laird had *hit* his mark four times out of six, right along. If the duel had come off, he would have so filled my skin with bullet-holes that it wouldn't have held my principles.

By breakfast-time the news was all over town that I had sent a challenge and Steve Gillis had carried it. Now that would entitle us to two years apiece in the penitentiary, according to the brand-new law. Judge North sent us no message as coming from himself, but a message *came* from a close friend of his. He said it would be a good idea for us to leave the territory by the first stage-coach. This would sail next morning, at four o'clock—and in the meantime we would be searched for, but not with avidity; and if we were in the Territory after that stage-coach left, we would be the first victims of the new law. Judge North was anxious to have some object-lessons for that law, and he would absolutely keep us in the prison the full two years.

Well, it seemed to me that our society was no longer desirable in Nevada; so we stayed in our quarters and observed proper caution all day—except that once Steve went over to the hotel to attend to another customer of mine. That was a Mr. Cutler. You see Laird was not the only person whom I had tried to reform during my occupancy of the editorial chair. I had looked around and selected several other people, and delivered a new zest of life into them through warm criticism and disapproval—so that when I laid down my editorial pen I had four horse-whippings and two duels owing to me. We didn't care for the horse-whippings; there was no glory in them; they were not worth the trouble of collecting. But honor required that some notice should be taken of that other duel. Mr. Cutler had come up from Carson City, and had sent a man over with a challenge from the hotel. Steve went over to pacify him. Steve weighed only ninety-five pounds, but it was well known throughout the territory that with his fists he could whip anybody that walked on two legs, let his weight and science be what they might. Steve was a Gillis, and when a Gillis confronted a man and had a proposition to make, the proposition always contained business. When Cutler found that Steve was my second he cooled down; he became calm and rational, and was ready to listen. Steve gave him fifteen minutes to get out of the hotel, and half an hour to get out of town or there would be results. So *that* duel went off successfully, because Mr. Cutler immediately left for Carson a convinced and reformed man.

I have never had anything to do with duels since. I thoroughly disapprove of duels. I consider them unwise, and I know they are dangerous. Also, sinful. If a man should challenge me now, I would go to that man and take him kindly and forgivingly by the hand and lead him to a quiet retired spot, and *kill* him.

MARK TWAIN

(to be continued)

North American Review

No. DCVI.

JANUARY 4, 1907

CHAPTERS FROM MY AUTOBIOGRAPHY—IX

BY MARK TWAIN

PREFATORY NOTE—Mr. Clemens began to write his autobiography many years ago, and he continues to add to it day by day. It was his original intention to permit no publication of his memoirs until after his death; but, after leaving "Pier No. 70," he concluded that a considerable portion might now suitably be given to the public. It is that portion, garnered from the quarter-million of words already written, which will appear in this REVIEW during the coming year. No part of the autobiography will be published in book form during the lifetime of the author.—EDITOR N. A. R.

[*Dictated December 13, 1906.*] As regards the coming American monarchy. It was before the Secretary of State had been heard from that the chairman of the banquet said:

"In this time of unrest it is of great satisfaction that such a man as you, Mr. Root, is chief adviser of the President."

Mr. Root then got up and in the most quiet and orderly manner touched off the successor to the San Francisco earthquake. As a result, the several State governments were well shaken up and considerably weakened. Mr. Root was prophesying. He was prophesying, and it seems to me that no shrewder and surer forecasting has been done in this country for a good many years.

He did not say, in so many words, that we are proceeding,

in a steady march, toward eventual and unavoidable replacement of the republic by monarchy; but I suppose he was aware that that is the case. He notes the several steps, the customary steps, which in all the ages have led to the consolidation of loose and scattered governmental forces into formidable centralizations of authority; but he stops there, and doesn't add up the sum. He is not unaware that heretofore the sum has been ultimate monarchy, and that the same figures can fairly be depended upon to furnish the same sum whenever and wherever they can be produced, so long as human nature shall remain as it is; but it was not needful that he do the adding, since any one can do it; neither would it have been gracious in him to do it.

In observing the changed conditions which in the course of time have made certain and sure the eventual seizure by the Washington government of a number of State duties and prerogatives which have been betrayed and neglected by the several States, he does not attribute those changes and the vast results which are to flow from them to any thought-out policy of any party or of any body of dreamers or schemers, but properly and rightly attributes them to that stupendous power—*Circumstance*—which moves by laws of its own, regardless of parties and policies, and whose decrees are final, and must be obeyed by all—and will be. The railway is a Circumstance, the steamship is a Circumstance, the telegraph is a Circumstance. They were mere happenings; and to the whole world, the wise and the foolish alike, they were entirely trivial, wholly inconsequential; indeed silly, comical, grotesque. No man, and no party, and no thought-out policy said, "Behold, we will build railways and steamships and telegraphs, and presently you will see the condition and way of life of every man and woman and child in the nation totally changed; unimaginable changes of law and custom will follow, in spite of anything that anybody can do to prevent it."

The changed conditions have come, and Circumstance knows what is following, and will follow. So does Mr. Root. His language is not unclear, it is crystal:

"Our whole life has swung away from the old State centres, and is crystallizing about national centres."

". . . . The old barriers which kept the States as separate communities are completely lost from sight."

". . . . That [State] power of regulation and control is gradually passing into the hands of the national government."

"Sometimes by an assertion of the inter-State commerce power, sometimes by an assertion of the taxing power, the national government is taking up the performance of duties which under the changed conditions the separate States are no longer capable of adequately performing."

"We are urging forward in a development of business and social life which tends more and more to the obliteration of State lines and the decrease of State power as compared with national power."

"It is useless for the advocates of State rights to inveigh against . . . the extension of national authority in the fields of necessary control where the States themselves fail in the performance of their duty."

He is not announcing a policy; he is not forecasting what a party of planners will bring about; he is merely telling what the people will require and compel. And he could have added— which would be perfectly true—that the people will not be moved to it by speculation and cogitation and planning, but by *Circumstance*—that power which arbitrarily compels all their actions, and over which they have not the slightest control.

"The end is not yet."

It is a true word. We are on the march, but at present we are only just getting started.

If the States continue to fail to do their duty as required by the people—

" . . . *constructions of the Constitution will be found* to vest the power where it will be exercised—in the national government."

I do not know whether that has a sinister meaning or not,

and so I will not enlarge upon it lest I should chance to be in the wrong. It sounds like ship-money come again, but it may not be so intended.

Human nature being what it is, I suppose we must expect to drift into monarchy by and by. It is a saddening thought, but we cannot change our nature: we are all alike, we human beings; and in our blood and bone, and ineradicable, we carry the seeds out of which monarchies and aristocracies are grown: worship of gauds, titles, distinctions, power. We have to worship these things and their possessors, we are all born so, and we cannot help it. We have to be despised by somebody whom we regard as above us, or we are not happy; we have to have somebody to worship and envy, or we cannot be content. In America we manifest this in all the ancient and customary ways. In public we scoff at titles and hereditary privilege, but privately we hanker after them, and when we get a chance we buy them for cash and a daughter. Sometimes we get a good man and worth the price, but we are ready to take him anyway, whether he be ripe or rotten, whether he be clean and decent, or merely a basket of noble and sacred and long-descended offal. And when we get him the whole nation publicly chaffs and scoffs—and privately envies; and also is proud of the honor which has been conferred upon us. We run over our list of titled purchases every now and then, in the newspapers, and discuss them and caress them, and are thankful and happy.

Like all the other nations, we worship money and the possessors of it—they being our aristocracy, and we have to have one. We like to read about rich people in the papers; the papers know it, and they do their best to keep this appetite liberally fed. They even leave out a football bull-fight now and then to get room for all the particulars of how—according to the display heading—"Rich Woman Fell Down Cellar—Not Hurt." The falling down the cellar is of no interest to us when the woman is not rich, but no rich woman can fall down cellar and we not yearn to know all about it and wish it was us.

In a monarchy the people willingly and rejoicingly revere

and take pride in their nobilities, and are not humiliated by the reflection that this humble and hearty homage gets no return but contempt. Contempt does not shame them, they are used to it, and they recognize that it is their proper due. We are all made like that. In Europe we easily and quickly learn to take that attitude toward the sovereigns and the aristocracies; moreover, it has been observed that when we get the attitude we go on and exaggerate it, presently becoming more servile than the natives, and vainer of it. The next step is to rail and scoff at republics and democracies. All of which is natural, for we have not ceased to be human beings by becoming Americans, and the human race was always intended to be governed by kingship, not by popular vote.

I suppose we must expect that unavoidable and irresistible Circumstances will gradually take away the powers of the States and concentrate them in the central government, and that the republic will then repeat the history of all time and become a monarchy; but I believe that if we obstruct these encroachments and steadily resist them the monarchy can be postponed for a good while yet.

[*Dictated December 1, 1906.*] An exciting event in our village (Hannibal) was the arrival of the mesmerizer. I think the year was 1850. As to that I am not sure, but I know the month—it was May; that detail has survived the wear of fifty-five years. A pair of connected little incidents of that month have served to keep the memory of it green for me all this time; incidents of no consequence, and not worth embalming, yet my memory has preserved them carefully and flung away things of real value to give them space and make them comfortable. The truth is, a person's memory has no more sense than his conscience, and no appreciation whatever of values and proportions. However, never mind those trifling incidents; my subject is the mesmerizer, now.

He advertised his show, and promised marvels. Admission as usual: 25 cents, children and negroes half price. The village had heard of mesmerism, in a general way, but had not encountered it yet. Not many people attended, the first night, but next day they had so many wonders to tell that everybody's curiosity was fired, and after that for a fortnight the magician had prosperous times. I was fourteen or fifteen years old—the age at which a boy is willing to endure all things, suffer all things, short of death by fire, if thereby he may be conspicuous and show off before the public; and so, when I saw the "subjects" perform their foolish antics on the platform and make the people laugh and shout and admire, I had a burning desire to be a subject myself. Every night, for three nights, I sat in the row of candidates on the platform, and held the magic disk in the palm of my hand, and gazed at it and tried to get sleepy, but it was a failure; I remained wide awake, and had to retire defeated, like the majority. Also, I had to sit there and be gnawed with envy of Hicks, our journeyman; I had to sit there and see him scamper and jump when Simmons the enchanter exclaimed, "See the snake! see the snake!" and hear him say, "My, how beautiful!" in response to the suggestion that he was observing a splendid sunset; and so on—the whole insane business. I couldn't laugh, I couldn't applaud; it filled me with bitterness to have others do it, and to have people make a hero of Hicks, and crowd around him when the show was over, and ask him for more and more particulars of the wonders he had seen in his visions, and manifest in many ways that they were proud to be acquainted with him. Hicks—the idea! I couldn't stand it; I was getting boiled to death in my own bile.

On the fourth night temptation came, and I was not strong enough to resist. When I had gazed at the disk awhile I pretended to be sleepy, and began to nod. Straightway came the professor and made passes over my head and down my body and legs and arms, finishing each pass with a snap of his fingers in the air, to discharge the surplus electricity; then he began to "draw" me with the disk, holding it in his fingers and telling me I could not take my eyes off it, try as I might; so I rose slowly, bent and gazing, and followed that disk all over the place, just as I had seen the others do. Then I was put through the other paces. Upon suggestion I fled from snakes; passed buckets at a fire; became excited over hot steamboat-races; made love to imaginary girls and kissed them; fished from the platform and landed mud-cats that outweighed me— and so on, all the customary marvels. But not in the customary way. I was cautious at first, and watchful, being afraid the professor would discover that I was an impostor and drive me from the platform in disgrace; but as soon as I realized that I was not in danger, I set myself the task of terminating Hicks's usefulness as a subject, and of usurping his place.

It was a sufficiently easy task. Hicks was born honest; I, without that incumbrance—so some people said. Hicks saw what he saw, and reported accordingly; I saw more than was visible, and added to it such details as could help. Hicks had no imagination, I had a double supply. He was born calm, I was born excited. No vision could start a rapture in him, and he was constipated as to language, anyway; but if I saw a vision I emptied the dictionary onto it and lost the remnant of my mind into the bargain.

At the end of my first half-hour Hicks was a thing of the past, a fallen hero, a broken idol, and I knew it and was glad, and said in my heart, Success to crime! Hicks could never have been mesmerized to the point where he could kiss an imaginary girl in public, or a real one either, but I was competent. Whatever Hicks had failed in, I made it a point to succeed in, let the cost be what it might, physically or morally. He had shown several bad defects, and I had made a note of them. For instance, if the magician asked, "What do you see?" and left him to invent a vision for himself, Hicks was dumb and blind, he couldn't see a thing nor say a word, whereas the magician soon found that when it came to seeing visions of a stunning and marketable sort I could get along better without his help than with it. Then there was another thing: Hicks wasn't worth a tallow dip on mute mental suggestion. Whenever Simmons stood behind him and gazed at the back of his skull and tried to drive a mental suggestion into it, Hicks sat with vacant face, and never suspected. If he had been noticing, he could have seen by the rapt faces of the audience that something was going on behind his back that required a response. Inasmuch as I was an impostor I dreaded to have this test put upon me, for I knew the professor would be "willing" me to do something, and as I couldn't know what it was, I should be exposed and denounced. However, when my time came, I took my chance. I perceived by the tense and expectant faces of the people that Simmons was behind me willing me with all his might. I tried my best to imagine what he wanted, but nothing suggested itself. I felt ashamed and miserable, then. I believed that the hour of my disgrace was come, and that in another moment I should go out of that place disgraced. I ought to be ashamed to confess it, but my next thought was, not how I could win the compassion of kindly hearts by going out humbly and in sorrow for my misdoings, but how I could go out most sensationally and spectacularly.

There was a rusty and empty old revolver lying on the table, among the "properties" employed in the performances. On May-day, two or three weeks before, there had been a celebration by the schools, and I had had a quarrel with a big boy who was the school-bully, and I had not come out of it with credit. That boy was now seated in the middle of the house, half-way down the main aisle. I crept stealthily and impressively toward the table, with a dark and murderous scowl on my face, copied from a popular romance, seized the revolver suddenly, flourished it, shouted the bully's name, jumped off the platform, and made a rush for him and chased him out of the house before the paralyzed people could interfere to save him. There was a storm of applause, and the magician, addressing the house, said, most impressively—

"That you may know how really remarkable this is, and how wonderfully developed a subject we have in this boy, I assure you that without a single spoken word to guide him he has carried out what I mentally commanded him to do, to the minutest detail. I could have stopped him at a moment in his vengeful career by a mere exertion of my will, therefore the poor fellow who has escaped was at no time in danger."

So I was not in disgrace. I returned to the platform a hero, and happier than I have ever been in this world since. As regards mental suggestion, my fears of it were gone. I judged that in case I failed to guess what the professor might be willing me to do, I could count on putting up something that would answer just as well. I was right, and exhibitions of unspoken suggestion became a favorite with the public. Whenever I perceived that I was being willed to do something I got up and did something—anything that occurred to me—and the magician, not being a fool, always ratified it. When people asked me, "How *can* you tell what he is willing you to do?" I said, "It's just as easy," and they always said, admiringly, "Well it beats *me* how you can do it."

Hicks was weak in another detail. When the professor made passes over him and said "his whole body is without sensation now—come forward and test him, ladies and gentlemen," the ladies and gentlemen always complied eagerly, and stuck pins into Hicks, and if they went deep Hicks was sure to wince, then that poor professor would have to explain that Hicks "wasn't sufficiently under the influence." But I didn't wince; I only suffered, and shed tears on the inside. The miseries that a conceited boy will endure to keep up his "reputation"! And so will a conceited man; I know it in my own person, and have seen it in a hundred thousand others. That professor ought to have protected me, and I often hoped he would, when the tests were unusually severe, but he didn't. It may be that he was deceived as well as the others, though I did not believe it nor think it possible. Those were dear good people, but they must have carried simplicity and credulity to the limit. They would stick a pin in my arm and bear on it until they drove it a third of its length in, and then be lost in wonder that by a mere exercise of willpower the professor could turn my arm to iron and make it insensible to pain. Whereas it was not insensible at all; I was suffering agonies of pain.

After that fourth night, that proud night, that triumphant night, I was the only subject. Simmons invited no more candidates to the platform. I performed alone, every night, the rest of the fortnight. In the beginning of the second week I conquered the last doubters. Up to that time a dozen wise old heads, the intellectual aristocracy of the town, had held out, as implacable unbelievers. I was as hurt by this as if I were engaged in some honest occupation. There is nothing surprising about this. Human beings feel dishonor the most, sometimes, when they most deserve it. That handful of overwise old gentlemen kept on shaking their heads all the first week, and saying they had seen no marvels there that could not have been produced by collusion; and they were pretty vain of their unbelief, too, and liked to show it and air it, and be superior to the ignorant and the gullible. Particularly old Dr. Peake, who was the ringleader of the irreconcilables, and very formidable; for he was an F.F.V., he was learned, white-haired and venerable, nobly and richly clad in the fashions of an earlier and a courtlier day, he was large and stately, and he not only seemed wise, but was what he seemed, in that regard. He had great influence, and his opinion upon any matter was worth much more than that of any other person in the community. When I conquered him, at last, I knew I was undisputed master of the field; and now, after more than fifty years, I acknowledge, with a few dry old tears, that I rejoiced without shame.

[*Dictated December 2, 1906.*] In 1847 we were living in a large white house on the corner of Hill and Main Streets—a house that still stands, but isn't large now, although it hasn't lost a plank; I saw it a year ago and noticed that shrinkage. My father died in it in March of the year mentioned, but our family did not move out of it until some months afterward. Ours was not the only family in the house, there was another— Dr. Grant's. One day Dr. Grant and Dr. Reyburn argued a matter on the street with sword-canes, and Grant was brought home multifariously punctured. Old Dr. Peake calked the leaks, and came every day for a while, to look after him. The Grants were Virginians, like Peake, and one day when Grant was getting well enough to be on his feet and sit around in the parlor and talk, the conversation fell upon Virginia and old times. I was present, but the group were probably quite unconscious of me, I being only a lad and a negligible quantity. Two of the group—Dr. Peake and Mrs. Crawford, Mrs. Grant's mother—had been of the audience when the Richmond theatre burned down, thirty-six years before, and they talked over the frightful details of that memorable tragedy. These were eyewitnesses, and with their eyes I saw it all with an intolerable vividness: I saw the black smoke rolling and tumbling toward the sky, I saw the flames burst through it and turn red, I heard the shrieks of the despairing, I glimpsed their faces at the windows, caught fitfully through the veiling smoke, I saw them jump to their death, or to mutilation worse than death. The picture is before me yet, and can never fade.

In due course they talked of the colonial mansion of the Peakes, with its stately columns and its spacious grounds, and by odds and ends I picked up a clearly defined idea of the place. I was strongly interested, for I had not before heard of such palatial things from the lips of people who had seen them with their own eyes. One detail, casually dropped, hit my imagination hard. In the wall, by the great front door, there was a round hole as big as a saucer—a British cannon-ball had made it, in the war of the Revolution. It was breath-taking; it made history real; history had never been real to me before.

Very well, three or four years later, as already mentioned, I was king-bee and sole "subject" in the mesmeric show; it was the beginning of the second week; the performance was half over; just then the majestic Dr. Peake, with his ruffled bosom and wristbands and his gold-headed cane, entered, and a deferential citizen vacated his seat beside the Grants and made the great chief take it. This happened while I was trying to invent something fresh in the way of a vision, in response to the professor's remark—

"Concentrate your powers. Look—look attentively. There—don't you see something? Concentrate—concentrate. Now then—describe it."

Without suspecting it, Dr. Peake, by entering the place, had reminded me of the talk of three years before. He had also furnished me capital and was become my confederate, an accomplice in my frauds. I began on a vision, a vague and dim one (that was part of the game at the beginning of a vision; it isn't best to see it too clearly at first, it might look as if you had come loaded with it). The vision developed, by degrees, and gathered swing, momentum, energy. It was the Richmond fire. Dr. Peake was cold, at first, and his fine face had a trace of polite scorn in it; but when he began to recognize that fire, that expression changed, and his eyes began to light up. As soon as I saw that, I threw the valves wide open and turned on all the steam, and gave those people a supper of fire and horrors that was calculated to last them one while! They couldn't gasp, when I got through—they were petrified. Dr. Peake had risen, and was standing,—and breathing hard. He said, in a great voice—

"My doubts are ended. No collusion could produce that miracle. It was totally impossible for him to know those details, yet he has described them with the clarity of an eyewitness—and with what unassailable truthfulness God knows I know!"

I saved the colonial mansion for the last night, and solidified and perpetuated Dr. Peake's conversion with the cannon-ball hole. He explained to the house that I could never have heard of that small detail, which differentiated this mansion from all other Virginian mansions and perfectly identified it, therefore the fact stood proven that I had *seen* it in my vision. Lawks!

It is curious. When the magician's engagement closed there was but one person in the village who did not believe in mesmerism, and I was the one. All the others were converted, but I was to remain an implacable and unpersuadable disbeliever in mesmerism and hypnotism for close upon fifty years. This was because I never would examine them, in after life. I couldn't. The subject revolted me. Perhaps because it brought back to me a passage in my life which for pride's sake I wished to forget; though I thought—or persuaded myself I thought—I should never come across a "proof" which wasn't thin and cheap, and probably had a fraud like me behind it.

The truth is, I did not have to wait long to get tired of my triumphs. Not thirty days, I think. The glory which is built upon a lie soon becomes a most unpleasant incumbrance. No doubt for a while I enjoyed having my exploits told and retold and told again in my presence and wondered over and exclaimed about, but I quite distinctly remember that there presently came a time when the subject was wearisome and odious to me and I could not endure the disgusting discomfort of it. I am well aware that the world-glorified doer of a deed of great and real splendor has just my experience; I know that he deliciously enjoys hearing about it for three or four weeks, and that pretty soon after that he begins to dread the mention of it, and by and by wishes he had been with the damned before he ever thought of doing that deed; I remember how General Sherman used to rage and swear over "When we were Marching through Georgia," which was played at him and sung at him everywhere he went; still, I think I suffered a shade more than the legitimate hero does, he being privileged to soften his misery with the reflection that his glory was at any rate golden and reproachless in its origin, whereas I had no such privilege, there being no possible way to make mine respectable.

How easy it is to make people believe a lie, and how hard it is to undo that work again! Thirty-five years after those evil exploits of mine I visited my old mother, whom I had not seen for ten years; and being moved by what seemed to me a rather noble and perhaps heroic impulse, I thought I would humble myelf and confess my ancient fault. It cost me a great effort to make up my mind; I dreaded the sorrow that would rise in her face, and the shame that would look out of her eyes; but after long and troubled reflection, the sacrifice seemed due and right, and I gathered my resolution together and made the confession.

To my astonishment there were no sentimentalities, no dramatics, no George Washington effects; she was not moved in the least degree; she simply did not believe me, and said so! I was not merely disappointed, I was nettled, to have my costly truthfulness flung out of the market in this placid and confident way when I was expecting to get a profit out of it. I asserted, and reasserted, with rising heat, my statement that every single thing I had done on those long-vanished nights was a lie and a swindle; and when she shook her head tranquilly and said she knew better, I put up my hand and *swore* to it— adding a triumphant "*Now* what do you say?"

It did not affect her at all; it did not budge her the fraction of an inch from her position. If this was hard for me to endure, it did not begin with the blister she put upon the raw when she began to put my sworn oath out of court with *arguments* to prove that I was under a delusion and did not know what I was talking about. Arguments! Arguments to show that a person on a man's outside can know better what is on his inside than he does himself! I had cherished some contempt for arguments before, I have not enlarged my respect for them since. She refused to believe that I had invented my visions myself; she said it was folly: that I was only a child at the time and could not have done it. She cited the Richmond fire and the colonial mansion and said they were quite beyond my capacities. Then I saw my chance! I said she was right—I didn't invent those, I got them from Dr. Peake. Even this great shot did no damage. She said Dr. Peake's evidence was better than mine, and he had said in plain words that it was impossible for me to have heard about those things. Dear, dear, what a grotesque and unthinkable situation: a confessed swindler convicted of honesty and condemned to acquittal by circumstantial evidence furnished by the swindled!

I realized, with shame and with impotent vexation, that I was defeated all along the line. I had but one card left, but it was a formidable one. I played it—and stood from under. It seemed ignoble to demolish her fortress, after she had defended it so valiantly; but the defeated know not mercy. I played that master card. It was the pin-sticking. I said, solemnly—

"I give you my honor, a pin was never stuck into me without causing me cruel pain."

She only said—

"It is thirty-five years. I believe you do think that, *now*, but I was there, and I know better. You never winced."

She was so calm! and I was so far from it, so nearly frantic.

"Oh, my goodness!" I said, "let me *show* you that I am speaking the truth. Here is my arm; drive a pin into it—drive it to the head—I shall not wince."

She only shook her gray head and said, with simplicity and conviction—

"You are a man, now, and could dissemble the hurt; but you were only a child then, and could not have done it."

And so the lie which I played upon her in my youth remained

with her as an unchallengeable truth to the day of her death. Carlyle said "a lie cannot live." It shows that he did not know how to tell them. If I had taken out a life policy on this one the premiums would have bankrupted me ages ago.

MARK TWAIN

(to be continued)

North American Review

No. DCVII.

JANUARY 18, 1907

CHAPTERS FROM MY AUTOBIOGRAPHY—X

BY MARK TWAIN

PREFATORY NOTE—Mr. Clemens began to write his autobiography many years ago, and he continues to add to it day by day. It was his original intention to permit no publication of his memoirs until after his death; but, after leaving "Pier No. 70," he concluded that a considerable portion might now suitably be given to the public. It is that portion, garnered from the quarter-million of words already written, which will appear in this REVIEW during the coming year. No part of the autobiography will be published in book form during the lifetime of the author.—EDITOR N. A. R.

[*Dictated March 28, 1906.*] Orion Clemens was born in Jamestown, Fentress County, Tennessee, in 1825. He was the family's first-born, and antedated me ten years. Between him and me came a sister, Margaret, who died, aged ten, in 1837, in that village of Florida, Missouri, where I was born; and Pamela, mother of Samuel E. Moffett, who was an invalid all her life and died in the neighborhood of New York a year ago, aged about seventy-five. Her character was without blemish, and she was of a most kindly and gentle disposition. Also there was a brother, Benjamin, who died in 1848 aged ten or twelve.

Orion's boyhood was spent in that wee little log hamlet of Jamestown up there among the "knobs"—so called—of East Tennessee. The family migrated to Florida, Missouri, then moved to Hannibal, Missouri, when Orion was twelve and a half years old. When he was fifteen or sixteen he was sent to St. Louis and there he learned the printer's trade. One of his characteristics was eagerness. He woke with an eagerness about some matter or other every morning; it consumed him all day; it perished in the night and he was on fire with a fresh new interest next morning before he could get his clothes on. He exploited in this way three hundred and sixty-five red-hot new eagernesses every year of his life. But I am forgetting another characteristic, a very pronounced one. That was his deep glooms, his despondencies, his despairs; these had their place in each and every day along with the eagernesses. Thus his day was divided—no, not divided, mottled—from sunrise to midnight with alternating brilliant sunshine and black cloud. Every day he was the most joyous and hopeful man that ever was, I think, and also every day he was the most miserable man that ever was.

While he was in his apprenticeship in St. Louis, he got well acquainted with Edward Bates, who was afterwards in Mr. Lincoln's first cabinet. Bates was a very fine man, an honorable and upright man, and a distinguished lawyer. He patiently allowed Orion to bring to him each new project; he discussed it with him and extinguished it by argument and irresistible logic—at first. But after a few weeks he found that this labor was not necessary; that he could leave the new project alone and it would extinguish itself the same night. Orion thought he would like to become a lawyer. Mr. Bates encouraged him, and he studied law nearly a week, then of course laid it aside to try something new. He wanted to become an orator. Mr. Bates gave him lessons. Mr. Bates walked the floor reading from an English book aloud and rapidly turning the English into French, and he recommended this exercise to Orion. But as Orion knew no French, he took up that study and wrought at it like a volcano for two or three days; then gave it up. During his apprenticeship in St. Louis he joined a number of churches, one after another, and taught in their Sunday-schools—changing his Sunday-school every time he changed his religion. He was correspondingly erratic in his politics—Whig to-day, Democrat next week, and anything fresh that he

could find in the political market the week after. I may remark
here that throughout his long life he was always trading reli-
gions and enjoying the change of scenery. I will also remark
that his sincerity was never doubted; his truthfulness was
never doubted; and in matters of business and money his honesty was never questioned. Notwithstanding his forever-
recurring caprices and changes, his principles were high,
always high, and absolutely unshakable. He was the strangest
compound that ever got mixed in a human mould. Such a person as that is given to acting upon impulse and without reflection; that was Orion's way. Everything he did he did with
conviction and enthusiasm and with a vainglorious pride in
the thing he was doing—and no matter what that thing was,
whether good, bad or indifferent, he repented of it every time
in sackcloth and ashes before twenty-four hours had sped. Pes-
simists are born, not made. Optimists are born, not made. But
I think he was the only person I have ever known in whom
pessimism and optimism were lodged in exactly equal proportions. Except in the matter of grounded principle, he was as
unstable as water. You could dash his spirits with a single
word; you could raise them into the sky again with another one.
You could break his heart with a word of disapproval; you
could make him as happy as an angel with a word of approval.
And there was no occasion to put any sense or any vestige of
mentality of any kind into these miracles; anything you might
say would answer.

He had another conspicuous characteristic, and it was the
father of those which I have just spoken of. This was an intense
lust for approval. He was so eager to be approved, so girlishly
anxious to be approved by anybody and everybody, without
discrimination, that he was commonly ready to forsake his
notions, opinions and convictions at a moment's notice in order
to get the approval of any person who disagreed with them. I
wish to be understood as reserving his fundamental principles
all the time. He never forsook those to please anybody. Born
and reared among slaves and slaveholders, he was yet an abo-
litionist from his boyhood to his death. He was always truthful; he was always sincere; he was always honest and honorable.

But in light matters—matters of small consequence, like religion and politics and such things—he never acquired a conviction that could survive a disapproving remark from a cat.

He was always dreaming; he was a dreamer from birth, and this characteristic got him into trouble now and then.

Once when he was twenty-three or twenty-four years old, and was become a journeyman, he conceived the romantic idea of coming to Hannibal without giving us notice, in order that he might furnish to the family a pleasant surprise. If he had given notice, he would have been informed that we had changed our residence and that that gruff old bass-voiced sailorman, Dr. G., our family physician, was living in the house which we had formerly occupied and that Orion's former room in that house was now occupied by Dr. G.'s two middle-aged maiden sisters. Orion arrived at Hannibal per steamboat in the middle of the night, and started with his customary eagerness on his excursion, his mind all on fire with his romantic project and building and enjoying his surprise in advance. He was always enjoying things in advance; it was the make of him. He never could wait for the event, but must build it out of dream-stuff and enjoy it beforehand—consequently sometimes when the event happened he saw that it was not as good as the one he had invented in his imagination, and so he had lost profit by not keeping the imaginary one and letting the reality go.

When he arrived at the house he went around to the back door and slipped off his boots and crept up-stairs and arrived at the room of those elderly ladies without having wakened any sleepers. He undressed in the dark and got into bed and snuggled up against somebody. He was a little surprised, but not much—for he thought it was our brother Ben. It was winter, and the bed was comfortable, and the supposed Ben added to the comfort—and so he was dropping off to sleep very well satisfied with his progress so far and full of happy dreams of what was going to happen in the morning. But something else was going to happen sooner than that, and it happened now. The maid that was being crowded fumed and fretted and struggled and presently came to a half-waking condition and protested against the crowding. That voice paralyzed Orion. He couldn't move a limb; he couldn't get his breath; and the crowded one discovered his new whiskers and began to scream. This removed the paralysis, and Orion was out of bed and clawing round in the dark for his clothes in a fraction of a second. Both maids began to scream, then, so Orion did not wait to get his whole wardrobe. He started with such parts of it as he could grab. He flew to the head of the stairs and started down, and was paralyzed again at that point, because he saw the faint yellow flame of a candle soaring up the stairs from below and he judged that Dr. G. was behind it, and he was. He had no clothes on to speak of, but no matter, he was well enough fixed for an occasion like this, because he had a butcher-knife in his hand. Orion shouted to him, and this saved his life, for the Doctor recognized his voice. Then in those deep-sea-going bass tones of his that I used to admire so much when I was a little boy, he explained to Orion the change that had been made, told him where to find the Clemens family, and closed with some quite unnecessary advice about posting himself before he undertook another adventure like that—advice which Orion probably never needed again as long as he lived.

One bitter December night, Orion sat up reading until three o'clock in the morning and then, without looking at a clock, sallied forth to call on a young lady. He hammered and hammered at the door; couldn't get any response; didn't understand it. Anybody else would have regarded that as an indication of some kind or other and would have drawn inferences and gone home. But Orion didn't draw inferences, he merely hammered and hammered, and finally the father of the girl appeared at the door in a dressing-gown. He had a candle in his hand and the dressing-gown was all the clothing he had on—except an expression of unwelcome which was so thick and so large that it extended all down his front to his instep and nearly obliterated the dressing-gown. But Orion didn't notice that this was an unpleasant expression. He merely walked in. The old gentleman took him into the parlor, set the candle on a table, and stood. Orion made the usual remarks about the weather, and sat down—sat down and talked and talked and went on talking—that old man looking at him vindictively and waiting for his chance—waiting treacherously and malignantly for his chance. Orion had not asked for the young lady. It was not customary. It was understood that a young fellow came to see the girl of the house, not the founder of it. At last Orion got up and made some remark to the effect that probably the young lady was busy and he would go now and call again. That was the old man's chance, and he said with fervency "Why good land, aren't you going to stop to breakfast?"

Orion did not come to Hannibal until two or three years after my father's death. Meantime he remained in St. Louis. He was a journeyman printer and earning wages. Out of his wage he supported my mother and my brother Henry, who was two years younger than I. My sister Pamela helped in this support by taking piano pupils. Thus we got along, but it was pretty hard sledding. I was not one of the burdens, because I was taken from school at once, upon my father's death, and placed in the office of the Hannibal "Courier," as printer's apprentice, and Mr. S., the editor and proprietor of the paper, allowed me the usual emolument of the office of apprentice—that is to say board and clothes, but no money. The clothes consisted of two suits a year, but one of the suits always failed to materialize and the other suit was not purchased so long as Mr. S.'s old clothes held out. I was only about half as big as Mr. S., consequently his shirts gave me the uncomfortable sense of living in a circus tent, and I had to turn up his pants to my ears to make them short enough.

There were two other apprentices. One was Steve Wilkins, seventeen or eighteen years old and a giant. When he was in Mr. S.'s clothes they fitted him as the candle-mould fits the candle—thus he was generally in a suffocated condition, particularly in the summer-time. He was a reckless, hilarious, admirable creature; he had no principles, and was delightful company. At first we three apprentices had to feed in the kitchen with the old slave cook and her very handsome and bright and well-behaved young mulatto daughter. For his own amusement—for he was not generally laboring for other people's amusement—Steve was constantly and persistently and loudly and elaborately making love to that mulatto girl and distressing the life out of her and worrying the old mother to death. She would say, "Now, Marse Steve, Marse Steve, can't you behave yourself?" With encouragement like that, Steve would naturally renew his attentions and emphasize them. It was killingly funny to Ralph and me. And, to speak truly, the old mother's distress about it was merely a pretence. She quite well understood that by the customs of slaveholding communities it was Steve's right to make love to that girl if he wanted to. But the girl's distress was very real. She had a refined nature, and she took all Steve's extravagant love-making in resentful earnest.

We got but little variety in the way of food at that kitchen table, and there wasn't enough of it anyway. So we apprentices used to keep alive by arts of our own—that is to say, we crept into the cellar nearly every night, by a private entrance which we had discovered, and we robbed the cellar of potatoes and onions and such things, and carried them down-town to the printing-office, where we slept on pallets on the floor, and cooked them at the stove and had very good times.

As I have indicated, Mr. S.'s economies were of a pretty close and rigid kind. By and by, when we apprentices were promoted from the basement to the ground floor and allowed to sit at the family table, along with the one journeyman, Harry H., the economies continued. Mrs. S. was a bride. She had attained to that distinction very recently, after waiting a good part of a lifetime for it, and she was the right woman in the right place, according to the economics of the place, for she did not trust the sugar-bowl to us, but sweetened our coffee herself. That is, she went through the motions. She didn't really sweeten it. She seemed to put one heaping teaspoonful of brown sugar into each cup, but, according to Steve, that was a deceit. He said she dipped the spoon in the coffee first to make the sugar stick, and then scooped the sugar out of the bowl with the spoon upside down, so that the effect to the eye was a heaped-up spoon, whereas the sugar on it was nothing but a layer. This all seems perfectly true to me, and yet that thing would be so difficult to perform that I suppose it really didn't happen, but was one of Steve's lies.

MARK TWAIN

(to be continued)

North American Review

No. DCVIII.

FEBRUARY 1, 1907

CHAPTERS FROM MY AUTOBIOGRAPHY—XI

BY MARK TWAIN

PREFATORY NOTE—Mr. Clemens began to write his
autobiography many years ago, and he continues to add to
it day by day. It was his original intention to permit no
publication of his memoirs until after is death; but, after
leaving "Pier No. 70," he concluded that a considerable
portion might now suitably be given to the public. It is
that portion, garnered from the quarter-million of words
already written, which will appear in this REVIEW during the coming year. No part of the autobiography will
be published in book form during the lifetime of the
author.—EDITOR N. A. R.

[*Dictated March 28th, 1906.*] About 1849 or 1850 Orion severed his connection with the printing-house in St. Louis and
came up to Hannibal, and bought a weekly paper called the
Hannibal "Journal," together with its plant and its good-will,
for the sum of five hundred dollars cash. He borrowed the
cash at ten per cent. interest, from an old farmer named Johnson who lived five miles out of town. Then he reduced the subscription price of the paper from two dollars to one dollar. He
reduced the rates for advertising in about the same proportion,
and thus he created one absolute and unassailable certainty—
to wit: that the business would never pay him a single cent of
profit. He took me out of the "Courier" office and engaged my
services in his own at three dollars and a half a week, which

was an extravagant wage, but Orion was always generous, always liberal with everybody except himself. It cost him nothing in my case, for he never was able to pay me a penny as long as I was with him. By the end of the first year he found he must make some economies. The office rent was cheap, but it was not cheap enough. He could not afford to pay rent of any kind, so he moved the whole plant into the house we lived in, and it cramped the dwelling-place cruelly. He kept that paper alive during four years, but I have at this time no idea how he accomplished it. Toward the end of each year he had to turn out and scrape and scratch for the fifty dollars of interest due Mr. Johnson, and that fifty dollars was about the only cash he ever received or paid out, I suppose, while he was proprietor of that newspaper, except for ink and printing-paper. The paper was a dead failure. It had to be that from the start. Finally he handed it over to Mr. Johnson, and went up to Muscatine, Iowa, and acquired a small interest in a weekly newspaper there. It was not a sort of property to marry on—but no matter. He came across a winning and pretty girl who lived in Quincy, Illinois, a few miles below Keokuk, and they became engaged. He was always falling in love with girls, but by some accident or other he had never gone so far as engagement before. And now he achieved nothing but misfortune by it, because he straightway fell in love with a Keokuk girl. He married the Keokuk girl and they began a struggle for life which turned out to be a difficult enterprise, and very unpromising.

To gain a living in Muscatine was plainly impossible, so Orion and his new wife went to Keokuk to live, for she wanted to be near her relatives. He bought a little bit of a job-printing plant—on credit, of course—and at once put prices down to where not even the apprentices could get a living out of it, and this sort of thing went on.

I had not joined the Muscatine migration. Just before that happened (which I think was in 1853) I disappeared one night and fled to St. Louis. There I worked in the composing-room of the "Evening News" for a time, and then started on my travels to see the world. The world was New York City, and there was a little World's Fair there. It had just been opened where the great reservoir afterward was, and where the sumptuous public library is now being built—Fifth Avenue and Forty-second Street. I arrived in New York with two or three dollars in pocket change and a ten-dollar bank-bill concealed in the lining of my coat. I got work at villainous wages in the establishment of John A. Gray and Green in Cliff Street, and I found board in a sufficiently villainous mechanics' boarding-house in Duane Street. The firm paid my wages in wildcat money at its face value, and my week's wage merely sufficed to pay board and lodging. By and by I went to Philadelphia and worked there some months as a "sub" on the "Inquirer" and the "Public Ledger." Finally I made a flying trip to Washington to see the sights there, and in 1854 I went back to the Mississippi Valley, sitting upright in the smoking-car two or three days and nights. When I reached St. Louis I was exhausted. I went to bed on board a steamboat that was bound for Muscatine. I fell asleep at once, with my clothes on, and didn't wake again for thirty-six hours.

. . . I worked in that little job-office in Keokuk as much as two years, I should say, without ever collecting a cent of wages, for Orion was never able to pay anything—but Dick Higham and I had good times. I don't know what Dick got, but it was probably only uncashable promises.

One day in the midwinter of 1856 or 1857—I think it was 1856—I was coming along the main street of Keokuk in the middle of the forenoon. It was bitter weather—so bitter that that street was deserted, almost. A light dry snow was blowing here and there on the ground and on the pavement, swirling this way and that way and making all sorts of beautiful figures, but very chilly to look at. The wind blew a piece of paper past me and it lodged against a wall of a house. Something about the look of it attracted my attention and I gathered it in. It was a fifty-dollar bill, the only one I had ever seen, and the largest assemblage of money I had ever encountered in one spot. I advertised it in the papers and suffered more than a thousand dollars' worth of solicitude and fear and distress during the next few days lest the owner should see the advertisement and come and take my fortune away. As many as four days went by without an applicant; then I could endure this kind of misery no longer. I felt sure that another four could not go by in this safe and secure way. I felt that I must take that money out of danger. So I bought a ticket for Cincinnati and went to that city. I worked there several months in the printing-office of Wrightson and Company. I had been reading Lieutenant Herndon's account of his explorations of the Amazon and had been mightily attracted by what he said of coca. I made up my mind that I would go to the head waters of the Amazon and collect coca and trade in it and make a fortune. I left for New Orleans in the steamer "Paul Jones" with this great idea filling my mind. One of the pilots of that boat was Horace Bixby. Little by little I got acquainted with him, and pretty soon I was doing a lot of steering for him in his daylight watches. When I got to New Orleans I inquired about ships leaving for Pará and discovered that there weren't any, and learned that there probably wouldn't be any during that century. It had not occurred to me to inquire about these particulars before leaving Cincinnati, so there I was. I couldn't get to the Amazon. I had no friends in New Orleans and no money to speak of. I went to Horace Bixby and asked him to make a pilot out of me. He said he would do it for a hundred dollars cash in advance. So I steered for him up to St. Louis, borrowed the money from my brother-in-law and closed the bargain. I had acquired this brother-in-law several years before. This was Mr. William A. Moffett, a merchant, a Virginian—a fine man in every way. He had married my sister Pamela, and the Samuel E. Moffett of whom I have been speaking was their son. Within eighteen months I became a competent pilot, and I served that office until the Mississippi River traffic was brought to a standstill by the breaking out of the civil war.

. . . Meantime Orion had gone down the river and established his little job-printing-office in Keokuk. On account of charging next to nothing for the work done in his job-office, he had almost nothing to do there. He was never able to comprehend that work done on a profitless basis deteriorates and is presently not worth anything, and that customers are then obliged to go where they can get better work, even if they must

pay better prices for it. He had plenty of time, and he took up
Blackstone again. He also put up a sign which offered his services to the public as a lawyer. He never got a case, in those
days, nor even an applicant, although he was quite willing to
transact law business for nothing and furnish the stationery
himself. He was always liberal that way.

Presently he moved to a wee little hamlet called Alexandria,
two or three miles down the river, and he put up that sign there.
He got no custom. He was by this time very hard aground. But
by this time I was beginning to earn a wage of two hundred
and fifty dollars a month as pilot, and so I supported him
thenceforth until 1861, when his ancient friend, Edward Bates,
then a member of Mr. Lincoln's first cabinet, got him the place
of Secretary of the new Territory of Nevada, and Orion and I
cleared for that country in the overland stage-coach, I paying
the fares, which were pretty heavy, and carrying with me what
money I had been able to save—this was eight hundred dollars, I should say—and it was all in silver coin and a good deal
of a nuisance because of its weight. And we had another nuisance, which was an Unabridged Dictionary. It weighed about
a thousand pounds, and was a ruinous expense, because the
stage-coach Company charged for extra baggage by the ounce.
We could have kept a family for a time on what that dictionary cost in the way of extra freight—and it wasn't a good dictionary anyway—didn't have any modern words in it—only
had obsolete ones that they used to use when Noah Webster
was a child.

The Government of the new Territory of Nevada was an
interesting menagerie. Governor Nye was an old and seasoned
politician from New York—politician, not statesman. He had
white hair; he was in fine physical condition; he had a winningly friendly face and deep lustrous brown eyes that could
talk as a native language the tongue of every feeling, every
passion, every emotion. His eyes could outtalk his tongue, and
this is saying a good deal, for he was a very remarkable talker,
both in private and on the stump. He was a shrewd man; he
generally saw through surfaces and perceived what was going

on inside without being suspected of having an eye on the matter.

When grown-up persons indulge in practical jokes, the fact gauges them. They have lived narrow, obscure, and ignorant lives, and at full manhood they still retain and cherish a job-lot of left-over standards and ideals that would have been discarded with their boyhood if they had then moved out into the world and a broader life. There were many practical jokers in the new Territory. I do not take pleasure in exposing this fact, for I liked those people; but what I am saying is true. I wish I could say a kindlier thing about them instead—that they were burglars, or hat-rack thieves, or something like that, that wouldn't be utterly uncomplimentary. I would prefer it, but I can't say those things, they would not be true. These people were practical jokers, and I will not try to disguise it. In other respects they were plenty good-enough people; honest people; reputable and likable. They played practical jokes upon each other with success, and got the admiration and applause and also the envy of the rest of the community. Naturally they were eager to try their arts on big game, and that was what the Governor was. But they were not able to score. They made several efforts, but the Governor defeated these efforts without any trouble and went on smiling his pleasant smile as if nothing had happened. Finally the joker chiefs of Carson City and Virginia City conspired together to see if their combined talent couldn't win a victory, for the jokers were getting into a very uncomfortable place: the people were laughing at them, instead of at their proposed victim. They banded themselves together to the number of ten and invited the Governor to what was a most extraordinary attention in those days—pickled oyster stew and champagne—luxuries very seldom seen in that region, and existing rather as fabrics of the imagination than as facts.

The Governor took me with him. He said disparagingly,

"It's a poor invention. It doesn't deceive. Their idea is to get me drunk and leave me under the table, and from their standpoint this will be very funny. But they don't know me. I am familiar with champagne and have no prejudices against it."

The fate of the joke was not decided until two o'clock in the morning. At that hour the Governor was serene, genial, comfortable, contented, happy and sober, although he was so full that he couldn't laugh without shedding champagne tears. Also, at that hour the last joker joined his comrades under the table, drunk to the last perfection. The Governor remarked,

"This is a dry place, Sam, let's go and get something to drink and go to bed."

The Governor's official menagerie had been drawn from the humblest ranks of his constituents at home—harmless good fellows who had helped in his campaigns, and now they had their reward in petty salaries payable in greenbacks that were worth next to nothing. Those boys had a hard time to make both ends meet. Orion's salary was eighteen hundred dollars a year, and he couldn't even support his dictionary on it. But the Irishwoman who had come out on the Governor's staff charged the menagerie only ten dollars a week apiece for board and lodging. Orion and I were of her boarders and lodgers; and so, on these cheap terms the silver I had brought from home held out very well.

At first I roamed about the country seeking silver, but at the end of '62 or the beginning of '63 when I came up from Aurora to begin a journalistic life on the Virginia City "Enterprise," I was presently sent down to Carson City to report the legislative session. Orion was soon very popular with the members of the legislature, because they found that whereas they couldn't usually trust each other, nor anybody else, they could trust him. He easily held the belt for honesty in that country, but it didn't do him any good in a pecuniary way, because he had no talent for either persuading or scaring legislators. But I was differently situated. I was there every day in the legislature to distribute compliment and censure with evenly balanced justice and spread the same over half a page of the "Enterprise" every morning, consequently I was an influence. I got the legislature to pass a wise and very necessary law requiring every corporation doing business in the Territory to record its charter in full, without skipping a word, in a record to be kept by the Secretary of the Territory—my brother. All the charters were framed in exactly the same words. For this record-service he was authorized to charge forty cents a folio of one hundred words for making the record; also five dollars for furnishing a certificate of each record, and so on. Everybody had a toll-road franchise but no toll-road. But the franchise had to be recorded and paid for. Everybody was a mining corporation, and had to have himself recorded and pay for it. Very well, we prospered. The record-service paid an average of a thousand dollars a month, in gold.

Governor Nye was often absent from the Territory. He liked to run down to San Francisco every little while and enjoy a rest from Territorial civilization. Nobody complained, for he was prodigiously popular. He had been a stage-driver in his early days in New York or New England, and had acquired the habit of remembering names and faces, and of making himself agreeable to his passengers. As a politician this had been valuable to him, and he kept his arts in good condition by practice. By the time he had been Governor a year, he had shaken hands with every human being in the Territory of Nevada, and after that he always knew these people instantly at sight and could call them by name. The whole population, of 20,000 persons, were his personal friends, and he could do anything he chose to do and count upon their being contented with it. Whenever he was absent from the Territory—which was generally—Orion served his office in his place, as Acting Governor, a title which was soon and easily shortened to "Governor." He recklessly built and furnished a house at a cost of twelve thousand dollars, and there was no other house in the sage-brush capital that could approach this property for style and cost.

When Governor Nye's four-year term was drawing to a close, the mystery of why he had ever consented to leave the great State of New York and help inhabit that jack-rabbit desert was solved: he had gone out there in order to become a United States Senator. All that was now necessary was to turn the Territory into a State. He did it without any difficulty. That undeveloped country and that sparse population were not well fitted for the heavy burden of a State Government, but no matter, the people were willing to have the change, and so the Governor's game was made.

Orion's game was made too, apparently, for he was as popular because of his honesty as the Governor was for more substantial reasons; but at the critical moment the inborn capriciousness of his character rose up without warning, and disaster followed.

MARK TWAIN

(to be continued)

North American Review

No. DCIX.

FEBRUARY 15, 1907

CHAPTERS FROM MY AUTOBIOGRAPHY—XII

BY MARK TWAIN

PREFATORY NOTE—Mr. Clemens began to write his autobiography many years ago, and he continues to add to it day by day. It was his original intention to permit no publication of his memoirs until after his death; but, after leaving "Pier No. 70," he concluded that a considerable portion might now suitably be given to the public. It is that portion, garnered from the quarter-million of words already written, which will appear in this REVIEW during the coming year. No part of the autobiography will be published in book form during the lifetime of the author.—EDITOR N. A. R.

ORION CLEMENS—RESUMED

[*Dictated April 5, 1906.*] There were several candidates for all the offices in the gift of the new State of Nevada save two— United States Senator, and Secretary of State. Nye was certain to get a Senatorship, and Orion was so sure to get the Secretaryship that no one but him was named for that office. But he was hit with one of his spasms of virtue on the very day that the Republican party was to make its nominations in the Convention, and refused to go near the Convention. He was urged, but all persuasions failed. He said his presence there would be an unfair and improper influence and that if he was to be nominated the compliment must come to him as a free and unspotted gift. This attitude would have settled his case for him without further effort, but he had another attack of virtue on the same day, that made it absolutely sure. It had been his habit for a great many years to change his religion with his shirt, and his ideas about temperance at the same time. He would be a teetotaler for a while and the champion of the cause; then he would change to the other side for a time. On nomination day he suddenly changed from a friendly attitude toward whiskey—which was the popular attitude—to uncompromising teetotalism, and went absolutely dry. His friends besought and implored, but all in vain. He could not be persuaded to cross the threshold of a saloon. The paper next morning contained the list of chosen nominees. His name was not in it. He had not received a vote.

His rich income ceased when the State government came into power. He was without an occupation. Something had to be done. He put up his sign as attorney-at-law, but he got no clients. It was strange. It was difficult to account for. I cannot account for it—but if I were going to guess at a solution I should guess that by the make of him he would examine both sides of a case so diligently and so conscientiously that when he got through with his argument neither he nor a jury would know which side he was on. I think that his client would find out his make in laying his case before him, and would take warning and withdraw it in time to save himself from probable disaster.

I had taken up my residence in San Francisco about a year before the time I have just been speaking of. One day I got a tip from Mr. Camp, a bold man who was always making big fortunes in ingenious speculations and losing them again in the course of six months by other speculative ingenuities. Camp told me to buy some shares in the Hale and Norcross. I bought fifty shares at three hundred dollars a share. I bought on a margin, and put up twenty per cent. It exhausted my funds. I wrote Orion and offered him half, and asked him to send his share of the money. I waited and waited. He wrote and said he was going to attend to it. The stock went along up pretty briskly. It went higher and higher. It reached a thousand dollars a share. It climbed to two thousand, then to three thousand; then to twice that figure. The money did not come, but I was not disturbed. By and by that stock took a turn and began to gallop down. Then I wrote urgently. Orion answered that he had sent the money long ago—said he had sent it to the Occidental Hotel. I inquired for it. They said it was not there. To cut a long story short, that stock went on down until it fell below the price I had paid for it. Then it began to eat up the margin, and when at last I got out I was very badly crippled.

When it was too late, I found out what had become of Orion's money. Any other human being would have sent a check, but he sent gold. The hotel clerk put it in the safe and went on vacation, and there it had reposed all this time enjoying its fatal work, no doubt. Another man might have thought to tell me that the money was not in a letter, but was in an express package, but it never occurred to Orion to do that.

Later, Mr. Camp gave me another chance. He agreed to buy our Tennessee land for two hundred thousand dollars, pay a part of the amount in cash and give long notes for the rest. His scheme was to import foreigners from grape-growing and wine-making districts in Europe, settle them on the land, and turn it into a wine-growing country. He knew what Mr. Longworth thought of those Tennessee grapes, and was satisfied. I sent the contracts and things to Orion for his signature, he being one of the three heirs. But they arrived at a bad time—in a doubly bad time, in fact. The temperance virtue was temporarily upon him in strong force, and he wrote and said that he would not be a party to debauching the country with wine. Also he said how could he know whether Mr. Camp was going to deal fairly and honestly with those poor people from Europe or not?—and so, without waiting to find out, he quashed the whole trade, and there it fell, never to be brought to life again. The land, from being suddenly worth two hundred thousand dollars, became as suddenly worth what it was before—nothing, and taxes to pay. I had paid the taxes and the other expenses for some years, but I dropped the Tennessee land there, and have never taken any interest in it since, pecuniarily or otherwise, until yesterday.

I had supposed, until yesterday, that Orion had frittered away the last acre, and indeed that was his own impression. But a gentleman arrived yesterday from Tennessee and brought a map showing that by a correction of the ancient surveys we still own a thousand acres, in a coal district, out of the hundred thousand acres which my father left us when he died in 1847. The gentleman brought a proposition; also he brought a reputable and well-to-do citizen of New York. The proposition was that the Tennesseean gentleman should sell that land; that the New York gentleman should pay all the expenses and fight all the lawsuits, in case any should turn up, and that of such profit as might eventuate the Tennesseean gentleman should take a third, the New-Yorker a third, and Sam Moffett and his sister and I—who are surviving heirs—the remaining third.

This time I hope we shall get rid of the Tennessee land for good and all and never hear of it again.

I came East in January, 1867. Orion remained in Carson City perhaps a year longer. Then he sold his twelve-thousand-dollar house and its furniture for thirty-five hundred in greenbacks at about sixty per cent. discount. He and his wife took passage in the steamer for home in Keokuk. About 1871 or '72 they came to New York. Orion had been trying to make a living in the law ever since he had arrived from the Pacific Coast, but he had secured only two cases. Those he was to try free of charge—but the possible result will never be known, because the parties settled the cases out of court without his help.

Orion got a job as proof-reader on the New York "Evening Post" at ten dollars a week. By and by he came to Hartford and wanted me to get him a place as reporter on a Hartford paper. Here was a chance to try my scheme again, and I did it. I made him go to the Hartford "Evening Post," without any letter of introduction, and propose to scrub and sweep and do all sorts of things for nothing, on the plea that he didn't need money but only needed work, and that that was what he was pining for. Within six weeks he was on the editorial staff of that paper at twenty dollars a week, and he was worth the money. He was presently called for by some other paper at better wages, but I made him go to the "Post" people and tell them about it. They stood the raise and kept him. It was the pleasantest berth he had ever had in his life. It was an easy berth. He was in every way comfortable. But ill-luck came. It was bound to come.

A new Republican daily was to be started in a New England city by a stock company of well-to-do politicians, and they offered him the chief editorship at three thousand a year. He was eager to accept. My beseechings and reasonings went for nothing. I said,

"You are as weak as water. Those people will find it out right away. They will easily see that you have no backbone; that they can deal with you as they would deal with a slave. You may last six months, but not longer. Then they will not dismiss you as they would dismiss a gentleman: they will fling you out as they would fling out an intruding tramp."

It happened just so. Then he and his wife migrated to Keokuk once more. Orion wrote from there that he was not resuming the law; that he thought that what his health needed was the open air, in some sort of outdoor occupation; that his father-in-law had a strip of ground on the river border a mile above Keokuk with some sort of a house on it, and his idea was to buy that place and start a chicken-farm and provide Keokuk with chickens and eggs, and perhaps butter—but I don't know whether you can raise butter on a chicken-farm or not. He said the place could be had for three thousand dollars cash, and I sent the money. He began to raise chickens, and he made a detailed monthly report to me, whereby it appeared that he was able to work off his chickens on the Keokuk people at a dollar and a quarter a pair. But it also appeared that it cost a dollar and sixty cents to raise the pair. This did not seem to discourage Orion, and so I let it go. Meantime he was borrowing a hundred dollars per month of me regularly, month by month. Now to show Orion's stern and rigid business ways—and he really prided himself on his large business capacities—the moment he received the advance of a hundred dollars at the beginning of each month, he always sent me his note for the amount, and with it he sent, *out of that money,*

three months' interest on the hundred dollars at six per cent.
per annum, these notes being always for three months.

As I say, he always sent a detailed statement of the month's
profit and loss on the chickens—at least the month's loss on
the chickens—and this detailed statement included the various
items of expense—corn for the chickens, boots for himself,
and so on; even car fares, and the weekly contribution of ten
cents to help out the missionaries who were trying to damn the
Chinese after a plan not satisfactory to those people.

I think the poultry experiment lasted about a year, possibly
two years. It had then cost me six thousand dollars.

Orion returned to the law business, and I suppose he remained
in that harness off and on for the succeeding quarter of a century, but so far as my knowledge goes he was only a lawyer in
name, and had no clients.

My mother died, in her eighty-eighth year, in the summer of
1890. She had saved some money, and she left it to me, because
it had come from me. I gave it to Orion and he said, with
thanks, that I had supported him long enough and now he was
going to relieve me of that burden, and would also hope to pay
back some of that expense, and maybe the whole of it. Accordingly, he proceeded to use up that money in building a considerable addition to the house, with the idea of taking boarders
and getting rich. We need not dwell upon this venture. It was
another of his failures. His wife tried hard to make the scheme
succeed, and if anybody could have made it succeed she would
have done it. She was a good woman, and was greatly liked. She
had a practical side, and she would have made that boarding-house
lucrative if circumstances had not been against her.

Orion had other projects for recouping me, but as they
always required capital I stayed out of them, and they did not
materialize. Once he wanted to start a newspaper. It was a
ghastly idea, and I squelched it with a promptness that was
almost rude. Then he invented a wood-sawing machine and
patched it together himself, and he really sawed wood with it.
It was ingenious; it was capable; and it would have made a
comfortable little fortune for him; but just at the wrong time
Providence interfered again. Orion applied for a patent and

found that the same machine had already been patented and had gone into business and was thriving.

Presently the State of New York offered a fifty-thousand-dollar prize for a practical method of navigating the Erie Canal with steam canal-boats. Orion worked at that thing for two or three years, invented and completed a method, and was once more ready to reach out and seize upon imminent wealth when somebody pointed out a defect: his steam canal-boat could not be used in the winter-time; and in the summer-time the commotion its wheels would make in the water would wash away the State of New York on both sides.

Innumerable were Orion's projects for acquiring the means to pay off the debt to me. These projects extended straight through the succeeding thirty years, but in every case they failed. During all those thirty years his well-established honesty kept him in offices of trust where other people's money had to be taken care of, but where no salary was paid. He was treasurer of all the benevolent institutions; he took care of the money and other property of widows and orphans; he never lost a cent for anybody, and never made one for himself. Every time he changed his religion the church of his new faith was glad to get him; made him treasurer at once, and at once he stopped the graft and the leaks in that church. He exhibited a facility in changing his political complexion that was a marvel to the whole community. Once the following curious thing happened, and he wrote me all about it himself.

One morning he was a Republican, and upon invitation he agreed to make a campaign speech at the Republican mass-meeting that night. He prepared the speech. After luncheon he became a Democrat and agreed to write a score of exciting mottoes to be painted upon the transparencies which the Democrats would carry in their torchlight procession that night. He wrote these shouting Democratic mottoes during the afternoon, and they occupied so much of his time that it was night before he had a chance to change his politics again; so he actually made a rousing Republican campaign speech in the open air while his Democratic transparencies passed by in front of him, to the joy of every witness present.

He was a most strange creature—but in spite of his eccentricities he was beloved, all his life, in whatsoever community he lived. And he was also held in high esteem, for at bottom he was a sterling man.

About twenty-five years ago—along there somewhere—I suggested to Orion that he write an autobiography. I asked him to try to tell the straight truth in it; to refrain from exhibiting himself in creditable attitudes exclusively, and to honorably set down all the incidents of his life which he had found interesting to him, including those which were burned into his memory because he was ashamed of them. I said that this had never been done, and that if he could do it his autobiography would be a most valuable piece of literature. I said I was offering him a job which I could not duplicate in my own case, but I would cherish the hope that he might succeed with it. I recognize now that I was trying to saddle upon him an impossibility. I have been dictating this autobiography of mine daily for three months; I have thought of fifteen hundred or two thousand incidents in my life which I am ashamed of, but I have not gotten one of them to consent to go on paper yet. I think that that stock will still be complete and unimpaired when I finish these memoirs, if I ever finish them. I believe that if I should put in all or any of those incidents I should be sure to strike them out when I came to revise this book.

Orion wrote his autobiography and sent it to me. But great was my disappointment; and my vexation, too. In it he was constantly making a hero of himself, exactly as I should have done and am doing now, and he was constantly forgetting to put in the episodes which placed him in an unheroic light. I knew several incidents of his life which were distinctly and painfully unheroic, but when I came across them in his autobiography they had changed color. They had turned themselves inside out, and were things to be intemperately proud of. In my dissatisfaction I destroyed a considerable part of that autobiography. But in what remains there are passages which are interesting, and I shall quote from them here and there and now and then, as I go along.

While we were living in Vienna in 1898 a cablegram came

from Keokuk announcing Orion's death. He was seventy-two years old. He had gone down to the kitchen in the early hours of a bitter December morning; he had built the fire, and had then sat down at a table to write something; and there he died, with the pencil in his hand and resting against the paper in the middle of an unfinished word—an indication that his release from the captivity of a long and troubled and pathetic and unprofitable life was mercifully swift and painless.

[*Dictated in 1904.*] A quarter of a century ago I was visiting John Hay at Whitelaw Reid's house in New York, which Hay was occupying for a few months while Reid was absent on a holiday in Europe. Temporarily also, Hay was editing Reid's paper, the New York "Tribune." I remember two incidents of that Sunday visit particularly well. I had known John Hay a good many years, I had known him when he was an obscure young editorial writer on the "Tribune" in Horace Greeley's time, earning three or four times the salary he got, considering the high character of the work which came from his pen. In those earlier days he was a picture to look at, for beauty of feature, perfection of form and grace of carriage and movement. He had a charm about him of a sort quite unusual to my Western ignorance and inexperience—a charm of manner, intonation, apparently native and unstudied elocution, and all that—the groundwork of it native, the ease of it, the polish of it, the winning naturalness of it, acquired in Europe where he had been Chargé d'Affaires some time at the Court of Vienna. He was joyous and cordial, a most pleasant comrade. One of the two incidents above referred to as marking that visit was this:

In trading remarks concerning our ages I confessed to forty-two and Hay to forty. Then he asked if I had begun to write my autobiography, and I said I hadn't. He said that I ought to begin at once, and that I had already lost two years. Then he said in substance this:

"At forty a man reaches the top of the hill of life and starts down on the sunset side. The ordinary man, the average man, not to particularize too closely and say the commonplace man, has at that age succeeded or failed; in either case he has lived all of his life that is likely to be worth recording; also in either case the life lived is worth setting down, and cannot fail to be interesting if he comes as near to telling the truth about himself as he can. And he *will* tell the truth in spite of himself, for his facts and his fictions will work loyally together for the protection of the reader; each fact and each fiction will be a dab of paint, each will fall in its right place, and together they will paint his portrait; not the portrait *he* thinks they are painting, but his real portrait, the inside of him, the soul of him, his character. Without intending to lie he will lie all the time; not bluntly, consciously, not dully unconsciously, but half-consciously—consciousness in twilight; a soft and gentle and merciful twilight which makes his general form comely, with his virtuous prominences and projections discernible and his ungracious ones in shadow. His truths will be recognizable as truths, his modifications of facts which would tell against him will go for nothing, the reader will see the fact through the film and know his man.

"There is a subtle devilish something or other about autobiographical composition that defeats all the writer's attempts to paint his portrait *his* way."

Hay meant that he and I were ordinary average commonplace people, and I did not resent my share of the verdict, but nursed my wound in silence. His idea that we had finished our work in life, passed the summit and were westward bound downhill, with me two years ahead of him and neither of us with anything further to do as benefactors to mankind, was all a mistake. I had written four books then, possibly five. I have been drowning the world in literary wisdom ever since, volume after volume; since that day's sun went down he has been the historian of Mr. Lincoln, and his book will never perish; he has been ambassador, brilliant orator, competent and admirable Secretary of State.

MARK TWAIN

(to be continued)

North American Review

No. DCX.

MARCH 1, 1907

CHAPTERS FROM MY
AUTOBIOGRAPHY—XIII

BY MARK TWAIN

PREFATORY NOTE—Mr. Clemens began to write his autobiography many years ago, and he continues to add to it day by day. It was his original intention to permit no publication of his memoirs until after his death; but, after leaving "Pier No. 70," he concluded that a considerable portion might now suitably be given to the public. It is that portion, garnered from the quarter-million of words already written, which will appear in this REVIEW during the coming year. No part of the autobiography will be published in book form during the lifetime of the author. —EDITOR N. A. R.

. . . As I have said, that vast plot of Tennessee land was held by my father twenty years—intact. When he died in 1847, we began to manage it ourselves. Forty years afterward, we had managed it all away except 10,000 acres, and gotten nothing to remember the sales by. About 1887—possibly it was earlier—the 10,000 went. My brother found a chance to trade it for a house and lot in the town of Corry, in the oil regions of Pennsylvania. About 1894 he sold this property for $250. That ended the Tennessee Land.

If any penny of cash ever came out of my father's wise investment but that, I have no recollection of it. No, I am over-looking a detail. It furnished me a field for Sellers and a book.

Out of my half of the book I got \$15,000 or \$20,000; out of the play I got \$75,000 or \$80,000—just about a dollar an acre. It is curious: I was not alive when my father made the investment, therefore he was not intending any partiality; yet I was the only member of the family that ever profited by it. I shall have occasion to mention this land again, now and then, as I go along, for it influenced our life in one way or another during more than a generation. Whenever things grew dark it rose and put out its hopeful Sellers hand and cheered us up, and said "Do not be afraid—trust in me—wait." It kept us hoping and hoping, during forty years, and forsook us at last. It put our energies to sleep and made visionaries of us—dreamers and indolent. We were always going to be rich next year—no occasion to work. It is good to begin life poor; it is good to begin life rich—these are wholesome; but to begin it *prospectively* rich! The man who has not experienced it cannot imagine the curse of it.

My parents removed to Missouri in the early thirties; I do not remember just when, for I was not born then, and cared nothing for such things. It was a long journey in those days, and must have been a rough and tiresome one. The home was made in the wee village of Florida, in Monroe county, and I was born there in 1835. The village contained a hundred people and I increased the population by one per cent. It is more than the best man in history ever did for any other town. It may not be modest in me to refer to this, but it is true. There is no record of a person doing as much—not even Shakespeare. But I did it for Florida, and it shows that I could have done it for any place—even London, I suppose.

Recently some one in Missouri has sent me a picture of the house I was born in. Heretofore I have always stated that it was a palace, but I shall be more guarded, now.

I remember only one circumstance connected with my life in it. I remember it very well, though I was but two and a half years old at the time. The family packed up everything and started in wagons for Hannibal, on the Mississippi, thirty miles away. Toward night, when they camped and counted up the children, one was missing. I was the one. I had been left behind.

Parents ought always to count the children before they start. I was having a good enough time playing by myself until I found that the doors were fastened and that there was a grisly deep silence brooding over the place. I knew, then, that the family were gone, and that they had forgotten me. I was well frightened, and I made all the noise I could, but no one was near and it did no good. I spent the afternoon in captivity and was not rescued until the gloaming had fallen and the place was alive with ghosts.

My brother Henry was six months old at that time. I used to remember his walking into a fire outdoors when he was a week old. It was remarkable in me to remember a thing like that, which occurred when I was so young. And it was still more remarkable that I should cling to the delusion, for thirty years, that I *did* remember it—for of course it never happened; he would not have been able to walk at that age. If I had stopped to reflect, I should not have burdened my memory with that impossible rubbish so long. It is believed by many people that an impression deposited in a child's memory within the first two years of its life cannot remain there five years, but that is an error. The incident of Benvenuto Cellini and the salamander must be accepted as authentic and trustworthy; and then that remarkable and indisputable instance in the experience of Helen Keller—however, I will speak of that at another time. For many years I believed that I remembered helping my grandfather drink his whiskey toddy when I was six weeks old, but I do not tell about that any more, now; I am grown old, and my memory is not as active as it used to be. When I was younger I could remember anything, whether it had happened or not; but my faculties are decaying, now, and soon I shall be so I cannot remember any but the things that happened. It is sad to go to pieces like this, but we all have to do it.

My uncle, John A. Quarles, was a farmer, and his place was in the country four miles from Florida. He had eight children, and fifteen or twenty negroes, and was also fortunate in other ways. Particularly in his character. I have not come across a better man than he was. I was his guest for two or three months every year, from the fourth year after we removed to Hannibal till I was eleven or twelve years old. I have never consciously used him or his wife in a book, but his farm has come very handy to me in literature, once or twice. In "Huck Finn" and in "Tom Sawyer Detective" I moved it down to Arkansas. It was all of six hundred miles, but it was no trouble, it was not a very large farm; five hundred acres, perhaps, but I could have done it if it had been twice as large. And as for the morality of it, I cared nothing for that; I would move a State if the exigencies of literature required it.

It was a heavenly place for a boy, that farm of my uncle John's. The house was a double log one, with a spacious floor (roofed in) connecting it with the kitchen. In the summer the table was set in the middle of that shady and breezy floor, and the sumptuous meals—well, it makes me cry to think of them. Fried chicken, roast pig, wild and tame turkeys, ducks and geese; venison just killed; squirrels, rabbits, pheasants, partridges, prairie-chickens; biscuits, hot batter cakes, hot buckwheat cakes, hot "wheat bread," hot rolls, hot corn pone; fresh corn boiled on the ear, succotash, butter-beans, string-beans, tomatoes, pease, Irish potatoes, sweet-potatoes; buttermilk, sweet milk, "clabber"; watermelons, muskmelons, cantaloups— all fresh from the garden—apple pie, peach pie, pumpkin pie, apple dumplings, peach cobbler—I can't remember the rest. The way that the things were cooked was perhaps the main splendor—particularly a certain few of the dishes. For instance, the corn bread, the hot biscuits and wheat bread, and the fried chicken. These things have never been properly cooked in the North—in fact, no one there is able to learn the art, so far as my experience goes. The North thinks it knows how to make corn bread, but this is gross superstition. Perhaps no bread in the world is quite as good as Southern corn bread, and perhaps no bread in the world is quite so bad as the Northern imitation of it. The North seldom tries to fry chicken, and this is well; the art cannot be learned north of the line of Mason and Dixon, nor anywhere in Europe. This is not hearsay; it is experience that is speaking. In Europe it is imagined that the custom of serving various kinds of bread blazing hot is "American," but that is too broad a spread; it is custom in the South, but is much less than that in the North. In the North and in Europe hot bread is considered unhealthy. This is probably another fussy superstition, like the European superstition that ice-water is unhealthy. Europe does not need ice-water, and does not drink it; and yet, notwithstanding this, its word for it is better than ours, because it describes it, whereas ours doesn't. Europe calls it "iced" water. Our word describes water made from melted ice—a drink which we have but little acquaintance with.

It seems a pity that the world should throw away so many good things merely because they are unwholesome. I doubt if God has given us any refreshment which, taken in moderation, is unwholesome, except microbes. Yet there are people who strictly deprive themselves of each and every eatable, drinkable and smokable which has in any way acquired a shady reputation. They pay this price for health. And health is all they get for it. How strange it is; it is like paying out your whole fortune for a cow that has gone dry.

The farmhouse stood in the middle of a very large yard, and the yard was fenced on three sides with rails and on the rear side with high palings; against these stood the smokehouse; beyond the palings was the orchard; beyond the orchard were the negro quarter and the tobacco-fields. The front yard was entered over a stile, made of sawed-off logs of graduated heights; I do not remember any gate. In a corner of the front yard were a dozen lofty hickory-trees and a dozen black-walnuts, and in the nutting season riches were to be gathered there.

Down a piece, abreast the house, stood a little log cabin against the rail fence; and there the woody hill fell sharply away, past the barns, the corn-crib, the stables and the tobacco-curing house, to a limpid brook which sang along over its gravelly bed and curved and frisked in and out and here and there and yonder in the deep shade of overhanging foliage and vines—a divine place for wading, and it had swimming-pools, too, which were forbidden to us and therefore much frequented by us. For we were little Christian children, and had early been taught the value of forbidden fruit.

In the little log cabin lived a bedridden white-headed slave woman whom we visited daily, and looked upon with awe, for we believed she was upwards of a thousand years old and had talked with Moses. The younger negroes credited these statistics, and had furnished them to us in good faith. We accommodated all the details which came to us about her; and so we believed that she had lost her health in the long desert trip coming out of Egypt, and had never been able to get it back again. She had a round bald place on the crown of her head, and we used to creep around and gaze at it in reverent silence, and reflect that it was caused by fright through seeing Pharaoh drowned. We called her "Aunt" Hannah, Southern fashion. She was superstitious like the other negroes; also, like them, she was deeply religious. Like them, she had great faith in prayer, and employed it in all ordinary exigencies, but not in cases where a dead certainty of result was urgent. Whenever witches were around she tied up the remnant of her wool in little tufts, with white thread, and this promptly made the witches impotent.

All the negroes were friends of ours, and with those of our own age we were in effect comrades. I say in effect, using the phrase as a modification. We were comrades, and yet not comrades; color and condition interposed a subtle line which both parties were conscious of, and which rendered complete fusion impossible. We had a faithful and affectionate good friend, ally and adviser in "Uncle Dan'l," a middle-aged slave whose head was the best one in the negro quarter, whose sympathies were wide and warm, and whose heart was honest and simple and knew no guile. He has served me well, these many, many years. I have not seen him for more than half a century, and yet spiritually I have had his welcome company a good part of that time, and have staged him in books under his own name and as "Jim," and carted him all around—to Hannibal, down the Mississippi on a raft, and even across the Desert of Sahara in a balloon—and he has endured it all with the patience and friendliness and loyalty which were his birthright. It was on the farm that I got my strong liking for his race and my appreciation of certain of its fine qualities. This feeling and this estimate have stood the test of sixty years and more and have suffered no impairment. The black face is as welcome to me now as it was then.

In my schoolboy days I had no aversion to slavery. I was not aware that there was anything wrong about it. No one arraigned it in my hearing; the local papers said nothing against it; the local pulpit taught us that God approved it, that it was a holy thing, and that the doubter need only look in the Bible if he wished to settle his mind—and then the texts were read aloud to us to make the matter sure; if the slaves themselves had an aversion to slavery they were wise and said nothing. In Hannibal we seldom saw a slave misused; on the farm, never.

There was, however, one small incident of my boyhood days which touched this matter, and it must have meant a good deal to me or it would not have stayed in my memory, clear and sharp, vivid and shadowless, all these slow-drifting years. We had a little slave boy whom we had hired from some one, there in Hannibal. He was from the Eastern Shore of Maryland, and had been brought away from his family and his friends, half-way across the American continent, and sold. He was a cheery spirit, innocent and gentle, and the noisiest creature that ever was, perhaps. All day long he was singing, whistling, yelling, whooping, laughing—it was maddening, devastating, unendurable. At last, one day, I lost all my temper, and went raging to my mother, and said Sandy had been singing for an hour without a single break, and I couldn't stand it, and *wouldn't* she please shut him up. The tears came into her eyes, and her lip trembled, and she said something like this—

"Poor thing, when he sings, it shows that he is not remembering, and that comforts me; but when he is still, I am afraid he is thinking, and I cannot bear it. He will never see his mother again; if he can sing, I must not hinder it, but be thankful for it. If you were older, you would understand me; then that friendless child's noise would make you glad."

It was a simple speech, and made up of small words, but it went home, and Sandy's noise was not a trouble to me any more. She never used large words, but she had a natural gift for making small ones do effective work. She lived to reach the

neighborhood of ninety years, and was capable with her tongue
to the last—especially when a meanness or an injustice roused
her spirit. She has come handy to me several times in my
books, where she figures as Tom Sawyer's "Aunt Polly." I fitted
her out with a dialect, and tried to think up other improvements for her, but did not find any. I used Sandy once, also; it
was in "Tom Sawyer"; I tried to get him to whitewash the fence,
but it did not work. I do not remember what name I called him
by in the book.

I can see the farm yet, with perfect clearness. I can see all
its belongings, all its details; the family room of the house,
with a "trundle" bed in one corner and a spinning-wheel in
another—a wheel whose rising and falling wail, heard from a
distance, was the mournfulest of all sounds to me, and made
me homesick and low-spirited, and filled my atmosphere with
the wandering spirits of the dead; the vast fireplace, piled high,
on winter nights, with flaming hickory logs from whose ends a
sugary sap bubbled out but did not go to waste, for we scraped
it off and ate it; the lazy cat spread out on the rough hearth-
stones, the drowsy dogs braced against the jambs and blink-
ing; my aunt in one chimney-corner knitting, my uncle in the
other smoking his corn-cob pipe; the slick and carpetless oak
floor faintly mirroring the dancing flame-tongues and freckled
with black indentations where fire-coals had popped out and
died a leisurely death; half a dozen children romping in the
background twilight; "split"-bottomed chairs here and there,
some with rockers; a cradle—out of service, but waiting, with
confidence; in the early cold mornings a snuggle of children, in
shirts and chemises, occupying the hearthstone and procrasti-
nating—they could not bear to leave that comfortable place
and go out on the wind-swept floor-space between the house
and kitchen where the general tin basin stood, and wash.

Along outside of the front fence ran the country road; dusty
in the summer-time, and a good place for snakes—they liked
to lie in it and sun themselves; when they were rattlesnakes or
puff adders, we killed them; when they were black snakes, or
racers, or belonged to the fabled "hoop" breed, we fled, without shame; when they were "house snakes" or "garters" we

carried them home and put them in Aunt Patsy's work-basket for a surprise; for she was prejudiced against snakes, and always when she took the basket in her lap and they began to climb out of it it disordered her mind. She never could seem to get used to them; her opportunities went for nothing. And she was always cold toward bats, too, and could not bear them; and yet I think a bat is as friendly a bird as there is. My mother was Aunt Patsy's sister, and had the same wild superstitions. A bat is beautifully soft and silky; I do not know any creature that is pleasanter to the touch, or is more grateful for caressings, if offered in the right spirit. I know all about these coleoptera, because our great cave, three miles below Hannibal, was multitudinously stocked with them, and often I brought them home to amuse my mother with. It was easy to manage if it was a school day, because then I had ostensibly been to school and hadn't any bats. She was not a suspicious person, but full of trust and confidence; and when I said "There's something in my coat pocket for you," she would put her hand in. But she always took it out again, herself; I didn't have to tell her. It was remarkable, the way she couldn't learn to like private bats.

I think she was never in the cave in her life; but everybody else went there. Many excursion parties came from considerable distances up and down the river to visit the cave. It was miles in extent, and was a tangled wilderness of narrow and lofty clefts and passages. It was an easy place to get lost in; anybody could do it—including the bats. I got lost in it myself, along with a lady, and our last candle burned down to almost nothing before we glimpsed the search-party's lights winding about in the distance.

"Injun Joe" the half-breed got lost in there once, and would have starved to death if the bats had run short. But there was no chance of that; there were myriads of them. He told me all his story. In the book called "Tom Sawyer" I starved him entirely to death in the cave, but that was in the interest of art; it never happened. "General" Gaines, who was our first town drunkard before Jimmy Finn got the place, was lost in there for the space of a week, and finally pushed his handkerchief out of a hole in a hilltop near Saverton, several miles down the river from the cave's mouth, and somebody saw it and dug him out. There is nothing the matter with his statistics except the handkerchief. I knew him for years, and he hadn't any. But it could have been his nose. That would attract attention.

Beyond the road where the snakes sunned themselves was a dense young thicket, and through it a dim-lighted path led a quarter of a mile; then out of the dimness one emerged abruptly upon a level great prairie which was covered with wild strawberry-plants, vividly starred with prairie pinks, and walled in on all sides by forests. The strawberries were fragrant and fine, and in the season we were generally there in the crisp freshness of the early morning, while the dew-beads still sparkled upon the grass and the woods were ringing with the first songs of the birds.

Down the forest slopes to the left were the swings. They were made of bark stripped from hickory saplings. When they became dry they were dangerous. They usually broke when a child was forty feet in the air, and this was why so many bones had to be mended every year. I had no ill-luck myself, but none of my cousins escaped. There were eight of them, and at one time and another they broke fourteen arms among them. But it cost next to nothing, for the doctor worked by the year— $25 for the whole family. I remember two of the Florida doctors, Chowning and Meredith. They not only tended an entire family for $25 a year, but furnished the medicines themselves. Good measure, too. Only the largest persons could hold a whole dose. Castor-oil was the principal beverage. The dose was half a dipperful, with half a dipperful of New Orleans molasses added to help it down and make it taste good, which it never did. The next standby was calomel; the next, rhubarb; and the next, jalap. Then they bled the patient, and put mustard-plasters on him. It was a dreadful system, and yet the death-rate was not heavy. The calomel was nearly sure to salivate the patient and cost him some of his teeth. There were no dentists. When teeth became touched with decay or were otherwise ailing, the doctor knew of but one thing to do: he fetched his tongs and dragged them out. If the jaw remained, it was not his fault.

Doctors were not called, in cases of ordinary illness; the family's grandmother attended to those. Every old woman was a doctor, and gathered her own medicines in the woods, and knew how to compound doses that would stir the vitals of a cast-iron dog. And then there was the "Indian doctor"; a grave savage, remnant of his tribe, deeply read in the mysteries of nature and the secret properties of herbs; and most back-woodsmen had high faith in his powers and could tell of won-derful cures achieved by him. In Mauritius, away off yonder in the solitudes of the Indian Ocean, there is a person who answers to our Indian doctor of the old times. He is a negro, and has had no teaching as a doctor, yet there is one disease which he is master of and can cure, and the doctors can't. They send for him when they have a case. It is a child's disease of a strange and deadly sort, and the negro cures it with a herb medicine which he makes, himself, from a prescription which has come down to him from his father and grandfather. He will not let any one see it. He keeps the secret of its compo-nents to himself, and it is feared that he will die without divulging it; then there will be consternation in Mauritius. I was told these things by the people there, in 1896.

We had the "faith doctor," too, in those early days—a woman. Her specialty was toothache. She was a farmer's old wife, and lived five miles from Hannibal. She would lay her hand on the patient's jaw and say "Believe!" and the cure was prompt. Mrs. Utterback. I remember her very well. Twice I rode out there behind my mother, horseback, and saw the cure performed. My mother was the patient.

Dr. Meredith removed to Hannibal, by and by, and was our family physician there, and saved my life several times. Still, he was a good man and meant well. Let it go.

I was always told that I was a sickly and precarious and tire-some and uncertain child, and lived mainly on allopathic med-icines during the first seven years of my life. I asked my mother about this, in her old age—she was in her 88th year—and said:

"I suppose that during all that time you were uneasy about me?"

"Yes, the whole time."

"Afraid I wouldn't live?"

After a reflective pause—ostensibly to think out the facts—
"No—afraid you would."

It sounds like a plagiarism, but it probably wasn't. The country schoolhouse was three miles from my uncle's farm. It stood in a clearing in the woods, and would hold about twenty-five boys and girls. We attended the school with more or less regularity once or twice a week, in summer, walking to it in the cool of the morning by the forest paths, and back in the gloaming at the end of the day. All the pupils brought their dinners in baskets—corn-dodger, buttermilk and other good things—and sat in the shade of the trees at noon and ate them. It is the part of my education which I look back upon with the most satisfaction. My first visit to the school was when I was seven. A strapping girl of fifteen, in the customary sunbonnet and calico dress, asked me if I "used tobacco"—meaning did I chew it. I said, no. It roused her scorn. She reported me to all the crowd, and said—

"Here is a boy seven years old who can't chaw tobacco."

By the looks and comments which this produced, I realized that I was a degraded object; I was cruelly ashamed of myself. I determined to reform. But I only made myself sick; I was not able to learn to chew tobacco. I learned to smoke fairly well, but that did not conciliate anybody, and I remained a poor thing, and characterless. I longed to be respected, but I never was able to rise. Children have but little charity for each other's defects.

As I have said, I spent some part of every year at the farm until I was twelve or thirteen years old. The life which I led there with my cousins was full of charm, and so is the memory of it yet. I can call back the solemn twilight and mystery of the deep woods, the earthy smells, the faint odors of the wild flowers, the sheen of rain-washed foliage, the rattling clatter of drops when the wind shook the trees, the far-off hammering of wood-peckers and the muffled drumming of wood-pheasants in the remoteness of the forest, the snap-shot glimpses of disturbed wild creatures skurrying through the grass,—I can call it all back and make it as real as it ever was, and as blessed. I can call back the prairie, and its loneliness and peace, and a vast hawk hanging motionless in the sky, with his wings spread wide and the blue of the vault showing through the fringe of their end-feathers. I can see the woods in their autumn dress, the oaks purple, the hickories washed with gold, the maples and the sumacs luminous with crimson fires, and I can hear the rustle made by the fallen leaves as we ploughed through them. I can see the blue clusters of wild grapes hanging amongst the foliage of the saplings, and I remember the taste of them and the smell. I know how the wild blackberries looked, and how they tasted; and the same with the pawpaws, the hazelnuts and the persimmons; and I can feel the thumping rain, upon my head, of hickory-nuts and walnuts when we were out in the frosty dawn to scramble for them with the pigs, and the gusts of wind loosed them and sent them down. I know the stain of blackberries, and how pretty it is; and I know the stain of walnut hulls, and how little it minds soap and water; also what grudged experience it had of either of them. I know the taste of maple sap, and when to gather it, and how to arrange the troughs and the delivery tubes, and how to boil down the juice, and how to hook the sugar after it is made; also how much better hooked sugar tastes than any that is honestly come by, let bigots say what they will. I know how a prize watermelon looks when it is sunning its fat rotundity among pumpkin-vines and "simblins"; I know how to tell when it is ripe without "plugging" it; I know how inviting it looks when it is cooling itself in a tub of water under the bed, waiting; I know how it looks when it lies on the table in the sheltered great floor-space between house and kitchen, and the children gathered for the sacrifice and their mouths watering; I know the crackling sound it makes when the carving-knife enters its end, and I can see the split fly along in front of the blade as the knife cleaves its way to the other end; I can see its halves fall apart and display the rich red meat and the black seeds, and the heart standing up, a luxury fit for the elect; I know how a boy looks, behind a yard-long slice of that melon, and I know how he feels; for I have been there.

I know the taste of the watermelon which has been honestly come by, and I know the taste of the watermelon which has been acquired by art. Both taste good, but the experienced know which tastes best. I know the look of green apples and peaches and pears on the trees, and I know how entertaining they are when they are inside of a person. I know how ripe ones look when they are piled in pyramids under the trees, and how pretty they are and how vivid their colors. I know how a frozen apple looks, in a barrel down cellar in the winter-time, and how hard it is to bite, and how the frost makes the teeth ache, and yet how good it is, notwithstanding. I know the disposition of elderly people to select the specked apples for the children, and I once knew ways to beat the game. I know the look of an apple that is roasting and sizzling on a hearth on a winter's evening, and I know the comfort that comes of eating it hot, along with some sugar and a drench of cream. I know the delicate art and mystery of so cracking hickory-nuts and walnuts on a flatiron with a hammer that the kernels will be delivered whole, and I know how the nuts, taken in conjunction with winter apples, cider and doughnuts, make old people's tales and old jokes sound fresh and crisp and enchanting, and juggle an evening away before you know what went with the time. I know the look of Uncle Dan'l's kitchen as it was on privileged nights when I was a child, and I can see the white and black children grouped on the hearth, with the firelight playing on their faces and the shadows flickering upon the walls, clear back toward the cavernous gloom of the rear, and I can hear Uncle Dan'l telling the immortal tales which Uncle Remus Harris was to gather into his books and charm the world with, by and by; and I can feel again the creepy joy which quivered through me when the time for the ghost-story of the "Golden Arm" was reached—and the sense of regret, too, which came over me, for it was always the last story of the evening, and there was nothing between it and the unwelcome bed.

I can remember the bare wooden stairway in my uncle's house, and the turn to the left above the landing, and the rafters and the slanting roof over my bed, and the squares of moonlight on the floor, and the white cold world of snow outside, seen through the curtainless window. I can remember the howling of the wind and the quaking of the house on stormy nights, and how snug and cozy one felt, under the blankets, listening, and how the powdery snow used to sift in, around the sashes, and lie in little ridges on the floor, and make the place look chilly in the morning, and curb the wild desire to get up—in case there was any. I can remember how very dark that room was, in the dark of the moon, and how packed it was with ghostly stillness when one woke up by accident away in the night, and forgotten sins came flocking out of the secret chambers of the memory and wanted a hearing; and how ill chosen the time seemed for this kind of business; and how dismal was the hoo-hooing of the owl and the wailing of the wolf, sent mourning by on the night wind.

I remember the raging of the rain on that roof, summer nights, and how pleasant it was to lie and listen to it, and enjoy the white splendor of the lightning and the majestic booming and crashing of the thunder. It was a very satisfactory room; and there was a lightning-rod which was reachable from the window, an adorable and skittish thing to climb up and down, summer nights, when there were duties on hand of a sort to make privacy desirable.

I remember the 'coon and 'possum hunts, nights, with the negroes, and the long marches through the black gloom of the woods, and the excitement which fired everybody when the distant bay of an experienced dog announced that the game was treed; then the wild scramblings and stumblings through briars and bushes and over roots to get to the spot; then the lighting of a fire and the felling of the tree, the joyful frenzy of the dogs and the negroes, and the weird picture it all made in the red glare—I remember it all well, and the delight that every one got out of it, except the 'coon.

I remember the pigeon seasons, when the birds would come in millions, and cover the trees, and by their weight break down the branches. They were clubbed to death with sticks; guns were not necessary, and were not used. I remember the squirrel hunts, and the prairie-chicken hunts, and the wild-turkey hunts, and all that; and how we turned out, mornings, while it was still dark, to go on these expeditions, and how chilly and dismal it was, and how often I regretted that I was well enough to go. A toot on a tin horn brought twice as many dogs as were needed, and in their happiness they raced and scampered about, and knocked small people down, and made no end of unnecessary noise. At the word, they vanished away toward the woods, and we drifted silently after them in the melancholy gloom. But presently the gray dawn stole over the world, the birds piped up, then the sun rose and poured light and comfort all around, everything was fresh and dewy and fragrant, and life was a boon again. After three hours of tramping we arrived back wholesomely tired, overladen with game, very hungry, and just in time for breakfast.

MARK TWAIN

(to be continued)

North American Review

No. DCXI.

MARCH 15, 1907

CHAPTERS FROM MY AUTOBIOGRAPHY—XIV

BY MARK TWAIN

PREFATORY NOTE—Mr. Clemens began to write his autobiography many years ago, and he continues to add to it day by day. It was his original intention to permit no publication of his memoirs until after his death; but, after leaving "Pier No. 70," he concluded that a considerable portion might now suitably be given to the public. It is that portion, garnered from the quarter-million of words already written, which will appear in this REVIEW during the coming year. No part of the autobiography will be published in book form during the lifetime of the author. —EDITOR N. A. R.

[*Dictated Thursday, December 6, 1906.*]

FROM SUSY'S BIOGRAPHY OF ME
Feb. 27, Sunday.

Clara's reputation as a baby was always a fine one, mine exactly the contrary. One often related story concerning her braveness as a baby and her own opinion of this quality of hers is this. Clara and I often got slivers in our hands and when mama took them out with a much dreaded needle, Clara was always very brave, and I very cowardly. One day Clara got one of these slivers in her hand, a very bad one, and while mama was taking it out, Clara stood perfectly still without even wincing; I saw how brave she was and turning to mamma said "Mamma isn't she a brave little thing!" presently mamma had

to give the little hand quite a dig with the needle and noticing
how perfectly quiet Clara was about it she exclaimed, Why
Clara! you *are* a brave little thing! Clara responded "No bodys
braver but God!"—

Clara's pious remark is the main detail, and Susy has accurately remembered its phrasing. The three-year-older's wound
was of a formidable sort, and not one which the mother's sur-
gery would have been equal to. The flesh of the finger had been
burst by a cruel accident. It was the doctor that sewed it up,
and to all appearances it was he, and the other independent
witnesses, that did the main part of the suffering; each stitch
that he took made Clara wince slightly, but it shrivelled the
others.

I take pride in Clara's remark, because it shows that although
she was only three years old, her fireside teachings were
already making her a thinker—a thinker and also an observer
of proportions. I am not claiming any credit for this. I furnished to the children worldly knowledge and wisdom, but
was not competent to go higher, and so I left their spiritual
education in the hands of the mother. A result of this modesty
of mine was made manifest to me in a very striking way, some
years afterward, when Jean was nine years old. We had recently
arrived in Berlin, at the time, and had begun housekeeping in
a furnished apartment. One morning at breakfast a vast card
arrived—an invitation. To be precise, it was a command from
the Emperor of Germany to come to dinner. During several
months I had encountered socially, on the Continent, men
bearing lofty titles; and all this while Jean was becoming more
and more impressed, and awed, and subdued, by these imposing events, for she had not been abroad before, and they were
new to her—wonders out of dreamland turned into realities.
The imperial card was passed from hand to hand, around the
table, and examined with interest; when it reached Jean she
exhibited excitement and emotion, but for a time was quite
speechless; then she said,

"Why, papa, if it keeps going on like this, pretty soon there
won't be anybody left for you to get acquainted with but God."

It was not complimentary to think I was not acquainted in that quarter, but she was young, and the young jump to conclusions without reflection.

Necessarily, I did myself the honor to obey the command of the Emperor Wilhelm II. Prince Heinrich, and six or eight other guests were present. The Emperor did most of the talking, and he talked well, and in faultless English. In both of these conspicuousnesses I was gratified to recognize a resemblance to myself—a very exact resemblance; no, almost exact, but not quite that—a modified exactness, with the advantage in favour of the Emperor. My English, like his, is nearly faultless; like him I talk well; and when I have guests at dinner I prefer to do all the talking myself. It is the best way, and the pleasantest. Also the most profitable for the others.

I was greatly pleased to perceive that his Majesty was familiar with my books, and that his attitude toward them was not uncomplimentary. In the course of his talk he said that my best and most valuable book was "Old Times on the Mississippi." I will refer to that remark again, presently.

An official who was well up in the Foreign Office at that time, and had served under Bismarck for fourteen years, was still occupying his old place under Chancellor Caprivi. Smith, I will call him of whom I am speaking, though that is not his name. He was a special friend of mine, and I greatly enjoyed his society, although in order to have it it was necessary for me to seek it as late as midnight, and not earlier. This was because Government officials of his rank had to work all day, after nine in the morning, and then attend official banquets in the evening; wherefore they were usually unable to get life-restoring fresh air and exercise for their jaded minds and bodies earlier than midnight; then they turned out, in groups of two or three, and gratefully and violently tramped the deserted streets until two in the morning. Smith had been in the Government service, at home and abroad, for more than thirty years, and he was now sixty years old, or close upon it. He could not remember a year in which he had had a vacation of more than a fortnight's length; he was weary all through to the bones and the marrow, now, and was yearning for a holiday of a whole three months—yearning so longingly and so poignantly that he had at last made up his mind to make a desperate cast for it and stand the consequences, whatever they might be. It was against all rules to *ask* for a vacation—quite against all etiquette; the shock of it would paralyze the Chancellery; stern etiquette and usage required another form: the applicant was not privileged to ask for a vacation, he must send in his *resignation*. The chancellor would know that the applicant was not really trying to resign, and didn't want to resign, but was merely trying in this left-handed way to get a vacation.

The night before the Emperor's dinner I helped Smith take his exercise, after midnight, and he was full of his project. He had sent in his resignation that day, and was trembling for the result; and naturally, because it might possibly be that the chancellor would be happy to fill his place with somebody else, in which case he could accept the resignation without comment and without offence. Smith was in a very anxious frame of mind; not that he feared that Caprivi was dissatisfied with him, for he had no such fear; it was the Emperor that he was afraid of; he did not know how he stood with the Emperor. He said that while apparently it was Caprivi who would decide his case, it was in reality the Emperor who would perform that service; that the Emperor kept personal watch upon everything, and that no official sparrow could fall to the ground without his privity and consent; that the resignation would be laid before his Majesty, who would accept it or decline to accept it, according to his pleasure, and that then his pleasure in the matter would be communicated by Caprivi. Smith said he would know his fate the next evening, after the imperial dinner; that when I should escort his Majesty into the large salon contiguous to the dining-room, I would find there about thirty men—Cabinet ministers, admirals, generals and other great officials of the Empire—and that these men would be standing talking together in little separate groups of two or three persons; that the Emperor would move from group to group and say a word to each, sometimes two words, sometimes ten words; and that the length of his speech, whether brief or not so brief, would indicate the exact standing in the

Emperor's regard, of the man accosted; and that by observing this thermometer an expert could tell, to half a degree, the state of the imperial weather in each case; that in Berlin, as in the imperial days of Rome, the Emperor was the sun, and that his smile or his frown meant good fortune or disaster to the man upon whom it should fall. Smith suggested that I watch the thermometer while the Emperor went his rounds of the groups; and added that if his Majesty talked four minutes with any person there present, it meant high favor, and that the sun was in the zenith, and cloudless, for that man.

I mentally recorded that four-minute altitude, and resolved to see if any man there on that night stood in sufficient favor to achieve it.

Very well. After the dinner I watched the Emperor while he passed from group to group, and privately I timed him with a watch. Two or three times he came near to reaching the four-minute altitude, but always he fell short a little. The last man he came to was Smith. He put his hand on Smith's shoulder and began to talk to him; and when he finished, the thermometer had scored seven minutes! The company then moved toward the smoking-room, where cigars, beer and anecdotes would be in brisk service until midnight, and as Smith passed me he whispered,

"That settles it. The chancellor will ask me how much of a vacation I want, and I sha'n't be afraid to raise the limit. I shall call for six months."

Smith's dream had been to spend his three months' vacation—in case he got a vacation instead of the other thing—in one of the great capitals of the Continent—a capital whose name I shall suppress, at present. The next day the chancellor asked him how much of a vacation he wanted, and where he desired to spend it. Smith told him. His prayer was granted, and rather more than granted. The chancellor augmented his salary and attached him to the German Embassy of that selected capital, giving him a place of high dignity bearing an imposing title, and with nothing to do except attend banquets of an extraordinary character at the Embassy, once or twice a year. The term of his vacation was not specified; he was to continue it until requested to come back to his work in the Foreign Office. This was in 1891. Eight years later Smith was passing through Vienna, and he called upon me. There had been no interruption of his vacation, as yet, and there was no likelihood that an interruption of it would occur while he should still be among the living.

[*Dictated Monday, December 17, 1906.*] As I have already remarked, "Old Times on the Mississippi" got the Kaiser's best praise. It was after midnight when I reached home; I was usually out until toward midnight, and the pleasure of being out late was poisoned, every night, by the dread of what I must meet at my front door—an indignant face, a resentful face, the face of the *portier*. The *portier* was a tow-headed young German, twenty-two or three years old; and it had been for some time apparent to me that he did not enjoy being hammered out of his sleep, nights, to let me in. He never had a kind word for me, nor a pleasant look. I couldn't understand it, since it was his business to be on watch and let the occupants of the several flats in at any and all hours of the night. I could not see why he so distinctly failed to get reconciled to it.

The fact is, I was ignorantly violating, every night, a custom in which he was commercially interested. I did not suspect this. No one had told me of the custom, and if I had been left to guess it, it would have taken me a very long time to make a success of it. It was a custom which was so well established and so universally recognized, that it had all the force and dignity of law. By authority of this custom, whosoever entered a Berlin house after ten at night must pay a trifling toll to the *portier* for breaking his sleep to let him in. This tax was either two and a half cents or five cents, I don't remember which; but I had never paid it, and didn't know I owed it, and as I had been residing in Berlin several weeks, I was so far in arrears that my presence in the German capital was getting to be a serious disaster to that young fellow.

I arrived from the imperial dinner sorrowful and anxious, made my presence known and prepared myself to wait in patience the tedious minute or two which the *portier* usually allowed himself to keep me tarrying—as a punishment. But this time there was no stage-wait; the door was instantly unlocked, unbolted, unchained and flung wide; and in it appeared the strange and welcome apparition of the *portier's* round face all sunshine and smiles and welcome, in place of the black frowns and hostility that I was expecting. Plainly he had not come out of his bed: he had been waiting for me, watching for me. He began to pour out upon me in the most enthusiastic and energetic way a generous stream of German welcome and homage, meanwhile dragging me excitedly to his small bedroom beside the front door; there he made me bend down over a row of German translations of my books and said,

"There—you wrote them! I have found it out! By God, I did not know it before, and I ask a million pardons! That one there, the 'Old Times on the Mississippi,' is the best book you ever wrote!"

The usual number of those curious accidents which we call coincidences have fallen to my share in this life, but for picturesqueness this one puts all the others in the shade: that a crowned head and a *portier*, the very top of an empire and the very bottom of it, should pass the very same criticism and deliver the very same verdict upon a book of mine—and almost in the same hour and the same breath—is a coincidence which out-coincidences any coincidence which I could have imagined with such powers of imagination as I have been favored with; and I have not been accustomed to regard them as being small or of an inferior quality. It is always a satisfaction to me to remember that whereas I do not know, for sure, what any other nation thinks of any one of my twenty-three volumes, I do at least know for a certainty what one nation of fifty millions thinks of one of them, at any rate; for if the mutual verdict of the top of an empire and the bottom of it does not establish for good and all the judgment of the entire nation concerning that book, then the axiom that we can get a sure estimate of a thing by arriving at a general average of all the opinions involved, is a fallacy.

[*Dictated Monday, February 10, 1907.*] Two months ago (December 6) I was dictating a brief account of a private dinner in Berlin, where the Emperor of Germany was host and I the chief guest. Something happened day before yesterday which moves me to take up that matter again.

At the dinner his Majesty chatted briskly and entertainingly along in easy and flowing English, and now and then he interrupted himself to address a remark to me, or to some other individual of the guests. When the reply had been delivered, he resumed his talk. I noticed that the table etiquette tallied with that which was the law of my house at home when we had guests: that is to say, the guests answered when the host favored them with a remark, and then quieted down and behaved themselves until they got another chance. If I had been in the Emperor's chair and he in mine, I should have felt infinitely comfortable and at home, and should have done a world of talking, and done it well; but I was guest now, and consequently I felt less at home. From old experience, I was familiar with the rules of the game, and familiar with their exercise from the high place of host; but I was not familiar with the trammelled and less satisfactory position of guest, therefore I felt a little strange and out of place. But there was no animosity—no, the Emperor was host, therefore according to my own rule he had a right to do the talking, and it was my honorable duty to intrude no interruptions or other improvements, except upon invitation; and of course it could be *my* turn some day: some day, on some friendly visit of inspection to America, it might be my pleasure and distinction to have him as guest at my table; then I would give him a rest, and a remarkably quiet time.

In one way there was a difference between his table and mine—for instance, atmosphere; the guests stood in awe of him, and naturally they conferred that feeling upon me, for, after all, I am only human, although I regret it. When a guest answered a question he did it with deferential voice and manner; he did not put any emotion into it, and he did not spin it out, but got it out of his system as quickly as he could, and then looked relieved. The Emperor was used to this atmosphere, and it did not chill his blood; maybe it was an inspiration to him, for he was alert, brilliant and full of animation; also he was most gracefully and felicitously complimentary to my books,—and I will remark here that the happy phrasing of a compliment is one of the rarest of human gifts, and the happy delivery of it another. In that other chapter I mentioned the high compliment which he paid to the book, "Old Times on the Mississippi," but there were other; among them some gratifying praise of my description in "A Tramp Abroad" of certain striking phases of German student life. I mention these things here because I shall have occasion to hark back to them presently.

[*Dictated Tuesday, February 12, 1907.*]

* * *

Those stars indicate the long chapter which I dictated yesterday, a chapter which is much too long for magazine purposes, and therefore must wait until this Autobiography shall appear in book form, five years hence, when I am dead: five years according to my calculation, twenty-seven years according to the prediction furnished me a week ago by the latest and most confident of all the palmists who have ever read my future in my hand. The Emperor's dinner, and its beer-and-anecdote appendix, covered six hours of diligent industry, and this accounts for the extraordinary length of that chapter.

A couple of days ago a gentleman called upon me with a message. He had just arrived from Berlin, where he had been acting for our Government in a matter concerning tariff revision, he being a member of the commission appointed by our Government to conduct our share of the affair. Upon the completion of the commission's labors, the Emperor invited the members of it to an audience, and in the course of the conversation he made a reference to me; continuing, he spoke of my chapter on the German language in "A Tramp Abroad," and characterized it by an adjective which is too complimentary for me to repeat here without bringing my modesty under suspicion. Then he paid some compliments to "The Innocents Abroad," and followed these with the remark that my account in one of my books of certain striking phases of German student life was the best and truest that had ever been written. By this I perceive that he remembers that dinner of sixteen years ago, for he said the same thing to me about the student-chapter at that time. Next he said he wished this gentleman to convey two messages to America from him and deliver them—one to the President, the other to me. The wording of the message to me was:

"Convey to Mr. Clemens my kindest regards. Ask him if he remembers that dinner, and ask him why he didn't do any talking."

Why, how could I talk when he was talking? He "held the age," as the poker-clergy say, and two can't talk at the same time with good effect. It reminds me of the man who was reproached by a friend, who said,

"I think it a shame that you have not spoken to your wife for fifteen years. How do you explain it? How do you justify it?"

That poor man said,

"I didn't want to interrupt her."

If the Emperor had been at my table, he would not have suffered from my silence, he would only have suffered from the sorrows of his own solitude. If I were not too old to travel I would go to Berlin and introduce the etiquette of my own table, which tallies with the etiquette observable at other royal tables. I would say, "Invite me again, your Majesty, and give me a chance"; then I would courteously waive rank and do all the talking myself. I thank his Majesty for his kind message, and am proud to have it and glad to express my sincere reciprocation of its sentiments.

[*Dictated January 17, 1906.*] . . . Rev. Joseph T. Harris and I have been visiting General Sickles. Once, twenty or twenty-five years ago, just as Harris was coming out of his gate Sunday morning to walk to his church and preach, a telegram was put into his hand. He read it immediately, and then, in a manner, collapsed. It said: "General Sickles died last night at midnight." [He had been a chaplain under Sickles through the war.]

It wasn't so. But no matter—it was so to Harris at the time. He walked along—walked to the church—but his mind was far away. All his affection and homage and worship of his General had come to the fore. His heart was full of these emotions. He hardly knew where he was. In his pulpit, he stood up and began the service, but with a voice over which he had almost no command. The congregation had never seen him thus moved, before, in his pulpit. They sat there and gazed at him and wondered what was the matter; because he was now reading, in this broken voice and with occasional tears trickling down his face, what to them seemed a quite unemotional chapter—that one about Moses begat Aaron, and Aaron begat Deuteronomy, and Deuteronomy begat St. Peter, and St. Peter begat Cain, and Cain begat Abel—and he was going along with this, and half crying—his voice continually breaking. The congregation left the church that morning without being able to account for this most extraordinary thing—as it seemed to them. That a man who had been a soldier for more than four years, and who had preached in that pulpit so many, many times on really moving subjects, without even the quiver of a lip, should break all down over the Begats, they couldn't understand. But there it is—any one can see how such a mystery as that would arouse the curiosity of those people to the boiling-point.

Harris has had many adventures. He has more adventures in a year than anybody else has in five. One Saturday night he noticed a bottle on his uncle's dressing-bureau. He thought the label said "Hair Restorer," and he took it in his room and gave his head a good drenching and sousing with it and carried it back and thought no more about it. Next morning when he got up his head was a bright green! He sent around everywhere and couldn't get a substitute preacher, so he had to go to his church himself and preach—and he did it. He hadn't a sermon in his barrel—as it happened—of any lightsome character, so he had to preach a very grave one—a very serious one—and it made the matter worse. The gravity of the sermon did not harmonize with the gayety of his head, and the people sat all through it with handkerchiefs stuffed in their mouths to try to keep down their joy. And Harris told me that he was sure he never had seen his congregation—the whole body of his congregation—the *entire* body of his congregation—absorbed in interest in his sermon, from beginning to end, before. Always there had been an aspect of indifference, here and there, or wandering, somewhere; but this time there was nothing of the kind. Those people sat there as if they thought, "Good for this day and train only: we must have all there is of this show, not waste any of it." And he said that when he came down out of the pulpit more people waited to shake him by the hand and tell him what a good sermon it was, than ever before. And it seemed a pity that these people should do these fictions in such a place—right in the church—when it was quite plain they were not interested in the sermon at all; they only wanted to get a near view of his head.

Well, Harris said—no, Harris didn't say, *I* say, that as the days went on and Sunday followed Sunday, the interest in Harris's hair grew and grew; because it didn't stay merely and monotonously green, it took on deeper and deeper shades of green; and then it would change and become reddish, and would go from that to some other color—purplish, yellowish, bluish, and so on—but it was never a solid color. It was always mottled. And each Sunday it was a little more interesting than it was the Sunday before—and Harris's head became famous, and people came from New York, and Boston, and South Carolina, and Japan, and so on, to look. There wasn't seating-capacity for all the people that came while his head was undergoing these various and fascinating mottlings. And it was a good thing in several ways, because the business had been languishing a little, and now a lot of people joined the church so that they could have the show, and it was the beginning of a prosperity for that church which has never diminished in all these years.

MARK TWAIN

(to be continued)

North American Review

No. DCXII.

APRIL 5, 1907

CHAPTERS FROM MY AUTOBIOGRAPHY—XV

BY MARK TWAIN

PREFATORY NOTE—Mr. Clemens began to write his autobiography many years ago, and he continues to add to it day by day. It was his original intention to permit no publication of his memoirs until after his death; but, after leaving "Pier No. 70," he concluded that a considerable portion might now suitably be given to the public. It is that portion, garnered from the quarter-million of words already written, which will appear in this REVIEW during the coming year. No part of the autobiography will be published in book form during the lifetime of the author.—EDITOR N. A. R.

[*Dictated October 8, 1906.*]

FROM SUSY'S BIOGRAPHY OF ME

Papa says that if the collera comes here he will take Sour Mash to the mountains.

This remark about the cat is followed by various entries, covering a month, in which Jean, General Grant, the sculptor Gerhardt, Mrs. Candace Wheeler, Miss Dora Wheeler, Mr. Frank Stockton, Mrs. Mary Mapes Dodge, and the widow of General Custer appear and drift in procession across the page, then vanish forever from the Biography; then Susy drops this remark in the wake of the vanished procession:

Sour Mash is a constant source of anxiety, care, and pleasure to papa.

I did, in truth, think a great deal of that old tortoise-shell harlot; but I haven't a doubt that in order to impress Susy I was pretending agonies of solicitude which I didn't honestly feel. Sour Mash never gave me any real anxiety; she was always able to take care of herself, and she was ostentatiously vain of the fact; vain of it to a degree which often made me ashamed of her, much as I esteemed her.

Many persons would like to have the society of cats during the summer vacation in the country, but they deny themselves this pleasure because they think they must either take the cats along when they return to the city, where they would be a trouble and an encumbrance, or leave them in the country, houseless and homeless. These people have no ingenuity, no invention, no wisdom; or it would occur to them to do as I do: rent cats by the month for the summer and return them to their good homes at the end of it. Early last May I rented a kitten of a farmer's wife, by the month; then I got a discount by taking three. They have been good company for about five months now, and are still kittens—at least they have not grown much, and to all intents and purposes are still kittens, and as full of romping energy and enthusiasm as they were in the beginning. This is remarkable. I am an expert in cats, but I have not seen a kitten keep its kittenhood nearly so long before.

These are beautiful creatures—these triplets. Two of them wear the blackest and shiniest and thickest of sealskin vestments all over their bodies except the lower half of their faces and the terminations of their paws. The black masks reach down below the eyes, therefore when the eyes are closed they are not visible; the rest of the face, and the gloves and stockings, are snow white. These markings are just the same on both cats—so exactly the same that when you call one the other is likely to answer, because they cannot tell each other apart. Since the cats are precisely alike, and can't be told apart by any of us, they do not need two names, so they have but one between them. We call both of them Sackcloth, and we call the gray one Ashes. I believe I have never seen such intelligent cats as these before. They are full of the nicest discriminations. When I read German aloud they weep; you can see the tears run down. It shows what pathos there is in the German tongue. I had not noticed before that all German is pathetic, no matter what the subject is nor how it is treated. It was these humble observers that brought the knowledge to me. I have tried all kinds of German on these cats; romance, poetry, philosophy, theology, market reports; and the result has always been the same—the cats sob, and let the tears run down, which shows that all German is pathetic. French is not a familiar tongue to me, and the pronunciation is difficult, and comes out of me encumbered with a Missouri accent; but the cats like it, and when I make impassioned speeches in that language they sit in a row and put up their paws, palm to palm, and frantically give thanks. Hardly any cats are affected by music, but these are; when I sing they go reverently away, showing how deeply they feel it. Sour Mash never cared for these things. She had many noble qualities, but at bottom she was not refined, and cared little or nothing for theology and the arts.

It is a pity to say it, but these cats are not above the grade of human beings, for I know by certain signs that they are not sincere in their exhibitions of emotion, but exhibit them merely to show off and attract attention—conduct which is distinctly human, yet with a difference: they do not know enough to conceal their desire to show off, but the grown human being does. What is ambition? It is only the desire to be conspicuous. The desire for fame is only the desire to be continuously conspicuous and attract attention and be talked about.

These cats are like human beings in another way: when Ashes began to work his fictitious emotions, and show off, the other members of the firm followed suit, in order to be in the fashion. That is the way with human beings; they are afraid to be outside; whatever the fashion happens to be, they conform to it, whether it be a pleasant fashion or the reverse, they lacking the courage to ignore it and go their own way. All human beings would like to dress in loose and comfortable and highly colored and showy garments, and they had their desire until a century ago, when a king, or some other influential ass, introduced sombre hues and discomfort and ugly designs into masculine clothing. The meek public surrendered to the outrage, and by consequence we are in that odious captivity to-day, and are likely to remain in it for a long time to come.

Fortunately the women were not included in the disaster, and so their graces and their beauty still have the enhancing help of delicate fabrics and varied and beautiful colors. Their clothing makes a great opera audience an enchanting spectacle, a delight to the eye and the spirit, a Garden of Eden for charm and color. The men, clothed in dismal black, are scattered here and there and everywhere over the Garden, like so many charred stumps, and they damage the effect, but cannot annihilate it.

In summer we poor creatures have a respite, and may clothe ourselves in white garments; loose, soft, and in some degree shapely; but in the winter—the sombre winter, the depressing winter, the cheerless winter, when white clothes and bright colors are especially needed to brighten our spirits and lift them up—we all conform to the prevailing insanity, and go about in dreary black, each man doing it because the others do it, and not because he wants to. They are really no sincerer than Sackcloth and Ashes. At bottom the Sackcloths do not care to exhibit their emotions when I am performing before them, they only do it because Ashes started it.

I would like to dress in a loose and flowing costume made all of silks and velvets, resplendent with all the stunning dyes of the rainbow, and so would every sane man I have ever known; but none of us dares to venture it. There is such a thing as carrying conspicuousness to the point of discomfort; and if I should appear on Fifth Avenue on a Sunday morning, at church-time, clothed as I would like to be clothed, the churches would be vacant, and I should have all the congregations tagging after me, to look, and secretly envy, and publicly scoff. It is the way human beings are made; they are always keeping their real feelings shut up inside, and publicly exploiting their fictitious ones.

Next after fine colors, I like plain white. One of my sorrows, when the summer ends, is that I must put off my cheery and comfortable white clothes and enter for the winter into the depressing captivity of the shapeless and degrading black ones. It is mid-October now, and the weather is growing cold up here in the New Hampshire hills, but it will not succeed in freezing me out of these white garments, for here the neighbors are few, and it is only of crowds that I am afraid. I made a brave experiment, the other night, to see how it would feel to shock a crowd with these unseasonable clothes, and also to see how long it might take the crowd to reconcile itself to them and stop looking astonished and outraged. On a stormy evening I made a talk before a full house, in the village, clothed like a ghost, and looking as conspicuously, all solitary and alone on that platform, as any ghost could have looked; and I found, to my gratification, that it took the house less than ten minutes to forget about the ghost and give its attention to the tidings I had brought.

I am nearly seventy-one, and I recognize that my age has given me a good many privileges; valuable privileges; privileges which are not granted to younger persons. Little by little I hope to get together courage enough to wear white clothes all through the winter, in New York. It will be a great satisfaction to me to show off in this way; and perhaps the largest of all the satisfactions will be the knowledge that every scoffer, of my sex, will secretly envy me and wish he dared to follow my lead.

That mention that I have acquired new and great privileges by grace of my age, is not an uncalculated remark. When I passed the seventieth mile-stone, ten months ago, I instantly realized that I had entered a new country and a new atmosphere. To all the public I was become recognizably old, undeniably old; and from that moment everybody assumed a new attitude toward me—the reverent attitude granted by custom to age—and straightway the stream of generous new privileges began to flow in upon me and refresh my life. Since then, I have lived an ideal existence; and I now believe what Choate said last March, and which at the time I didn't credit: that the best of life begins at seventy; for then your work is done; you know that you have done your best, let the quality of the work be what it may; that you have earned your holiday—a holiday

of peace and contentment—and that thenceforth, to the setting of your sun, nothing will break it, nothing interrupt it.

[*Dictated January 22, 1907.*] In an earlier chapter I inserted
some verses beginning "Love Came at Dawn" which had been
found among Susy's papers after her death. I was not able to
say that they were hers, but I judged that they might be, for the
reason that she had not enclosed them in quotation marks
according to her habit when storing up treasures gathered from
other people. Stedman was not able to determine the authorship for me, as the verses were new to him, but the authorship
has now been traced. The verses were written by William Wil-
fred Campbell, a Canadian poet, and they form a part of the
contents of his book called "Beyond the Hills of Dream."

The authorship of the beautiful lines which my wife and I
inscribed upon Susy's gravestone was untraceable for a time.
We had found them in a book in India, but had lost the book
and with it the author's name. But in time an application to the
editor of "Notes and Queries" furnished me the author's name,
and it has been added to the verses upon the gravestone.

Last night, at a dinner-party where I was present, Mr. Peter
Dunne Dooley handed to the host several dollars, in satisfaction of a lost bet. I seemed to see an opportunity to better my
condition, and I invited Dooley, apparently disinterestedly, to
come to my house Friday and play billiards. He accepted, and
I judge that there is going to be a deficit in the Dooley treasury
as a result. In great qualities of the heart and brain, Dooley is
gifted beyond all propriety. He is brilliant; he is an expert with
his pen, and he easily stands at the head of all the satirists of
this generation—but he is going to walk in darkness Friday
afternoon. It will be a fraternal kindness to teach him that
with all his light and culture, he does not know all the valuable things; and it will also be a fraternal kindness to him to
complete his education for him—and I shall do this on Friday,
and send him home in that perfected condition.

I possess a billiard secret which can be valuable to the
Dooley sept, after I shall have conferred it upon Dooley—for a
consideration. It is a discovery which I made by accident,

thirty-eight years ago, in my father-in-law's house in Elmira. There was a scarred and battered and ancient billiard-table in the garret, and along with it a peck of checked and chipped balls, and a rackful of crooked and headless cues. I played solitaire up there every day with that difficult outfit. The table was not level, but slanted sharply to the southeast; there wasn't a ball that was round, or would complete the journey you started it on, but would always get tired and stop half-way and settle, with a jolty wabble, to a standstill on its chipped side. I tried making counts with four balls, but found it difficult and discouraging, so I added a fifth ball, then a sixth, then a seventh, and kept on adding until at last I had twelve balls on the table and a thirteenth to play with. My game was caroms— caroms solely—caroms plain, or caroms with cushion to help—anything that could furnish a count. In the course of time I found to my astonishment that I was never able to run fifteen, under any circumstances. By huddling the balls advantageously in the beginning, I could now and then coax fourteen out of them, but I couldn't reach fifteen by either luck or skill. Sometimes the balls would get scattered into difficult positions and defeat me in that way; sometimes if I managed to keep them together, I would freeze; and always when I froze, and had to play away from the contact, there was sure to be nothing to play at but a wide and uninhabited vacancy.

One day Mr. Dalton called on my brother-in-law, on a matter of business, and I was asked if I could entertain him awhile, until my brother-in-law should finish an engagement with another gentleman. I said I could, and took him up to the billiard-table. I had played with him many times at the club, and knew that he could play billiards tolerably well—only tolerably well—but not any better than I could. He and I were just a match. He didn't know our table; he didn't know those balls; he didn't know those warped and headless cues; he didn't know the southeastern slant of the table, and how to allow for it. I judged it would be safe and profitable to offer him a bet on my scheme. I emptied the avalanche of thirteen balls on the table and said:

"Take a ball and begin, Mr. Dalton. How many can you run with an outlay like that?"

He said, with the half-affronted air of a mathematician who has been asked how much of the multiplication table he can recite without a break:

"I suppose a million—eight hundred thousand, anyway."

I said "You shall have the privilege of placing the balls to suit yourself, and I want to bet you a dollar that you can't run fifteen."

I will not dwell upon the sequel. At the end of an hour his face was red, and wet with perspiration; his outer garments lay scattered here and there over the place; he was the angriest man in the State, and there wasn't a rag or remnant of an injurious adjective left in him anywhere—and I had all his small change.

When the summer was over, we went home to Hartford, and one day Mr. George Robertson arrived from Boston with two or three hours to spare between then and the return train, and as he was a young gentleman to whom we were in debt for much social pleasure, it was my duty, and a welcome duty, to make his two or three hours interesting for him. So I took him up-stairs and set up my billiard scheme for his comfort. Mine was a good table, in perfect repair; the cues were in perfect condition; the balls were ivory, and flawless—but I knew that Mr. Robertson was my prey, just the same, for by exhaustive tests with this outfit I had found that my limit was thirty-one. I had proved to my satisfaction that whereas I could not fairly expect to get more than six or eight or a dozen caroms out of a run, I could now and then reach twenty and twenty-five, and after a long procession of failures finally achieve a run of thirty-one; but in no case had I ever got beyond thirty-one. Robertson's game, as I knew, was a little better than mine, so I resolved to require him to make thirty-two. I believed it would entertain him. He was one of these brisk and hearty and cheery and self-satisfied young fellows who are brimful of confidence, and who plunge with grateful eagerness into any enterprise that offers a showy test of their abilities. I emptied the balls on the table and said,

"Take a cue and a ball, George, and begin. How many caroms do you think you can make out of that layout?"

He laughed the laugh of the gay and the care-free, as became his youth and inexperience, and said,

"I can punch caroms out of that bunch a week without a break."

I said "Place the balls to suit yourself, and begin."

Confidence is a necessary thing in billiards, but overconfidence is bad. George went at his task with much too much lightsomeness of spirit and disrespect for the situation. On his first shot he scored three caroms; on his second shot he scored four caroms; and on his third shot he missed as simple a carom as could be devised. He was very much astonished, and said he would not have supposed that careful play could be needed with an acre of bunched balls in front of a person.

He began again, and played more carefully, but still with too much lightsomeness; he couldn't seem to learn to take the situation seriously. He made about a dozen caroms and broke down. He was irritated with himself now, and he thought he caught me laughing. He didn't. I do not laugh publicly at my client when this game is going on; I only do it inside—or save it for after the exhibition is over. But he thought he had caught me laughing, and it increased his irritation. Of course I knew he thought I was laughing privately—for I was experienced; they all think that, and it has a good offect; it sharpens their annoyance and debilitates their play.

He made another trial and failed. Once more he was astonished; once more he was humiliated—and as for his anger, it rose to summer-heat. He arranged the balls again, grouping them carefully, and said he would win this time, or die. When a client reaches this condition, it is a good time to damage his nerve further, and this can always be done by saying some little mocking thing or other that has the outside appearance of a friendly remark—so I employed this art. I suggested that a bet might tauten his nerves, and that I would offer one, but that as I did not want it to be an expense to him, but only a help, I would make it small—a cigar, if he were willing—a cigar that he would fail again; not an expensive one, but a

cheap native one, of the Crown Jewel breed, such as is manufactured in Hartford for the clergy. It set him afire all over! I
could see the blue flame issue from his eyes. He said,

"Make it a hundred!—and no Connecticut cabbage-leaf
product, but Havana, $25 the box!"

I took him up, but said I was sorry to see him do this,
because it did not seem to me right or fair for me to rob him
under our own roof, when he had been so kind to us. He said,
with energy and acrimony:

"You take care of your own pocket, if you'll be so good, and
leave me to take care of mine."

And he plunged at the congress of balls with a vindictive-
ness which was infinitely contenting to me. He scored a
failure—and began to undress. I knew it would come to that,
for he was in the condition now that Mr. Dooley will be in at
about that stage of the contest on Friday afternoon. A clothes-
rack will be provided for Mr. Dooley to hang his things on as
fast as he shall from time to time shed them. George raised his
voice four degrees and flung out the challenge—

"Double or quits!"

"Done," I responded, in the gentle and compassionate voice
of one who is apparently getting sorrier and sorrier.

There was an hour and a half of straight disaster after that,
and if it was a sin to enjoy it, it is no matter—I did enjoy it. It is
half a lifetime ago, but I enjoy it yet, every time I think of it.
George made failure after failure. His fury increased with each
failure as he scored it. With each defeat he flung off one or
another rag of his raiment, and every time he started on a fresh
inning he made it "double or quits" once more. Twice he reached
thirty and broke down; once he reached thirty-one and broke
down. These "nears" made him frantic, and I believe I was
never so happy in my life, except the time, a few years later,
when the Rev. J. H. Twichell and I walked to Boston and he had
the celebrated conversation with the hostler at the Inn at Ash-
ford, Connecticut.

At last, when we were notified that Patrick was at the door
to drive him to his train, George owed me five thousand cigars

at twenty-five cents apiece, and I was so sorry I could have hugged him. But he shouted,

"Give me ten minutes more!" and added stormily, "it's double or quits again, and I'll win out free of debt or owe you ten thousand cigars, and you'll pay the funeral expenses."

He began on his final effort, and I believe that in all my experience among both amateurs and experts, I have never seen a cue so carefully handled in my lifetime as George handled his upon this intensely interesting occasion. He got safely up to twenty-five, and then ceased to breathe. So did I. He labored along, and added a point, another point, still another point, and finally reached thirty-one. He stopped there, and we took a breath. By this time the balls were scattered all down the cushions, about a foot or two apart, and there wasn't a shot in sight anywhere that any man might hope to make. In a burst of anger and confessed defeat, he sent his ball flying around the table at random, and it crotched a ball that was packed against the cushion and sprang across to a ball against the bank on the opposite side, and counted!

His luck had set him free, and he didn't owe me anything. He had used up all his spare time, but we carried his clothes to the carriage, and he dressed on his way to the station, greatly wondered at and admired by the ladies, as he drove along— but he got his train.

I am very fond of Mr. Dooley, and shall await his coming with affectionate and pecuniary interest.

P.S. Saturday. He has been here. Let us not talk about it.

MARK TWAIN

(to be continued)

North American Review

No. DCXIII.

APRIL 19, 1907

CHAPTERS FROM MY
AUTOBIOGRAPHY—XVI

BY MARK TWAIN

PREFATORY NOTE—Mr. Clemens began to write his autobiography many years ago, and he continues to add to it day by day. It was his original intention to permit no publication of his memoirs until after his death; but, after leaving "Pier No. 70," he concluded that a considerable portion might now suitably be given to the public. It is that portion, garnered from the quarter-million of words already written, which will appear in this REVIEW during the coming year. No part of the autobiography will be published in book form during the lifetime of the author. —EDITOR N. A. R.

[*Dictated January 12th, 1905.*] . . . But I am used to having my statements discounted. My mother began it before I was seven years old. Yet all through my life my facts have had a substratum of truth, and therefore they were not without preciousness. Any person who is familiar with me knows how to strike my average, and therefore knows how to get at the jewel of any fact of mine and dig it out of its blue-clay matrix. My mother knew that art. When I was seven or eight, or ten, or twelve years old—along there—a neighbor said to her,

"Do you ever believe anything that that boy says?"

My mother said,

"He is the well-spring of truth, but you can't bring up the

whole well with one bucket"—and she added, "I know his average, therefore he never deceives me. I discount him thirty per cent. for embroidery, and what is left is perfect and price-less truth, without a flaw in it anywhere."

Now to make a jump of forty years, without breaking the connection: that word "embroidery" was used again in my presence and concerning me, when I was fifty years old, one night at Rev. Frank Goodwin's house in Hartford, at a meet-ing of the Monday Evening Club. The Monday Evening Club still exists. It was founded about forty-five years ago by that theological giant, Rev. Dr. Bushnell, and some comrades of his, men of large intellectual calibre and more or less distinc-tion, local or national. I was admitted to membership in it in the fall of 1871 and was an active member thenceforth until I left Hartford in the summer of 1891. The membership was restricted, in those days, to eighteen—possibly twenty. The meetings began about the 1st of October and were held in the private houses of the members every fortnight thereafter throughout the cold months until the 1st of May. Usually there were a dozen members present—sometimes as many as fifteen. There was an essay and a discussion. The essayists followed each other in alphabetical order through the season. The essay-ist could choose his own subject and talk twenty minutes on it, from MS. or orally, according to his preference. Then the dis-cussion followed, and each member present was allowed ten minutes in which to express his views. The wives of these peo-ple were always present. It was their privilege. It was also their privilege to keep still; they were not allowed to throw any light upon the discussion. After the discussion there was a sup-per, and talk, and cigars. This supper began at ten o'clock promptly, and the company broke up and went away at mid-night. At least they did except upon one occasion. In my recent Birthday speech I remarked upon the fact that I have always bought cheap cigars, and that is true. I have never bought costly ones.

Well, that night at the Club meeting—as I was saying—George, our colored butler, came to me when the supper was nearly over, and I noticed that he was pale. Normally his complexion was a clear black, and very handsome, but now it had modified to old amber. He said:

"Mr. Clemens, what are we going to do? There is not a cigar in the house but those old Wheeling long nines. Can't nobody smoke them but you. They kill at thirty yards. It is too late to telephone—we couldn't get any cigars out from town—what can we do? Ain't it best to say nothing, and let on that we didn't think?"

"No," I said, "that would not be honest. Fetch out the long nines"—which he did.

I had just come across those "long nines" a few days or a week before. I hadn't seen a long nine for years. When I was a cub pilot on the Mississippi in the late '50's, I had had a great affection for them, because they were not only—to my mind—perfect, but you could get a basketful of them for a cent—or a dime, they didn't use cents out there in those days. So when I saw them advertised in Hartford I sent for a thousand at once. They came out to me in badly battered and disreputable-looking old square pasteboard boxes, two hundred in a box. George brought a box, which was caved in on all sides, looking the worst it could, and began to pass them around. The conversation had been brilliantly animated up to that moment—but now a frost fell upon the company. That is to say, not all of a sudden, but the frost fell upon each man as he took up a cigar and held it poised in the air—and there, in the middle, his sentence broke off. That kind of thing went on all around the table, until when George had completed his crime the whole place was full of a thick solemnity and silence.

Those men began to light the cigars. Rev. Dr. Parker was the first man to light. He took three or four heroic whiffs—then gave it up. He got up with the remark that he had to go to the bedside of a sick parishioner. He started out. Rev. Dr. Burton was the next man. He took only one whiff, and followed Parker. He furnished a pretext, and you could see by the sound of his voice that he didn't think much of the pretext, and was vexed with Parker for getting in ahead with a fictitious ailing client. Rev. Mr. Twichell followed, and said he had to go now because he must take the midnight train for Boston. Boston was the first place that occurred to him, I suppose.

It was only a quarter to eleven when they began to distribute pretexts. At ten minutes to eleven all those people were out of the house. When nobody was left but George and me I was cheerful—I had no compunctions of conscience, no griefs of any kind. But George was beyond speech, because he held the honor and credit of the family above his own, and he was ashamed that this smirch had been put upon it. I told him to go to bed and try to sleep it off. I went to bed myself. At breakfast in the morning when George was passing a cup of coffee, I saw it tremble in his hand. I knew by that sign that there was something on his mind. He brought the cup to me and asked impressively,

"Mr. Clemens, how far is it from the front door to the upper gate?"

I said, "It is a hundred and twenty-five steps."

He said, "Mr. Clemens, you can start at the front door and you can go plumb to the upper gate and tread on one of them cigars every time."

It wasn't true in detail, but in essentials it was.

The subject under discussion on the night in question was Dreams. The talk passed from mouth to mouth in the usual serene way.

I do not now remember what form my views concerning dreams took at the time. I don't remember now what my notion about dreams was then, but I do remember telling a dream by way of illustrating some detail of my speech, and I also remember that when I had finished it Rev. Dr. Burton made that doubting remark which contained that word I have already spoken of as having been uttered by my mother, in some such connection, forty or fifty years before. I was probably engaged in trying to make those people believe that now and then, by some accident, or otherwise, a dream which was prophetic turned up in the dreamer's mind. The date of my memorable dream was about the beginning of May, 1858. It was a remarkable dream, and I had been telling it several times every year for more than fifteen years—and now I was telling it again, here in the club.

In 1858 I was a steersman on board the swift and popular New Orleans and St. Louis packet, "Pennsylvania," Captain Klinefelter. I had been lent to Mr. Brown, one of the pilots of the "Pennsylvania," by my owner, Mr. Horace E. Bixby, and I had been steering for Brown about eighteen months, I think. Then in the early days of May, 1858, came a tragic trip—the last trip of that fleet and famous steamboat. I have told all about it in one of my books called "Old Times on the Mississippi." But it is not likely that I told the dream in that book. It is impossible that I can ever have published it, I think, because I never wanted my mother to know about the dream, and she lived several years after I published that volume.

I had found a place on the "Pennsylvania" for my brother Henry, who was two years my junior. It was not a place of profit, it was only a place of promise. He was "mud" clerk. Mud clerks received no salary, but they were in the line of promotion. They could become, presently, third clerk and second clerk, then chief clerk—that is to say, purser. The dream begins when Henry had been mud clerk about three months. We were lying in port at St. Louis. Pilots and steersmen had nothing to do during the three days that the boat lay in port in St. Louis and New Orleans, but the mud clerk had to begin his labors at dawn and continue them into the night, by the light of pine-knot torches. Henry and I, moneyless and unsalaried, had billeted ourselves upon our brother-in-law, Mr. Moffett, as night lodgers while in port. We took our meals on board the boat. No, I mean I lodged at the house, not Henry. He spent the *evenings* at the house, from nine until eleven, then went to the boat to be ready for his early duties. On the night of the dream he started away at eleven, shaking hands with the family, and said good-by according to custom. I may mention that hand-shaking as a good-by was not merely the custom of that family, but the custom of the region—the custom of Missouri, I may say. In all my life, up to that time, I had never seen one member of the Clemens family kiss another one—except once. When my father lay dying in our home in Hannibal—the 24th of

March, 1847—he put his arm around my sister's neck and drew her down and kissed her, saying "Let me die." I remember that, and I remember the death rattle which swiftly followed those words, which were his last. These good-bys of Henry's were always executed in the family sitting-room on the second floor, and Henry went from that room and downstairs without further ceremony. But this time my mother went with him to the head of the stairs and said good-by *again*. As I remember it she was moved to this by something in Henry's manner, and she remained at the head of the stairs while he descended. When he reached the door he hesitated, and climbed the stairs and shook hands good-by once more.

In the morning, when I awoke I had been dreaming, and the dream was so vivid, so like reality, that it deceived me, and I thought it *was* real. In the dream I had seen Henry a corpse. He lay in a metallic burial-case. He was dressed in a suit of my clothing, and on his breast lay a great bouquet of flowers, mainly white roses, with a red rose in the centre. The casket stood upon a couple of chairs. I dressed, and moved toward that door, thinking I would go in there and look at it, but I changed my mind. I thought I could not yet bear to meet my mother. I thought I would wait awhile and make some preparation for that ordeal. The house was in Locust Street, a little above 13th, and I walked to 14th, and to the middle of the block beyond, before it suddenly flashed upon me that there was nothing real about this—it was only a dream. I can still feel something of the grateful upheaval of joy of that moment, and I can also still feel the remnant of doubt, the suspicion that maybe it *was* real, after all. I returned to the house almost on a run, flew up the stairs two or three steps at a jump, and rushed into that sitting-room—and was made glad again, for there was no casket there.

We made the usual eventless trip to New Orleans—no, it was not eventless, for it was on the way down that I had the fight with Mr. Brown which resulted in his requiring that I be left ashore at New Orleans. In New Orleans I always had a job. It was my privilege to watch the freight-piles from seven in the evening until seven in the morning, and get three dollars for it. It was a three-night job and occurred every thirty-five days. Henry always joined my watch about nine in the evening, when his own duties were ended, and we often walked my rounds and chatted together until midnight. This time we were to part, and so the night before the boat sailed I gave Henry some advice. I said, "In case of disaster to the boat, don't lose your head—leave that unwisdom to the passengers— they are competent—they'll attend to it. But you rush for the hurricane-deck, and astern to one of the life-boats lashed aft the wheel-house, and obey the mate's orders—thus you will be useful. When the boat is launched, give such help as you can in getting the women and children into it, and be sure you don't try to get into it yourself. It is summer weather, the river is only a mile wide, as a rule, and you can swim that without any trouble." Two or three days afterward the boat's boilers exploded at Ship Island, below Memphis, early one morning— and what happened afterward I have already told in "Old Times on the Mississippi." As related there, I followed the "Pennsylvania" about a day later, on another boat, and we began to get news of the disaster at every port we touched at, and so by the time we reached Memphis we knew all about it.

I found Henry stretched upon a mattress on the floor of a great building, along with thirty or forty other scalded and wounded persons, and was promptly informed, by some indiscreet person, that he had inhaled steam; that his body was badly scalded, and that he would live but a little while; also, I was told that the physicians and nurses were giving their whole attention to persons who had a chance of being saved. They were short-handed in the matter of physicians and nurses; and Henry and such others as were considered to be fatally hurt were receiving only such attention as could be spared, from time to time, from the more urgent cases. But Dr. Peyton, a fine and large-hearted old physician of great reputation in the community, gave me his sympathy and took vigorous hold of the case, and in about a week he had brought Henry around. Dr. Peyton never committed himself with prognostications which might not materialize, but at eleven o'clock one night he told me that Henry was out of danger, and would get well. Then he said, "At midnight these poor fellows lying here and there all over this place will begin to mourn and mutter and lament and make outcries, and if this commotion should disturb Henry it will be bad for him; therefore ask the physician on watch to give him an eighth of a grain of morphine, but this is not to be done unless Henry shall show signs that he is being disturbed."

Oh well, never mind the rest of it. The physicians on watch were young fellows hardly out of the medical college, and they made a mistake—they had no way of measuring the eighth of a grain of morphine, so they guessed at it and gave him a vast quantity heaped on the end of a knife-blade, and the fatal effects were soon apparent. I think he died about dawn, I don't remember as to that. He was carried to the dead-room and I went away for a while to a citizen's house and slept off some of my accumulated fatigue—and meantime something was happening. The coffins provided for the dead were of unpainted white pine, but in this instance some of the ladies of Memphis had made up a fund of sixty dollars and bought a metallic case, and when I came back and entered the dead-room Henry lay in that open case, and he was dressed in a suit of my clothing. He had borrowed it without my knowledge during our last sojourn in St. Louis; and I recognized instantly that my dream of several weeks before was here exactly reproduced, so far as these details went—and I think I missed one detail; but that one was immediately supplied, for just then an elderly lady entered the place with a large bouquet consisting mainly of white roses, and in the centre of it was a red rose, and she laid it on his breast.

I told the dream there in the Club that night just as I have told it here.

Rev. Dr. Burton swung his leonine head around, focussed me with his eye, and said:

"When was it that this happened?"

"In June, '58."

"It is a good many years ago. Have you told it several times since?"

"Yes, I have, a good many times."

"How many?"

"Why, I don't know how many."

"Well, strike an average. How many times a year do you think you have told it?"

"Well, I have told it as many as six times a year, possibly oftener."

"Very well, then you've told it, we'll say, seventy or eighty times since it happened?"

"Yes," I said, "that's a conservative estimate."

"Now then, Mark, a very extraordinary thing happened to me a great many years ago, and I used to tell it a number of times—a good many times—every year, for it was so wonderful that it always astonished the hearer, and that astonishment gave me a distinct pleasure every time. I never suspected that that tale was acquiring any auxiliary advantages through repetition until one day after I had been telling it ten or fifteen years it struck me that either I was getting old, and slow in delivery, or that the tale was longer than it was when it was born. Mark, I diligently and prayerfully examined that tale with this result: that I found that its proportions were now, as nearly as I could make out, one part fact, straight fact, fact pure and undiluted, golden fact, and twenty-four parts embroidery. I never told that tale afterwards—I was never able to tell it again, for I had lost confidence in it, and so the pleasure of telling it was gone, and gone permanently. How much of this tale of yours is embroidery?"

"Well," I said, "I don't know. I don't think any of it is embroidery. I think it is all just as I have stated it, detail by detail."

"Very well," he said, "then it is all right, but I wouldn't tell it any more; because if you keep on, it will begin to collect embroidery sure. The safest thing is to stop now."

That was a great many years ago. And to-day is the first time that I have told that dream since Dr. Burton scared me into fatal doubts about it. No, I don't believe I can say that. I don't believe that I ever really had any doubts whatever concerning the salient points of the dream, for those points are of such a nature that they are *pictures*, and pictures can be remembered, when they are vivid, much better than one can remember remarks and unconcreted facts. Although it has been so many years since I have told that dream, I can see those pictures now just as clearly defined as if they were before me in this room. I have not told the entire dream. There was a good deal more of it. I mean I have not told all that happened in the dream's fulfilment. After the incident in the death-room I may mention one detail, and that is this. When I arrived in St. Louis with the casket it was about eight o'clock in the morning, and I ran to my brother-in-law's place of business, hoping to find him there, but I missed him, for while I was on the way to his office he was on his way from the house to the boat. When I got back to the boat the casket was gone. He had conveyed it out to his house. I hastened thither, and when I arrived the men were just removing the casket from the vehicle to carry it up-stairs. I stopped that procedure, for I did not want my mother to see the dead face, because one side of it was drawn and distorted by the effects of the opium. When I went up-stairs, there stood the two chairs—placed to receive the coffin—just as I had seen them in my dream; and if I had arrived two or three minutes later, the casket would have been resting upon them, precisely as in my dream of several weeks before.

MARK TWAIN

(to be continued)

North American Review

No. DCXIV.

MAY 3, 1907

CHAPTERS FROM MY AUTOBIOGRAPHY—XVII

BY MARK TWAIN

PREFATORY NOTE—Mr. Clemens began to write his autobiography many years ago, and he continues to add to it day by day. It was his original intention to permit no publication of his memoirs until after his death; but, after leaving "Pier No. 70," he concluded that a considerable portion might now suitably be given to the public. It is that portion, garnered from the quarter-million of words already written, which will appear in this REVIEW during the coming year. No part of the autobiography will be published in book form during the lifetime of the author. —EDITOR N. A. R.

FROM SUSY'S BIOGRAPHY OF ME

Sept. 9, '85.—Mamma is teaching Jean a little natural history and is making a little collection of insects for her. But mamma does not allow Jean to kill any insects she only collects those insects that are found dead. Mamma has told us all, perticularly Jean, to bring her all the little dead insects that she finds. The other day as we were all sitting at supper Jean broke into the room and ran triumfantly up to Mamma and presented her with a plate full of dead flies. Mamma thanked Jean very enthusiastically although she with difficulty concealed her amusement. Just then Sour Mash entered the room and Jean believing her hungry asked Mamma for permission to give her the flies.

Mamma laughingly consented and the flies almost immediately dissapeared.

[*Monday, October 15, 1906.*] Sour Mash's presence indicates that this adventure occurred at Quarry Farm. Susy's Biography interests itself pretty exclusively with historical facts; where they happen is not a matter of much concern to her. When other historians refer to the Bunker Hill Monument they know it is not necessary to mention that that monument is in Boston. Susy recognizes that when she mentions Sour Mash it is not necessary to localize her. To Susy, Sour Mash is the Bunker Hill Monument of Quarry Farm.

Ordinary cats have some partiality for living flies, but none for dead ones; but Susy does not trouble herself to apologize for Sour Mash's eccentricities of taste. This Biography was for *us*, and Susy knew that nothing that Sour Mash might do could startle us or need explanation, we being aware that she was not an ordinary cat, but moving upon a plane far above the prejudices and superstitions which are law to common catdom.

Once in Hartford the flies were so numerous for a time, and so troublesome, that Mrs. Clemens conceived the idea of paying George* a bounty on all the flies he might kill. The children saw an opportunity here for the acquisition of sudden wealth. They supposed that their mother merely wanted to accumulate dead flies, for some æsthetic or scientific reason or other, and they judged that the more flies she could get the happier she would be; so they went into business with George on a commission. Straightway the dead flies began to arrive in such quantities that Mrs. Clemens was pleased beyond words with the success of her idea. Next, she was astonished that one house could furnish so many. She was paying an extravagantly high bounty, and it presently began to look as if by this addition to our expenses we were now probably living beyond our income. After a few days there was peace and comfort; not a fly was discoverable in the house; there wasn't a straggler left.

* The colored butler.

Still, to Mrs. Clemens's surprise, the dead flies continued to arrive by the plateful, and the bounty expense was as crushing as ever. Then she made inquiry, and found that our innocent little rascals had established a Fly Trust, and had hired all the children in the neighborhood to collect flies on a cheap and unburdensome commission.

Mrs. Clemens's experience in this matter was a new one for her, but the governments of the world had tried it, and wept over it, and discarded it, every half-century since man was created. Any Government could have told her that the best way to increase wolves in America, rabbits in Australia, and snakes in India, is to pay a bounty on their scalps. Then every patriot goes to raising them.

FROM SUSY'S BIOGRAPHY OF ME

Sept. 10, '85.—The other evening Clara and I brought down our new soap buble water and we all blew soap bubles. Papa blew his soap bubles and filled them with tobacco smoke and as the light shone on them they took very beautiful opaline colors. Papa would hold them and then let us catch them in our hand and they felt delightful to the touch the mixture of the smoke and water had a singularly pleasant effect.

It is human life. We are blown upon the world; we float buoyantly upon the summer air a little while, complacently showing off our grace of form and our dainty iridescent colors; then we vanish with a little puff, leaving nothing behind but a memory—and sometimes not even that. I suppose that at those solemn times when we wake in the deeps of the night and reflect, there is not one of us who is not willing to confess that he is really only a soap-bubble, and as little worth the making.

I remember those days of twenty-one years ago, and a certain pathos clings about them. Susy, with her manifold young charms and her iridescent mind, was as lovely a bubble as any we made that day—and as transitory. She passed, as they passed, in her youth and beauty, and nothing of her is left but a heartbreak and a memory. That long-vanished day came vividly back to me a few weeks ago when, for the first time in twenty-one years, I found myself again amusing a child with smoke-charged soap-bubbles.

Susy's next date is November 29th, 1885, the eve of my fiftieth birthday. It seems a good while ago. I must have been rather young for my age then, for I was trying to tame an old-fashioned bicycle nine feet high. It is to me almost unbelievable, at my present stage of life, that there have really been people willing to trust themselves upon a dizzy and unstable altitude like that, and that I was one of them. Twichell and I took lessons every day. He succeeded, and became a master of the art of riding that wild vehicle, but I had no gift in that direction and was never able to stay on mine long enough to get any satisfactory view of the planet. Every time I tried to steal a look at a pretty girl, or any other kind of scenery, that single moment of inattention gave the bicycle the chance it had been waiting for, and I went over the front of it and struck the ground on my head or my back before I had time to realize that something was happening. I didn't always go over the front way; I had other ways, and practised them all; but no matter which way was chosen for me there was always one monotonous result—the bicycle skinned my leg and leaped up into the air and came down on top of me. Sometimes its wires were so sprung by this violent performance that it had the collapsed look of an umbrella that had had a misunderstanding with a cyclone. After each day's practice I arrived at home with my skin hanging in ribbons, from my knees down. I plastered the ribbons on where they belonged, and bound them there with handkerchiefs steeped in Pond's Extract, and was ready for more adventures next day. It was always a surprise to me that I had so much skin, and that it held out so well. There was always plenty, and I soon came to understand that the supply was going to remain sufficient for all my needs. It turned out that I had nine skins, in layers, one on top of the other like the leaves of a book, and some of the doctors said it was quite remarkable.

I was full of enthusiasm over this insane amusement. My teacher was a young German from the bicycle factory, a gentle, kindly, patient creature, with a pathetically grave face. He never smiled; he never made a remark; he always gathered me tenderly up when I plunged off, and helped me on again without a word. When he had been teaching me twice a day for three weeks I introduced a new gymnastic—one that he had never seen before—and so at last a compliment was wrung from him, a thing which I had been risking my life for days to achieve. He gathered me up and said mournfully: "Mr. Clemens, you can fall off a bicycle in more different ways than any person I ever saw before."

A boy's life is not all comedy; much of the tragic enters into it. The drunken tramp—mentioned in "Tom Sawyer" or "Huck Finn"—who was burned up in the village jail, lay upon my conscience a hundred nights afterward and filled them with hideous dreams—dreams in which I saw his appealing face as I had seen it in the pathetic reality, pressed against the window-bars, with the red hell glowing behind him—a face which seemed to say to me, "If you had not give me the matches, this would not have happened; you are responsible for my death." I was *not* responsible for it, for I had meant him no harm, but only good, when I let him have the matches; but no matter, mine was a trained Presbyterian conscience, and knew but the one duty—to hunt and harry its slave upon all pretexts and on all occasions; particularly when there was no sense or reason in it. The tramp—who was to blame—suffered ten minutes; I, who was not to blame, suffered three months.

The shooting down of poor old Smarr in the main street at noonday supplied me with some more dreams; and in them I always saw again the grotesque closing picture—the great family Bible spread open on the profane old man's breast by some thoughtful idiot, and rising and sinking to the labored breathings, and adding the torture of its leaden weight to the dying struggles. We are curiously made. In all the throng of gaping and sympathetic onlookers there was not one with common sense enough to perceive that an anvil would have been in better taste there than the Bible, less open to sarcastic criticism, and swifter in its atrocious work. In my nightmares I gasped and struggled for breath under the crush of that vast book for many a night.

All within the space of a couple of years we had two or three other tragedies, and I had the ill-luck to be too near by on each occasion. There was the slave man who was struck down with a chunk of slag for some small offence; I saw him die. And the young California emigrant who was stabbed with a bowie knife by a drunken comrade: I saw the red life gush from his breast. And the case of the rowdy young Hyde brothers and their harmless old uncle: one of them held the old man down with his knees on his breast while the other one tried repeatedly to kill him with an Allen revolver which wouldn't go off. I happened along just then, of course.

Then there was the case of the young California emigrant who got drunk and proposed to raid the "Welshman's house" all alone one dark and threatening night. This house stood halfway up Holliday's Hill ("Cardiff" Hill), and its sole occupants were a poor but quite respectable widow and her young and blameless daughter. The invading ruffian woke the whole village with his ribald yells and coarse challenges and obscenities. I went up there with a comrade—John Briggs, I think—to look and listen. The figure of the man was dimly visible; the women were on their porch, but not visible in the deep shadow of its roof, but we heard the elder woman's voice. She had loaded an old musket with slugs, and she warned the man that if he stayed where he was while she counted ten it would cost him his life. She began to count, slowly: he began to laugh. He stopped laughing at "six"; then through the deep stillness, in a steady voice, followed the rest of the tale: "seven . . . eight . . . nine"—a long pause, we holding our breath— "ten!" A red spout of flame gushed out into the night, and the man dropped, with his breast riddled to rags. Then the rain and the thunder burst loose and the waiting town swarmed up the hill in the glare of the lightning like an invasion of ants. Those people saw the rest; I had had my share and was satisfied. I went home to dream, and was not disappointed.

My teaching and training enabled me to see deeper into these tragedies than an ignorant person could have done. I knew what they were for. I tried to disguise it from myself, but down in the secret deeps of my heart I knew—and I *knew* that

I knew. They were inventions of Providence to beguile me to a better life. It sounds curiously innocent and conceited, now, but to me there was nothing strange about it; it was quite in accordance with the thoughtful and judicious ways of Providence as I understood them. It would not have surprised me, nor even over-flattered me, if Providence had killed off that whole community in trying to save an asset like me. Educated as I had been, it would have seemed just the thing, and well worth the expense. *Why* Providence should take such an anxious interest in such a property—that idea never entered my head, and there was no one in that simple hamlet who would have dreamed of putting it there. For one thing, no one was equipped with it.

It is quite true I took all the tragedies to myself; and tallied them off, in turn as they happened, saying to myself in each case, with a sigh, "Another one gone—and on my account; this ought to bring me to repentance; His patience will not always endure." And yet privately I believed it would. That is, I believed it in the daytime; but not in the night. With the going down of the sun my faith failed, and the clammy fears gathered about my heart. It was then that I repented. Those were awful nights, nights of despair, nights charged with the bitterness of death. After each tragedy I recognized the warning and repented; repented and begged; begged like a coward, begged like a dog; and not in the interest of those poor people who had been extinguished for my sake, but only in my own interest. It seems selfish, when I look back on it now.

My repentances were very real, very earnest; and after each tragedy they happened every night for a long time. But as a rule they could not stand the daylight. They faded out and shredded away and disappeared in the glad splendor of the sun. They were the creatures of fear and darkness, and they could not live out of their own place. The day gave me cheer and peace, and at night I repented again. In all my boyhood life I am not sure that I ever tried to lead a better life in the daytime—or wanted to. In my age I should never think of wishing to do such a thing. But in my age, as in my youth, night brings me many a deep remorse. I realize that from the cradle up I have been like the rest of the race—never quite sane in the night. When "Injun Joe" died . . . But never mind: in another chapter I have already described what a raging hell of repentance I passed through then. I believe that for months I was as pure as the driven snow. After dark.

It was back in those far-distant days—1848 or '9—that Jim Wolf came to us. He was from Shelbyville, a hamlet thirty or forty miles back in the country, and he brought all his native sweetnesses and gentlenesses and simplicities with him. He was approaching seventeen, a grave and slender lad, trustful, honest, a creature to love and cling to. And he was incredibly bashful.

It is to this kind that untoward things happen. My sister gave a "candy-pull" on a winter's night. I was too young to be of the company, and Jim was too diffident. I was sent up to bed early, and Jim followed of his own motion. His room was in the new part of the house, and his window looked out on the roof of the L annex. That roof was six inches deep in snow, and the snow had an ice-crust upon it which was as slick as glass. Out of the comb of the roof projected a short chimney, a common resort for sentimental cats on moonlight nights—and this was a moonlight night. Down at the eaves, below the chimney, a canopy of dead vines spread away to some posts, making a cozy shelter, and after an hour or two the rollicking crowd of young ladies and gentlemen grouped themselves in its shade, with their saucers of liquid and piping-hot candy disposed about them on the frozen ground to cool. There was joyous chaffing and joking and laughter—peal upon peal of it.

About this time a couple of old disreputable tom-cats got up on the chimney and started a heated argument about something; also about this time I gave up trying to get to sleep, and went visiting to Jim's room. He was awake and fuming about the cats and their intolerable yowling. I asked him, mockingly, why he didn't climb out and drive them away. He was nettled, and said over-boldly that for two cents he *would*.

It was a rash remark, and was probably repented of before it was fairly out of his mouth. But it was too late—he was committed. I knew him; and I knew he would rather break his neck than back down, if I egged him on judiciously.

"Oh, of course you would! Who's doubting it?"

It galled him, and he burst out, with sharp irritation—

"Maybe *you* doubt it!"

"I? Oh no, I shouldn't think of such a thing. You are always doing wonderful things. With your mouth."

He was in a passion, now. He snatched on his yarn socks and began to raise the window, saying in a voice unsteady with anger—

"*You* think I dasn't—*you* do! Think what you blame please—*I* don't care what you think. I'll show you!"

The window made him rage; it wouldn't stay up. I said—

"Never mind, I'll hold it."

Indeed, I would have done anything to help. I was only a boy, and was already in a radiant heaven of anticipation. He climbed carefully out, clung to the window-sill until his feet were safely placed, then began to pick his perilous way on all fours along the glassy comb, a foot and a hand on each side of it. I believe I enjoy it now as much as I did then: yet it is a good deal over fifty years ago. The frosty breeze flapped his short shirt about his lean legs; the crystal roof shone like polished marble in the intense glory of the moon; the unconscious cats sat erect upon the chimney, alertly watching each other, lashing their tails and pouring out their hollow grievances; and slowly and cautiously Jim crept on, flapping as he went, the gay and frolicsome young creatures under the vine-canopy unaware, and outraging these solemnities with their misplaced laughter. Every time Jim slipped I had a hope; but always on he crept and disappointed it. At last he was within reaching distance. He paused, raised himself carefully up, measured his distance deliberately, then made a frantic grab at the nearest cat—and missed. Of course he lost his balance. His heels flew up, he struck on his back, and like a rocket he darted down the roof feet first, crashed through the dead vines and landed in a sitting posture in fourteen saucers of red-hot candy, in the midst of all that party—and dressed as *he* was: this lad who could not look a girl in the face with his clothes on. There was a wild scramble and a storm of shrieks, and Jim fled up the stairs, dripping broken crockery all the way.

The incident was ended. But I was not done with it yet, though I supposed I was. Eighteen or twenty years later I arrived in New York from California, and by that time I had failed in all my other undertakings and had stumbled into literature without intending it. This was early in 1867. I was offered a large sum to write something for the "Sunday Mercury," and I answered with the tale of "Jim Wolf and the Cats." I also collected the money for it—twenty-five dollars. It seemed over-pay, but I did not say anything about that, for I was not so scrupulous then as I am now.

A year or two later "Jim Wolf and the Cats" appeared in a Tennessee paper in a new dress—as to spelling; spelling borrowed from Artemus Ward. The appropriator of the tale had a wide reputation in the West, and was exceedingly popular. Deservedly so, I think. He wrote some of the breeziest and funniest things I have ever read, and did his work with distinguished ease and fluency. His name has passed out of my memory.

A couple of years went by; then the original story—my own version—cropped up again and went floating around in the original spelling, and with my name to it. Soon first one paper and then another fell upon me vigorously for "stealing" Jim Wolf and the Cats from the Tennessee man. I got a merciless basting, but I did not mind it. It's all in the game. Besides, I had learned, a good while before that, that it is not wise to keep the fire going under a slander unless you can get some large advantage out of keeping it alive. Few slanders can stand the wear of silence.

But I was not done with Jim and the Cats yet. In 1873 I was lecturing in London, in the Queen's Concert Rooms, Hanover Square, and was living at the Langham Hotel, Portland Place. I had no domestic household, and no official household except George Dolby, lecture-agent, and Charles Warren Stoddard, the California poet, now (1900) Professor of English Literature in the Roman Catholic University, Washington. Ostensibly

Stoddard was my private secretary; in reality he was merely my comrade—I hired him in order to have his company. As secretary there was nothing for him to do except to scrap-book the daily reports of the great trial of the Tichborne Claimant for perjury. But he made a sufficient job out of that, for the reports filled six columns a day and he usually post-poned the scrap-booking until Sunday; then he had 36 col-umns to cut out and paste in—a proper labor for Hercules. He did his work well, but if he had been older and feebler it would have killed him once a week. Without doubt he does his liter-ary lectures well, but also without doubt he prepares them fif-teen minutes before he is due on his platform and thus gets into them a freshness and sparkle which they might lack if they underwent the staling process of overstudy.

He was good company when he was awake. He was refined, sensitive, charming, gentle, generous, honest himself and unsuspicious of other people's honesty, and I think he was the purest male I have known, in mind and speech. George Dolby was something of a contrast to him, but the two were very friendly and sociable together, nevertheless. Dolby was large and ruddy, full of life and strength and spirits, a tireless and energetic talker, and always overflowing with good-nature and bursting with jollity. It was a choice and satisfactory menag-erie, this pensive poet and this gladsome gorilla. An indelicate story was a sharp distress to Stoddard; Dolby told him twenty-five a day. Dolby always came home with us after the lecture, and entertained Stoddard till midnight. Me too. After he left, I walked the floor and talked, and Stoddard went to sleep on the sofa. I hired him for company.

Dolby had been agent for concerts, and theatres, and Charles Dickens and all sorts of shows and "attractions" for many years; he had known the human being in many aspects, and he didn't much believe in him. But the poet did. The waifs and estrays found a friend in Stoddard: Dolby tried to per-suade him that he was dispensing his charities unworthily, but he was never able to succeed.

One night a young American got access to Stoddard at the Concert Rooms and told him a moving tale. He said he was living on the Surrey side, and for some strange reason his remittances had failed to arrive from home; he had no money, he was out of employment, and friendless; his girl-wife and his new baby were actually suffering for food; for the love of heaven could he lend him a sovereign until his remittances should resume? Stoddard was deeply touched, and gave him a sovereign on my account. Dolby scoffed, but Stoddard stood his ground. Each told me his story later in the evening, and I backed Stoddard's judgment. Dolby said we were women in disguise, and not a sane kind of women, either.

The next week the young man came again. His wife was ill with the pleurisy, the baby had the bots, or something, I am not sure of the name of the disease; the doctor and the drugs had eaten up the money, the poor little family was starving. If Stoddard "in the kindness of his heart could only spare him another sovereign," etc., etc. Stoddard was much moved, and spared him a sovereign for me. Dolby was outraged. He spoke up and said to the customer—

"Now, young man, you are going to the hotel with us and state your case to the other member of the family. If you don't make him believe in you I sha'n't honour this poet's drafts in your interest any longer, for I don't believe in you myself."

The young man was quite willing. I found no fault in him. On the contrary, I believed in him at once, and was solicitous to heal the wounds inflicted by Dolby's too frank incredulity; therefore I did everything I could think of to cheer him up and entertain him and make him feel at home and comfortable. I spun many yarns; among others the tale of Jim Wolf and the Cats. Learning that he had done something in a small way in literature, I offered to try to find a market for him in that line. His face lighted joyfully at that, and he said that if I could only sell a small manuscript to Tom Hood's Annual for him it would be the happiest event of his sad life and he would hold me in grateful remembrance always. That was a most pleasant night for three of us, but Dolby was disgusted and sarcastic.

Next week the baby died. Meantime I had spoken to Tom Hood and gained his sympathy. The young man had sent his manuscript to him, and the very day the child died the money for the MS. came—three guineas. The young man came with a poor little strip of crape around his arm and thanked me, and said that nothing could have been more timely than that money, and that his poor little wife was grateful beyond words for the service I had rendered. He wept, and in fact Stoddard and I wept with him, which was but natural. Also Dolby wept. At least he wiped his eyes and wrung out his handkerchief, and sobbed stertorously and made other exaggerated shows of grief. Stoddard and I were ashamed of Dolby, and tried to make the young man understand that he meant no harm, it was only his way. The young man said sadly that he was not minding it, his grief was too deep for other hurts; that he was only thinking of the funeral, and the heavy expenses which—

We cut that short and told him not to trouble about it, leave it all to us; send the bills to Mr. Dolby and—

"Yes," said Dolby, with a mock tremor in his voice, "send them to me, and I will pay them. What, are you going? You must not go alone in your worn and broken condition; Mr. Stoddard and I will go with you. Come, Stoddard. We will comfort the bereaved mamma and get a lock of the baby's hair."

It was shocking. We were ashamed of him again, and said so. But he was not disturbed. He said—

"Oh, I know this kind, the woods are full of them. I'll make this offer: if he will show me his family I will give him twenty pounds. Come!" The young man said he would not remain to be insulted; and he said good-night and took his hat. But Dolby said he would go with him, and stay by him until he found the family. Stoddard went along to soothe the young man and modify Dolby. They drove across the river and all over Southwark, but did not find the family. At last the young man confessed there wasn't any.

The thing he sold to Tom Hood's Annual was "Jim and the Cats." And he did not put my name to it.

So that small tale was sold three times. I am selling it again, now. It is one of the best properties I have come across.

MARK TWAIN

(to be continued)

North American Review

No. DCXV.

MAY 17, 1907

CHAPTERS FROM MY
AUTOBIOGRAPHY—XVIII

BY MARK TWAIN

PREFATORY NOTE—Mr. Clemens began to write his autobiography many years ago, and he continues to add to it day by day. It was his original intention to permit no publication of his memoirs until after his death; but, after leaving "Pier No. 70," he concluded that a considerable portion might now suitably be given to the public. It is that portion, garnered from the quarter-million of words already written, which will appear in this REVIEW during the coming year. No part of the autobiography will be published in book form during the lifetime of the author.—EDITOR N. A. R.

[*Dictated December 21, 1906.*] I wish to insert here some pages of Susy's Biography of me in which the biographer does not scatter, according to her custom, but sticks pretty steadily to a single subject until she has fought it to a finish:

Feb. 27, '86.—Last summer while we were in Elmira an article came out in the "Christian Union" by name "What ought he to have done" treating of the government of children, or rather giving an account of a fathers battle with his little baby boy, by the mother of the child and put in the form of a question as to whether the father disciplined the child corectly or not, different people wrote their opinions of the fathers behavior, and told what they thought he should have done. Mamma had long known how to disciplin children, for in fact the bringing up of children had been one of her specialties for many years. She had a great many theories, but one of them was, that if a child was big enough to be nauty, it was big enough to be whipped and here we all agreed with her. I remember one morning when Dr.—— came up to the farm he had a long discussion with mamma, upon the following topic. Mamma gave *this* as illustrative of one important rule for punishing a child. She said we will suppose the boy has thrown a handkerchief onto the floor, I tell him to pick it up, he refuses. I tell him again, he refuses. Then I say you must either pick up the handkerchief or have a whipping. My theory is never to make a child have a whipping and pick up the handkerchief too. I say "If you do not pick it up, I must punish you," if he doesn't he gets the whipping, but *I* pick up the handkerchief, if he does he gets no punishment. I tell him to do a thing if he disobeys me he is punished for so doing, but not forced to obey me afterwards.

When Clara and I had been very nauty or were being very nauty, the nurse would go and call Mamma and she would appear suddenly and look at us (she had a way of looking at us when she was displeased as if she could see right through us) till we were ready to sink through the floor from embarasment, and total absence of knowing what to say. This look was usually followed with "Clara" or "Susy what do you mean by this? do you want to come to the bath-room with me?" Then followed the climax for Clara and I both new only too well what going to the bath-room meant.

But mamma's first and foremost object was to make the child understand that he is being punished for *his* sake, and because the mother so loves him that she cannot allow him to do wrong; also that it is as hard for her to punish him as for him to be punished and even harder. Mamma never allowed herself to punish us when she was angry with us she never struck us because she was enoyed at us and felt like striking us if we had been nauty and had enoyed her, so that she thought she felt or would show the least bit of temper toward us while punnishing us, she always postponed the punishment until *she* was no more chafed by our behavior. She never humored herself by striking or punishing us because or while she was the least bit enoyed with us.

Our very worst nautinesses were punished by being taken to the bath-room and being whipped by the paper cutter. But after the whipping was over, mamma did not allow us to leave her until we were perfectly happy, and perfectly understood why we had been whipped. I never remember having felt the least bit bitterly toward mamma for punishing me. I always felt I had deserved my punishment, and was much happier for having received it. For after mamma had punished us and shown her displeasure, she showed no signs of further displeasure, but acted as if we had not displeased her in any way.

Ordinary punishments answered very well for Susy. She was a thinker, and would reason out the purpose of them, apply the lesson, and achieve the reform required. But it was much less easy to devise punishments that would reform Clara. This was because she was a philosopher who was always turning her attention to finding something good and satisfactory and entertaining in everything that came her way; consequently it was sometimes pretty discouraging to the troubled mother to find that after all her pains and thought in inventing what she meant to be a severe and reform-compelling punishment, the child had entirely missed the severities through her native disposition to get interest and pleasure out of them as novelties. The mother, in her anxiety to find a penalty that would take sharp hold and do its work effectively, at last resorted, with a sore heart, and with a reproachful conscience, to that punishment which the incorrigible criminal in the penitentiary dreads above all the other punitive miseries which the warden inflicts upon him for his good—solitary confinement in the dark chamber. The grieved and worried mother shut Clara up in a very small clothes-closet and went away and left her there—for fifteen minutes—it was all that the mother-heart could endure. Then she came softly back and listened—listened for the sobs, but there weren't any; there were muffled and inarticulate sounds, but they could not be construed into sobs. The mother waited half an hour longer; by that time she was suffering so intensely with sorrow and compassion for the little prisoner that she was not able to wait any longer for the distressed sounds which she had counted upon to inform her when there had been punishment enough and the reform accomplished. She opened the closet to set the prisoner free and take her back into her loving favor and forgiveness, but the result was not the one expected. The captive had manufactured a fairy cavern out of the closet, and friendly fairies out of the clothes hanging from the hooks, and was having a most sinful and unrepentant good time, and requested permission to spend the rest of the day there!

FROM SUSY'S BIOGRAPHY OF ME

But Mamma's oppinions and ideas upon the subject of bringing up children has always been more or less of a joke in our family, perticularly since Papa's article in the "Christian Union," and I am sure Clara and I have related the history of our old family paper-cutter, our punishments and privations with rather more pride and triumph than any other sentiment, because of Mamma's way of rearing us.

When the article "What ought he to have done?" came out Mamma read it, and was very much interested in it. And when papa heard that she had read it he went to work and secretly wrote his opinion of what the father ought to have done. He told Aunt Susy, Clara and I, about it but mamma was not to see it or hear any thing about it till it came out. He gave it to Aunt Susy to read, and after Clara and I had gone up to get ready for bed he brought it up for us to read. He told what he thought the father ought to have done by telling what mamma would have done. The article was a beautiful tribute to mamma and every word in it true. But still in writing about mamma he partly forgot that the article was going to be published, I think, and expressed himself more fully than he would do the second time he wrote it; I think the article has done and will do a great deal of good, and I think it would have been perfect for the family and friend's enjoyment, but a little bit too private to have been published as it was. And Papa felt so too, because the very next day or a few days after, he went down to New York to see if he couldn't get it back before it was published but it was too late, and he had to return without it. When the Christian Union reached the farm and papa's article in it all ready and waiting to be read to mamma papa hadn't the courage to show it to her (for he knew she wouldn't like it at all) at first, and he didn't but he might have let it go and never let her see it, but finally he gave his consent to her seeing it, and told Clara and I we could take it to her, which we did, with tardiness, and we all stood around mamma while she read it, all wondering what she would say and think about it.

She was too much surprised, (and pleased privately, too) to say much at first, but as we all expected publicly, (or rather when she remembered that this article was to be read by every one that took the Christian Union) she was rather shocked and a little displeased.

Clara and I had great fun the night papa gave it to us to read and then hide, so mamma couldn't see it, for just as we were in the midst of reading it mamma appeared papa following anxiously and asked why we were not in bed? then a scuffle ensued for we told her it was a secret and tried to hide it; but she chased us wherever we went, till she thought it was time for us to go to bed, then she surrendered and left us to tuck it under Clara's matress.

A little while after the article was published letters began to come in to papa crittisizing it, there were some very pleasant ones but a few very disagreable. One of these, the very worst, mamma got hold of and read, to papa's great regret, it was full of the most disagreble things, and so very enoying to papa that he for a time felt he must do something to show the author of it his great displeasure at being so insulted. But he finally decided not to, because he felt the man had some cause for feeling enoyed at, for papa had spoken of him, (he was the baby's father) rather slightingly in his Christian Union Article.

After all this, papa and mamma both wished I think they might never hear or be spoken to on the subject of the Christian Union article, and whenever any has spoken to me and told me "How much they did enjoy my father's article in the Christian

Union" I almost laughed in their faces when I remembered what a great variety of oppinions had been expressed upon the subject of the Christian Union article of papa's.

The article was written in July or August and just the other day papa received quite a bright letter from a gentleman who has read the C. U. article and gave his opinion of it in these words.

It is missing. She probably put the letter between the leaves of the Biography and it got lost out. She threw away the hostile letters, but tried to keep the pleasantest one for her book; surely there has been no kindlier biographer than this one. Yet to a quite creditable degree she is loyal to the responsibilities of her position as historian—not eulogist—and honorably gives me a quiet prod now and then. But how many, many, many she has withheld that I deserved! I could prize them now; there would be no acid in her words, and it is loss to me that she did not set them all down. Oh, Susy, you sweet little biographer, you break my old heart with your gentle charities!

I think a great deal of her work. Her canvases are on their easels, and her brush flies about in a care-free and random way, delivering a dash here, a dash there and another yonder, and one might suppose that there would be no definite result; on the contrary I think that an intelligent reader of her little book must find that by the time he has finished it he has somehow accumulated a pretty clear and nicely shaded idea of the several members of this family—including Susy herself—and that the random dashes on the canvases have developed into portraits. I feel that my own portrait, with some of the defects fined down and others left out, is here; and I am sure that any who knew the mother will recognize her without difficulty, and will say that the lines are drawn with a just judgment and a sure hand. Little creature though Susy was, the penetration which was born in her finds its way to the surface more than once in these pages.

Before Susy began the Biography she let fall a remark now and then concerning my character which showed that she had it under observation. In the Record which we kept of the children's sayings there is an instance of this. She was twelve years old at the time. We had established a rule that each member of the family must bring a fact to breakfast—a fact drawn from a book or from any other source; any fact would answer. Susy's first contribution was in substance as follows. Two great exiles and former opponents in war met in Ephesus—Scipio and Hannibal. Scipio asked Hannibal to name the greatest general the world had produced.

"Alexander"—and he explained why.

"And the next greatest?"

"Pyrrhus"—and he explained why.

"But where do you place yourself, then?"

"If I had conquered you I would place myself before the others."

Susy's grave comment was—

"That *attracted* me, it was just like papa—he is so frank about his books."

So frank in admiring them, she meant.

[*Thursday, March 28, 1907.*] Some months ago I commented upon a chapter of Susy's Biography wherein she very elaborately discussed an article about the training and disciplining of children, which I had published in the "Christian Union" (this was twenty-one years ago), an article which was full of worshipful praises of Mrs. Clemens as a mother, and which little Clara, and Susy, and I had been hiding from this lovely and admirable mother because we knew she would disapprove of public and printed praises of herself. At the time that I was dictating these comments, several months ago, I was trying to call back to my memory some of the details of that article, but I was not able to do it, and I wished I had a copy of the article so that I could see what there was about it which gave it such large interest for Susy.

Yesterday afternoon I elected to walk home from the luncheon at the St. Regis, which is in 55th Street and Fifth Avenue, for it was a fine spring day and I hadn't had a walk for a year or two, and felt the need of exercise. As I walked along down Fifth Avenue the desire to see that "Christian Union" article came into my head again. I had just reached the corner of 42nd Street then, and there was the usual jam of wagons, carriages, and automobiles there. I stopped to let it thin out before trying to cross the street, but a stranger, who didn't require as much room as I do, came racing by and darted into a crack among the vehicles and made the crossing. But on his way past me he thrust a couple of ancient newspaper clippings into my hand, and said,

"There, you don't know me, but I have saved them in my scrap-book for twenty years, and it occurred to me this morning that perhaps you would like to see them, so I was carrying them down-town to mail them, I not expecting to run across you in this accidental way, of course; but I will give them into your own hands now. Good-by!"—and he disappeared among the wagons.

Those scraps which he had put into my hand were ancient newspaper copies of that "Christian Union" article! It is a handsome instance of mental telegraphy—or if it isn't that, it is a handsome case of coincidence.

FROM THE BIOGRAPHY

March 14th, '86.—Mr. Laurence Barrette and Mr. and Mrs. Hutton were here a little while ago, and we had a very interesting visit from them. Papa said Mr. Barette never had acted so well before when he had seen him, as he did the first night he was staying with us. And Mrs.—— said she never had seen an actor on the stage, whom she more wanted to speak with.

Papa has been very much interested of late, in the "Mind Cure" theory. And in fact so have we all. A young lady in town has worked wonders, by using the "Mind Cure" upon people; she is constantly busy now curing peoples deseases in this way—and curing her own even, which to me seems the most remarkable of all.

A little while past, papa was delighted with the knowledge of what he thought the best way of curing a cold, which was by starving it. This starving did work beautifully, and freed him from a great many severe colds. Now he says it wasn't the starving that helped his colds, but the trust in the starving, the mind cure connected with the starving.

I shouldn't wonder if we finally became firm believers in Mind Cure. The next time papa has a cold, I haven't a doubt, he will send for Miss H—— the young lady who is doctoring in the "Mind Cure" theory, to cure him of it.

Mamma was over at Mrs. George Warners to lunch the other day, and Miss H—— was there too. Mamma asked if anything as natural as near sightedness could be cured she said oh yes just as well as other deseases.

When mamma came home, she took me into her room, and told me that perhaps my near-sightedness could be cured by the "Mind Cure" and that she was going to have me try the treatment any way, there could be no harm in it, and there might be great good. If her plan succeeds there certainly will be a great deal in "Mind Cure" to my oppinion, for I am *very* near sighted and so is mamma, and I never expected there could be any more cure for it than for blindness, but now I dont know but what theres a cure for *that*.

It was a disappointment; her near-sightedness remained with her to the end. She was born with it, no doubt; yet, strangely enough, she must have been four years old, and possibly five, before we knew of its existence. It is not easy to understand how that could have happened. I discovered the defect by accident. I was half-way up the hall stairs one day at home, and was leading her by the hand, when I glanced back through the open door of the dining-room and saw what I thought she would recognize as a pretty picture. It was "Stray Kit," the slender, the graceful, the sociable, the beautiful, the incomparable, the cat of cats, the tortoise-shell, curled up as round as a wheel and sound asleep on the fire-red cover of the dining-table, with a brilliant stream of sunlight falling across her. I exclaimed about it, but Susy said she could see nothing there, neither cat nor table-cloth. The distance was so slight—not more than twenty feet, perhaps—that if it had been any other child I should not have credited the statement.

FROM THE BIOGRAPHY

March 14th, '86.—Clara sprained her ankle, a little while ago, by running into a tree, when coasting, and while she was unable to walk with it she played solotaire with cards a great deal. While Clara was sick and papa saw her play solotaire so much, he got very much interested in the game, and finally began to play it himself a little, then Jean took it up, and at last *mamma*, even played it ocasionally; Jean's and papa's love for it rapidly increased, and now Jean brings the cards every night to the table and papa and mamma help her play, and before dinner is at an end, papa has gotten a separate pack of cards, and is playing alone, with great interest. Mamma and Clara next are made subject to the contagious solatair, and there are four solotaireans at the table; while you hear nothing but "Fill up the place" etc. It is dreadful! after supper Clara goes into the library, and gets a little red mahogany table, and placing it under the gas fixture seats herself and begins to play again, then papa follows with another table of the same discription, and they play solatair till bedtime.

We have just had our Prince and Pauper pictures taken; two groups and some little single ones. The groups (the Interview and Lady Jane Grey scene) were pretty good, the lady Jane scene was perfect, just as pretty as it could be, the Interview was not so good; and two of the little single pictures were very good indeed, but one was very bad. Yet on the whole we think they were a success.

Papa has done a great deal in his life I think, that is good, and very remarkable, but I think if he had had the advantages with which he could have developed the gifts which he has made no use of in writing his books, or in any other way for other peoples pleasure and benefit outside of his own family and intimate friends, he could have done *more* than he has and a great deal more even. He is known to the public as a humorist, but he has much more in him that is earnest than that is humorous. He has a keen sense of the ludicrous, notices funny stories and incidents knows how to tell them, to improve upon them, and does not forget them. He has been through a great many of the funny adventures related in "Tom Sayer" and in "Huckleberry Finn," *himself* and he lived among just such boys, and in just such villages all the days of his early life. His "Prince and Pauper is his most orriginal, and best production; it shows the most of any of his books what kind of pictures are in his mind, usually. Not that the pictures of England in the 16th Century and the adventures of a little prince and pauper are the kind of things he mainly thinks about; but that *that* book, and those pictures represent the train of thought and imagination he would be likely to be thinking of to-day, to-morrow, or next day, more nearly than those given in "Tom Sawyer or "Huckleberry Finn."

Papa can make exceedingly bright jokes, and he enjoys funny things, and when he is with people he jokes and laughs a great deal, but still he is more interested in earnest books and earnest subjects to talk upon, than in humorous ones.

When we are all alone at home, nine times out of ten, he talks about some very earnest subjects, (with an ocasional joke thrown in) and he a good deal more often talks upon such subjects than upon the other kind.

He is as much of a Pholosopher as anything I think. I think he could have done a great deal in this direction if he had studied while young, for he seems to enjoy reasoning out things, no matter what; in a great many such directions he has greater ability than in the gifts which have made him famous.

Thus at fourteen she had made up her mind about me, and in no timorous or uncertain terms had set down her reasons for her opinion. Fifteen years were to pass before any other critic—except Mr. Howells, I think—was to reutter that daring opinion and print it. Right or wrong, it was a brave position for that little analyzer to take. She never withdrew it afterward, nor modified it. She has spoken of herself as lacking physical courage, and has evinced her admiration of Clara's; but she had moral courage, which is the rarest of human qualities, and she kept it functionable by exercising it. I think that in questions of morals and politics she was usually on my side; but when she was not she had her reasons and maintained her ground. Two years after she passed out of my life I wrote a

Philosophy. Of the three persons who have seen the manuscript only one understood it, and all three condemned it. If she could have read it, she also would have condemned it, possibly,—probably, in fact—but she would have understood it. It would have had no difficulties for her on that score; also she would have found a tireless pleasure in analyzing and discussing its problems.

MARK TWAIN

(to be continued)

North American Review

No. DCXVI.

JUNE 7, 1907

CHAPTERS FROM MY AUTOBIOGRAPHY—XIX

BY MARK TWAIN

PREFATORY NOTE—Mr. Clemens began to write his autobiography many years ago, and he continues to add to it day by day. It was his original intention to permit no publication of his memoirs until after his death; but, after leaving "Pier No. 70," he concluded that a considerable portion might now suitably be given to the public. It is that portion, garnered from the quarter-million of words already written, which will appear in this REVIEW during the present year. No part of the autobiography will be published in book form during the lifetime of the author.—EDITOR N. A. R.

FROM SUSY'S BIOGRAPHY OF ME

March 23, '86.—The other day was my birthday, and I had a little birthday party in the evening and papa acted some very funny charades with Mr. Gherhardt, Mr. Jesse Grant (who had come up from New York and was spending the evening with us) and Mr. Frank Warner. One of them was "on his knees" honys-sneeze. There were a good many other funny ones, all of which I dont remember. Mr. Grant was very pleasant, and began playing the charades in the most delightful way.

Susy's spelling has defeated me, this time. I cannot make out what "honys-sneeze" stands for. Impromptu charades were almost a nightly pastime of ours, from the children's earliest days—they played in them with me when they were only five or six years old. As they increased in years and practice their love for the sport almost amounted to a passion, and they acted their parts with a steadily increasing ability. At first they required much drilling; but later they were generally ready as soon as the parts were assigned, and they acted them according to their own devices. Their stage facility and absence of constraint and self-consciousness in the "Prince and Pauper" was a result of their charading practice.

At ten and twelve Susy wrote plays, and she and Daisy Warner and Clara played them in the library or up-stairs in the school-room, with only themselves and the servants for audience. They were of a tragic and tremendous sort, and were performed with great energy and earnestness. They were dramatized (freely) from English history, and in them Mary Queen of Scots and Elizabeth had few holidays. The clothes were borrowed from the mother's wardrobe and the gowns were longer than necessary, but that was not regarded as a defect. In one of these plays Jean (three years old, perhaps) was Sir Francis Bacon. She was not dressed for the part, and did not have to say anything, but sat silent and decorous at a tiny table and was kept busy signing death-warrants. It was a really important office, for few entered those plays and got out of them alive.

March 26.—Mamma and Papa have been in New York for two or three days, and Miss Corey has been staying with us. They are coming home to-day at two o'clock.

Papa has just begun to play chess, and he is very fond of it, so he has engaged to play with Mrs. Charles Warner every morning from 10 to 12, he came down to supper last night, full of this pleasant prospect, but evidently with something on his mind. Finally he said to mamma in an appologetical tone, Susy Warner and I have a plan.

"Well" mamma said "what now, I wonder?"

Papa said that Susy Warner and he were going to name the chess men after some of the old bible heroes and then play chess on Sunday.

April 18, '86.—Mamma and papa Clara and Daisy have gone to New York to see the "Mikado." They are coming home to-night at half past seven.

Last winter when Mr. Cable was lecturing with papa, he wrote this letter to him just before he came to visit us.

DEAR UNCLE,—That's one nice thing about me, I never bother any one, to offer me a good thing twice. You dont ask me to stay over Sunday, but then you dont ask me to leave Saturday night, and knowing the nobility of your nature as I do—thank you, I'll stay till Monday morning.

Your's and the dear familie's

GEORGE W. CABLE.

[*December 22, 1906.*] It seems a prodigious while ago! Two or three nights ago I dined at a friend's house with a score of other men, and at my side was Cable—actually almost an old man, really almost an old man, that once so young chap! 62 years old, frost on his head, seven grandchildren in stock, and a brand-new wife to re-begin life with!

[*Dictated Nov. 19, 1906.*]

Ever since papa and mamma were married, papa has written his books and then taken them to mamma in manuscript and she has expergated them. Papa read "Huckleberry Finn" to us in manuscript just before it came out, and then he would leave parts of it with mamma to expergate, while he went off up to the study to work, and sometimes Clara and I would be sitting with mamma while she was looking the manuscript over, and I remember so well, with what pangs of regret we used to see her turn down the leaves of the pages, which meant that some delightfully dreadful part must be scratched out. And I remember one part pertickularly which was perfectly fascinating it was dreadful, that Clara and I used to delight in, and oh with what dispair we saw mamma turn down the leaf on which it was written, we thought the book would be almost ruined without it. But we gradually came to feel as mamma did.

It would be a pity to replace the vivacity and quaintness and felicity of Susy's innocent free spelling with the dull and petrified uniformities of the spelling-book. Nearly all the grimness is taken out of the "expergating" of my books by the subtle mollification accidentally infused into the word by Susy's modification of the spelling of it.

I remember the special case mentioned by Susy, and can see the group yet—two-thirds of it pleading for the life of the culprit sentence that was so fascinatingly dreadful and the other third of it patiently explaining why the court could not grant the prayer of the pleaders; but I do not remember what the condemned phrase was. It had much company, and they all went to the gallows; but it is possible that that specially dreadful one which gave those little people so much delight was cunningly devised and put into the book for just that function, and not with any hope or expectation that it would get by the "expergator" alive. It is possible, for I had that custom.

Susy's quaint and effective spelling falls quite opportunely into to-day's atmosphere, which is heavy with the rumblings and grumblings and mutterings of the Simplified Spelling Reform. Andrew Carnegie started this storm, a couple of years ago, by moving a simplifying of English orthography, and establishing a fund for the prosecution and maintenance of the crusade. He began gently. He addressed a circular to some hundreds of his friends, asking them to simplify the spelling of a dozen of our badly spelt words—I think they were only words which end with the superfluous *ugh*. He asked that these friends use the suggested spellings in their private correspondence.

By this, one perceives that the beginning was sufficiently quiet and unaggressive.

Next stage: a small committee was appointed, with Brander Matthews for managing director and spokesman. It issued a list of three hundred words, of average silliness as to spelling, and proposed new and sane spellings for these words. The President of the United States, unsolicited, adopted these simplified three hundred officially, and ordered that they be used in the official documents of the Government. It was now remarked, by all the educated and the thoughtful except the clergy that Sheol was to pay. This was most justly and comprehensively descriptive. The indignant British lion rose, with a roar that was heard across the Atlantic, and stood there on his little isle, gazing, red-eyed, out over the glooming seas, snow-flecked with driving spindrift, and lashing his tail—a most scary spectacle to see.

The lion was outraged because we, a nation of children, without any grown-up people among us, with no property in the language, but using it merely by courtesy of its owner the English nation, were trying to defile the sacredness of it by removing from it peculiarities which had been its ornament and which had made it holy and beautiful for ages.

In truth there is a certain sardonic propriety in preserving our orthography, since ours is a mongrel language which started with a child's vocabulary of three hundred words, and now consists of two hundred and twenty-five thousand; the whole lot, with the exception of the original and legitimate three hundred, borrowed, stolen, smouched from every unwatched language under the sun, the spelling of each individual word of the lot locating the source of the theft and preserving the memory of the revered crime.

Why is it that I have intruded into this turmoil and manifested a desire to get our orthography purged of its asininities? Indeed I do not know why I should manifest any interest in the matter, for at bottom I disrespect our orthography most heartily, and as heartily disrespect everything that has been said by anybody in defence of it. Nothing professing to be a defence of our ludicrous spellings has had any basis, so far as my observation goes, except sentimentality. In these "arguments" the term venerable is used instead of mouldy, and hallowed instead of devilish; whereas there is nothing properly venerable or antique about a language which is not yet four hundred years old, and about a jumble of imbecile spellings which were grotesque in the beginning, and which grow more and more grotesque with the flight of the years.

[*Dictated Monday, November 30, 1906.*]

Jean and Papa were walking out past the barn the other day
when Jean saw some little newly born baby ducks, she exclaimed
as she perceived them "I dont see why God gives us so much
ducks when Patrick kills them so."

Susy is mistaken as to the origin of the ducks. They were not
a gift, I bought them. I am not finding fault with her, for that
would be most unfair. She is remarkably accurate in her statements as a historian, as a rule, and it would not be just to
make much of this small slip of hers; besides I think it was a
quite natural slip, for by heredity and habit ours was a religious household, and it was a common thing with us whenever
anybody did a handsome thing, to give the credit of it to Providence, without examining into the matter. This may be called
automatic religion—in fact that is what it is; it is so used to its
work that it can do it without your help or even your privity;
out of all the facts and statistics that may be placed before it, it
will always get the one result, since it has never been taught to
seek any other. It is thus the unreflecting cause of much injustice. As we have seen, it betrayed Susy into an injustice toward
me. It had to be automatic, for she would have been far from
doing me an injustice when in her right mind. It was a dear
little biographer, and she meant me no harm, and I am not
censuring her now, but am only desirous of correcting in
advance an erroneous impression which her words would be
sure to convey to a reader's mind. No elaboration of this matter is necessary; it is sufficient to say *I* provided the ducks.

It was in Hartford. The greensward sloped down-hill from
the house to the sluggish little river that flowed through the
grounds, and Patrick, who was fertile in good ideas, had early
conceived the idea of having home-made ducks for our table.
Every morning he drove them from the stable down to the
river, and the children were always there to see and admire the
waddling white procession; they were there again at sunset to
see Patrick conduct the procession back to its lodgings in the
stable. But this was not always a gay and happy holiday show,

with joy in it for the witnesses; no, too frequently there was a tragedy connected with it, and then there were tears and pain for the children. There was a stranded log or two in the river, and on these certain families of snapping-turtles used to congregate and drowse in the sun and give thanks, in their dumb way, to Providence for benevolence extended to them. It was but another instance of misplaced credit; it was the young ducks that those pious reptiles were so thankful for—whereas they were *my* ducks. I bought the ducks.

When a crop of young ducks, not yet quite old enough for the table but approaching that age, began to join the procession, and paddle around in the sluggish water, and give thanks—not to me—for that privilege, the snapping-turtles would suspend their songs of praise and slide off the logs and paddle along under the water and chew the feet of the young ducks. Presently Patrick would notice that two or three of those little creatures were not moving about, but were apparently at anchor, and were not looking as thankful as they had been looking a short time before. He early found out what that sign meant—a submerged snapping-turtle was taking his breakfast, and silently singing his gratitude. Every day or two Patrick would rescue and fetch up a little duck with incomplete legs to stand upon—nothing left of their extremities but gnawed and bleeding stumps. Then the children said pitying things and wept—and at dinner we finished the tragedy which the turtles had begun. Thus, as will be seen—out of season, at least—it was really the turtles that gave us so much ducks. At my expense.

Papa has written a new version of "There is a happy land" it is—

> "There is a boarding-house
> Far, far away,
> Where they have ham and eggs,
> Three times a day,
> Oh dont those boarders yell
> When they hear the dinner-bell,
> They give that land-lord rats
> Three times a day."

Again Susy has made a small error. It was not I that wrote the song. I heard Billy Rice sing it in the negro minstrel show, and I brought it home and sang it—with great spirit—for the elevation of the household. The children admired it to the limit, and made me sing it with burdensome frequency. To their minds it was superior to the Battle Hymn of the Republic.

How many years ago that was! Where now is Billy Rice? He was a joy to me, and so were the other stars of the nigger-show—Billy Birch, David Wambold, Backus, and a delightful dozen of their brethren, who made life a pleasure to me forty years ago, and later. Birch, Wambold, and Backus are gone years ago; and with them departed to return no more forever, I suppose, the real nigger-show—the genuine nigger-show, the extravagant nigger-show,—the show which to me had no peer and whose peer has not yet arrived, in my experience. We have the grand opera; and I have witnessed, and greatly enjoyed, the first act of everything which Wagner created; but the effect on me has always been so powerful that one act was quite sufficient; whenever I have witnessed two acts I have gone away physically exhausted; and whenever I have ventured an entire opera the result has been the next thing to suicide. But if I could have the nigger-show back again, in its pristine purity and perfection, I should have but little further use for opera. It seems to me that to the elevated mind and the sensitive spirit the hand-organ and the nigger-show are a standard and a summit to whose rarefied altitude the other forms of musical art may not hope to reach.

[*Dictated September 5, 1906.*] It is years since I have examined "The Children's Record." I have turned over a few of its pages this morning. This book is a record in which Mrs. Clemens and I registered some of the sayings and doings of the children, in the long ago, when they were little chaps. Of course, we wrote these things down at the time because they were of momentary interest—things of the passing hour, and of no permanent value—but at this distant day I find that they still possess an interest for me and also a value, because it turns out that they were *registrations of character*. The qualities then revealed by fitful glimpses, in childish acts and speeches, remained as a permanency in the children's characters in the drift of the years, and were always afterwards clearly and definitely recognizable.

There is a masterful streak in Jean that now and then moves her to set my authority aside for a moment and end a losing argument in that prompt and effective fashion. And here in this old book I find evidence that she was just like that before she was quite four years old.

From The Children's Record. Quarry Farm, July 7, 1884.— Yesterday evening our cows (after being inspected and worshipped by Jean from the shed for an hour,) wandered off down into the pasture, and left her bereft. I thought I was going to get back home, now, but that was an error. Jean knew of some more cows, in a field somewhere, and took my hand and led me thitherward. When we turned the corner and took the right-hand road, I saw that we should presently be out of range of call and sight; so I began to argue against continuing the expedition, and Jean began to argue in favor of it—she using English for light skirmishing, and German for "business." I kept up my end with vigor, and demolished her arguments in detail, one after the other, till I judged I had her about cornered. She hesitated a moment, then answered up sharply:

"Wir werden nichts mehr darüber sprechen!" (We won't talk any more about it!)

It nearly took my breath away; though I thought I might possibly have misunderstood. I said:

"Why, you little rascal! *Was hast du gesagt?*"

But she said the same words over again, and in the same decided way. I suppose I ought to have been outraged; but I wasn't, I was charmed. And I suppose I ought to have spanked her; but I didn't, I fraternized with the enemy, and we went on and spent half an hour with the cows.

That incident is followed in the "Record" by the following paragraph, which is another instance of a juvenile characteristic maintaining itself into mature age. Susy was persistently and conscientiously truthful throughout her life with the exception of one interruption covering several months, and perhaps a year. This was while she was still a little child. Suddenly—not gradually—she began to lie; not furtively, but frankly, openly, and on a scale quite disproportioned to her size. Her mother was so stunned, so nearly paralyzed for a day or two, that she did not know what to do with the emergency. Reasonings, persuasions, beseechings, all went for nothing; they produced no effect; the lying went tranquilly on. Other remedies were tried, but they failed. There is a tradition that success was finally accomplished by whipping. I think the Record says so, but if it does it is because the Record is incomplete. Whipping was indeed tried, and was faithfully kept up during two or three weeks, but the results were merely temporary; the reforms achieved were discouragingly brief.

Fortunately for Susy, an incident presently occurred which put a complete stop to all the mother's efforts in the direction of reform. This incident was the chance discovery in Darwin of a passage which said that when a child exhibits a sudden and unaccountable disposition to forsake the truth and restrict itself to lying, the explanation must be sought away back in the past; that an ancestor of the child had had the same disease, at the same tender age; that it was irremovable by persuasion or punishment, and that it had ceased as suddenly and as mysteriously as it had come, when it had run its appointed course. I think Mr. Darwin said that nothing was necessary but to leave the matter alone and let the malady have its way and perish by the statute of limitations.

We had confidence in Darwin, and after that day Susy was relieved of our reformatory persecutions. She went on lying without let or hindrance during several months, or a year; then the lying suddenly ceased, and she became as conscientiously and exactingly truthful as she had been before the attack, and she remained so to the end of her life.

The paragraph in the Record to which I have been leading up is in my handwriting, and is of a date so long posterior to the time of the lying malady that she had evidently forgotten that truth-speaking had ever had any difficulties for her.

Mama was speaking of a servant who had been pretty unvera-cious, but was now "trying to tell the truth." Susy was a good deal surprised, and said she shouldn't think anybody would have to *try* to tell the truth.

In the Record the children's acts and speeches quite defi-nitely define their characters. Susy's indicated the presence of mentality—thought—and they were generally marked by grav-ity. She was timid, on her physical side, but had an abundance of moral courage. Clara was sturdy, independent, orderly, practical, persistent, plucky—just a little animal, and very sat-isfactory. Charles Dudley Warner said Susy was made of mind, and Clara of matter.

When Motley, the kitten, died, some one said that the thoughts of the two children need not be inquired into, they could be divined: that Susy was wondering if this was the *end* of Motley, and had his life been worth while; whereas Clara was merely interested in seeing to it that there should be a creditable funeral.

In those days Susy was a dreamer, a thinker, a poet and phi-losopher, and Clara—well, Clara wasn't. In after-years a pas-sion for music developed the latent spirituality and intellectuality in Clara, and her practicality took second and, in fact, even third place. Jean was from the beginning orderly, steady, dili-gent, persistent; and remains so. She picked up languages eas-ily, and kept them.

Susy aged eleven, Jean three.—Susy said the other day when she saw Jean bringing a cat to me of her own motion, "Jean has found out already that mamma loves morals and papa loves cats."

It is another of Susy's remorselessly sound verdicts.

As a child, Jean neglected my books. When she was nine years old Will Gillette invited her and the rest of us to a dinner at the Murray Hill Hotel in New York, in order that we might get acquainted with Mrs. Leslie and her daughters. Elsie Leslie was nine years old, and was a great celebrity on the stage. Jean was astonished and awed to see that little slip of a thing sit up at table and take part in the conversation of the grown people, capably and with ease and tranquillity. Poor Jean was obliged to keep still, for the subjects discussed never happened to hit her level, but at last the talk fell within her limit and she had her chance to contribute to it. "Tom Sawyer" was mentioned. Jean spoke gratefully up and said,

"I know who wrote that book—Harriet Beecher Stowe!"

One evening Susy had prayed, Clara was curled up for sleep; she was reminded that it was her turn to pray now. She said "Oh! one's enough," and dropped off to slumber.

Clara five years old.—We were in Germany. The nurse, Rosa, was not allowed to speak to the children otherwise than in German. Clara grew very tired of it; by and by the little creature's patience was exhausted, and she said "Aunt Clara, I wish God had made Rosa in English."

Clara four years old, Susy six.—This morning when Clara discovered that this is my birthday, she was greatly troubled because she had provided no gift for me, and repeated her sorrow several times. Finally she went musing to the nursery and presently returned with her newest and dearest treasure, a large toy horse, and said, "You shall have this horse for your birthday, papa."

I accepted it with many thanks. After an hour she was racing up and down the room with the horse, when Susy said,

"Why Clara, you gave that horse to papa, and now you've tooken it again."

Clara.— "I never give it to him for always; I give it to him for his birthday."

In Geneva, in September, I lay abed late one morning, and as Clara was passing through the room I took her on my bed a moment. Then the child went to Clara Spaulding and said,

"Aunt Clara, papa is a good deal of trouble to me."

"Is he? Why?"

"Well, he wants me to get in bed with him, and I can't do that with jelmuls [gentlemen]—I don't like jelmuls anyway."

"What, you don't like gentlemen! Don't you like Uncle Theodore Crane?"

"Oh yes, but he's not a jelmul, he's a friend."

MARK TWAIN

(to be continued)

North American Review

No. DCXVIII.

JULY 5, 1907

CHAPTERS FROM MY AUTOBIOGRAPHY—XX

BY MARK TWAIN

PREFATORY NOTE—Mr. Clemens began to write his autobiography many years ago, and he continues to add to it day by day. It was his original intention to permit no publication of his memoirs until after his death; but, after leaving "Pier No. 70," he concluded that a considerable portion might now suitably be given to the public. It is that portion, garnered from the quarter-million of words already written, which will appear in this REVIEW during the coming year. No part of the autobiography will be published in book form during the lifetime of the author. —EDITOR N. A. R.

[*Notes on "Innocents Abroad." Dictated in Florence, Italy, April, 1904.*]—I will begin with a note upon the dedication. I wrote the book in the months of March and April, 1868, in San Francisco. It was published in August, 1869. Three years afterward Mr. Goodman, of Virginia City, Nevada, on whose newspaper I had served ten years before, came East, and we were walking down Broadway one day when he said: "How did you come to steal Oliver Wendell Holmes's dedication and put it in your book?"

I made a careless and inconsequential answer, for I supposed he was joking. But he assured me that he was in earnest. He said: "I'm not discussing the question of whether you stole it or didn't—for that is a question that can be settled in the first bookstore we come to—I am only asking you *how* you came to steal it, for that is where my curiosity is focalized."

I couldn't accommodate him with this information, as I hadn't it in stock. I could have made oath that I had not stolen anything, therefore my vanity was not hurt nor my spirit troubled. At bottom I supposed that he had mistaken another book for mine, and was now getting himself into an untenable place and preparing sorrow for himself and triumph for me. We entered a bookstore and he asked for "The Innocents Abroad" and for the dainty little blue and gold edition of Dr. Oliver Wendell Holmes's poems. He opened the books, exposed their dedications and said: "Read them. It is plain that the author of the second one stole the first one, isn't it?"

I was very much ashamed, and unspeakably astonished. We continued our walk, but I was not able to throw any gleam of light upon that original question of his. I could not remember ever having seen Dr. Holmes's dedication. I knew the poems, but the dedication was new to me.

I did not get hold of the key to that secret until months afterward, then it came in a curious way, and yet it was a natural way; for the natural way provided by nature and the construction of the human mind for the discovery of a forgotten event is to employ another forgotten event for its resurrection.

I received a letter from the Rev. Dr. Rising, who had been rector of the Episcopal church in Virginia City in my time, in which letter Dr. Rising made reference to certain things which had happened to us in the Sandwich Islands six years before; among things he made casual mention of the Honolulu Hotel's poverty in the matter of literature. At first I did not see the bearing of the remark, it called nothing to my mind. But presently it did—with a flash! There was but one book in Mr. Kirchhof's hotel, and that was the first volume of Dr. Holmes's blue and gold series. I had had a fortnight's chance to get well acquainted with its contents, for I had ridden around the big island (Hawaii) on horseback and had brought back so many saddle boils that if there had been a duty on them it would have bankrupted me to pay it. They kept me in my room, unclothed, and in persistent pain for two weeks, with no company but cigars and the little volume of poems. Of course I read them almost constantly; I read them from beginning to end, then read them backwards, then began in the middle and read them both ways, then read them wrong end first and upside down. In a word, I read the book to rags, and was infinitely grateful to the hand that wrote it.

Here we have an exhibition of what repetition can do, when persisted in daily and hourly over a considerable stretch of time, where one is merely reading for entertainment, without thought or intention of preserving in the memory that which is read. It is a process which in the course of years dries all the juice out of a familiar verse of Scripture, leaving nothing but a sapless husk behind. In that case you at least know the origin of the husk, but in the case in point I apparently preserved the husk but presently forgot whence it came. It lay lost in some dim corner of my memory a year or two, then came forward when I needed a dedication, and was promptly mistaken by me as a child of my own happy fancy.

I was new, I was ignorant, the mysteries of the human mind were a sealed book to me as yet, and I stupidly looked upon myself as a tough and unforgivable criminal. I wrote to Dr. Holmes and told him the whole disgraceful affair, implored him in impassioned language to believe that I had never intended to commit this crime, and was unaware that I had committed it until I was confronted with the awful evidence. I have lost his answer, I could better have afforded to lose an uncle. Of these I had a surplus, many of them of no real value to me, but that letter was beyond price, beyond uncledom, and unsparable. In it Dr. Holmes laughed the kindest and healingest laugh over the whole matter, and at considerable length and in happy phrase assured me that there was no crime in unconscious plagiarism; that I committed it every day, that he committed it every day, that every man alive on the earth who writes or speaks commits it every day and not merely once or twice but every time he opens his mouth; that all our phrasings are spiritualized shadows cast multitudinously from our readings; that no happy phrase of ours is ever quite original with us, there is nothing of our own in it except some slight change born of our temperament, character, environment, teachings and associations; that this slight change differentiates it from another man's manner of saying it, stamps it with our special style, and makes it our own for the time being; all the rest of it being old, moldy, antique, and smelling of the breath of a thousand generations of them that have passed it over their teeth before!

In the thirty-odd years which have come and gone since then, I have satisfied myself that what Dr. Holmes said was true.

I wish to make a note upon the preface of the "Innocents." In the last paragraph of that brief preface, I speak of the proprietors of the "Daily Alta California" having "waived their rights" in certain letters which I wrote for that journal while absent on the "Quaker City" trip. I was young then, I am white-headed now, but the insult of that word rankles yet, now that I am reading that paragraph for the first time in many years, reading it for the first time since it was written, perhaps. There were rights, it is true—such rights as the strong are able to acquire over the weak and the absent. Early in '66 George Barnes invited me to resign my reportership on his paper, the San Francisco "Morning Call," and for some months thereafter I was without money or work; then I had a pleasant turn of fortune. The proprietors of the "Sacramento Union," a great and influential daily journal, sent me to the Sandwich Islands to write four letters a month at twenty dollars apiece. I was there four or five months, and returned to find myself about the best known honest man on the Pacific Coast. Thomas McGuire, proprietor of several theatres, said that now was the time to make my fortune—strike while the iron was hot!—break into the lecture field! I did it. I announced a lecture on the Sandwich Islands, closing the advertisement with the remark, "Admission one dollar; doors open at half-past 7, the trouble begins at 8." A true prophecy. The trouble certainly did begin at 8, when I found myself in front of the only audience I had ever faced, for the fright which pervaded me from head to foot was paralyzing. It lasted two minutes and was as bitter as death, the memory of it is indestructible, but it had its compensations, for it made me immune from timidity before audiences for all time to come. I lectured in all the principal Californian towns and in Nevada, then lectured once or twice more in San Francisco, then retired from the field rich—for me—and laid out a plan to sail Westward from San Francisco, and go around the world. The proprietors of the "Alta" engaged me to write an account of the trip for that paper—fifty letters of a column and a half each, which would be about two thousand words per letter, and the pay to be twenty dollars per letter.

I went East to St. Louis to say good-bye to my mother, and then I was bitten by the prospectus of Captain Duncan of the "Quaker City" excursion, and I ended by joining it. During the trip I wrote and sent the fifty letters; six of them miscarried, and I wrote six new ones to complete my contract. Then I put together a lecture on the trip and delivered it in San Francisco at great and satisfactory pecuniary profit, then I branched out into the country and was aghast at the result: I had been entirely forgotten, I never had people enough in my houses to sit as a jury of inquest on my lost reputation! I inquired into this curious condition of things and found that the thrifty owners of that prodigiously rich "Alta" newspaper had *copy-righted* all those poor little twenty-dollar letters, and had threatened with prosecution any journal which should venture to copy a paragraph from them!

And there I was! I had contracted to furnish a large book, concerning the excursion, to the American Publishing Co. of Hartford, and I supposed I should need all those letters to fill it out with. I was in an uncomfortable situation—that is, if the proprietors of this stealthily acquired copyright should refuse to let me use the letters. That is just what they did; Mr. Mac—something—I have forgotten the rest of his name—said his firm were going to make a book out of the letters in order to get back the thousand dollars which they had paid for them. I said that if they had acted fairly and honorably, and had allowed the country press to use the letters or portions of them, my lecture-skirmish on the coast would have paid me ten thousand dollars, whereas the "Alta" had lost me that amount. Then he offered a compromise: he would publish the book and allow me ten per cent. royalty on it. The compromise did not appeal to me, and I said so. I was now quite unknown outside of San Francisco, the book's sale would be confined to that city, and my royalty would not pay me enough to board me three months; whereas my Eastern contract, if carried out, could be profitable to me, for I had a sort of reputation on the Atlantic seaboard acquired through the publication of six excursion-letters in the New York "Tribune" and one or two in the "Herald."

In the end Mr. Mac agreed to suppress his book, on certain conditions: in my preface I must thank the "Alta" for waiving its "rights" and granting me permission. I objected to the thanks. I could not with any large degree of sincerity thank the "Alta" for bankrupting my lecture-raid. After considerable debate my point was conceded and the thanks left out.

Noah Brooks was the editor of the "Alta" at the time, a man of sterling character and equipped with a right heart, also a good historian where facts were not essential. In biographical sketches of me written many years afterward (1902), he was quite eloquent in praises of the generosity of the "Alta" people in giving to me without compensation a book which, as history had afterward shown, was worth a fortune. After all the fuss, I did not levy heavily upon the "Alta" letters. I found that they were newspaper matter, not book matter. They had been written here and there and yonder, as opportunity had given me a chance working-moment or two during our feverish flight around about Europe or in the furnace-heat of my state-room on board the "Quaker City," therefore they were loosely constructed, and needed to have some of the wind and water squeezed out of them. I used several of them—ten or twelve, perhaps. I wrote the rest of "The Innocents Abroad" in sixty days, and I could have added a fortnight's labor with the pen and gotten along without the letters altogether. I was very young in those days, exceedingly young, marvellously young, younger than I am now, younger than I shall ever be again, by hundreds of years. I worked every night from eleven or twelve until broad day in the morning, and as I did two hundred thousand words in the sixty days, the average was more than three thousand words a day—nothing for Sir Walter Scott, nothing for Louis Stevenson, nothing for plenty of other people, but quite handsome for me. In 1897, when we were living in Tedworth Square, London, and I was writing the book called "Following the Equator" my average was eighteen hundred words a day; here in Florence (1904), my average seems to be fourteen hundred words per sitting of four or five hours.*

I was deducing from the above that I have been slowing down steadily in these thirty-six years, but I perceive that my statistics have a defect: three thousand words in the spring of 1868 when I was working seven or eight or nine hours at a sitting has little or no advantage over the sitting of today, covering half the time and producing half the output. Figures often beguile me, particularly when I have the arranging of them myself; in which case the remark attributed to Disraeli would often apply with justice and force:

"There are three kinds of lies: lies, damned lies, and statistics."

[*Dictated, January 23, 1907.*]—The proverb says that Providence protects children and idiots. This is really true. I know it because I have tested it. It did not protect George through the most of his campaign, but it saved him in his last inning, and the veracity of the proverb stood confirmed.

I have several times been saved by this mysterious interposition, when I was manifestly in extreme peril. It has been common, all my life, for smart people to perceive in me an easy prey for selfish designs, and I have walked without suspicion into the trap set for me, yet have often come out unscathed, against all the likelihoods. More than forty years ago, in San Francisco, the office staff adjourned, upon conclusion of its work at two o'clock in the morning, to a great bowling establishment where there were twelve alleys. I was invited, rather perfunctorily, and as a matter of etiquette—by which I mean that I was invited politely, but not urgently. But when I diffi-

---

* With the pen, I mean. This Autobiography is dictated, not written.

dently declined, with thanks, and explained that I knew nothing about the game, those lively young fellows became at once eager and anxious and urgent to have my society. This flattered me, for I perceived no trap, and I innocently and gratefully accepted their invitation. I was given an alley all to myself. The boys explained the game to me, and they also explained to me that there would be an hour's play, and that the player who scored the fewest ten-strikes in the hour would have to provide oysters and beer for the combination. This disturbed me very seriously, since it promised me bankruptcy, and I was sorry that this detail had been overlooked in the beginning. But my pride would not allow me to back out now, so I stayed in, and did what I could to look satisfied and glad I had come. It is not likely that I looked as contented as I wanted to, but the others looked glad enough to make up for it, for they were quite unable to hide their evil joy. They showed me how to stand, and how to stoop, and how to aim the ball, and how to let fly; and then the game began. The results were astonishing. In my ignorance I delivered the balls in apparently every way except the right one; but no matter—during half an hour I never started a ball down the alley that didn't score a ten-strike, every time, at the other end. The others lost their grip early, and their joy along with it. Now and then one of them got a ten-strike, but the occurrence was so rare that it made no show alongside of my giant score. The boys surrendered at the end of the half-hour, and put on their coats and gathered around me and in courteous, but sufficiently definite, language expressed their opinion of an experience-worn and seasoned expert who would stoop to lying and deception in order to rob kind and well-meaning friends who had put their trust in him under the delusion that he was an honest and honorable person. I was not able to convince them that I had not lied, for now my character was gone, and they refused to attach any value to anything I said. The proprietor of the place stood by for a while saying nothing, then he came to my defence. He said: "It looks like a mystery, gentlemen, but it isn't a mystery after it's explained. That is a *grooved* alley; you've only to start a ball down it any way you please and the groove will do the rest; it will slam the ball against the northeast curve of the head pin every time, and nothing can save the ten from going down."

It was true. The boys made the experiment and they found that there was no art that could send a ball down that alley and fail to score a ten-strike with it. When I had told those boys that I knew nothing about that game I was speaking only the truth; but it was ever thus, all through my life: whenever I have diverged from custom and principle and uttered a truth, the rule has been that the hearer hadn't strength of mind enough to believe it.

A quarter of a century ago I arrived in London to lecture a few weeks under the management of George Dolby, who had conducted the Dickens readings in America five or six years before. He took me to the Albemarle and fed me, and in the course of the dinner he enlarged a good deal, and with great satisfaction, upon his reputation as a player of fifteen-ball pool, and when he learned by my testimony that I had never seen the game played, and knew nothing of the art of pocketing balls, he enlarged more and more, and still more, and kept on enlarging, until I recognized that I was either in the presence of the very father of fifteen-ball pool or in the presence of his most immediate descendant. At the end of the dinner Dolby was eager to introduce me to the game and show me what he could do. We adjourned to the billiard-room and he framed the balls in a flat pyramid and told me to fire at the apex ball and then go on and do what I could toward pocketing the fifteen, after which he would take the cue and show me what a past-master of the game could do with those balls. I did as required. I began with the diffidence proper to my ignorant estate, and when I had finished my inning all the balls were in the pockets and Dolby was burying me under a volcanic irruption of acid sarcasms.

So I was a liar in Dolby's belief. He thought he had been sold, and at a cheap rate; but he divided his sarcasms quite fairly and quite equally between the two of us. He was full of ironical admiration of his childishness and innocence in letting a wandering and characterless and scandalous American load him up with deceptions of so transparent a character that they ought not to have deceived the house cat. On the other hand, he was remorselessly severe upon me for beguiling him, by studied and discreditable artifice, into bragging and boasting about his poor game in the presence of a professional expert disguised in lies and frauds, who could empty more balls in billiard pockets in an hour than he could empty into a basket in a day.

In the matter of fifteen-ball pool I never got Dolby's confidence wholly back, though I got it in other ways, and kept it until his death. I have played that game a number of times since, but that first time was the only time in my life that I have ever pocketed all the fifteen in a single inning.

My unsuspicious nature has made it necessary for Providence to save me from traps a number of times. Thirty years ago, a couple of Elmira bankers invited me to play the game of "Quaker" with them. I had never heard of the game before, and said that if it required intellect, I should not be able to entertain them. But they said it was merely a game of chance, and required no mentality—so I agreed to make a trial of it. They appointed four in the afternoon for the sacrifice. As the place, they chose a ground-floor room with a large window in it. Then they went treacherously around and advertised the "sell" which they were going to play upon me.

I arrived on time, and we began the game—with a large and eager free-list to superintend it. These superintendents were outside, with their noses pressed against the window-pane. The bankers described the game to me. So far as I recollect, the pattern of it was this: they had a pile of Mexican dollars on the table; twelve of them were of even date, fifty of them were of odd dates. The bankers were to separate a coin from the pile and hide it under a hand, and I must guess "odd" or "even." If I guessed correctly, the coin would be mine; if incorrectly, I lost a dollar. The first guess I made was "even," and was right. I guessed again, "even," and took the money. They fed me another one and I guessed "even" again, and took the money. I guessed "even" the fourth time, and took the money. It seemed to me that "even" was a good guess, and I might as well stay by it, which I did. I guessed "even" twelve times, and took the twelve dollars. I was doing as they secretly desired. Their experience of human nature had convinced them that any human being as innocent as my face proclaimed me to be, would repeat his first guess if it won, and would go on repeating it if it should continue to win. It was their belief that an innocent would be almost sure at the beginning to guess "even," and not "odd," and that if an innocent should guess "even" twelve times in succession and win every time, he would go on guessing "even" to the end—so it was their purpose to let me win those twelve even dates and then advance the odd dates, one by one, until I should lose fifty dollars, and furnish those superintendents something to laugh about for a week to come.

But it did not come out in that way; for by the time I had won the twelfth dollar and last even date, I withdrew from the game because it was so one-sided that it was monotonous, and did not entertain me. There was a burst of laughter from the superintendents at the window when I came out of the place, but I did not know what they were laughing at nor whom they were laughing at, and it was a matter of no interest to me anyway. Through that incident I acquired an enviable reputation for smartness and penetration, but it was not my due, for I had not penetrated anything that the cow could not have penetrated.

MARK TWAIN

(to be continued)

North American Review

No. DCXX.

AUGUST 2, 1907

CHAPTERS FROM MY
AUTOBIOGRAPHY—XXI

BY MARK TWAIN

PREFATORY NOTE—Mr. Clemens began to write his
autobiography many years ago, and he continues to add to
it day by day. It was his original intention to permit no
publication of his memoirs until after his death; but, after
leaving "Pier No. 70," he concluded that a considerable
portion might now suitably be given to the public. It is that
portion, garnered from the quarter-million of words
already written, which will appear in this REVIEW during
the present year. No part of the autobiography will be
published in book form during the lifetime of the author.
—EDITOR N. A. R.

FROM SUSY'S BIOGRAPHY OF ME

Feb. 12, '86.

Mamma and I have both been very much troubled of late
because papa since he has been publishing Gen. Grant's book
has seemed to forget his own books and work entirely, and the
other evening as papa and I were promonading up and down the
library he told me that he didn't expect to write but one more
book, and then he was ready to give up work altogether, die, or
do anything, he said that he had written more than he had ever
expected to, and the only book that he had been pertickularly
anxious to write was one locked up in the safe down stairs, not
yet published.

But this intended future of course will never do, and although papa usually holds to his own opinions and intents with outsiders, when mamma realy desires anything and says that it must be, papa allways gives up his plans (at least so far) and does as she says is right (and she is usually right, if she dissagrees with him at all). It was because he knew his great tendency to being convinced by her, that he published without her knowledge that article in the "Christian Union" concerning the government of children. So judging by the proofs of past years, I think that we will be able to persuade papa to go back to work as before, and not leave off writing with the end of his next story. Mamma says that she sometimes feels, and I do too, that she would rather have papa depend on his writing for a living than to have him think of giving it up.

[*Dictated, November 8, 1906.*] I have a defect of a sort which I think is not common; certainly I hope it isn't: it is rare that I can call before my mind's eye the form and face of either friend or enemy. If I should make a list, now, of persons whom I know in America and abroad—say to the number of even an entire thousand—it is quite unlikely that I could reproduce five of them in my mind's eye. Of my dearest and most intimate friends, I could name eight whom I have seen and talked with four days ago, but when I try to call them before me they are formless shadows. Jean has been absent, this past eight or ten days, in the country, and I wish I could reproduce her in the mirror of my mind, but I can't do it.

It may be that this defect is not constitutional, but a result of lifelong absence of mind and indolent and inadequate observation. Once or twice in my life it has been an embarrassment to me. Twenty years ago, in the days of Susy's Biography of Me, there was a dispute one morning at the breakfast-table about the color of a neighbor's eyes. I was asked for a verdict, but had to confess that if that valued neighbor and old friend had eyes I was not sure that I had ever seen them. It was then mockingly suggested that perhaps I didn't even know the color of the eyes of my own family, and I was required to shut my own at once and testify. I was able to name the color of Mrs.

Clemens's eyes, but was not able to even suggest a color for Jean's, or Clara's, or Susy's.

All this talk is suggested by Susy's remark: "The other evening as papa and I were promonading up and down the library." Down to the bottom of my heart I am thankful that I can see *that* picture! And it is not dim, but stands out clear in the unfaded light of twenty-one years ago. In those days Susy and I used to "promonade" daily up and down the library, with our arms about each other's waists, and deal in intimate communion concerning affairs of State, or the deep questions of human life, or our small personal affairs.

It was quite natural that I should think I had written myself out when I was only fifty years old, for everybody who has ever written has been smitten with that superstition at about that age. Not even yet have I really written myself out. I have merely stopped writing because dictating is pleasanter work, and because dictating has given me a strong aversion to the pen, and because two hours of talking per day is enough, and because—But I am only damaging my mind with this digging around in it for pretexts where no pretext is needed, and where the simple truth is for this one time better than any invention, in this small emergency. I shall never finish my five or six unfinished books, for the reason that by forty years of slavery to the pen I have earned my freedom. I detest the pen and I wouldn't use it again to sign the death warrant of my dearest enemy.

[*Dictated, March 8, 1906.*] For thirty years, I have received an average of a dozen letters a year from strangers who remember me, or whose fathers remember me as boy and young man. But these letters are almost always disappointing. I have not known these strangers nor their fathers. I have not heard of the names they mention; the reminiscences to which they call attention have had no part in my experience; all of which means that these strangers have been mistaking me for somebody else. But at last I have the refreshment, this morning, of a letter from a man who deals in names that were familiar to me in my boyhood. The writer encloses a newspaper clipping which has been wandering through the press for four or five weeks, and he wants to know if Capt. Tonkray, lately deceased, was (as stated in the clipping) the original of "Huckleberry Finn."

I have replied that "Huckleberry Finn" was Frank F. As this inquirer evidently knew the Hannibal of the forties, he will easily recall Frank. Frank's father was at one time Town Drunkard, an exceedingly well-defined and unofficial office of those days. He succeeded "General" Gaines, and for a time he was sole and only incumbent of the office; but afterward Jimmy Finn proved competency and disputed the place with him, so we had two town drunkards at one time—and it made as much trouble in that village as Christendom experienced in the fourteenth century when there were two Popes at the same time.

In "Huckleberry Finn" I have drawn Frank exactly as he was. He was ignorant, unwashed, insufficiently fed; but he had as good a heart as ever any boy had. His liberties were totally unrestricted. He was the only really independent person—boy or man—in the community, and by consequence he was tranquilly and continuously happy, and was envied by all the rest of us. We liked him; we enjoyed his society. And as his society was forbidden us by our parents, the prohibition trebled and quadrupled its value, and therefore we sought and got more of his society than of any other boy's. I heard, four years ago, that he was Justice of the Peace in a remote village in the State of——, and was a good citizen and was greatly respected.

During Jimmy Finn's term he (Jimmy) was not exclusive; he was not finical; he was not hypercritical; he was largely and handsomely democratic—and slept in the deserted tan-yard with the hogs. My father tried to reform him once, but did not succeed. My father was not a professional reformer. In him the spirit of reform was spasmodic. It only broke out now and then, with considerable intervals between. Once he tried to reform Injun Joe. That also was a failure. It was a failure, and we boys were glad. For Injun Joe, drunk, was interesting and a benefaction to us, but Injun Joe, sober, was a dreary spectacle. We watched my father's experiments upon him with a good deal of anxiety, but it came out all right and we were satisfied.

Injun Joe got drunk oftener than before, and became intolerably interesting.

I think that in "Tom Sawyer" I starved Injun Joe to death in the cave. But that may have been to meet the exigencies of romantic literature. I can't remember now whether the real Injun Joe died in the cave or out of it, but I do remember that the news of his death reached me at a most unhappy time— that is to say, just at bedtime on a summer night when a prodigious storm of thunder and lightning accompanied by a deluging rain that turned the streets and lanes into rivers, caused me to repent and resolve to lead a better life. I can remember those awful thunder-bursts and the white glare of the lightning yet, and the wild lashing of the rain against the window-panes. By my teachings I perfectly well knew what all that wild riot was for—Satan had come to get Injun Joe. I had no shadow of doubt about it. It was the proper thing when a person like Injun Joe was required in the under world, and I should have thought it strange and unaccountable if Satan had come for him in a less impressive way. With every glare of lightning I shrivelled and shrunk together in mortal terror, and in the interval of black darkness that followed I poured out my lamentings over my lost condition, and my supplications for just one more chance, with an energy and feeling and sincerity quite foreign to my nature.

But in the morning I saw that it was a false alarm and concluded to resume business at the old stand and wait for another reminder.

The axiom says "History repeats itself." A week or two ago Mr. Blank-Blank dined with us. At dinner he mentioned a circumstance which flashed me back over about sixty years and landed me in that little bedroom on that tempestuous night, and brought to my mind how creditable to me was my conduct through the whole night, and how barren it was of moral spot or fleck during that entire period: he said Mr. X was sexton, or something, of the Episcopal church in his town, and had been for many years the competent superintendent of all the church's worldly affairs, and was regarded by the whole congregation as a stay, a blessing, a priceless treasure. But he had a couple of defects—not large defects, but they seemed large when flung against the background of his profoundly religious character: he drank a good deal, and he could outswear a brakeman. A movement arose to persuade him to lay aside these vices, and after consulting with his pal, who occupied the same position as himself in the other Episcopal church, and whose defects were duplicates of his own and had inspired regret in the congregation he was serving, they concluded to try for reform— not wholesale, but half at a time. They took the liquor pledge and waited for results. During nine days the results were entirely satisfactory, and they were recipients of many compliments and much congratulation. Then on New-year's eve they had business a mile and a half out of town, just beyond the State line. Everything went well with them that evening in the barroom of the inn—but at last the celebration of the occasion by those villagers came to be of a burdensome nature. It was a bitter cold night and the multitudinous hot toddies that were circulating began by and by to exert a powerful influence upon the new prohibitionists. At last X's friend remarked,

"X, does it occur to you that we are *outside the diocese?*"

That ended reform No. 1. Then they took a chance in reform No. 2. For a while that one prospered, and they got much applause. I now reach the incident which sent me back a matter of sixty years, as I have remarked a while ago.

One morning Mr. Blank-Blank met X on the street and said,

"You have made a gallant struggle against those defects of yours. I am aware that you failed on No. 1, but I am also aware that you are having better luck with No. 2."

"Yes," X said; "No. 2 is all right and sound up to date, and we are full of hope."

Blank-Blank said, "X, of course you have your troubles like other people, but they never show on the outside. I have never seen you when you were not cheerful. Are you always cheerful? Really always cheerful?"

"Well, no," he said, "no, I can't say that I am always cheerful, but—well, you know that kind of a night that comes: *say*—you wake up 'way in the night and the whole world is sunk in gloom and there are storms and earthquakes and all sorts of disasters in the air threatening, and you get cold and clammy; and when that happens to me I recognize how sinful I am and it all goes clear to my heart and wrings it and I have such terrors and terrors!—oh, they are indescribable, those terrors that assail me, and I slip out of bed and get on my knees and pray and pray and promise that I *will* be good, if I can only have another chance. And then, you know, in the morning the sun shines out *so* lovely, and the birds sing and the whole world is so beautiful, and—*b' God, I rally!*"

Now I will quote a brief paragraph from this letter which I have a minute ago spoken of. The writer says:

> You no doubt are at a loss to know who I am. I will tell you. In my younger days I was a resident of Hannibal, Mo., and you and I were schoolmates attending Mr. Dawson's school along with Sam and Will Bowen and Andy Fuqua and others whose names I have forgotten. I was then about the smallest boy in school, for my age, and they called me little Aleck for short.

I only dimly remember him, but I knew those other people as well as I knew the town drunkards. I remember Dawson's schoolhouse perfectly. If I wanted to describe it I could save myself the trouble by conveying the description of it to these pages from "Tom Sawyer." I can remember the drowsy and inviting summer sounds that used to float in through the open windows from that distant boy-Paradise, Cardiff Hill (Holliday's Hill), and mingle with the murmurs of the studying pupils and make them the more dreary by the contrast. I remember Andy Fuqua, the oldest pupil—a man of twenty-five. I remember the youngest pupil, Nannie Owsley, a child of seven. I remember George Robards, eighteen or twenty years old, the only pupil who studied Latin. I remember—in some cases vividly, in others vaguely—the rest of the twenty-five boys and girls. I remember Mr. Dawson very well. I remember his boy, Theodore, who was as good as he could be. In fact, he was inordinately good, extravagantly good, offensively good, detestably good—and he had pop-eyes—and I would have drowned him if I had had a chance. In that school we were all about on an equality, and, so far as I remember, the passion of envy had no place in our hearts, except in the case of Arch Fuqua—the other one's brother. Of course we all went barefoot in the summer-time. Arch Fuqua was about my own age—ten or eleven. In the winter we could stand him, because he wore shoes then, and his great gift was hidden from our sight and we were enabled to forget it. But in the summer-time he was a bitterness to us. He was our envy, for he could double back his big toe and let it fly and you could hear it snap thirty yards. There was not another boy in the school that could approach this feat. He had not a rival as regards a physical distinction—except in Theodore Eddy, who could work his ears like a horse. But he was no real rival, because you couldn't hear him work his ears; so all the advantage lay with Arch Fuqua.

I am not done with Dawson's school; I will return to it in a later chapter.

[*Dictated at Hamilton, Bermuda, January 6, 1907.*] "That reminds me." In conversation we are always using that phrase, and seldom or never noticing how large a significance it bears. It stands for a curious and interesting fact, to wit: that sleeping or waking, dreaming or talking, the thoughts which swarm through our heads are almost constantly, almost continuously, accompanied by a like swarm of reminders of incidents and episodes of our past. A man can never know what a large traffic this commerce of association carries on in our minds until he sets out to write his autobiography; he then finds that a thought is seldom born to him that does not immediately remind him of some event, large or small, in his past experience. Quite naturally these remarks remind me of various things, among others this: that sometimes a thought, by the power of association, will bring back to your mind a lost word or a lost name which you have not been able to recover by any other process known to your mental equipment. Yesterday we had an instance of this. Rev. Joseph H. Twichell is with me on this flying trip to Bermuda. He was with me on my last visit to Bermuda, and to-day we were trying to remember when it was. We thought it was somewhere in the neighborhood of thirty years ago, but that was as near as we could get at the date. Twichell said that the landlady in whose boarding-house we sojourned in that ancient time could doubtless furnish us the date, and we must look her up. We wanted to see her, any-way, because she and her blooming daughter of eighteen were the only persons whose acquaintance we had made at that time, for we were travelling under fictitious names, and people who wear aliases are not given to seeking society and bringing themselves under suspicion. But at this point in our talk we encountered an obstruction: we could not recall the landlady's name. We hunted all around through our minds for that name, using all the customary methods of research, but without suc-cess; the name was gone from us, apparently permanently. We finally gave the matter up, and fell to talking about something else. The talk wandered from one subject to another, and finally arrived at Twichell's school-days in Hartford—the Hartford of something more than half a century ago—and he mentioned several of his schoolmasters, dwelling with special interest upon the peculiarities of an aged one named Olney. He remarked that Olney, humble village schoolmaster as he was, was yet a man of superior parts, and had published text-books which had enjoyed a wide currency in America in their day. I said I remembered those books, and had studied Olney's Geography in school when I was a boy. Then Twichell said,

"That reminds me—our landlady's name was a name that was associated with school-books of some kind or other fifty or sixty years ago. I wonder what it was. I believe it began with K."

Association did the rest, and did it instantly. I said,

"Kirkham's Grammar!"

That settled it. Kirkham was the name; and we went out to seek for the owner of it. There was no trouble about that, for Bermuda is not large, and is like the earlier Garden of Eden, in that everybody in it knows everybody else, just as it was in the serpent's headquarters in Adam's time. We easily found Miss Kirkham—she that had been the blooming girl of a generation before—and she was still keeping boarders; but her mother had passed from this life. She settled the date for us, and did it with certainty, by help of a couple of uncommon circumstances, events of that ancient time. She said we had sailed from Bermuda on the 24th of May, 1877, which was the day on which her only nephew was born—and he is now thirty years of age. The other unusual circumstance—she called it an unusual circumstance, and I didn't say anything—was that on that day the Rev. Mr. Twichell (bearing the assumed name of Peters) had made a statement to her which she regarded as a fiction. I remembered the circumstance very well. We had bidden the young girl good-by and had gone fifty yards, perhaps, when Twichell said he had forgotten something (I doubted it) and must go back. When he rejoined me he was silent, and this alarmed me, because I had not seen an example of it before. He seemed quite uncomfortable, and I asked him what the trouble was. He said he had been inspired to give the girl a pleasant surprise, and so had gone back and said to her—

"That young fellow's name is not Wilkinson—that's Mark Twain."

She did not lose her mind; she did not exhibit any excitement at all, but said quite simply, quite tranquilly,

"Tell it to the marines, Mr. Peters—if that should happen to be *your* name."

It was very pleasant to meet her again. We were white-headed, but she was not; in the sweet and unvexed spiritual atmosphere of the Bermudas one does not achieve gray hairs at forty-eight.

I had a dream last night, and of course it was born of association, like nearly everything else that drifts into a person's head, asleep or awake. On board ship, on the passage down, Twichell was talking about the swiftly developing possibilities of aerial navigation, and he quoted those striking verses of Tennyson's which forecast a future when air-borne vessels of war shall meet and fight above the clouds and redden the earth below with a rain of blood. This picture of carnage and blood and death reminded me of something which I had read a fortnight ago—statistics of railway accidents compiled by the United States Government, wherein the appalling fact was set forth that on our 200,000 miles of railway we annually kill

10,000 persons outright and injure 80,000. The war-ships in the air suggested the railway horrors, and three nights afterward the railway horrors suggested my dream. The work of association was going on in my head, unconsciously, all that time. It was an admirable dream, what there was of it.

In it I saw a funeral procession; I saw it from a mountain peak; I saw it crawling along and curving here and there, serpentlike, through a level vast plain. I seemed to see a hundred miles of the procession, but neither the beginning of it nor the end of it was within the limits of my vision. The procession was in ten divisions, each division marked by a sombre flag, and the whole represented ten years of our railway activities in the accident line; each division was composed of 80,000 cripples, and was bearing its own year's 10,000 mutilated corpses to the grave: in the aggregate 800,000 cripples and 100,000 dead, drenched in blood!

MARK TWAIN

(to be continued)

CHAPTERS FROM MY AUTOBIOGRAPHY—XXII

BY MARK TWAIN

PREFATORY NOTE—Mr. Clemens began to write his autobiography many years ago, and he continues to add to it day by day. It was his original intention to permit no publication of his memoirs until after his death; but, after leaving "Pier No. 70," he concluded that a considerable portion might now suitably be given to the public. It is that portion, garnered from the quarter-million of words already written, which will appear in this REVIEW during the present year. No part of the autobiography will be published in book form during the lifetime of the author. —EDITOR N. A. R.

[*Dictated, October 10, 1906.*] Susy has named a number of the friends who were assembled at Onteora at the time of our visit, but there were others—among them Laurence Hutton, Charles Dudley Warner, and Carroll Beckwith, and their wives. It was a bright and jolly company. Some of those choice spirits are still with us; the others have passed from this life: Mrs. Clemens, Susy, Mr. Warner, Mary Mapes Dodge, Laurence Hutton, Dean Sage—peace to their ashes! Susy is in error in thinking Mrs. Dodge was not there at that time; we were her guests.

We arrived at nightfall, dreary from a tiresome journey; but the dreariness did not last. Mrs. Dodge had provided a home-made banquet, and the happy company sat down to it, twenty strong, or more. Then the thing happened which always happens at large dinners, and is always exasperating: everybody talked to his elbow-mates and all talked at once, and gradually raised their voices higher, and higher, and higher, in the desperate effort to be heard. It was like a riot, an insurrection; it was an intolerable volume of noise. Presently I said to the lady next me—

"I will subdue this riot, I will silence this racket. There is only one way to do it, but I know the art. You must tilt your head toward mine and seem to be deeply interested in what I am saying; I will talk in a low voice; then, just because our neighbors won't be able to hear me, they will *want* to hear me. If I mumble long enough—say two minutes—you will see that the dialogues will one after another come to a standstill, and there will be silence, not a sound anywhere but my mumbling."

Then in a very low voice I began:

"When I went out to Chicago, eleven years ago, to witness the Grant festivities, there was a great banquet on the first night, with six hundred ex-soldiers present. The gentleman who sat next me was Mr. X. X. He was very hard of hearing, and he had a habit common to deaf people of shouting his remarks instead of delivering them in an ordinary voice. He would handle his knife and fork in reflective silence for five or six minutes at a time and then suddenly fetch out a shout that would make you jump out of the United States."

By this time the insurrection at Mrs. Dodge's table—at least that part of it in my immediate neighborhood—had died down, and the silence was spreading, couple by couple, down the long table. I went on in a lower and still lower mumble, and most impressively—

"During one of Mr. X. X.'s mute intervals, a man opposite us approached the end of a story which he had been telling his elbow-neighbor. He was speaking in a low voice—there was much noise—I was deeply interested, and straining my ears to catch his words, stretching my neck, holding my breath, to hear, unconscious of everything but the fascinating tale. I heard him say, 'At this point he seized her by her long hair— she shrieking and begging—bent her neck across his knee, and with one awful sweep of the razor—'

250   AUTOBIOGRAPHICAL WRITINGS

"HOW DO YOU LIKE CHICA-A-AGO?!!!"

That was X. X.'s interruption, hearable at thirty miles. By the time I had reached that place in my mumblings Mrs. Dodge's dining-room was so silent, so breathlessly still, that if you had dropped a thought anywhere in it you could have heard it smack the floor. When I delivered that yell the entire dinner company jumped as one person, and punched their heads through the ceiling, damaging it, for it was only lath and plaster, and it all came down on us, and much of it went into the victuals and made them gritty, but no one was hurt. Then I explained why it was that I had played that game, and begged them to take the moral of it home to their hearts and be rational and merciful thenceforth, and cease from screaming in mass, and agree to let one person talk at a time and the rest listen in grateful and unvexed peace. They granted my prayer, and we had a happy time all the rest of the evening; I do not think I have ever had a better time in my life. This was largely because the new terms enabled me to keep the floor—now that I had it—and do all the talking myself. I do like to hear myself talk. Susy has exposed this in her Biography of me.

Dean Sage was a delightful man, yet in one way a terror to his friends, for he loved them so well that he could not refrain from playing practical jokes on them. We have to be pretty deeply in love with a person before we can do him the honor of joking familiarly with him. Dean Sage was the best citizen I have known in America. It takes courage to be a good citizen, and he had plenty of it. He allowed no individual and no corporation to infringe his smallest right and escape unpunished. He was very rich, and very generous, and benevolent, and he gave away his money with a prodigal hand; but if an individual or corporation infringed a right of his, to the value of ten cents, he would spend thousands of dollars' worth of time and labor and money and persistence on the matter, and would not lower his flag until he had won his battle or lost it.

He and Rev. Mr. Harris had been classmates in college, and to the day of Sage's death they were as fond of each other as an engaged pair. It follows, without saying, that whenever Sage found an opportunity to play a joke upon Harris, Harris was sure to suffer.

Along about 1873 Sage fell a victim to an illness which reduced him to a skeleton, and defied all the efforts of the physicians to cure it. He went to the Adirondacks and took Harris with him. Sage had always been an active man, and he couldn't idle any day wholly away in inanition, but walked every day to the limit of his strength. One day, toward nightfall, the pair came upon a humble log cabin which bore these words painted upon a shingle: "Entertainment for Man and Beast." They were obliged to stop there for the night, Sage's strength being exhausted. They entered the cabin and found its owner and sole occupant there, a rugged and sturdy and simple-hearted man of middle age. He cooked supper and placed it before the travellers—salt junk, boiled beans, corn bread and black coffee. Sage's stomach could abide nothing but the most delicate food, therefore this banquet revolted him, and he sat at the table unemployed, while Harris fed ravenously, limitlessly, gratefully; for he had been chaplain in a fighting regiment all through the war, and had kept in perfection the grand and uncritical appetite and splendid physical vigor which those four years of tough fare and activity had furnished him. Sage went supperless to bed, and tossed and writhed all night upon a shuck mattress that was full of attentive and interested corncobs. In the morning Harris was ravenous again, and devoured the odious breakfast as contentedly and as delightedly as he had devoured its twin the night before. Sage sat upon the porch, empty, and contemplated the performance and meditated revenge. Presently he beckoned to the landlord and took him aside and had a confidential talk with him. He said,

"I am the paymaster. What is the bill?"

"Two suppers, fifty cents; two beds, thirty cents; two breakfasts, fifty cents—total, a dollar and thirty cents."

Sage said, "Go back and make out the bill and fetch it to me here on the porch. Make it thirteen dollars."

"Thirteen dollars! Why, it's impossible! I am no robber. I am charging you what I charge everybody. It's a dollar and thirty cents, and that's all it is."

"My man, I've got something to say about this as well as you. It's thirteen dollars. You'll make out your bill for that, and you'll *take* it, too, or you'll not get a cent."

The man was troubled, and said, "I don't understand this. I can't make it out."

"Well, I understand it. I know what I am about. It's thirteen dollars, and I want the bill made out for that. There's no other terms. Get it ready and bring it out here. I will examine it and be outraged. You understand? I will dispute the bill. You must stand to it. You must refuse to take less. I will begin to lose my temper; you must begin to lose yours. I will call you hard names; you must answer with harder ones. I will raise my voice; you must raise yours. You must go into a rage—foam at the mouth, if you can; insert some soap to help it along. Now go along and follow your instructions."

The man played his assigned part, and played it well. He brought the bill and stood waiting for results. Sage's face began to cloud up, his eyes to snap, and his nostrils to inflate like a horse's; then he broke out with—

"*Thirteen dollars!* You mean to say that you charge thirteen dollars for these damned inhuman hospitalities of yours? Are you a professional buccaneer? Is it your custom to—"

The man burst in with spirit: "Now, I don't want any more out of you—that's a plenty. The bill is thirteen dollars and you'll *pay* it—that's all; a couple of characterless adventurers bilking their way through this country and attempting to dictate terms to a gentleman! a gentleman who received you supposing you were gentlemen yourselves, whereas in my opinion hell's full of—"

Sage broke in—

"Not another word of that!—I won't have it. I regard you as the lowest-down thief that ever—"

"Don't you use that word again! By ——, I'll take you by the neck and—"

Harris came rushing out, and just as the two were about to grapple he pushed himself between them and began to implore—

"Oh, Dean, don't, *don't*—now, Mr. Smith, control yourself! Oh, think of your family, Dean!—think what a scandal—"

But they burst out with maledictions, imprecations and all the hard names they could dig out of the rich accumulations of their educated memories, and in the midst of it the man shouted—

"When *gentlemen* come to this house, I treat them *as* gentlemen. When people come to this house with the ordinary appetites of gentlemen, I charge them a dollar and thirty cents for what I furnished you; but when a man brings a hell-fired Famine here that gorges a barrel of pork and four barrels of beans at two sittings—"

Sage broke in, in a voice that was eloquent with remorse and self-reproach, "I never thought of that, and I ask your pardon; I am ashamed of myself and of my friend. Here's your thirteen dollars, and my apologies along with it."

[*Dictated March 12, 1906.*] I have always taken a great interest in other people's duels. One always feels an abiding interest in any heroic thing which has entered into his own experience.

In 1878, fourteen years after my unmaterialized duel, Messieurs Fortu and Gambetta fought a duel which made heroes of both of them in France, but made them rather ridiculous throughout the rest of the world. I was living in Munich that fall and winter, and I was so interested in that funny tragedy that I wrote a long account of it, and it is in one of my books, somewhere—an account which had some inaccuracies in it, but as an exhibition of the *spirit* of that duel, I think it was correct and trustworthy. And when I was living in Vienna, thirty-four years after my ineffectual duel, my interest in that kind of incident was still strong; and I find here among my Autobiographical manuscripts of that day a chapter which I began concerning it, but did not finish. I wanted to finish it, but held it open in the hope that the Italian ambassador, M. Nigra, would find time to furnish me the *full* history of Señor Cavalotti's adventures in that line. But he was a busy man; there was always an interruption before he could get well started; so my hope was never fulfilled. The following is the unfinished chapter:

As concerns duelling. This pastime is as common in Austria to-day as it is in France. But with this difference, that here in the Austrian States the duel is dangerous, while in France it is not. Here it is tragedy, in France it is comedy; here it is a solemnity, there it is monkey-shines; here the duellist risks his life, there he does not even risk his shirt. Here he fights with pistol or sabre, in France with a hairpin—a blunt one. Here the desperately wounded man tries to walk to the hospital; there they paint the scratch so that they can find it again, lay the sufferer on a stretcher, and conduct him off the field with a band of music.

At the end of a French duel the pair hug and kiss and cry, and praise each other's valor; then the surgeons make an examination and pick out the scratched one, and the other one helps him on to the litter and pays his fare; and in return the scratched one treats to champagne and oysters in the evening, and then "the incident is closed," as the French say. It is all polite, and gracious, and pretty, and impressive. At the end of an Austrian duel the antagonist that is alive gravely offers his hand to the other man, utters some phrases of courteous regret, then bids him good-by and goes his way, and that incident also is closed. The French duellist is painstakingly protected from danger, by the rules of the game. His antagonist's weapon cannot reach so far as his body; if he get a scratch it will not be above his elbow. But in Austria the rules of the game do not provide against danger, they carefully provide *for* it, usually. Commonly the combat must be kept up until one of the men is disabled; a non-disabling slash or stab does not retire him.

For a matter of three months I watched the Viennese journals, and whenever a duel was reported in their telegraphic columns I scrap-booked it. By this record I find that duelling in Austria is not confined to journalists and old maids, as in France, but is indulged in by military men, journalists, students, physicians, lawyers, members of the legislature, and even the Cabinet, the Bench and the police. Duelling is forbidden by law; and so it seems odd to see the makers and administrators of the laws dancing on their work in this way. Some months ago Count Bodeni, at that time Chief of the Government, fought a pistol-duel here in the capital city of the Empire with representative

Wolf, and both of those distinguished Christians came near getting turned out of the Church—for the Church as well as the State forbids duelling.

In one case, lately, in Hungary, the police interfered and stopped a duel after the first innings. This was a sabre-duel between the chief of police and the city attorney. Unkind things were said about it by the newspapers. They said the police remembered their duty uncommonly well when their own officials were the parties concerned in duels. But I think the underlings showed good bread-and-butter judgment. If their superiors had carved each other well, the public would have asked, Where were the police? and their places would have been endangered; but custom does not require them to be around where mere unofficial citizens are explaining a thing with sabres.

There was another duel—a double duel—going on in the immediate neighborhood at the time, and in this case the police obeyed custom and did not disturb it. Their bread and butter was not at stake there. In this duel a physician fought a couple of surgeons, and wounded both—one of them lightly, the other seriously. An undertaker wanted to keep people from interfering, but that was quite natural again.

Selecting at random from my record, I next find a duel at Tarnopol between military men. An officer of the Tenth Dragoons charged an officer of the Ninth Dragoons with an offence against the laws of the card-table. There was a defect or a doubt somewhere in the matter, and this had to be examined and passed upon by a Court of Honor. So the case was sent up to Lemberg for this purpose. One would like to know what the defect was, but the newspaper does not say. A man here who has fought many duels and has a graveyard, says that probably the matter in question was as to whether the accusation was true or not; that if the charge was a very grave one—cheating, for instance—proof of its truth would rule the guilty officer out of the field of honor; the Court would not allow a gentleman to fight with such a person. You see what a solemn thing it is; you see how particular they are; any little careless act can lose you your privilege of getting yourself shot, here. The Court seems to have gone into the matter in a searching and careful fashion, for several months elapsed before it reached a decision. It then sanctioned a duel and the accused killed his accuser.

Next I find a duel between a prince and a major; first with pistols—no result satisfactory to either party; then with sabres, and the major badly hurt.

Next, a sabre-duel between journalists—the one a strong man, the other feeble and in poor health. It was brief; the strong one drove his sword through the weak one, and death was immediate.

Next, a duel between a lieutenant and a student of medicine. According to the newspaper report these are the details. The student was in a restaurant one evening: passing along, he halted at a table to speak with some friends; near by sat a dozen military men; the student conceived that one of these was "staring" at him; he asked the officer to step outside and explain. This officer and another one gathered up their caps and sabres and went out with the student. Outside—this is the student's account—the student introduced himself to the offending officer and said, "You seemed to stare at me"; for answer, the officer struck at the student with his fist; the student parried the blow; both officers drew their sabres and attacked the young fellow, and one of them gave him a wound on the left arm; then they withdrew. This was Saturday night. The duel followed on Monday, in the military riding-school—the customary duelling-ground all over Austria, apparently. The weapons were pistols. The duelling terms were somewhat beyond custom in the matter of severity, if I may gather that from the statement that the combat was fought *"unter sehr schweren Bedingungen"*—to wit, "Distance, 15 steps—with 3 steps advance." There was but one exchange of shots. The student was hit. "He put his hand on his breast, his body began to bend slowly forward, then collapsed in death and sank to the ground."

It is pathetic. There are other duels in my list, but I find in each and all of them one and the same ever-recurring defect— the *principals* are never present, but only their sham representatives. The *real* principals in any duel are not the duellists themselves, but their families. They do the mourning, the suffering, theirs is the loss and theirs the misery. They stake all that, the duellist stakes nothing but his life, and that is a trivial thing compared with what his death must cost those whom he leaves behind him. Challenges should not mention the duellist; he has nothing much at stake, and the real vengeance cannot reach him. The challenge should summon the offender's old gray mother, and his young wife and his little children,—these, or any to whom he is a dear and worshipped possession—and should say, "You have done me no harm, but I am the meek slave of a custom which requires me to crush the happiness out of your hearts and condemn you to years of pain and grief, in order that I may wash clean with your tears a stain which has been put upon me by another person."

The logic of it is admirable: a person has robbed me of a penny; I must beggar ten innocent persons to make good my loss. Surely nobody's "honor" is worth all that.

Since the duellist's family are the real principals in a duel, the State ought to compel them to be present at it. Custom, also, ought to be so amended as to require it; and without it no duel ought to be allowed to go on. If that student's unoffending mother had been present and watching the officer through her tears as he raised his pistol, he—why, he would have fired in the air. We know that. For we know how we are all made. Laws ought to be based upon the ascertained facts of our nature. It would be a simple thing to make a duelling law which would stop duelling.

As things are now, the mother is never invited. She submits to this; and without outward complaint, for she, too, is the vassal of custom, and custom requires her to conceal her pain when she learns the disastrous news that her son must go to the duelling-field, and by the powerful force that is lodged in habit and custom she is enabled to obey this trying requirement—a requirement which exacts a miracle of her, and gets it. Last January a neighbor of ours who has a young son in the army was wakened by this youth at three o'clock one morning, and she sat up in bed and listened to his message:

"I have come to tell you something, mother, which will distress you, but you must be good and brave, and bear it. I have been affronted by a fellow officer, and we fight at three this afternoon. Lie down and sleep, now, and think no more about it."

She kissed him good night and lay down paralyzed with grief and fear, but said nothing. But she did not sleep; she prayed and mourned till the first streak of dawn, then fled to the nearest church and implored the Virgin for help; and from that church she went to another and another and another; church after church, and still church after church, and so spent all the day until three o'clock on her knees in agony and tears; then dragged herself home and sat down comfortless and desolate, to count the minutes, and wait, with an outward show of calm, for what had been ordained for her—happiness, or endless misery. Presently she heard the clank of a sabre—she had not known before what music was in that sound!—and her son put his head in and said:

"X was in the wrong, and he apologized."

So that incident was closed; and for the rest of her life the mother will always find something pleasant about the clank of a sabre, no doubt.

In one of my listed duels—however, let it go, there is nothing particularly striking about it except that the seconds interfered. And prematurely, too, for neither man was dead. This was certainly irregular. Neither of the men liked it. It was a duel with cavalry sabres, between an editor and a lieutenant. The editor walked to the hospital, the lieutenant was carried. In this country an editor who can write well is valuable, but he is not likely to remain so unless he can handle a sabre with charm.

The following very recent telegram shows that also in France duels are humanely stopped as soon as they approach the (French) danger-point:

"*Reuter's Telegram.*—PARIS, *March 5.*—The duel between Colonels Henry and Picquart took place this morning in the Riding School of the Ecole Militaire, the doors of which were strictly guarded in order to prevent intrusion. The combatants, who fought with swords, were in position at ten o'clock.

"At the first reengagement Lieutenant-Colonel Henry was slightly scratched in the fore arm, and just at the same moment his own blade appeared to touch his adversary's neck. Senator Rane, who was Colonel Picquart's second, stopped the fight, but as it was found that his principal had not been touehed, the combat continued. A very sharp encounter ensued, in which Colonel Henry was wounded in the elbow, and the duel terminated."

After which, the stretcher and the band. In lurid contrast with this delicate flirtation, we have this fatal duel of day before yesterday in Italy, where the earnest Austrian duel is in vogue. I knew Cavalotti slightly, and this gives me a sort of personal interest in his duel. I first saw him in Rome several years ago. He was sitting on a block of stone in the Forum, and was writing something in his note-book—a poem or a challenge, or something like that—and the friend who pointed him out to me said, "That is Cavalotti—he has fought thirty duels; do not disturb him." I did not disturb him.

[*May 13, 1907.*] It is a long time ago. Cavalotti—poet, orator, satirist, statesman, patriot—was a great man, and his death was deeply lamented by his countrymen: many monuments to his memory testify to this. In his duels he killed several of his antagonists and disabled the rest. By nature he was a little irascible. Once when the officials of the library of Bologna threw out his books the gentle poet went up there and challenged the whole fifteen! His parliamentary duties were exacting, but he proposed to keep coming up and fighting duels between trains until all those officials had been retired from the activities of life. Although he always chose the sword to fight with, he had never had a lesson with that weapon. When game was called he waited for nothing, but always plunged at his opponent and rained such a storm of wild and original thrusts and whacks upon him that the man was dead or crippled before he could bring his science to bear. But his latest antagonist discarded science, and won. He held his sword straight forward like a lance when Cavalotti made his plunge—with the result that he impaled himself upon it. It entered his mouth and passed out at the back of his neck. Death was instantaneous.

[*Dictated December 20, 1906.*] Six months ago, when I was recalling early days in San Francisco, I broke off at a place where I was about to tell about Captain Osborn's odd adventure at the "What Cheer," or perhaps it was at another cheap feeding-place—the "Miners' Restaurant." It was a place where one could get good food on the cheapest possible terms, and its popularity was great among the multitudes whose purses were light. It was a good place to go to, to observe mixed humanity. Captain Osborn and Bret Harte went there one day and took a meal, and in the course of it Osborn fished up an interesting reminiscence of a dozen years before and told about it. It was to this effect:

He was a midshipman in the navy when the Californian gold craze burst upon the world and set it wild with excitement. His ship made the long journey around the Horn and was approaching her goal, the Golden Gate, when an accident happened.

"It happened to me," said Osborn. "I fell overboard. There was a heavy sea running, but no one was much alarmed about me, because we had on board a newly patented life-saving device which was believed to be competent to rescue anything that could fall overboard, from a midshipman to an anchor. Ours was the only ship that had this device; we were very proud of it, and had been anxious to give its powers a practical test. This thing was lashed to the garboard-strake of the main-to'gallant mizzen-yard amidships, and there was nothing to do but cut the lashings and heave it over; it would do the rest. One day the cry of 'Man overboard!' brought all hands on deck. Instantly the lashings were cut and the machine flung joyously over. Damnation, it went to the bottom like an anvil! By the time that the ship was brought to and a boat manned, I was become but a bobbing speck on the waves half a mile astern and losing my strength very fast; but by good luck there was a common seaman on board who had practical ideas in his head and hadn't waited to see what the patent machine was going to do, but had run aft and sprung over after me the moment the alarm was cried through the ship. I had a good deal of a start of him, and the seas made his progress slow and difficult, but he stuck to his work and fought his way to me, and just in the nick of time he put his saving arms about me when I was about to go down. He held me up until the boat reached us and rescued us. By that time I was unconscious, and I was still unconscious when we arrived at the ship. A dangerous fever followed, and I was delirious for three days; then I came to myself and at once inquired for my benefactor, of course. He was gone. We were lying at anchor in the Bay and every man had deserted to the gold-mines except the commissioned officers. I found out nothing about my benefactor but his name—Burton Sanders—a name which I have held in grateful memory ever since. Every time I have been on the Coast, these twelve or thirteen years, I have tried to get track of him, but have never succeeded. I wish I could find him and make him understand that his brave act has never been forgotten by me. Harte, I would rather see him and take him by the hand than any other man on the planet."

At this stage or a little later there was an interruption. A waiter near by said to another waiter, pointing,

"Take a look at that tramp that's coming in. Ain't that the one that bilked the house, last week, out of ten cents?"

"I believe it is. Let him alone—don't pay any attention to him; wait till we can get a good look at him."

The tramp approached timidly and hesitatingly, with the air of one unsure and apprehensive. The waiters watched him furtively. When he was passing behind Harte's chair one of them said,

"He's the one!"—and they pounced upon him and proposed to turn him over to the police as a bilk. He begged piteously. He confessed his guilt, but said he had been driven to his crime by necessity—that when he had eaten the plate of beans and slipped out without paying for it, it was because he was starving, and hadn't the ten cents to pay for it with. But the waiters would listen to no explanations, no palliations; he must be placed in custody. He brushed his hand across his eyes and said meekly that he would submit, being friendless. Each waiter took him by an arm and faced him about to conduct him away. Then his melancholy eyes fell upon Captain Osborn, and a light of glad and eager recognition flashed from them. He said,

"Weren't you a midshipman once, sir, in the old 'Lancaster'?"

"Yes," said Osborn. "Why?"

"Didn't you fall overboard?"

"Yes, I did. How do you come to know about it?"

"Wasn't there a new patent machine aboard, and didn't they throw it over to save you?"

"Why, yes," said Osborn, laughing gently, "but it didn't do it."

"No, sir, it was a sailor that done it."

"It certainly was. Look here, my man, you are getting distinctly interesting. Were you of our crew?"

"Yes, sir, I was."

"I reckon you may be right. You do certainly know a good deal about that incident. What is your name?"

"Burton Sanders."

The Captain sprang up, excited, and said,

"Give me your hand! Give me both your hands! I'd rather shake them than inherit a fortune!"—and then he cried to the waiters, "Let him go!—take your hands off! He is my guest, and can have anything and everything this house is able to furnish. I am responsible."

There was a love-feast, then. Captain Osborn ordered it regardless of expense, and he and Harte sat there and listened while the man told stirring adventures of his life and fed himself up to the eyebrows. Then Osborn wanted to be benefactor in his turn, and pay back some of his debt. The man said it could all be paid with ten dollars—that it had been so long since he had owned that amount of money that it would seem a fortune to him, and he should be grateful beyond words if the Captain could spare him that amount. The Captain spared him ten broad twenty-dollar gold pieces, and made him take them in spite of his modest protestations, and gave him his address and said he must never fail to give him notice when he needed grateful service.

Several months later Harte stumbled upon the man in the street. He was most comfortably drunk, and pleasant and chatty. Harte remarked upon the splendidly and movingly dramatic incident of the restaurant, and said,

"How curious and fortunate and happy and interesting it was that you two should come together, after that long separation, and at exactly the right moment to save you from disaster and turn your defeat by the waiters into a victory. A preacher could make a great sermon out of that, for it does look as if the hand of Providence was in it."

The hero's face assumed a sweetly genial expression, and he said,

"Well now, it wasn't Providence this time. I was running the arrangements myself."

"How do you mean?"

"Oh, I hadn't ever seen the gentleman before. I was at the next table, with my back to you the whole time he was telling about it. I saw my chance, and slipped out and fetched the two waiters with me and offered to give them a commission out of what I could get out of the Captain if they would do a quarrel act with me and give me an opening. So, then, after a minute or two I straggled back, and you know the rest of it as well as I do."

MARK TWAIN

(to be continued)

North American Review

No. DCXXIII.

OCTOBER, 1907

CHAPTERS FROM MY AUTOBIOGRAPHY—XXIII

BY MARK TWAIN

PREFATORY NOTE—Mr. Clemens began to write his autobiography many years ago, and he continues to add to it day by day. It was his original intention to permit no publication of his memoirs until after his death; but, after leaving "Pier No. 70," he concluded that a considerable portion might now suitably be given to the public. It is that portion, garnered from the quarter-million of words already written, which will appear in this REVIEW during the present year. No part of the autobiography will be published in book form during the lifetime of the author.—EDITOR N. A. R.

[*Dictated March 9, 1906.*] . . . I am talking of a time sixty years ago, and upwards. I remember the names of some of those schoolmates, and, by fitful glimpses, even their faces rise dimly before me for a moment—only just long enough to be recognized; then they vanish. I catch glimpses of George Robards, the Latin pupil—slender, pale, studious, bending over his book and absorbed in it, his long straight black hair hanging down below his jaws like a pair of curtains on the sides of his face. I can see him give his head a toss and flirt one of the curtains back around his head—to get it out of his way, apparently; really to show off. In that day it was a great thing among the boys to have hair of so flexible a sort that it could be flung back in that way, with a flirt of the head. George Robards was the envy of us all. For there was no hair among us that was so competent for this exhibition as his—except, perhaps, the yellow locks of Will Bowen and John Robards. My hair was a dense ruck of short curls, and so was my brother Henry's. We tried all kinds of devices to get these crooks straightened out so that they would flirt, but we never succeeded. Sometimes, by soaking our heads and then combing and brushing our hair down tight and flat to our skulls, we could get it straight, temporarily, and this gave us a comforting moment of joy; but the first time we gave it a flirt it all shrivelled into curls again and our happiness was gone.

John Robards was the little brother of George; he was a wee chap with silky golden curtains to his face which dangled to his shoulders and below, and could be flung back ravishingly. When he was twelve years old he crossed the plains with his father amidst the rush of the gold-seekers of '49; and I remember the departure of the cavalcade when it spurred westward. We were all there to see and to envy. And I can still see that proud little chap sailing by on a great horse, with his long locks streaming out behind. We were all on hand to gaze and envy when he returned, two years later, in unimaginable glory—*for he had travelled!* None of us had ever been forty miles from home. But he had crossed the Continent. He had been in the gold-mines, that fairyland of our imagination. And he had done a still more wonderful thing. He had been in ships—in ships on the actual ocean; in ships on three actual oceans. For he had sailed down the Pacific and around the Horn among icebergs and through snow-storms and wild wintry gales, and had sailed on and turned the corner and flown northward in the trades and up through the blistering equatorial waters—and there in his brown face were the proofs of what he had been through. We would have sold our souls to Satan for the privilege of trading places with him.

I saw him when I was out on that Missouri trip four years ago. He was old then—though not quite so old as I—and the burden of life was upon him. He said his granddaughter, twelve years old, had read my books and would like to see me.

It was a pathetic time, for she was a prisoner in her room and marked for death. And John knew that she was passing swiftly away. Twelve years old—just her grandfather's age when he rode away on that great journey with his yellow hair flapping behind him. In her I seemed to see that boy again. It was as if he had come back out of that remote past and was present before me in his golden youth. Her malady was heart disease, and her brief life came to a close a few days later.

Another of those schoolboys was John Garth. He became a prosperous banker and a prominent and valued citizen; and a few years ago he died, rich and honored. *He died.* It is what I have to say about so many of those boys and girls. The widow still lives, and there are grandchildren. In her pantalette days and my barefoot days she was a schoolmate of mine. I saw John's tomb when I made that Missouri visit.

Her father, Mr. Kercheval, had an apprentice in the early days when I was nine years old, and he had also a slave woman who had many merits. But I can't feel very kindly or forgivingly toward either that good apprentice boy or that good slave woman, for they saved my life. One day when I was playing on a loose log which I supposed was attached to a raft—but it wasn't—it tilted me into Bear Creek. And when I had been under water twice and was coming up to make the third and fatal descent my fingers appeared above the water and that slave woman seized them and pulled me out. Within a week I was in again, and that apprentice had to come along just at the wrong time, and he plunged in and dived, pawed around on the bottom and found me, and dragged me out and emptied the water out of me, and I was saved again. I was drowned seven times after that before I learned to swim—once in Bear Creek and six times in the Mississippi. I do not now know who the people were who interfered with the intentions of a Providence wiser than themselves, but I hold a grudge against them yet. When I told the tale of these remarkable happenings to Rev. Dr. Burton of Hartford, he said he did not believe it. *He slipped on the ice the very next year and sprained his ankle.*

Will Bowen was another schoolmate, and so was his brother, Sam, who was his junior by a couple of years. Before the Civil

War broke out, both became St. Louis and New Orleans pilots. Both are dead, long ago.

[*Dictated March 16, 1906.*] We will return to those school-children of sixty years ago. I recall Mary Miller. She was not my first sweetheart, but I think she was the first one that furnished me a broken heart. I fell in love with her when she was eighteen and I was nine, but she scorned me, and I recognized that this was a cold world. I had not noticed that temperature before. I believe I was as miserable as even a grown man could be. But I think that this sorrow did not remain with me long. As I remember it, I soon transferred my worship to Artimisia Briggs, who was a year older than Mary Miller. When I revealed my passion to her she did not scoff at it. She did not make fun of it. She was very kind and gentle about it. But she was also firm, and said she did not want to be pestered by children.

And there was Mary Lacy. She was a schoolmate. But she also was out of my class because of her advanced age. She was pretty wild and determined and independent. But she married, and at once settled down and became in all ways a model matron and was as highly respected as any matron in the town. Four years ago she was still living, and had been married fifty years.

Jimmie McDaniel was another schoolmate. His age and mine about tallied. His father kept the candy-shop and he was the most envied little chap in the town—after Tom Blankenship ("Huck Finn")—for although we never saw him eating candy, we supposed that it was, nevertheless, his ordinary diet. He pretended that he never ate it, and didn't care for it because there was nothing forbidden about it—there was plenty of it and he could have as much of it as he wanted. He was the first human being to whom I ever told a humorous story, so far as I can remember. This was about Jim Wolfe and the cats; and I gave him that tale the morning after that memorable episode. I thought he would laugh his teeth out. I had never been so proud and happy before, and have seldom been so proud and happy since. I saw him four years ago when I was out there. He wore a beard, gray and venerable, that came half-way down to his knees, and yet it was not difficult for me to recognize him.

He had been married fifty-four years. He had many children and grandchildren and great-grandchildren, and also even posterity, they all said—thousands—yet the boy to whom I had told the cat story when we were callow juveniles was still present in that cheerful little old man.

Artimisia Briggs got married not long after refusing me. She married Richmond, the stone mason, who was my Methodist Sunday-school teacher in the earliest days, and he had one distinction which I envied him: at some time or other he had hit his thumb with his hammer and the result was a thumb nail which remained permanently twisted and distorted and curved and pointed, like a parrot's beak. I should not consider it an ornament now, I suppose, but it had a fascination for me then, and a vast value, because it was the only one in the town. He was a very kindly and considerate Sunday-school teacher, and patient and compassionate, so he was the favorite teacher with us little chaps. In that school they had slender oblong pasteboard blue tickets, each with a verse from the Testament printed on it, and you could get a blue ticket by reciting two verses. By reciting five verses you could get three blue tickets, and you could trade these at the bookcase and borrow a book for a week. I was under Mr. Richmond's spiritual care every now and then for two or three years, and he was never hard upon me. I always recited the same five verses every Sunday. He was always satisfied with the performance. He never seemed to notice that these were the same five foolish virgins that he had been hearing about every Sunday for months. I always got my tickets and exchanged them for a book. They were pretty dreary books, for there was not a bad boy in the entire bookcase. They were *all* good boys and good girls and drearily uninteresting, but they were better society than none, and I was glad to have their company and disapprove of it.

Twenty years ago Mr. Richmond had become possessed of Tom Sawyer's cave in the hills three miles from town, and had made a tourist-resort of it. In 1849 when the gold-seekers were streaming through our little town of Hannibal, many of our grown men got the gold fever, and I think that all the boys had it. On the Saturday holidays in summer-time we used to borrow skiffs whose owners were not present and go down the river three miles to the cave hollow (Missourian for "valley"), and there we staked out claims and pretended to dig gold, panning out half a dollar a day at first; two or three times as much, later, and by and by whole fortunes, as our imaginations became inured to the work. Stupid and unprophetic lads! We were doing this in play and never suspecting. Why, that cave hollow and all the adjacent hills were made of gold! But we did not know it. We took it for dirt. We left its rich secret in its own peaceful possession and grew up in poverty and went wandering about the world struggling for bread—and this because we had not the gift of prophecy. That region was all dirt and rocks to us, yet all it needed was to be ground up and scientifically handled and it was gold. That is to say, the whole region was a cement-mine—and they make the finest kind of Portland cement there now, five thousand barrels a day, with a plant that cost $2,000,000.

For a little while Reuel Gridley attended that school of ours. He was an elderly pupil; he was perhaps twenty-two or twenty-three years old. Then came the Mexican War and he volunteered. A company of infantry was raised in our town and Mr. Hickman, a tall, straight, handsome athlete of twenty-five, was made captain of it and had a sword by his side and a broad yellow stripe down the leg of his gray pants. And when that company marched back and forth through the streets in its smart uniform—which it did several times a day for drill—its evolutions were attended by all the boys whenever the school hours permitted. I can see that marching company yet, and I can almost feel again the consuming desire that I had to join it. But they had no use for boys of twelve and thirteen, and before I had a chance in another war the desire to kill people to whom I had not been introduced had passed away.

I saw the splendid Hickman in his old age. He seemed about the oldest man I had ever seen—an amazing and melancholy contrast with the showy young captain I had seen preparing his warriors for carnage so many, many years before. Hickman is dead—it is the old story. As Susy said, "What is it all for?"

Reuel Gridley went away to the wars and we heard of him no more for fifteen or sixteen years. Then one day in Carson City while I was having a difficulty with an editor on the sidewalk—an editor better built for war than I was—I heard a voice say, "Give him the best you've got, Sam, I'm at your back." It was Reuel Gridley. He said he had not recognized me by my face but by my drawling style of speech.

He went down to the Reese River mines about that time and presently he lost an election bet in his mining camp, and by the terms of it he was obliged to buy a fifty-pound sack of self-raising flour and carry it through the town, preceded by music, and deliver it to the winner of the bet. Of course the whole camp was present and full of fluid and enthusiasm. The winner of the bet put up the sack at auction for the benefit of the United States Sanitary Fund, and sold it. The excitement grew and grew. The sack was sold over and over again for the benefit of the Fund. The news of it came to Virginia City by telegraph. It produced great enthusiasm, and Reuel Gridley was begged by telegraph to bring the sack and have an auction in Virginia City. He brought it. An open barouche was provided, also a brass band. The sack was sold over and over again at Gold Hill, then was brought up to Virginia City toward night and sold—and sold again, and again, and still again, netting twenty or thirty thousand dollars for the Sanitary Fund. Gridley carried it across California and sold it at various towns. He sold it for large sums in Sacramento and in San Francisco. He brought it East, sold it in New York and in various other cities, then carried it out to a great Fair at St. Louis, and went on selling it; and finally made it up into small cakes and sold those at a dollar apiece. First and last, the sack of flour which had originally cost ten dollars, perhaps, netted more than two hundred thousand dollars for the Sanitary Fund. Reuel Gridley has been dead these many, many years—it is the old story.

In that school were the first Jews I had ever seen. It took me a good while to get over the awe of it. To my fancy they were clothed invisibly in the damp and cobwebby mould of antiquity. They carried me back to Egypt, and in imagination I moved among the Pharaohs and all the shadowy celebrities of that remote age. The name of the boys was Levin. We had a collective name for them which was the only really large and handsome witticism that was ever born in that Congressional district. We called them "Twenty-two"—and even when the joke was old and had been worn threadbare we always followed it with the explanation, to make sure that it would be understood, "Twice Levin—twenty-two."

There were other boys whose names remain with me. Irving Ayres—but no matter, he is dead. Then there was George Butler, whom I remember as a child of seven wearing a blue leather belt with a brass buckle, and hated and envied by all the boys on account of it. He was a nephew of General Ben Butler and fought gallantly at Ball's Bluff and in several other actions of the Civil War. He is dead, long and long ago.

Will Bowen (dead long ago), Ed Stevens (dead long ago) and John Briggs were special mates of mine. John is still living.

In 1845, when I was ten years old, there was an epidemic of measles in the town and it made a most alarming slaughter among the little people. There was a funeral almost daily, and the mothers of the town were nearly demented with fright. My mother was greatly troubled. She worried over Pamela and Henry and me, and took constant and extraordinary pains to keep us from coming into contact with the contagion. But upon reflection I believed that her judgment was at fault. It seemed to me that I could improve upon it if left to my own devices. I cannot remember now whether I was frightened about the measles or not, but I clearly remember that I grew very tired of the suspense I suffered on account of being continually under the threat of death. I remember that I got so weary of it and so anxious to have the matter settled one way or the other, and promptly, that this anxiety spoiled my days and my nights. I had no pleasure in them. I made up my mind to end this suspense and be done with it. Will Bowen was dangerously ill with the measles and I thought I would go down there and catch them. I entered the house by the front way and slipped along through rooms and halls, keeping sharp watch against discovery, and at last I reached Will's bed-chamber in the rear of the house on the second floor and got into it uncaptured. But that was as far as my victory reached. His mother caught me there a moment later and snatched me out of the house and gave me a most competent scolding and drove me away. She was so scared that she could hardly get her words out, and her face was white. I saw that I must manage better next time, and I did. I hung about the lane at the rear of the house and watched through cracks in the fence until I was convinced that the conditions were favorable; then I slipped through the back yard and up the back way and got into the room and into the bed with Will Bowen without being observed. I don't know how long I was in the bed. I only remember that Will Bowen, as society, had no value for me, for he was too sick to even notice that I was there. When I heard his mother coming I covered up my head, but that device was a failure. It was dead summer-time—the cover was nothing more than a limp blanket or sheet, and anybody could see that there were two of us under it. It didn't remain two very long. Mrs. Bowen snatched me out of the bed and conducted me home herself, with a grip on my collar which she never loosened until she delivered me into my mother's hands along with her opinion of that kind of a boy.

It was a good case of measles that resulted. It brought me within a shade of death's door. It brought me to where I no longer took any interest in anything, but, on the contrary, felt a total absence of interest—which was most placid and enchanting. I have never enjoyed anything in my life any more than I enjoyed dying that time. I *was*, in effect, dying. The word had been passed and the family notified to assemble around the bed and see me off. I knew them all. There was no doubtfulness in my vision. They were all crying, but that did not affect me. I took but the vaguest interest in it, and that merely because I was the centre of all this emotional attention and was gratified by it and vain of it.

When Dr. Cunningham had made up his mind that nothing more could be done for me he put bags of hot ashes all over me. He put them on my breast, on my wrists, on my ankles; and so, very much to his astonishment—and doubtless to my regret—he dragged me back into this world and set me going again.

[*Dictated July 26, 1907.*] In an article entitled "England's Ovation to Mark Twain," Sydney Brooks—but never mind that, now.

I was in Oxford by seven o'clock that evening (June 25, 1907), and trying on the scarlet gown which the tailor had been constructing, and found it right—right and surpassingly becoming. At half past ten the next morning we assembled at All Souls College and marched thence, gowned, mortar-boarded and in double file, down a long street to the Sheldonian Theatre, between solid walls of the populace, very much hurrah'd and limitlessly kodak'd. We made a procession of considerable length and distinction and picturesqueness, with the Chancellor, Lord Curzon, late Viceroy of India, in his rich robe of black and gold, in the lead, followed by a pair of trim little boy train-bearers, and the train-bearers followed by the young Prince Arthur of Connaught, who was to be made a D.C.L. The detachment of D.C.L.'s were followed by the Doctors of Science, and these by the Doctors of Literature, and these in turn by the Doctors of Music. Sidney Colvin marched in front of me; I was coupled with Sidney Lee, and Kipling followed us; General Booth, of the Salvation Army, was in the squadron of D.C.L.'s.

Our journey ended, we were halted in a fine old hall whence we could see, through a corridor of some length, the massed audience in the theatre. Here for a little time we moved about and chatted and made acquaintanceships; then the D.C.L.'s were summoned, and they marched through that corridor and the shouting began in the theatre. It would be some time before the Doctors of Literature and of Science would be called for, because each of those D.C.L.'s had to have a couple of Latin speeches made over him before his promotion would be complete—one by the Regius Professor of Civil Law, the other by the Chancellor. After a while I asked Sir William Ramsay if a person might smoke here and not get shot. He said, "Yes," but that whoever did it and got caught would be fined a guinea, and perhaps hanged later. He said he knew of a place where we could accomplish at least as much as half of a smoke before any informers would be likely to chance upon us, and he was ready to show the way to any who might be willing to risk the guinea and the hanging. By request he led the way, and Kipling, Sir Norman Lockyer and I followed. We crossed an unpopulated quadrangle and stood under one of its exits—an archway of massive masonry—and there we lit up and began to take comfort. The photographers soon arrived, but they were courteous and friendly and gave us no trouble, and we gave them none. They grouped us in all sorts of ways and photographed us at their diligent leisure, while we smoked and talked. We were there more than an hour; then we returned to headquarters, happy, content, and greatly refreshed. Presently we filed into the theatre, under a very satisfactory hurrah, and waited in a crimson column, dividing the crowded pit through the middle, until each of us in his turn should be called to stand before the Chancellor and hear our merits set forth in sonorous Latin. Meantime, Kipling and I wrote autographs until some good kind soul interfered in our behalf and procured for us a rest.

I will now save what is left of my modesty by quoting a paragraph from Sydney Brooks's "Ovation."

* * *

Let those stars take the place of it for the present. Sydney Brooks has done it well. It makes me proud to read it; as proud as I was in that old day, sixty-two years ago, when I lay dying, the centre of attraction, with one eye piously closed upon the fleeting vanities of this life—an excellent effect—and the other open a crack to observe the tears, the sorrow, the admiration—all for me—all for me!

Ah, that was the proudest moment of my long life—until Oxford!

* * *

Most Americans have been to Oxford and will remember what a dream of the Middle Ages it is, with its crooked lanes, its gray and stately piles of ancient architecture and its meditation-breeding air of repose and dignity and unkinship with the noise and fret and hurry and bustle of these modern days. As a dream of the Middle Ages Oxford was not perfect until Pageant day arrived and furnished certain details which had been for generations lacking. These details began to appear at mid-afternoon on the 27th. At that time singles, couples, groups and squadrons of the three thousand five hundred costumed characters who were to take part in the Pageant began to ooze and drip and stream through house doors, all over the old town, and wend toward the meadows outside the walls. Soon the lanes were thronged with costumes which Oxford had from time to time seen and been familiar with in bygone centuries—fashions of dress which marked off centuries as by dates, and mile-stoned them back, and back, and back, until history faded into legend and tradition, when Arthur was a fact and the Round Table a reality. In this rich commingling of quaint and strange and brilliantly colored fashions in dress the dress-changes of Oxford for twelve centuries stood livid and realized to the eye; Oxford as a dream of the Middle Ages was complete now as it had never, in our day, before been complete; at last there was no discord; the mouldering old buildings, and the picturesque throngs drifting past them, were in harmony; soon—astonishingly soon!—the only persons that seemed out of place, and grotesquely and offensively and criminally out of place were such persons as came intruding along clothed in the ugly and odious fashions of the twentieth century; they were a bitterness to the feelings, an insult to the eye.

The make-ups of illustrious historic personages seemed perfect, both as to portraiture and costume; one had no trouble in recognizing them. Also, I was apparently quite easily recognizable myself. The first corner I turned brought me suddenly face to face with Henry VIII, a person whom I had been implacably disliking for sixty years; but when he put out his hand with royal courtliness and grace and said, "Welcome, well-beloved stranger, to my century and to the hospitalities of my realm," my old prejudices vanished away and I forgave him. I think now that Henry the Eighth has been over-abused, and that most of us, if we had been situated as he was, domestically, would not have been able to get along with as limited a graveyard as he forced himself to put up with. I feel now that he was one of the nicest men in history. Personal contact with a king is more effective in removing baleful prejudices than is any amount of argument drawn from tales and histories. If I had a child I would name it Henry the Eighth, regardless of sex.

Do you remember Charles the First?—and his broad slouch with the plume in it? and his slender, tall figure? and his body clothed in velvet doublet with lace sleeves, and his legs in leather, with long rapier at his side and his spurs on his heels? I encountered him at the next corner, and knew him in a moment—knew him as perfectly and as vividly as I should know the Grand Chain in the Mississippi if I should see it from the pilot-house after all these years. He bent his body and gave his hat a sweep that fetched its plume within an inch of the ground, and gave me a welcome that went to my heart. This king has been much maligned; I shall understand him better hereafter, and shall regret him more than I have been in the habit of doing these fifty or sixty years. He did some things in his time, which might better have been left undone, and which cast a shadow upon his name—we all know that, we all concede it—but our error has been in regarding them as crimes and in calling them by that name, whereas I perceive now that they were only indiscretions. At every few steps I met persons of deathless name whom I had never encountered before outside of pictures and statuary and history, and these were most thrilling and charming encounters. I had hand-shakes with Henry the Second, who had not been seen in the Oxford streets for nearly eight hundred years; and with the Fair Rosamond, whom I now believe to have been chaste and blameless, although I had thought differently about it before; and with Shakespeare, one of the pleasantest foreigners I have ever gotten acquainted with; and with Roger Bacon; and with Queen Elizabeth, who talked five minutes and never swore once—a fact which gave me a new and good opinion of her and moved me to forgive her for beheading the Scottish Mary, if she really did it, which I now doubt; and with the quaintly and anciently clad young King Harold Harefoot, of near nine hundred years ago, who came flying by on a bicycle and smoking a pipe, but at once checked up and got off to shake with me; and also I met a bishop who had lost his way because this was the first time he had been inside the walls of Oxford for as much as twelve hundred years or thereabouts. By this time I had grown so used to the obliterated ages and their best-known people that if I had met Adam I should not have been either surprised or embarrassed; and if he had come in a racing automobile and a cloud of dust, with nothing on but his fig-leaf, it would have seemed to me all right and harmonious.

MARK TWAIN

(to be continued)

CHAPTERS FROM MY AUTOBIOGRAPHY—XXIV

BY MARK TWAIN

PREFATORY NOTE—Mr. Clemens began to write his autobiography many years ago, and he continues to add to it day by day. It was his original intention to permit no publication of his memoirs until after his death; but, after leaving "Pier No. 70," he concluded that a considerable portion might now suitably be given to the public. It is that portion, garnered from the quarter-million of words already written, which will appear in this REVIEW during the present year. No part of the autobiography will be published in book form during the lifetime of the author.
—EDITOR N. A. R.

FROM SUSY'S BIOGRAPHY OF ME [1885–6]

Mamma and papa have returned from Onteora and they have had a delightful visit. Mr. Frank Stockton was down in Virginia and could not reach Onteora in time, so they did not see him, and Mrs. Mary Mapes Dodge was ill and couldn't go to Onteora, but Mrs. General Custer was there, and mamma said that she was a very attractive, sweet appearing woman.

[*Dictated October 9, 1906.*] Onteora was situated high up in the Catskill Mountains, in the centre of a far-reaching solitude. I do not mean that the region was wholly uninhabited; there were farmhouses here and there, at generous distances apart. Their occupants were descendants of ancestors who had built the houses in Rip Van Winkle's time, or earlier; and those ancestors were not more primitive than were this posterity of theirs. The city people were as foreign and unfamiliar and strange to them as monkeys would have been, and they would have respected the monkeys as much as they respected these elegant summer-resorters. The resorters were a puzzle to them, their ways were so strange and their interests so trivial. They drove the resorters over the mountain roads and listened in shamed surprise at their bursts of enthusiasm over the scenery. The farmers had had that scenery on exhibition from their mountain roosts all their lives, and had never noticed anything remarkable about it. By way of an incident: a pair of these primitives were overheard chatting about the resorters, one day, and in the course of their talk this remark was dropped:

"I was a-drivin' a passel of 'em round about yisterday evenin', quiet ones, you know, still and solemn, and all to wunst they busted out to make your hair lift and I judged hell was to pay. Now what do you reckon it was? It wa'n't anything but jest one of them common damned yaller sunsets."

In those days—

[*Tuesday, October 16, 1906.*] . . . Warner is gone. Stockton is gone. I attended both funerals. Warner was a near neighbor, from the autumn of '71 until his death, nineteen years afterward. It is not the privilege of the most of us to have many intimate friends—a dozen is our aggregate—but I think he could count his by the score. It is seldom that a man is so beloved by both sexes and all ages as Warner was. There was a charm about his spirit, and his ways, and his words, that won all that came within the sphere of its influence. Our children adopted him while they were little creatures, and thenceforth, to the end, he was "Cousin Charley" to them. He was "Uncle Charley" to the children of more than one other friend. Mrs. Clemens was very fond of him, and he always called her by her first name—shortened. Warner died, as she died, and as I would die—without premonition, without a moment's warning.

Uncle Remus still lives, and must be over a thousand years old. Indeed, I know that this must be so, because I have seen a new photograph of him in the public prints within the last month or so, and in that picture his aspects are distinctly and strikingly geological, and one can see he is thinking about the mastodons and plesiosaurians that he used to play with when he was young.

It is just a quarter of a century since I have seen Uncle Remus. He visited us in our home in Hartford and was reverently devoured by the big eyes of Susy and Clara, for I made a deep and awful impression upon the little creatures—who knew his book by heart through my nightly declamation of its tales to them—by revealing to them privately that he was the real Uncle Remus whitewashed so that he could come into people's houses the front way.

He was the bashfulest grown person I have ever met. When there were people about he stayed silent, and seemed to suffer until they were gone. But he was lovely, nevertheless; for the sweetness and benignity of the immortal Remus looked out from his eyes, and the graces and sincerities of his character shone in his face.

It may be that Jim Wolf was as bashful as Harris. It hardly seems possible, yet as I look back fifty-six years and consider Jim Wolf, I am almost persuaded that he was. He was our long slim apprentice in my brother's printing-office in Hannibal. He was seventeen, and yet he was as much as four times as bashful as I was, though I was only fourteen. He boarded and slept in the house, but he was always tongue-tied in the presence of my sister, and when even my gentle mother spoke to him he could not answer save in frightened monosyllables. He would not enter a room where a girl was; nothing could persuade him to do such a thing. Once when he was in our small parlor alone, two majestic old maids entered and seated themselves in such a way that Jim could not escape without passing by them. He would as soon have thought of passing by one of Harris's plesiosaurians ninety feet long. I came in presently, was charmed with the situation, and sat down in a corner to watch Jim suffer, and enjoy it. My mother followed a minute later and sat down with the visitors and began to talk. Jim sat upright in his chair, and during a quarter of an hour he did not change his position by a shade—neither General Grant nor a bronze image could have maintained that immovable pose more successfully. I mean as to body and limbs; with the face there was a difference. By fleeting revealments of the face I saw that something was happening—something out of the common. There would be a sudden twitch of the muscles of the face, an instant distortion, which in the next instant had passed and left no trace. These twitches gradually grew in frequency, but no muscle outside of the face lost any of its rigidity, or betrayed any interest in what was happening to Jim. I mean if something *was* happening to him, and I knew perfectly well that that was the case. At last a pair of tears began to swim slowly down his cheeks amongst the twitchings, but Jim sat still and let them run; then I saw his right hand steal along his thigh until half-way to his knee, then take a vigorous grip upon the cloth.

That was a *wasp* that he was grabbing! A colony of them were climbing up his legs and prospecting around, and every time he winced they stabbed him to the hilt—so for a quarter of an hour one group of excursionists after another climbed up Jim's legs and resented even the slightest wince or squirm that he indulged himself with, in his misery. When the entertainment had become nearly unbearable, he conceived the idea of gripping them between his fingers and putting them out of commission. He succeeded with many of them, but at great cost, for, as he couldn't see the wasp, he was as likely to take hold of the wrong end of him as he was the right; then the dying wasp gave him a punch to remember the incident by.

If those ladies had stayed all day, and if all the wasps in Missouri had come and climbed up Jim's legs, nobody there would ever have known it but Jim and the wasps and me. There he would have sat until the ladies left.

When they finally went away we went up-stairs and he took his clothes off, and his legs were a picture to look at. They looked as if they were mailed all over with shirt buttons, each with a single red hole in the centre. The pain was intolerable—no, would have been intolerable, but the pain of the presence of those ladies had been so much harder to bear that the pain of the wasps' stings was quite pleasant and enjoyable by comparison.

Jim never could enjoy wasps. I remember once—

FROM SUSY'S BIOGRAPHY OF ME [1885–6]

Mamma has given me a very pleasant little newspaper scrap about papa, to copy. I will put it in here.

[*Thursday, October 11, 1906.*] It was a rather strong compliment; I think I will leave it out. It was from James Redpath.

The chief ingredients of Redpath's make-up were honesty, sincerity, kindliness, and pluck. He wasn't afraid. He was one of Ossawatomie Brown's right-hand men in the bleeding Kansas days; he was all through that struggle. He carried his life in his hands, and from one day to another it wasn't worth the price of a night's lodging. He had a small body of daring men under him, and they were constantly being hunted by the "jayhawkers," who were proslavery Missourians, guerillas, modern free lances.

[*Friday, October 12, 1906*] . . . I can't think of the name of that daredevil guerilla who led the jayhawkers and chased Redpath up and down the country, and, in turn, was chased by Redpath. By grace of the chances of war, the two men never met in the field, though they several times came within an ace of it.

Ten or twelve years later, Redpath was earning his living in Boston as chief of the lecture business in the United States. Fifteen or sixteen years after his Kansas adventures I became a public lecturer, and he was my agent. Along there somewhere was a press dinner, one November night, at the Tremont Hotel in Boston, and I attended it. I sat near the head of the table, with Redpath between me and the chairman; a stranger sat on my other side. I tried several times to talk with the stranger, but he seemed to be out of words and I presently ceased from troubling him. He was manifestly a very shy man, and, moreover, he might have been losing sleep the night before.

The first man called up was Redpath. At the mention of the name the stranger started, and showed interest. He fixed a fascinated eye on Redpath, and lost not a word of his speech. Redpath told some stirring incidents of his career in Kansas, and said, among other things:

"Three times I came near capturing the gallant jayhawker

chief, and once he actually captured *me*, but didn't know me and let me go, because he said he was hot on Redpath's trail and couldn't afford to waste time and rope on inconsequential small fry."

My stranger was called up next, and when Redpath heard his name he, in turn, showed a startled interest. The stranger said, bending a caressing glance upon Redpath and speaking gently—I may even say sweetly:

"You realize that I was that jayhawker chief. I am glad to know you now and take you to my heart and call you friend"—then he added, in a voice that was pathetic with regret, "but if I had only known you then, what tumultuous happiness I should have had in your society!—while it lasted."

The last quarter of a century of my life has been pretty constantly and faithfully devoted to the study of the human race—that is to say, the study of myself, for, in my individual person, I am the entire human race compacted together. I have found that there is no ingredient of the race which I do not possess in either a small way or a large way. When it is small, as compared with the same ingredient in somebody else, there is still enough of it for all the purposes of examination. In my contacts with the species I find no one who possesses a quality which I do not possess. The shades of difference between other people and me serve to make variety and prevent monotony, but that is all; broadly speaking, we are all alike; and so by studying myself carefully and comparing myself with other people, and noting the divergences, I have been enabled to acquire a knowledge of the human race which I perceive is more accurate and more comprehensive than that which has been acquired and revealed by any other member of our species. As a result, my private and concealed opinion of myself is not of a complimentary sort. It follows that my estimate of the human race is the duplicate of my estimate of myself.

I am not proposing to discuss all of the peculiarities of the human race, at this time; I only wish to touch lightly upon one or two of them. To begin with, I wonder why a man should prefer a good billiard-table to a poor one; and why he should prefer straight cues to crooked ones; and why he should prefer round balls to chipped ones; and why he should prefer a level table to one that slants; and why he should prefer responsive cushions to the dull and unresponsive kind. I wonder at these things, because when we examine the matter we find that the essentials involved in billiards are as competently and exhaustively furnished by a bad billiard outfit as they are by the best one. One of the essentials is amusement. Very well, if there is any more amusement to be gotten out of the one outfit than out of the other, the facts are in favor of the bad outfit. The bad outfit will always furnish thirty per cent. more fun for the players and for the spectators than will the good outfit. Another essential of the game is that the outfit shall give the players full opportunity to exercise their best skill, and display it in a way to compel the admiration of the spectators. Very well, the bad outfit is nothing behind the good one in this regard. It is a difficult matter to estimate correctly the eccentricities of chipped balls and a slanting table, and make the right allowance for them and secure a count; the finest kind of skill is required to accomplish the satisfactory result. Another essential of the game is that it shall add to the interest of the game by furnishing opportunities to bet. Very well, in this regard no good outfit can claim any advantage over a bad one. I know, by experience, that a bad outfit is as valuable as the best one; that an outfit that couldn't be sold at auction for seven dollars is just as valuable for all the essentials of the game as an outfit that is worth a thousand.

I acquired some of this learning in Jackass Gulch, California, more than forty years ago. Jackass Gulch had once been a rich and thriving surface-mining camp. By and by its gold deposits were exhausted; then the people began to go away, and the town began to decay, and rapidly; in my time it had disappeared. Where the bank, and the city hall, and the church, and the gambling-dens, and the newspaper office, and the streets of brick blocks had been, was nothing now but a wide and beautiful expanse of green grass, a peaceful and charming solitude. Half a dozen scattered dwellings were still inhabited, and there was still one saloon of a ruined and rickety character struggling for life, but doomed. In its bar was a billiard outfit that was the counterpart of the one in my father-in-law's garret. The balls were chipped, the cloth was darned and patched, the table's surface was undulating, and the cues were headless and had the curve of a parenthesis—but the forlorn remnant of marooned miners played games there, and those games were more entertaining to look at than a circus and a grand opera combined. Nothing but a quite extraordinary skill could score a carom on that table—a skill that required the nicest estimate of force, distance, and how much to allow for the various slants of the table and the other formidable peculiarities and idiosyncrasies furnished by the contradictions of the outfit. Last winter, here in New York, I saw Hoppe and Schaefer and Sutton and the three or four other billiard champions of world-wide fame contend against each other, and certainly the art and science displayed were a wonder to see; yet I saw nothing there in the way of science and art that was more wonderful than shots which I had seen Texas Tom make on the wavy surface of that poor old wreck in the perishing saloon at Jackass Gulch forty years before. Once I saw Texas Tom make a string of seven points on a single inning!—all calculated shots, and not a fluke or a scratch among them. I often saw him make runs of four, but when he made his great string of seven, the boys went wild with enthusiasm and admiration. The joy and the noise exceeded that which the great gathering at Madison Square produced when Sutton scored five hundred points at the eighteen-inch game, on a world-famous night last winter. With practice, that champion could score nineteen or twenty on the Jackass Gulch table; but to start with, Texas Tom would show him miracles that would astonish him; also it might have another handsome result: it might persuade the great experts to discard their own trifling game and bring the Jackass Gulch outfit here and exhibit their skill in a game worth a hundred of the discarded one, for profound and breathless interest, and for displays of almost superhuman skill.

In my experience, games played with a fiendish outfit furnish ecstasies of delight which games played with the other kind cannot match. Twenty-seven years ago my budding little family spent the summer at Bateman's Point, near Newport, Rhode Island. It was a comfortable boarding-place, well stocked with sweet mothers and little children, but the male sex was scarce; however, there was another young fellow besides myself, and he and I had good times—Higgins was his name, but that was not his fault. He was a very pleasant and companionable person. On the premises there was what had once been a bowling-alley. It was a single alley, and it was estimated that it had been out of repair for sixty years—but not the balls, the balls were in good condition; there were forty-one of them, and they ranged in size from a grapefruit up to a lignum-vitae sphere that you could hardly lift. Higgins and I played on that alley day after day. At first, one of us located himself at the bottom end to set up the pins in case anything should happen to them, but nothing happened. The surface of that alley consisted of a rolling stretch of elevations and depressions, and neither of us could, by any art known to us, persuade a ball to stay on the alley until it should accomplish something. Little balls and big, the same thing always happened—the ball left the alley before it was half-way home and went thundering down alongside of it the rest of the way and made the gamekeeper climb out and take care of himself. No matter, we persevered, and were rewarded. We examined the alley, noted and located a lot of its peculiarities, and little by little we learned how to deliver a ball in such a way that it would travel home and knock down a pin or two. By and by we succeeded in improving our game to a point where we were able to get all of the pins with thirty-five balls—so we made it a thirty-five-ball game. If the player did not succeed with thirty-five, he had lost the game. I suppose that all the balls, taken together, weighed five hundred pounds, or maybe a ton—or along there somewhere—but anyway it was hot weather, and by the time that a player had sent thirty-five of them home he was in a drench of perspiration, and physically exhausted.

Next, we started cocked hat—that is to say, a triangle of three pins, the other seven being discarded. In this game we used the three smallest balls and kept on delivering them until we got the three pins down. After a day or two of practice we were able to get the chief pin with an output of four balls, but it cost us a great many deliveries to get the other two; but by and by we succeeded in perfecting our art—at least we perfected it to our limit. We reached a scientific excellence where we could get the three pins down with twelve deliveries of the three small balls, making thirty-six shots to conquer the cocked hat.

Having reached our limit for daylight work, we set up a couple of candles and played at night. As the alley was fifty or sixty feet long, we couldn't see the pins, but the candles indicated their locality. We continued this game until we were able to knock down the invisible pins with thirty-six shots. Having now reached the limit of the candle game, we changed and played it left-handed. We continued the left-handed game until we conquered its limit, which was fifty-four shots. Sometimes we sent down a succession of fifteen balls without getting anything at all. We easily got out of that old alley five times the fun that anybody could have gotten out of the best alley in New York.

One blazing hot day, a modest and courteous officer of the regular army appeared in our den and introduced himself. He was about thirty-five years old, well built and militarily erect and straight, and he was hermetically sealed up in the uniform of that ignorant old day—a uniform made of heavy material, and much properer for January than July. When he saw the venerable alley, and glanced from that to the long procession of shining balls in the trough, his eye lit with desire, and we judged that he was our meat. We politely invited him to take a hand, and he could not conceal his gratitude; though his breeding, and the etiquette of his profession, made him try. We explained the game to him, and said that there were forty-one balls, and that the player was privileged to extend his inning and keep on playing until he had used them all up—repeatedly—and that for every ten-strike he got a prize. We didn't name the prize—it wasn't necessary, as no prize would ever be needed or called for. He started a sarcastic smile, but quenched it, according to the etiquette of his profession. He merely remarked that he would like to select a couple of medium balls and one small one, adding that he didn't think he would need the rest.

Then he began, and he was an astonished man. He couldn't get a ball to stay on the alley. When he had fired about fifteen balls and hadn't yet reached the cluster of pins, his annoyance began to show out through his clothes. He wouldn't let it show in his face; but after another fifteen balls he was not able to control his face; he didn't utter a word, but he exuded mute blasphemy from every pore. He asked permission to take off his coat, which was granted; then he turned himself loose, with bitter determination, and although he was only an infantry officer he could have been mistaken for a battery, he got up such a volleying thunder with those balls. Presently he removed his cravat; after a little he took off his vest; and still he went bravely on. Higgins was suffocating. My condition was the same, but it would not be courteous to laugh; it would be better to burst, and we came near it. That officer was good pluck. He stood to his work without uttering a word, and kept the balls going until he had expended the outfit four times, making four times forty-one shots; then he had to give it up, and he did; for he was no longer able to stand without wobbling. He put on his clothes, bade us a courteous good-by, invited us to call at the Fort, and started away. Then he came back, and said,

"What is the prize for the ten-strike?"

We had to confess that we had not selected it yet.

He said, gravely, that he thought there was no occasion for hurry about it.

I believe Bateman's alley was a better one than any other in America, in the matter of the essentials of the game. It compelled skill; it provided opportunity for bets; and if you could get a stranger to do the bowling for you, there was more and wholesomer and delightfuler entertainment to be gotten out of his industries than out of the finest game by the best expert, and played upon the best alley elsewhere in existence.

MARK TWAIN

(to be continued)

North American Review

No. DCXXV.

DECEMBER, 1907

CHAPTERS FROM MY AUTOBIOGRAPHY—XXV

BY MARK TWAIN

PREFATORY NOTE—Mr. Clemens began to write his autobiography many years ago, and he continues to add to it day by day. It was his original intention to permit no publication of his memoirs until after his death; but, after leaving "Pier No. 70," he concluded that a considerable portion might now suitably be given to the public. It is that portion, garnered from the quarter-million of words already written, which will appear in this REVIEW during the present year. No part of the autobiography will be published in book form during the lifetime of the author.
—EDITOR N. A. R.

January 11, 1906. Answer to a letter received this morning:

DEAR MRS. H.,—I am forever your debtor for reminding me of that curious passage in my life. During the first year or two after it happened, I could not bear to think of it. My pain and shame were so intense, and my sense of having been an imbecile so settled, established and confirmed, that I drove the episode entirely from my mind—and so all these twenty-eight or twenty-nine years I have lived in the conviction that my performance of that time was coarse, vulgar and destitute of humor. But your suggestion that you and your family found humor in it twenty-eight years ago moved me to look into the matter. So I commissioned a Boston typewriter to delve among the Boston papers of that bygone time and send me a copy of it.

It came this morning, and if there is any vulgarity about it I am not able to discover it. If it isn't innocently and ridiculously funny, I am no judge. I will see to it that you get a copy.

Address of Samuel L. Clemens ("Mark Twain")
From a report of the dinner given by the Publishers
of the Atlantic Monthly in honor of the
Seventieth Anniversary of the
Birth of John Greenleaf Whittier, at the
Hotel Brunswick, Boston, December 17, 1877,
as published in the
BOSTON EVENING TRANSCRIPT,
December 18, 1877

Mr. Chairman—This is an occasion peculiarly meet for the digging up of pleasant reminiscences concerning literary folk; therefore I will drop lightly into history myself. Standing here on the shore of the Atlantic and contemplating certain of its largest literary billows, I am reminded of a thing which happened to me thirteen years ago, when I had just succeeded in stirring up a little Nevadian literary puddle myself, whose spume-flakes were beginning to blow thinly Californiawards. I started an inspection tramp through the southern mines of California. I was callow and conceited, and I resolved to try the virtue of my *nom de guerre*. I very soon had an opportunity. I knocked at a miner's lonely log cabin in the foothills of the Sierras just at nightfall. It was snowing at the time. A jaded, melancholy man of fifty, barefooted, opened the door to me. When he heard my *nom de guerre* he looked more dejected than before. He let me in—pretty reluctantly, I thought—and after the customary bacon and beans, black coffee and hot whiskey, I took a pipe. This sorrowful man had not said three words up to this time. Now he spoke up and said, in the voice of one who is secretly suffering, "You're the fourth—I'm going to move." "The fourth what?" said I. "The fourth littery man that has been here in twenty-four hours—I'm going to move." "You don't tell me!" said I; "who were the others?" "Mr. Longfellow, Mr. Emerson and Mr. Oliver Wendell Holmes—consound the lot!"

You can easily believe I was interested. I supplicated—three hot whiskeys did the rest—and finally the melancholy miner began. Said he—

"They came here just at dark yesterday evening, and I let them in of course. Said they were going to the Yosemite. They were a rough lot, but that's nothing; everybody looks rough that travels afoot. Mr. Emerson was a seedy little bit of a chap, redheaded. Mr. Holmes was as fat as a balloon; he weighed as much as three hundred, and had double chins all the way down to his stomach. Mr. Longfellow was built like a prize-fighter. His head was cropped and bristly, like as if he had a wig made of hair-brushes. His nose lay straight down his face, like a finger with the end joint tilted up. They had been drinking, I could see that. And what queer talk they used! Mr. Holmes inspected this cabin, then he took me by the buttonhole, and says he—

> "'Through the deep caves of thought
> I hear a voice that sings,
> Build thee more stately mansions,
> O my soul!'

"Says I, 'I can't afford it, Mr. Holmes, and moreover I don't want to.' Blamed if I liked it pretty well, either, coming from a stranger, that way. However, I started to get out my bacon and beans, when Mr. Emerson came and looked on awhile, and then *he* takes me aside by the buttonhole and says—

> "'Give me agates for my meat;
> Give me cantharids to eat;
> From air and ocean bring me foods,
> From all zones and altitudes.'

"Says I, 'Mr. Emerson, if you'll excuse me, this ain't no hotel.' You see it sort of riled me—I warn't used to the ways of littery swells. But I went on a-sweating over my work, and next comes Mr. Longfellow and buttonholes me, and interrupts me. Says he,

> "'Honor be to Mudjekeewis!
> You shall hear how Pau-Puk-Keewis—'

"But I broke in, and says I, 'Beg your pardon, Mr. Longfellow, if you'll be so kind as to hold your yawp for about five minutes and let me get this grub ready, you'll do me proud.' Well, sir, after they'd filled up I set out the jug. Mr. Holmes looks at it and then he fires up all of a sudden and yells—

> "'Flash out a stream of blood-red wine!
> For I would drink to other days.'

"By George, I was getting kind of worked up. I don't deny it, I was getting kind of worked up. I turns to Mr. Holmes, and says I, 'Looky here, my fat friend, I'm a-running this shanty, and if the court knows herself, you'll take whiskey straight or you'll go dry.' Them's the very words I said to him. Now I don't want to sass such famous littery people, but you see they kind of forced me. There ain't nothing onreasonable 'bout me; I don't mind a passel of guests a-treadin' on my tail three or four times, but when it comes to *standing* on it it's different, 'and if the court knows herself,' I says, 'you'll take whiskey straight or you'll go dry.' Well, between drinks they'd swell around the cabin and strike attitudes and spout; and pretty soon they got out a greasy old deck and went to playing euchre at ten cents a corner—on trust. I began to notice some pretty suspicious things. Mr. Emerson dealt, looked at his hand, shook his head, says—

> "'I am the doubter and the doubt—'

and ca'mly bunched the hands and went to shuffling for a new layout. Says he—

> "'They reckon ill who leave me out;
> They know not well the subtle ways I keep.
> I pass and deal *again!*'

Hang'd if he didn't go ahead and do it, too! O, he was a cool one! Well, in about a minute, things were running pretty tight, but all of a sudden I see by Mr. Emerson's eye he judged he had 'em. He had already corralled two tricks and each of the others one. So now he kind of lifts a little in his chair and says—

  "'I tire of globes and aces!—
   Too long the game is played!'

—and down he fetched a right bower. Mr. Longfellow smiles as sweet as pie and says—

  "'Thanks, thanks to thee, my worthy friend,
   For the lesson thou hast taught,'

—and blamed if he didn't down with *another* right bower! Emerson claps his hand on his bowie, Longfellow claps his on his revolver, and I went under a bunk. There was going to be trouble; but that monstrous Holmes rose up, wobbling his double chins, and says he, 'Order, gentlemen; the first man that draws, I'll lay down on him and smother him!' All quiet on the Potomac, you bet!

 "They were pretty how-come-you-so, by now, and they begun to blow. Emerson says, 'The nobbiest thing I ever wrote was Barbara Frietchie.' Says Longfellow, 'It don't begin with my Biglow Papers.' Says Holmes, 'My Thanatopsis lays over 'em both.' They mighty near ended in a fight. Then they wished they had some more company—and Mr. Emerson pointed to me and says—

  "'Is yonder squalid peasant all
   That this proud nursery could breed?'

He was a-whetting his bowie on his boot—so I let it pass. Well, sir, next they took it into their heads that they would like some music; so they made me stand up and sing 'When Johnny Comes Marching Home' till I dropped—at thirteen minutes past four this morning. That's what I've been through, my friend. When I woke at seven, they were leaving, thank goodness, and Mr. Longfellow had my only boots on, and his'n under his arm. Says I, 'Hold on, there, Evangeline, what are you going to do with *them?*' He says, 'Going to make tracks with 'em; because—

> "'Lives of great men all remind us
>   We can make our lives sublime;
>   And, departing, leave behind us
>   Footprints on the sands of time.'

As I said, Mr. Twain, you are the fourth in twenty-four hours— and I'm going to move; I ain't suited to a littery atmosphere."

I said to the miner, "Why, my dear sir, *these* were not the gracious singers to whom we and the world pay loving reverence and homage; these were impostors."

The miner investigated me with a calm eye for a while; then said he, "Ah! impostors, were they? Are *you?*"

I did not pursue the subject, and since then I have not travelled on my *nom de guerre* enough to hurt. Such was the reminiscence I was moved to contribute, Mr. Chairman. In my enthusiasm I may have exaggerated the details a little, but you will easily forgive me that fault, since I believe it is the first time I have ever deflected from perpendicular fact on an occasion like this.

What I have said to Mrs. H. is true. I did suffer during a year or two from the deep humiliations of that episode. But at last, in 1888, in Venice, my wife and I came across Mr. and Mrs. A. P. C., of Concord, Massachusetts, and a friendship began then of the sort which nothing but death terminates. The C.'s were very bright people and in every way charming and companionable. We were together a month or two in Venice and several months in Rome, afterwards, and one day that lamented break of mine was mentioned. And when I was on the point of lathering those people for bringing it to my mind when I had gotten the memory of it almost squelched, I perceived with joy that the C.'s were indignant about the way that my performance had been received in Boston. They poured out their opinions most freely and frankly about the frosty attitude of the people who were present at that performance, and about the Boston newspapers for the position they had taken in regard to the matter. That position was that I had been irreverent beyond belief, beyond imagination. Very well, I had accepted that as a fact for a year or two, and had been thoroughly miserable about it whenever I thought of it—which was not frequently, if I could help it. Whenever I thought of it I wondered how I ever could have been inspired to do so unholy a thing. Well, the C.'s comforted me, but they did not persuade me to continue to think about the unhappy episode. I resisted that. I tried to get it out of my mind, and let it die, and I succeeded. Until Mrs. H.'s letter came, it had been a good twenty-five years since I had thought of that matter; and when she said that the thing was funny I wondered if possibly she might be right. At any rate, my curiosity was aroused, and I wrote to Boston and got the whole thing copied, as above set forth.

I vaguely remember some of the details of that gathering— dimly I can see a hundred people—no, perhaps fifty—shadowy figures sitting at tables feeding, ghosts now to me, and name-less forever more. I don't know who they were, but I can very distinctly see, seated at the grand table and facing the rest of us, Mr. Emerson, supernaturally grave, unsmiling; Mr. Whit-tier, grave, lovely, his beautiful spirit shining out of his face; Mr. Longfellow, with his silken white hair and his benignant face; Dr. Oliver Wendell Holmes, flashing smiles and affection and all good-fellowship everywhere like a rose-diamond whose facets are being turned toward the light first one way and then another—a charming man, and always fascinating, whether he was talking or whether he was sitting still (what *he* would call still, but what would be more or less motion to other people). I can see those figures with entire distinctness across this abyss of time.

One other feature is clear—Willie Winter (for these past thousand years dramatic editor of the "New York Tribune," and still occupying that high post in his old age) was there. He was much younger then than he is now, and he showed it. It was always a pleasure to me to see Willie Winter at a banquet.

During a matter of twenty years I was seldom at a banquet where Willie Winter was not also present, and where he did not read a charming poem written for the occasion. He did it this time, and it was up to standard: dainty, happy, choicely phrased, and as good to listen to as music, and sounding exactly as if it was pouring unprepared out of heart and brain.

Now at that point ends all that was pleasurable about that notable celebration of Mr. Whittier's seventieth birthday—because *I* got up at that point and followed Winter, with what I have no doubt I supposed would be the gem of the evening—the gay oration above quoted from the Boston paper. I had written it all out the day before and had perfectly memorized it, and I stood up there at my genial and happy and self-satisfied ease, and began to deliver it. Those majestic guests, that row of venerable and still active volcanoes, listened, as did everybody else in the house, with attentive interest. Well, I delivered myself of—we'll say the first two hundred words of my speech. I was expecting no returns from that part of the speech, but this was not the case as regarded the rest of it. I arrived now at the dialogue: 'The old miner said, "You are the fourth, I'm going to move." "The fourth what?" said I. He answered, "The fourth littery man that has been here in twenty-four hours. I am going to move." "Why, you don't tell me," said I. "Who were the others?" "Mr. Longfellow, Mr. Emerson, Mr. Oliver Wendell Holmes, consound the lot—"'

Now then the house's *attention* continued, but the expression of interest in the faces turned to a sort of black frost. I wondered what the trouble was. I didn't know. I went on, but with difficulty—I struggled along, and entered upon that miner's fearful description of the bogus Emerson, the bogus Holmes, the bogus Longfellow, always hoping—but with a gradually perishing hope—that somebody would laugh, or that somebody would at least smile, but nobody did. I didn't know enough to give it up and sit down, I was too new to public speaking, and so I went on with this awful performance, and carried it clear through to the end, in front of a body of people who seemed turned to stone with horror. It was the sort of expression their faces would have worn if I had been making these remarks about the Deity and the rest of the Trinity; there is no milder way in which to describe the petrified condition and the ghastly expression of those people.

When I sat down it was with a heart which had long ceased to beat. I shall never be as dead again as I was then. I shall never be as miserable again as I was then. I speak now as one who doesn't know what the condition of things may be in the next world, but in this one I shall never be as wretched again as I was then. Howells, who was near me, tried to say a comforting word, but couldn't get beyond a gasp. There was no use—he understood the whole size of the disaster. He had good intentions, but the words froze before they could get out. It was an atmosphere that would freeze anything. If Benvenuto Cellini's salamander had been in that place he would not have survived to be put into Cellini's autobiography. There was a frightful pause. There was an awful silence, a desolating silence. Then the next man on the list had to get up—there was no help for it. That was Bishop—Bishop had just burst handsomely upon the world with a most acceptable novel, which had appeared in the "Atlantic Monthly," a place which would make any novel respectable and any author noteworthy. In this case the novel itself was recognized as being, without extraneous help, respectable. Bishop was away up in the public favor, and he was an object of high interest, consequently there was a sort of national expectancy in the air; we may say our American millions were standing, from Maine to Texas and from Alaska to Florida, holding their breath, their lips parted, their hands ready to applaud when Bishop should get up on that occasion, and for the first time in his life speak in public. It was under these damaging conditions that he got up to "make good," as the vulgar say. I had spoken several times before, and that is the reason why I was able to go on without dying in my tracks, as I ought to have done—but Bishop had had no experience. He was up facing those awful deities— facing those other people, those strangers—facing human beings for the first time in his life, with a speech to utter. No doubt it was well packed away in his memory, no doubt it was fresh and usable, until I had been heard from. I suppose that after that, and under the smothering pall of that dreary silence, it began to waste away and disappear out of his head like the rags breaking from the edge of a fog, and presently there wasn't any fog left. He didn't go on—he didn't last long. It was not many sentences after his first before he began to hesitate, and break, and lose his grip, and totter, and wobble, and at last he slumped down in a limp and mushy pile.

Well, the programme for the occasion was probably not more than one-third finished, but it ended there. Nobody rose. The next man hadn't strength enough to get up, and everybody looked so dazed, so stupefied, paralyzed, it was impossible for anybody to do anything, or even try. Nothing could go on in that strange atmosphere. Howells mournfully, and without words, hitched himself to Bishop and me and supported us out of the room. It was very kind—he was most generous. He towed us tottering away into some room in that building, and we sat down there. I don't know what my remark was now, but I know the nature of it. It was the kind of remark you make when you know that nothing in the world can help your case. But Howells was honest—he had to say the heart-breaking things he did say: that there was no help for this calamity, this shipwreck, this cataclysm; that this was the most disastrous thing that had ever happened in anybody's history—and then he added, "That is, for *you*—and consider what you have done for Bishop. It is bad enough in your case, you deserve to suffer. You have committed this crime, and you deserve to have all you are going to get. But here is an innocent man. Bishop had never done you any harm, and see what you have done to him. He can never hold his head up again. The world can never look upon Bishop as being a live person. He is a corpse."

That is the history of that episode of twenty-eight years ago, which pretty nearly killed me with shame during that first year or two whenever it forced its way into my mind.

Now, then, I take that speech up and examine it. As I said, it arrived this morning, from Boston. I have read it twice, and unless I am an idiot, it hasn't a single defect in it from the first word to the last. It is just as good as good can be. It is smart; it is saturated with humor. There isn't a suggestion of coarseness or vulgarity in it anywhere. What could have been the matter with that house? It is amazing, it is incredible, that they didn't shout with laughter, and those deities the loudest of them all. Could the fault have been with me? Did I lose courage when I saw those great men up there whom I was going to describe in such a strange fashion? If that happened, if I showed doubt, that can account for it, for you can't be successfully funny if you show that you are afraid of it. Well, I can't account for it, but if I had those beloved and revered old literary immortals back here now on the platform at Carnegie Hall I would take that same old speech, deliver it, word for word, and melt them till they'd run all over that stage. Oh, the fault must have been with *me*, it is not in the speech at all.

[*Dictated October 3, 1907.*] In some ways, I was always honest; even from my earliest years I could never bring myself to use money which I had acquired in questionable ways; many a time I tried, but principle was always stronger than desire. Six or eight months ago, Lieutenant-General Nelson A. Miles was given a great dinner-party in New York, and when he and I were chatting together in the drawing-room before going out to dinner he said,

"I've known you as much as thirty years, isn't it?"

I said, "Yes, that's about it, I think."

He mused a moment or two and then said,

"I wonder we didn't meet in Washington in 1867; you were there at that time, weren't you?"

I said, "Yes, but there was a difference; I was not known then; I had not begun to bud—I was an obscurity; but you had been adding to your fine Civil War record; you had just come back from your brilliant Indian campaign in the Far West, and had been rewarded with a brigadier-generalship in the regular army, and everybody was talking about you and praising you. If you had met me, you wouldn't be able to remember it now—unless some unusual circumstance of the meeting had burnt it into your memory. It is forty years ago, and people don't remember nobodies over a stretch of time like that."

I didn't wish to continue the conversation along that line, so I changed the subject. I could have proven to him, without any trouble, that we did meet in Washington in 1867, but I thought it might embarrass one or the other of us, so I didn't do it. I remember the incident very well. This was the way of it:

I had just come back from the Quaker City Excursion, and had made a contract with Bliss of Hartford to write "The Innocents Abroad." I was out of money, and I went down to Washington to see if I could earn enough there to keep me in bread and butter while I should write the book. I came across William Clinton, brother of the astronomer, and together we invented a scheme for our mutual sustenance; we became the fathers and originators of what is a common feature in the newspaper world now—the syndicate. We became the old original first Newspaper Syndicate on the planet; it was on a small scale, but that is usual with untried new enterprises. We had twelve journals on our list; they were all weeklies, all obscure and poor, and all scattered far away among the back settlements. It was a proud thing for those little newspapers to have a Washington correspondence, and a fortunate thing for us that they felt in that way about it. Each of the twelve took two letters a week from us, at a dollar per letter; each of us wrote one letter per week and sent off six duplicates of it to these benefactors, thus acquiring twenty-four dollars a week to live on—which was all we needed, in our cheap and humble quarters.

Clinton was one of the dearest and loveliest human beings I have ever known, and we led a charmed existence together, in a contentment which knew no bounds. Clinton was refined by nature and breeding; he was a gentleman by nature and breeding; he was highly educated; he was of a beautiful spirit; he was pure in heart and speech. He was a Scotchman, and a Presbyterian; a Presbyterian of the old and genuine school, being honest and sincere in his religion, and loving it, and finding serenity and peace in it. He hadn't a vice—unless a large and grateful sympathy with Scotch whiskey may be called by that name. I didn't regard it as a vice, because he was a Scotchman, and Scotch whiskey to a Scotchman is as innocent as milk is to the rest of the human race. In Clinton's case it was a virtue, and not an economical one. Twenty-four dollars a week would really have been riches to us if we hadn't had to support that jug; because of the jug we were always sailing pretty close to the wind, and any tardiness in the arrival of any part of our income was sure to cause us some inconvenience.

I remember a time when a shortage occurred; we had to have three dollars, and we had to have it before the close of the day. I don't know now how we happened to want all that money at one time; I only know we had to have it. Clinton told me to go out and find it—and he said he would also go out and see what he could do. He didn't seem to have any doubt that we would succeed, but I knew that that was his religion working in him; I hadn't the same confidence; I hadn't any idea where to turn to raise all that bullion, and I said so. I think he was ashamed of me, privately, because of my weak faith. He told me to give myself no uneasiness, no concern; and said in a simple, confident, and unquestioning way, "the Lord will provide." I saw that he fully believed the Lord would provide, but it seemed to me that if he had had my experience—

But never mind that; before he was done with me his strong faith had had its influence, and I went forth from the place almost convinced that the Lord really would provide.

I wandered around the streets for an hour, trying to think up some way to get that money, but nothing suggested itself. At last I lounged into the big lobby of the Ebbitt House, which was then a new hotel, and sat down. Presently a dog came loafing along. He paused, glanced up at me and said, with his eyes, "Are you friendly?" I answered, with my eyes, that I was. He gave his tail a grateful little wag and came forward and rested his jaw on my knee and lifted his brown eyes to my face in a winningly affectionate way. He was a lovely creature—as beautiful as a girl, and he was made all of silk and velvet. I stroked his smooth brown head and fondled his drooping ears, and we were a pair of lovers right away. Pretty soon Brigadier-General Miles, the hero of the land, came strolling by in his blue and gold splendors, with everybody's admiring gaze upon him. He saw the dog and stopped, and there was a light in his eye which showed that he had a warm place in his heart for dogs like this gracious creature; then he came forward and patted the dog and said,

"He is very fine—he is a wonder; would you sell him?"

I was greatly moved; it seemed a marvellous thing to me, the way Clinton's prediction had come true. I said,

"Yes."

The General said,

"What do you ask for him?"

"Three dollars."

The General was manifestly surprised. He said,

"Three dollars? Only three dollars? Why, that dog is a most uncommon dog; he can't possibly be worth less than fifty. If he were mine, I wouldn't take a hundred for him. I'm afraid you are not aware of his value. Reconsider your price if you like, I don't wish to wrong you."

But if he had known me he would have known that I was no more capable of wronging him than he was of wronging me. I responded with the same quiet decision as before,

"No—three dollars. That is his price."

"Very well, since you insist upon it," said the General, and he gave me three dollars and led the dog away, and disappeared up-stairs.

In about ten minutes a gentle-faced middle-aged gentleman came along, and began to look around here and there and under tables and everywhere, and I said to him,

"Is it a dog you are looking for?"

His face was sad, before, and troubled; but it lit up gladly now, and he answered,

"Yes—have you seen him?"

"Yes," I said, "he was here a minute ago, and I saw him follow a gentleman away. I think I could find him for you if you would like me to try."

I have seldom seen a person look so grateful—and there was gratitude in his voice, too, when he conceded that he would like me to try. I said I would do it with great pleasure, but that as it might take a little time I hoped he would not mind paying me something for my trouble. He said he would do it most gladly—repeating that phrase "most gladly"—and asked me how much. I said—

"Three dollars."

He looked surprised, and said,

"Dear me, it is nothing! I will pay you ten, quite willingly."

But I said,

"No, three is the price"—and I started for the stairs without waiting for any further argument, for Clinton had said that that was the amount that the Lord would provide, and it seemed to me that it would be sacrilegious to take a penny more than was promised.

I got the number of the General's room from the office-clerk, as I passed by his wicket, and when I reached the room I found the General there caressing his dog, and quite happy. I said,

"I am sorry, but I have to take the dog again."

He seemed very much surprised, and said,

"Take him again? Why, he is my dog; you sold him to me, and at your own price."

"Yes," I said, "it is true—but I have to have him, because the man wants him again."

"What man?"

"The man that owns him; he wasn't my dog."

The General looked even more surprised than before, and for a moment he couldn't seem to find his voice; then he said,

"Do you mean to tell me that you were selling another man's dog—and knew it?"

"Yes, I knew it wasn't my dog."

"Then why did you sell him?"

I said,

"Well, that is a curious question to ask. I sold him because you wanted him. You offered to buy the dog; you can't deny that. I was not anxious to sell him—I had not even thought of selling him, but it seemed to me that if it could be any accommodation to you—"

He broke me off in the middle, and said,

"*Accommodation* to me? It is the most extraordinary spirit of accommodation I have ever heard of—the idea of your selling a dog that didn't belong to you—"

I broke him off there, and said,

"There is no relevancy about this kind of argument; you said yourself that the dog was probably worth a hundred dollars, I only asked you three; was there anything unfair about that? You offered to pay more, you know you did. I only asked you three; you can't deny it."

"Oh, what in the world has that to do with it! The crux of the matter is that you didn't own the dog—can't you see that? You seem to think that there is no impropriety in selling property that isn't yours provided you sell it cheap. Now, then—"

I said,

"Please don't argue about it any more. You can't get around the fact that the price was perfectly fair, perfectly reasonable—considering that I didn't own the dog—and so arguing about it is only a waste of words. I have to have him back again because the man wants him; don't you see that I haven't any choice in the matter? Put yourself in my place. Suppose you had sold a dog that didn't belong to you; suppose you—"

"Oh," he said, "don't muddle my brains any more with your idiotic reasonings! Take him along, and give me a rest."

So I paid back the three dollars and led the dog down-stairs and passed him over to his owner, and collected three for my trouble.

I went away then with a good conscience, because I had acted honorably; I never could have used the three that I sold the dog for, because it was not rightly my own, but the three I got for restoring him to his rightful owner was righteously and properly mine, because I had earned it. That man might never have gotten that dog back at all, if it hadn't been for me. My principles have remained to this day what they were then. I was always honest; I know I can never be otherwise. It is as I said in the beginning—I was never able to persuade myself to use money which I had acquired in questionable ways.

Now, then, that is the tale. Some of it is true.

MARK TWAIN

YOUTHFUL
MEMORIES

AN UNPLEASANT
ADVENTURE

It is hard to forget repulsive things. I remember yet how I ran off from school once, when I was a boy, and then, pretty late at night, concluded to climb into the window of my father's office and sleep on a lounge, because I had a delicacy about going home and getting thrashed. As I lay on the lounge and my eyes grew accustomed to the darkness, I fancied I could see a long, dusky, shapeless thing stretched upon the floor. A cold shiver went through me. I turned my face to the wall. That did not answer. I was afraid that that thing would creep over and seize me in the dark. I turned back and stared at it for minutes and minutes—they seemed hours. It appeared to me that the lagging moonlight never, never would get to it. I turned to the wall and counted twenty, to pass the feverish time away. I looked—the pale square was nearer. I turned again and counted fifty—it was almost touching it. With desperate will I turned again and counted one hundred, and faced about, all in a tremble. A white human hand lay in the moonlight! Such an awful sinking at the heart—such a sudden gasp for breath! I felt—I can not tell *what* I felt. When I recovered strength enough, I faced the wall again. But no boy could have remained so, with that mysterious hand behind him. I counted again, and looked—the most of a naked arm was exposed. I put my hands over my eyes and counted till I could stand it no longer, and then—the pallid face of a man was there, with the corners of the mouth drawn down, and the eyes fixed and glassy in death! I raised to a sitting posture and glowered on that corpse till the light crept down the bare breast,—line by line—inch by inch—past the nipple,—and then it disclosed a ghastly stab!

I went away from there. I do not say that I went away in any sort of a hurry, but I simply went—that is sufficient. I went out at the window, and I carried the sash along with me. I did not need the sash, but it was handier to take it than it was to leave it, and so I took it.—I was not scared, but I was considerably agitated.

When I reached home, they whipped me, but I enjoyed it. It seemed perfectly delightful. That man had been stabbed near the office that afternoon, and they carried him in there to doctor him, but he only lived an hour. I have slept in the same room with him often, since then—in my dreams.

MY FIRST LITERARY VENTURE

I was a very smart child at the age of thirteen—an unusually smart child, I thought at the time. It was then that I did my first newspaper scribbling, and most unexpectedly to me it stirred up a fine sensation in the community. It did, indeed, and I was very proud of it, too. I was a printer's "devil," and a progressive and aspiring one. My uncle had me on his paper (the *Weekly Hannibal Journal*, two dollars a year in advance— five hundred subscribers, and they paid in cordwood, cabbages, and unmarketable turnips), and on a lucky summer's day he left town to be gone a week, and asked me if I thought I could edit one issue of the paper judiciously. Ah! didn't I want to try! Higgins was the editor on the rival paper. He had lately been jilted, and one night a friend found an open note on the poor fellow's bed, in which he stated that he could no longer endure life and had drowned himself in Bear Creek. The friend ran down there and discovered Higgins wading back to shore! He had concluded he wouldn't. The village was full of it for several days, but Higgins did not suspect it. I thought this was a fine opportunity. I wrote an elaborately wretched account of the whole matter, and then illustrated it with villainous cuts engraved on the bottoms of wooden type with a jack-knife— one of them a picture of Higgins wading out into the creek in his shirt, with a lantern, sounding the depth of the water with a walking-stick. I thought it was desperately funny, and was densely unconscious that there was any moral obliquity about such a publication. Being satisfied with this effort I looked around for other worlds to conquer, and it struck me that it would make good, interesting matter to charge the editor of a neighboring country paper with a piece of gratuitous rascality and "see him squirm."

I did it, putting the article into the form of a parody on the Burial of "Sir John Moore"—and a pretty crude parody it was, too.

Then I lampooned two prominent citizens outrageously—not because they had done anything to deserve it, but merely because I thought it was my duty to make the paper lively.

Next I gently touched up the newest stranger—the lion of the day, the gorgeous journeyman tailor from Quincy. He was a simpering coxcomb of the first water, and the "loudest" dressed man in the State. He was an inveterate woman-killer. Every week he wrote lushy "poetry" for the "Journal," about his newest conquest. His rhymes for my week were headed, "To MARY IN H—— L," meaning to Mary in Hannibal, of course. But while setting up the piece I was suddenly riven from head to heel by what I regarded as a perfect thunderbolt of humor, and I compressed it into a snappy foot-note at the bottom—thus:—"We will let this thing pass, just this once; but we wish Mr. J. Gordon Runnels to understand distinctly that we have a character to sustain, and from this time forth when he wants to commune with his friends in h—l, he must select some other medium than the columns of this journal!"

The paper came out, and I never knew any little thing attract so much attention as those playful trifles of mine.

For once the Hannibal Journal was in demand—a novelty it had not experienced before. The whole town was stirred. Higgins dropped in with a double-barrelled shot-gun early in the forenoon. When he found that it was an infant (as he called me) that had done him the damage, he simply pulled my ears and went away; but he threw up his situation that night and left town for good. The tailor came with his goose and a pair of shears; but he despised me too, and departed for the South that night. The two lampooned citizens came with threats of libel, and went away incensed at my insignificance. The country editor pranced in with a warwhoop next day, suffering for blood to drink; but he ended by forgiving me cordially and inviting me down to the drug store to wash away all animosity in a friendly bumper of "Fahnestock's Vermifuge." It was his little joke. My uncle was very angry when he got back—unreasonably so, I thought, considering what an impetus I had given the paper, and considering also that gratitude for his preservation ought to have been uppermost in his mind, inasmuch as by his delay he had so wonderfully escaped dissection, tomahawking, libel, and getting his head shot off. But he softened when he looked at the accounts and saw that I had actually booked the unparalleled number of thirty-three new subscribers, and had the vegetables to show for it, cordwood, cabbage, beans, and unsalable turnips enough to run the family for two years!

CUB PILOTING DAYS

THE BOYS' AMBITION

When I was a boy, there was but one permanent ambition among my comrades in our village* on the west bank of the Mississippi River. That was, to be a steamboatman. We had transient ambitions of other sorts, but they were only transient. When a circus came and went, it left us all burning to become clowns; the first negro minstrel show that ever came to our section left us all suffering to try that kind of life; now and then we had a hope that, if we lived and were good, God would permit us to be pirates. These ambitions faded out, each in its turn; but the ambition to be a steamboatman always remained.

Once a day a cheap, gaudy packet arrived upward from St. Louis, and another downward from Keokuk. Before these events, the day was glorious with expectancy; after them, the day was a dead and empty thing. Not only the boys, but the whole village, felt this. After all these years I can picture that old time to myself now, just as it was then: the white town drowsing in the sunshine of a summer's morning; the streets empty, or pretty nearly so; one or two clerks sitting in front of the Water Street stores, with their splint-bottomed chairs tilted back against the wall, chins on breasts, hats slouched over their faces, asleep—with shingle-shavings enough around to show what broke them down; a sow and a litter of pigs loafing along the sidewalk, doing a good business in watermelon rinds and seeds; two or three lonely little freight piles scattered about the "levee"; a pile of "skids" on the slope of the stone-paved wharf, and the fragrant town drunkard asleep in the shadow of them;

* Hannibal, Missouri.

two or three wood flats at the head of the wharf, but nobody to listen to the peaceful lapping of the wavelets against them; the great Mississippi, the majestic, the magnificent Mississippi, rolling its mile-wide tide along, shining in the sun; the dense forest away on the other side; the "point" above the town, and the "point" below, bounding the river-glimpse and turning it into a sort of sea, and withal a very still and brilliant and lonely one. Presently a film of dark smoke appears above one of those remote "points"; instantly a negro drayman, famous for his quick eye and prodigious voice, lifts up the cry, "S-t-e-a-m-boat a-comin'!" and the scene changes! The town drunkard stirs, the clerks wake up, a furious clatter of drays follows, every house and store pours out a human contribution, and all in a twinkling the dead town is alive and moving. Drays, carts, men, boys, all go hurrying from many quarters to a common centre, the wharf. Assembled there, the people fasten their eyes upon the coming boat as upon a wonder they are seeing for the first time. And the boat *is* rather a handsome sight, too. She is long and sharp and trim and pretty; she has two tall, fancy-topped chimneys, with a gilded device of some kind swung between them; a fanciful pilot-house, all glass and "gingerbread," perched on top of the "texas" deck behind them; the paddle-boxes are gorgeous with a picture or with gilded rays above the boat's name; the boiler deck, the hurricane deck, and the texas deck are fenced and ornamented with clean white railings; there is a flag gallantly flying from the jack-staff; the furnace doors are open and the fires glaring bravely; the upper decks are black with passengers; the captain stands by the big bell, calm, imposing, the envy of all; great volumes of the blackest smoke are rolling and tumbling out of the chimneys—a husbanded grandeur created with a bit of pitch pine just before arriving at a town; the crew are grouped on the forecastle; the broad stage is run far out over the port bow, and an envied deck-hand stands picturesquely on the end of it with a coil of rope in his hand; the pent steam is screaming through the gauge-cocks; the captain lifts his hand, a bell rings, the wheels stop; then they turn back, churning the water to foam, and the steamer is at rest. Then such a scramble as there is to get aboard, and to get ashore, and to take in freight and to discharge freight, all at one and the same time; and such a yelling and cursing as the mates facilitate it all with! Ten minutes later the steamer is under way again, with no flag on the jack-staff and no black smoke issuing from the chimneys. After ten more minutes the town is dead again, and the town drunkard asleep by the skids once more.

My father was a justice of the peace, and I supposed he possessed the power of life and death over all men, and could hang anybody that offended him. This was distinction enough for me as a general thing; but the desire to be a steamboatman kept intruding, nevertheless. I first wanted to be a cabin-boy, so that I could come out with a white apron on and shake a table-cloth over the side, where all my old comrades could see me; later I thought I would rather be the deck-hand who stood on the end of the stage-plank with the coil of rope in his hand, because he was particularly conspicuous. But these were only day-dreams—they were too heavenly to be contemplated as real possibilities. By and by one of our boys went away. He was not heard of for a long time. At last he turned up as apprentice engineer or "striker" on a steamboat. This thing shook the bottom out of all my Sunday-school teachings. That boy had been notoriously worldly, and I just the reverse; yet he was exalted to this eminence, and I left in obscurity and misery. There was nothing generous about this fellow in his greatness. He would always manage to have a rusty bolt to scrub while his boat tarried at our town, and he would sit on the inside guard and scrub it, where we all could see him and envy him and loathe him. And whenever his boat was laid up he would come home and swell around the town in his blackest and greasiest clothes, so that nobody could help remembering that he was a steamboatman; and he used all sorts of steamboat technicalities in his talk, as if he were so used to them that he forgot common people could not understand them. He would speak of the "labboard" side of a horse in an easy, natural way that would make one wish he was dead. And he was always talking about "St. Looy" like an old citizen; he would refer casually to occasions when he was "coming down Fourth Street," or when he was "passing by the Planter's House," or when there was a fire and he took a turn on the brakes of "the old Big Missouri"; and then he would go on and lie about how many towns the size of ours were burned down there that day. Two or three of the boys had long been persons of consideration among us because they had been to St. Louis once and had a vague general knowledge of its wonders, but the day of their glory was over now. They lapsed into a humble silence, and learned to disappear when the ruthless "cub"-engineer approached. This fellow had money, too, and hair oil. Also an ignorant silver watch and a showy brass watch chain. He wore a leather belt and used no suspenders. If ever a youth was cordially admired and hated by his comrades, this one was. No girl could withstand his charms. He "cut out" every boy in the village. When his boat blew up at last, it diffused a tranquil contentment among us such as we had not known for months. But when he came home the next week, alive, renowned, and appeared in church all battered up and bandaged, a shining hero, stared at and wondered over by everybody, it seemed to us that the partiality of Providence for an undeserving reptile had reached a point where it was open to criticism.

This creature's career could produce but one result, and it speedily followed. Boy after boy managed to get on the river. The minister's son became an engineer. The doctor's, and the post-master's sons became "mud clerks"; the wholesale liquor-dealer's son became a bar-keeper on a boat; four sons of the chief merchant, and two sons of the county judge, became pilots. Pilot was the grandest position of all. The pilot, even in those days of trivial wages, had a princely salary—from a hundred and fifty to two hundred and fifty dollars a month, and no board to pay. Two months of his wages would pay a preacher's salary for a year. Now some of us were left disconsolate. We could not get on the river—at least our parents would not let us.

So, by and by, I ran away. I said I would never come home again till I was a pilot and could come in glory. But somehow I could not manage it. I went meekly aboard a few of the boats that lay packed together like sardines at the long St. Louis wharf, and humbly enquired for the pilots, but got only a cold shoulder and short words from mates and clerks. I had to make the best of this sort of treatment for the time being, but I had comforting day-dreams of a future when I should be a great and honored pilot, with plenty of money, and could kill some of these mates and clerks and pay for them.

I WANT TO BE A CUB-PILOT

Months afterward the hope within me struggled to a reluctant death, and I found myself without an ambition. But I was ashamed to go home. I was in Cincinnati, and I set to work to map out a new career. I had been reading about the recent exploration of the river Amazon by an expedition sent out by our government. It was said that the expedition, owing to difficulties, had not thoroughly explored a part of the country lying about the head-waters, some four thousand miles from the mouth of the river. It was only about fifteen hundred miles from Cincinnati to New Orleans, where I could doubtless get a ship. I had thirty dollars left; I would go and complete the exploration of the Amazon. This was all the thought I gave to the subject. I never was great in matters of detail. I packed my valise, and took passage on an ancient tub called the "Paul Jones," for New Orleans. For the sum of sixteen dollars I had the scarred and tarnished splendors of "her" main saloon principally to myself, for she was not a creature to attract the eye of wiser travellers.

When we presently got under way and went poking down the broad Ohio, I became a new being, and the subject of my own admiration. I was a traveller! A word never had tasted so good in my mouth before. I had an exultant sense of being bound for mysterious lands and distant climes which I never have felt in so uplifting a degree since. I was in such a glorified condition that all ignoble feelings departed out of me, and I was able to look down and pity the untravelled with a compassion that had hardly a trace of contempt in it. Still, when we stopped at villages and wood-yards, I could not help lolling carelessly upon the railings of the boiler deck to enjoy the envy of the country boys on the bank. If they did not seem to discover me, I presently sneezed to attract their attention, or moved to a position where they could not help seeing me. And as soon as I knew they saw me I gaped and stretched, and gave other signs of being mightily bored with travelling.

I kept my hat off all the time, and stayed where the wind and the sun could strike me, because I wanted to get the bronzed and weather-beaten look of an old traveller. Before the second day was half gone I experienced a joy which filled me with the purest gratitude; for I saw that the skin had begun to blister and peel off my face and neck. I wished that the boys and girls at home could see me now.

We reached Louisville in time—at least the neighborhood of it. We stuck hard and fast on the rocks in the middle of the river, and lay there four days. I was now beginning to feel a strong sense of being a part of the boat's family, a sort of infant son to the captain and younger brother to the officers. There is no estimating the pride I took in this grandeur, or the affection that began to swell and grow in me for those people. I could not know how the lordly steamboatman scorns that sort of presumption in a mere landsman. I particularly longed to acquire the least trifle of notice from the big stormy mate, and I was on the alert for an opportunity to do him a service to that end. It came at last. The riotous powwow of setting a spar was going on down on the forecastle, and I went down there and stood around in the way—or mostly skipping out of it—till the mate suddenly roared a general order for somebody to bring him a capstan bar. I sprang to his side and said: "Tell me where it is—I'll fetch it!"

If a rag-picker had offered to do a diplomatic service for the Emperor of Russia, the monarch could not have been more astounded than the mate was. He even stopped swearing. He stood and stared down at me. It took him ten seconds to scrape his disjointed remains together again. Then he said impressively: "Well, if this don't beat hell!" and turned to his work with the air of a man who had been confronted with a problem too abstruse for solution.

I crept away, and courted solitude for the rest of the day. I did not go to dinner; I stayed away from supper until everybody else had finished. I did not feel so much like a member of the boat's family now as before. However, my spirits returned, in instalments, as we pursued our way down the river. I was sorry I hated the mate so, because it was not in (young) human nature not to admire him. He was huge and muscular, his face was bearded and whiskered all over; he had a red woman and a blue woman tattooed on his right arm, one on each side of a blue anchor with a red rope to it; and in the matter of profanity he was sublime. When he was getting out cargo at a landing, I was always where I could see and hear. He felt all the majesty of his great position, and made the world feel it, too. When he gave even the simplest order, he discharged it like a blast of lightning, and sent a long, reverberating peal of profanity thundering after it. I could not help contrasting the way in which the average landsman would give an order with the mate's way of doing it. If the landsman should wish the gang-plank moved a foot farther forward, he would probably say: "James, or William, one of you push that plank forward, please"; but put the mate in his place, and he would roar out: "Here, now, start that gang-plank for'ard! Lively, now! *What*'re you about! Snatch it! *snatch* it! There! there! Aft again! aft again! Don't you hear me? Dash it to dash! are you going to *sleep* over it! '*Vast* heaving. '*Vast* heaving, I tell you! Going to heave it clear astern? WHERE're you going with that barrel! *for'ard* with it 'fore I make you swallow it, you dash-dash-dash-*dashed* split between a tired mud-turtle and a crippled hearse-horse!"

I wished I could talk like that.

When the soreness of my adventure with the mate had somewhat worn off, I began timidly to make up to the humblest official connected with the boat—the night watchman. He snubbed my advances at first, but I presently ventured to offer him a new chalk pipe, and that softened him. So he allowed me to sit with him by the big bell on the hurricane deck, and in time he melted into conversation. He could not well have helped it, I hung with such homage on his words and so plainly showed that I felt honored by his notice. He told me the names of dim capes and shadowy islands as we glided by them in the solemnity of the night, under the winking stars, and by and by got to talking about himself. He seemed over-sentimental for a man whose salary was six dollars a week—or rather he might have seemed so to an older person than I. But I drank in his words hungrily, and with a faith that might have moved mountains if it had been applied judiciously. What was it to me that he was soiled and seedy and fragrant with gin? What was it to me that his grammar was bad, his construction worse, and his profanity so void of art that it was an element of weakness rather than strength in his conversation? He was a wronged man, a man who had seen trouble, and that was enough for me. As he mellowed into his plaintive history his tears dripped upon the lantern in his lap, and I cried, too, from sympathy. He said he was the son of an English nobleman—either an earl or an alderman, he could not remember which, but believed was both; his father, the nobleman, loved him, but his mother hated him from the cradle; and so while he was still a little boy he was sent to "one of them old, ancient colleges"—he couldn't remember which; and by and by his father died and his mother seized the property and "shook" him, as he phrased it. After his mother shook him, members of the nobility with whom he was acquainted used their influence to get him the position of "loblolly-boy in a ship"; and from that point my watchman threw off all trammels of date and locality and branched out into a narrative that bristled all along with incredible adventures; a narrative that was so reeking with bloodshed and so crammed with hair-breadth escapes and the most engaging and unconscious personal villanies, that I sat speechless, enjoying, shuddering, wondering, worshipping.

It was a sore blight to find out afterward that he was a low, vulgar, ignorant, sentimental, half-witted humbug, an untravelled native of the wilds of Illinois, who had absorbed wildcat literature and appropriated its marvels, until in time he had woven odds and ends of the mess into this yarn, and then gone on telling it to fledglings like me, until he had come to believe it himself.

A CUB-PILOT'S EXPERIENCE

What with lying on the rocks four days at Louisville, and some other delays, the poor old "Paul Jones" fooled away about two weeks in making the voyage from Cincinnati to New Orleans. This gave me a chance to get acquainted with one of the pilots, and he taught me how to steer the boat, and thus made the fascination of river life more potent than ever for me.

It also gave me a chance to get acquainted with a youth who had taken deck passage—more's the pity; for he easily borrowed six dollars of me on a promise to return to the boat and pay it back to me the day after we should arrive. But he probably died or forgot, for he never came. It was doubtless the former, since he had said his parents were wealthy, and he only travelled deck passage because it was cooler.*

I soon discovered two things. One was that a vessel would not be likely to sail for the mouth of the Amazon under ten or twelve years; and the other was that the nine or ten dollars still left in my pocket would not suffice for so impossible an exploration as I had planned, even if I could afford to wait for a ship. Therefore it followed that I must contrive a new career. The "Paul Jones" was now bound for St. Louis. I planned a siege against my pilot, and at the end of three hard days he surrendered. He agreed to teach me the Mississippi River from New Orleans to St. Louis for five hundred dollars, payable out of the first wages I should receive after graduating. I entered upon the small enterprise of "learning" twelve or thirteen hundred miles of the great Mississippi River with the easy confidence of my time of life. If I had really known what I was about to require of my faculties, I should not have had the courage to begin. I supposed that all a pilot had to do was to keep his boat in the river, and I did not consider that that could be much of a trick, since it was so wide.

The boat backed out from New Orleans at four in the afternoon, and it was "our watch" until eight. Mr. Bixby, my chief, "straightened her up," ploughed her along past the sterns of the other boats that lay at the Levee, and then said, "Here,

---

* "Deck" passage—*i.e.*, steerage passage.

take her; shave those steamships as close as you'd peel an apple." I took the wheel, and my heart-beat fluttered up into the hundreds; for it seemed to me that we were about to scrape the side off every ship in the line, we were so close. I held my breath and began to claw the boat away from the danger; and I had my own opinion of the pilot who had known no better than to get us into such peril, but I was too wise to express it. In half a minute I had a wide margin of safety intervening between the "Paul Jones" and the ships; and within ten seconds more I was set aside in disgrace, and Mr. Bixby was going into danger again and flaying me alive with abuse of my cowardice. I was stung, but I was obliged to admire the easy confidence with which my chief loafed from side to side of his wheel, and trimmed the ships so closely that disaster seemed ceaselessly imminent. When he had cooled a little he told me that the easy water was close ashore and the current outside, and therefore we must hug the bank, up-stream, to get the benefit of the former, and stay well out, down-stream, to take advantage of the latter. In my own mind I resolved to be a down-stream pilot and leave the up-streaming to people dead to prudence.

Now and then Mr. Bixby called my attention to certain things. Said he, "This is Six-Mile Point." I assented. It was pleasant enough information, but I could not see the bearing of it. I was not conscious that it was a matter of any interest to me. Another time he said, "This is Nine-Mile Point." Later he said, "This is Twelve-Mile Point." They were all about level with the water's edge; they all looked about alike to me; they were monotonously unpicturesque. I hoped Mr. Bixby would change the subject. But no; he would crowd up around a point, hugging the shore with affection, and then say: "The slack water ends here, abreast this bunch of China-trees; now we cross over." So he crossed over. He gave me the wheel once or twice, but I had no luck. I either came near chipping off the edge of a sugar plantation, or I yawed too far from shore, and so dropped back into disgrace again and got abused.

The watch was ended at last, and we took supper and went to bed. At midnight the glare of a lantern shone in my eyes, and the night watchman said:—

"Come, turn out!"

And then he left. I could not understand this extraordinary procedure; so I presently gave up trying to, and dozed off to sleep. Pretty soon the watchman was back again, and this time he was gruff. I was annoyed. I said:—

"What do you want to come bothering around here in the middle of the night for? Now, as like as not, I'll not get to sleep again to-night."

The watchman said:—

"Well, if this an't good, I'm blessed."

The "off-watch" was just turning in, and I heard some brutal laughter from them, and such remarks as "Hello, watchman! an't the new cub turned out yet? He's delicate, likely. Give him some sugar in a rag, and send for the chambermaid to sing rock-a-by, baby, to him."

About this time Mr. Bixby appeared on the scene. Something like a minute later I was climbing the pilot-house steps with some of my clothes on and the rest in my arms. Mr. Bixby was close behind, commenting. Here was something fresh— this thing of getting up in the middle of the night to go to work. It was a detail in piloting that had never occurred to me at all. I knew that boats ran all night, but somehow I had never happened to reflect that somebody had to get up out of a warm bed to run them. I began to fear that piloting was not quite so romantic as I had imagined it was; there was something very real and work-like about this new phase of it.

It was a rather dingy night, although a fair number of stars were out. The big mate was at the wheel, and he had the old tub pointed at a star and was holding her straight up the middle of the river. The shores on either hand were not much more than half a mile apart, but they seemed wonderfully far away and ever so vague and indistinct. The mate said:—

"We've got to land at Jones's plantation, sir."

The vengeful spirit in me exulted. I said to myself, "I wish you joy of your job, Mr. Bixby; you'll have a good time finding Mr. Jones's plantation such a night as this; and I hope you never *will* find it as long as you live."

Mr. Bixby said to the mate:—

"Upper end of the plantation, or the lower?"

"Upper."

"I can't do it. The stumps there are out of water at this stage. It's no great distance to the lower, and you'll have to get along with that."

"All right, sir. If Jones don't like it, he'll have to lump it, I reckon."

And then the mate left. My exultation began to cool and my wonder to come up. Here was a man who not only proposed to find this plantation on such a night, but to find either end of it you preferred. I dreadfully wanted to ask a question, but I was carrying about as many short answers as my cargo-room would admit of, so I held my peace. All I desired to ask Mr. Bixby was the simple question whether he was ass enough to really imagine he was going to find that plantation on a night when all plantations were exactly alike and all of the same color. But I held in. I used to have fine inspirations of prudence in those days.

Mr. Bixby made for the shore and soon was scraping it, just the same as if it had been daylight. And not only that, but singing—

"Father in heaven, the day is declining," etc.

It seemed to me that I had put my life in the keeping of a peculiarly reckless outcast. Presently he turned on me and said:—

"What's the name of the first point above New Orleans?"

I was gratified to be able to answer promptly, and I did. I said I didn't know.

"Don't *know?*"

This manner jolted me. I was down at the foot again, in a moment. But I had to say just what I had said before.

"Well, you're a smart one!" said Mr. Bixby. "What's the name of the *next* point?"

Once more I didn't know.

"Well, this beats anything. Tell me the name of *any* point or place I told you."

I studied a while and decided that I couldn't.

"Look here! What do you start out from, above Twelve-Mile Point, to cross over?"

"I—I—don't know."

"You—you—don't know?" mimicking my drawling manner of speech. "What *do* you know?"

"I—I—nothing, for certain."

"By the great Cæsar's ghost, I believe you! You're the stupidest dunderhead I ever saw or ever heard of, so help me Moses! The idea of *you* being a pilot—*you!* Why, you don't know enough to pilot a cow down a lane."

Oh, but his wrath was up! He was a nervous man, and he shuffled from one side of his wheel to the other as if the floor was hot. He would boil a while to himself, and then overflow and scald me again.

"Look here! What do you suppose I told you the names of those points for?"

I tremblingly considered a moment, and then the devil of temptation provoked me to say:—

"Well—to—to—be entertaining, I thought."

This was a red rag to the bull. He raged and stormed so (he was crossing the river at the time) that I judge it made him blind, because he ran over the steering-oar of a trading-scow. Of course the traders sent up a volley of red-hot profanity. Never was a man so grateful as Mr. Bixby was: because he was brim full, and here were subjects who could *talk back*. He threw open a window, thrust his head out, and such an irruption followed as I never had heard before. The fainter and farther away the scowmen's curses drifted, the higher Mr. Bixby lifted his voice and the weightier his adjectives grew. When he closed the window he was empty. You could have drawn a seine through his system and not caught curses enough to disturb your mother with. Presently he said to me in the gentlest way:—

"My boy, you must get a little memorandum-book; and every time I tell you a thing, put it down right away. There's only one way to be a pilot, and that is to get this entire river by heart. You have to know it just like A B C."

That was a dismal revelation to me; for my memory was

never loaded with anything but blank cartridges. However, I did not feel discouraged long. I judged that it was best to make some allowances, for doubtless Mr. Bixby was "stretching." Presently he pulled a rope and struck a few strokes on the big bell. The stars were all gone now, and the night was as black as ink. I could hear the wheels churn along the bank, but I was not entirely certain that I could see the shore. The voice of the invisible watchman called up from the hurricane deck:—

"What's this, sir?"

"Jones's plantation."

I said to myself, "I wish I might venture to offer a small bet that it isn't." But I did not chirp. I only waited to see. Mr. Bixby handled the engine bells, and in due time the boat's nose came to the land, a torch glowed from the forecastle, a man skipped ashore, a darky's voice on the bank said, "Gimme de k'yarpet-bag, Mars' Jones," and the next moment we were standing up the river again, all serene. I reflected deeply a while, and then said,—but not aloud,— "Well, the finding of that plantation was the luckiest accident that ever happened; but it couldn't happen again in a hundred years." And I fully believed it *was* an accident, too.

By the time we had gone seven or eight hundred miles up the river, I had learned to be a tolerably plucky upstream steersman, in daylight, and before we reached St. Louis I had made a trifle of progress in night-work, but only a trifle. I had a note-book that fairly bristled with the names of towns, "points," bars, islands, bends, reaches, etc.; but the information was to be found only in the note-book—none of it was in my head. It made my heart ache to think I had only got half of the river set down; for as our watch was four hours off and four hours on, day and night, there was a long four-hour gap in my book for every time I had slept since the voyage began.

My chief was presently hired to go on a big New Orleans boat, and I packed my satchel and went with him. She was a grand affair. When I stood in her pilot-house I was so far above the water that I seemed perched on a mountain; and her decks stretched so far away, fore and aft, below me, that I wondered how I could ever have considered the little "Paul

Jones" a large craft. There were other differences, too. The
"Paul Jones"'s pilot-house was a cheap, dingy, battered rattle-
trap, cramped for room; but here was a sumptuous glass tem-
ple; room enough to have a dance in; showy red and gold
window curtains; an imposing sofa; leather cushions and a
back to the high bench where visiting pilots sit, to spin yarns
and "look at the river"; bright, fanciful "cuspadores" instead
of a broad wooden box filled with sawdust; nice new oilcloth
on the floor; a hospitable big stove for winter; a wheel as high
as my head, costly with inlaid work; a wire tiller-rope; bright
brass knobs for the bells; and a tidy, white-aproned, black
"texas-tender," to bring up tarts and ices and coffee during
mid-watch, day and night. Now this was "something like";
and so I began to take heart once more to believe that piloting
was a romantic sort of occupation after all. The moment we
were under way I began to prowl about the great steamer and
fill myself with joy. She was as clean and as dainty as a drawing-
room; when I looked down her long, gilded saloon, it was like
gazing through a splendid tunnel; she had an oil-picture, by
some gifted sign-painter, on every state-room door; she glit-
tered with no end of prism-fringed chandeliers; the clerk's
office was elegant, the bar was marvellous, and the bar-keeper
had been barbered and upholstered at incredible cost. The
boiler deck (*i.e.*, the second story of the boat, so to speak), was
as spacious as a church, it seemed to me; so with the forecastle; and there was no pitiful handful of deck-hands, firemen,
and roust-abouts down there, but a whole battalion of men.
The fires were fiercely glaring from a long row of furnaces,
and over them were eight huge boilers! This was unutterable
pomp. The mighty engines—but enough of this. I had never
felt so fine before. And when I found that the regiment of natty
servants respectfully "sir'd" me, my satisfaction was complete.

A DARING DEED

When I returned to the pilot-house St. Louis was gone, and I
was lost. Here was a piece of river which was all down in my
book, but I could make neither head nor tail of it: you understand, it was turned around. I had seen it when coming up-
stream, but I had never faced about to see how it looked when
it was behind me. My heart broke again, for it was plain that I
had got to learn this troublesome river *both ways*.

The pilot-house was full of pilots, going down to "look at
the river." What is called the "upper river" (the two hundred
miles between St. Louis and Cairo, where the Ohio comes in)
was low; and the Mississippi changes its channel so constantly
that the pilots used to always find it necessary to run down to
Cairo to take a fresh look, when their boats were to lie in port
a week; that is, when the water was at a low stage. A deal of
this "looking at the river," was done by poor fellows who seldom had a berth, and whose only hope of getting one lay in
their being always freshly posted and therefore ready to drop
into the shoes of some reputable pilot, for a single trip, on
account of such pilot's sudden illness, or some other necessity.
And a good many of them constantly ran up and down inspecting the river, not because they ever really hoped to get a berth,
but because (they being guests of the boat) it was cheaper to
"look at the river" than stay ashore and pay board. In time
these fellows grew dainty in their tastes, and only infested
boats that had an established reputation for setting good
tables. All visiting pilots were useful, for they were always
ready and willing, winter or summer, night or day, to go out in
the yawl and help buoy the channel or assist the boat's pilots in
any way they could. They were likewise welcome because all
pilots are tireless talkers, when gathered together, and as they
talk only about the river they are always understood and are
always interesting. Your true pilot cares nothing about anything on earth but the river, and his pride in his occupation
surpasses the pride of kings.

We had a fine company of these river inspectors along this

trip. There were eight or ten; and there was abundance of room for them in our great pilot-house. Two or three of them wore polished silk hats, elaborate shirtfronts, diamond breast-pins, kid gloves, and patent-leather boots. They were choice in their English, and bore themselves with a dignity proper to men of solid means and prodigious reputation as pilots. The others were more or less loosely clad, and wore upon their heads tall felt cones that were suggestive of the days of the Commonwealth.

I was a cipher in this august company, and felt subdued, not to say torpid. I was not even of sufficient consequence to assist at the wheel when it was necessary to put the tiller hard down in a hurry; the guest that stood nearest did that when occasion required—and this was pretty much all the time, because of the crookedness of the channel and the scant water. I stood in a corner; and the talk I listened to took the hope all out of me. One visitor said to another:—

"Jim, how did you run Plum Point, coming up?"

"It was in the night, there, and I ran it the way one of the boys on the "Diana" told me; started out about fifty yards above the wood-pile on the false point, and held on the cabin under Plum Point till I raised the reef—quarter less twain—then straightened up for the middle bar till I got well abreast the old one-limbed cotton-wood in the bend, then got my stern on the cotton-wood, and head on the low place above the point, and came through a-booming—nine and a half."

"Pretty square crossing, an't it?"

"Yes, but the upper bar's working down fast."

Another pilot spoke up and said:—

"I had better water than that, and ran it lower down; started out from the false point—mark twain—raised the second reef abreast the big snag in the bend, and had quarter less twain."

One of the gorgeous ones remarked:—

"I don't want to find fault with your leadsmen, but that's a good deal of water for Plum Point, it seems to me."

There was an approving nod all around as this quiet snub dropped on the boaster and "settled" him. And so they went on talk-talk-talking. Meantime, the thing that was running in my mind was, "Now, if my ears hear aright, I have not only to get the names of all the towns and islands and bends, and so on, by heart, but I must even get up a warm personal acquaintanceship with every old snag and one-limbed cotton-wood and obscure woodpile that ornaments the banks of this river for twelve hundred miles; and more than that, I must actually know where these things are in the dark, unless these guests are gifted with eyes that can pierce through two miles of solid blackness; I wish the piloting business was in Jericho and I had never thought of it."

At dusk Mr. Bixby tapped the big bell three times (the signal to land), and the captain emerged from his drawing-room in the forward end of the texas, and looked up enquiringly. Mr. Bixby said:—

"We will lay up here all night, captain."

"Very well, sir."

That was all. The boat came to shore and was tied up for the night. It seemed to me a fine thing that the pilot could do as he pleased, without asking so grand a captain's permission. I took my supper and went immediately to bed, discouraged by my day's observations and experiences. My late voyage's note-booking was but a confusion of meaningless names. It had tangled me all up in a knot every time I had looked at it in the day-time. I now hoped for respite in sleep: but no, it revelled all through my head till sunrise again, a frantic and tireless nightmare.

Next morning I felt pretty rusty and low-spirited. We went booming along, taking a good many chances, for we were anxious to "get out of the river" (as getting out to Cairo was called) before night should overtake us. But Mr. Bixby's partner, the other pilot, presently grounded the boat, and we lost so much time getting her off that it was plain the darkness would overtake us a good long way above the mouth. This was a great misfortune, especially to certain of our visiting pilots, whose boats would have to wait for their return, no matter how long that might be. It sobered the pilot-house talk a good deal. Coming up-stream, pilots did not mind low water or any kind of darkness; nothing stopped them but fog. But down-stream work was different; a boat was too nearly help-less, with a stiff current pushing behind her; so it was not cus-tomary to run down-stream at night in low water.

There seemed to be one small hope, however: if we could get through the intricate and dangerous Hat Island crossing before night, we could venture the rest, for we would have plainer sail-ing and better water. But it would be insanity to attempt Hat Island at night. So there was a deal of looking at watches all the rest of the day, and a constant ciphering upon the speed we were making; Hat Island was the eternal subject; sometimes hope was high and sometimes we were delayed in a bad cross-ing, and down it went again. For hours all hands lay under the burden of this suppressed excitement; it was even communi-cated to me, and I got to feeling so solicitous about Hat Island, and under such an awful pressure of responsibility, that I wished I might have five minutes on shore to draw a good, full, reliev-ing breath, and start over again. We were standing no regular watches. Each of our pilots ran such portions of the river as he had run when coming up-stream, because of his greater famil-iarity with it; but both remained in the pilot-house constantly.

An hour before sunset Mr. Bixby took the wheel, and Mr. W—— stepped aside. For the next thirty minutes every man held his watch in his hand and was restless, silent, and uneasy. At last somebody said, with a doomful sigh,—

"Well, yonder's Hat Island—and we can't make it."

All the watches closed with a snap, everybody sighed and muttered something about it's being "too bad, too bad—ah, if we could *only* have got here half an hour sooner!" and the place was thick with the atmosphere of disappointment. Some started to go out, but loitered, hearing no bell-tap to land. The sun dipped behind the horizon, the boat went on. Enquiring looks passed from one guest to another; and one who had his hand on the door-knob and had turned it, waited, then pres-ently took away his hand and let the knob turn back again. We bore steadily down the bend. More looks were exchanged, and nods of surprised admiration—but no words. Insensibly the men drew together behind Mr. Bixby, as the sky darkened and one or two dim stars came out. The dead silence and sense of waiting became oppressive. Mr. Bixby pulled the cord, and two deep, mellow notes from the big bell floated off on the night. Then a pause, and one more note was struck. The watchman's voice followed, from the hurricane deck:

"Labboard lead, there! Stabboard lead!"

The cries of the leadsmen began to rise out of the distance, and were gruffly repeated by the word-passers on the hurricane deck.

"M-a-r-k three! . . . . M-a-r-k three! . . . . Quarter-less-three! . . . . Half twain! . . . . Quarter twain! . . . . M-a-r-k twain! . . . . Quarter-less"—

Mr. Bixby pulled two bell-ropes, and was answered by faint jinglings far below in the engine-room, and our speed slackened. The steam began to whistle through the gauge-cocks. The cries of the leadsmen went on—and it is a weird sound, always, in the night. Every pilot in the lot was watching now, with fixed eyes, and talking under his breath. Nobody was calm and easy but Mr. Bixby. He would put his wheel down and stand on a spoke, and as the steamer swung into her (to me) utterly invisible marks—for we seemed to be in the midst of a wide and gloomy sea—he would meet and fasten her there. Out of the murmur of half-audible talk, one caught a coherent sentence now and then—such as:

"There; she's over the first reef all right!"

After a pause, another subdued voice:—

"Her stern's coming down just *exactly* right, by *George!*"

"Now she's in the marks; over she goes!"

Somebody else muttered:—

"Oh, it was done beautiful—*beautiful!*"

Now the engines were stopped altogether, and we drifted with the current. Not that I could see the boat drift, for I could not, the stars being all gone by this time. This drifting was the dismalest work; it held one's heart still. Presently I discovered a blacker gloom than that which surrounded us. It was the head of the island. We were closing right down upon it. We entered its deeper shadow, and so imminent seemed the peril that I was likely to suffocate; and I had the strongest impulse to do *something*, anything, to save the vessel. But still Mr.

Bixby stood by his wheel, silent, intent as a cat, and all the pilots stood shoulder to shoulder at his back.

"She'll not make it!" somebody whispered.

The water grew shoaler and shoaler, by the leadsman's cries, till it was down to—

"Eight-and-a-half! . . . . E-i-g-h-t feet! . . . . E-i-g-h-t feet! . . . . Seven-and"—

Mr. Bixby said warningly through his speaking tube to the engineer:—

"Stand by, now!"

"Ay, ay, sir!"

"Seven-and-a-half! Seven feet! *Six*-and"—

We touched bottom! Instantly Mr. Bixby set a lot of bells ringing, shouted through the tube, "*Now*, let her have it—every ounce you've got!" then to his partner, "Put her hard down! snatch her! snatch her!" The boat rasped and ground her way through the sand, hung upon the apex of disaster a single tremendous instant, and then over she went! And such a shout as went up at Mr. Bixby's back never loosened the roof of a pilot-house before!

There was no more trouble after that. Mr. Bixby was a hero that night; and it was some little time, too, before his exploit ceased to be talked about by river men.

Fully to realize the marvellous precision required in laying the great steamer in her marks in that murky waste of water, one should know that not only must she pick her intricate way through snags and blind reefs, and then shave the head of the island so closely as to brush the overhanging foliage with her stern, but at one place she must pass almost within arm's reach of a sunken and invisible wreck that would snatch the hull timbers from under her if she should strike it, and destroy a quarter of a million dollars' worth of steamboat and cargo in five minutes, and maybe a hundred and fifty human lives into the bargain.

The last remark I heard that night was a compliment to Mr. Bixby, uttered in soliloquy and with unction by one of our guests. He said:—

"By the Shadow of Death, but he's a lightning pilot!"

PERPLEXING LESSONS

At the end of what seemed a tedious while, I had managed to pack my head full of islands, towns, bars, "points," and bends; and a curiously inanimate mass of lumber it was, too. However, inasmuch as I could shut my eyes and reel off a good long string of these names without leaving out more than ten miles of river in every fifty, I began to feel that I could take a boat down to New Orleans if I could make her skip those little gaps. But of course my complacency could hardly get start enough to lift my nose a trifle into the air, before Mr. Bixby would think of something to fetch it down again. One day he turned on me suddenly with this settler:—

"What is the shape of Walnut Bend?"

He might as well have asked me my grandmother's opinion of protoplasm. I reflected respectfully, and then said I didn't know it had any particular shape. My gunpowdery chief went off with a bang, of course, and then went on loading and firing until he was out of adjectives.

I had learned long ago that he only carried just so many rounds of ammunition, and was sure to subside into a very placable and even remorseful old smooth-bore as soon as they were all gone. That word "old" is merely affectionate; he was not more than thirty-four. I waited. By and by he said,—

"My boy, you've got to know the *shape* of the river perfectly. It is all there is left to steer by on a very dark night. Everything else is blotted out and gone. But mind you, it hasn't the same shape in the night that it has in the day-time."

"How on earth am I ever going to learn it, then?"

"How do you follow a hall at home in the dark? Because you know the shape of it. You can't see it."

"Do you mean to say that I've got to know all the million trifling variations of shape in the banks of this interminable river as well as I know the shape of the front hall at home?"

"On my honor, you've got to know them *better* than any man ever did know the shapes of the halls in his own house."

"I wish I was dead!"

"Now I don't want to discourage you, but"—

"Well, pile it on me; I might as well have it now as another time."

"You see, this has got to be learned; there isn't any getting around it. A clear starlight night throws such heavy shadows that, if you didn't know the shape of a shore perfectly, you would claw away from every bunch of timber, because you would take the black shadow of it for a solid cape; and you see you would be getting scared to death every fifteen minutes by the watch. You would be fifty yards from shore all the time when you ought to be within fifty feet of it. You can't see a snag in one of those shadows, but you know exactly where it is, and the shape of the river tells you when you are coming to it. Then there's your pitch-dark night; the river is a very different shape on a pitch-dark night from what it is on a starlight night. All shores seem to be straight lines, then, and mighty dim ones, too; and you'd *run* them for straight lines, only you know better. You boldly drive your boat right into what seems to be a solid, straight wall (you knowing very well that in reality there is a curve there), and that wall falls back and makes way for you. Then there's your gray mist. You take a night when there's one of these grisly, drizzly, gray mists, and then there isn't *any* particular shape to a shore. A gray mist would tangle the head of the oldest man that ever lived. Well, then, different kinds of *moonlight* change the shape of the river in different ways. You see"—

"Oh, don't say any more, please! Have I got to learn the shape of the river according to all these five hundred thousand different ways? If I tried to carry all that cargo in my head it would make me stoop-shouldered."

"*No!* you only learn *the* shape of the river; and you learn it with such absolute certainty that you can always steer by the shape that's *in your head*, and never mind the one that's before your eyes."

"Very well, I'll try it; but after I have learned it, can I depend on it? Will it keep the same form and not go fooling around?"

Before Mr. Bixby could answer, Mr. W—— came in to take the watch, and he said:

"Bixby, you'll have to look out for President's Island, and all that country clear away up above the Old Hen and Chickens. The banks are caving and the shape of the shores changing like everything. Why, you wouldn't know the point above 40. You can go up inside the old sycamore snag, now."*

So that question was answered. Here were leagues of shore changing shape. My spirits were down in the mud again. Two things seemed pretty apparent to me. One was, that in order to be a pilot a man had got to learn more than any one man ought to be allowed to know; and the other was, that he must learn it all over again in a different way every twenty-four hours.

That night we had the watch until twelve. Now it was an ancient river custom for the two pilots to chat a bit when the watch changed. While the relieving pilot put on his gloves and lit his cigar, his partner, the retiring pilot, would say something like this:—

"I judge the upper bar is making down a little at Hale's Point; had quarter twain with the lower lead and mark twain† with the other."

"Yes, I thought it was making down a little, last trip. Meet any boats?"

"Met one abreast the head of 21, but she was away over hugging the bar, and I couldn't make her out entirely. I took her for the "Sunny South"—hadn't any skylights forward of the chimneys."

And so on. And as the relieving pilot took the wheel his partner‡ would mention that we were in such-and-such a bend, and say we were abreast of such-and-such a man's wood-yard or plantation. This was courtesy; I supposed it was *necessity*. But Mr. W—— came on watch full twelve minutes late on this particular night—a tremendous breach of etiquette; in fact, it is the unpardonable sin among pilots. So Mr. Bixby gave him

---

* It may not be necessary, but still it can do no harm to explain that "inside" means between the snag and the shore.—M. T.

† Two fathoms. Quarter twain is 2¼ fathoms, 13½ feet. Mark three is three fathoms.

‡ "Partner" is technical for "the other pilot."

no greeting whatever, but simply surrendered the wheel and
marched out of the pilot-house without a word. I was appalled;
it was a villanous night for blackness, we were in a particularly wide and blind part of the river, where there was no shape
or substance to anything, and it seemed incredible that Mr.
Bixby should have left that poor fellow to kill the boat, trying
to find out where he was. But I resolved that I would stand by
him any way. He should find that he was not wholly friendless.
So I stood around, and waited to be asked where we were. But
Mr. W—— plunged on serenely through the solid firmament of
black cats that stood for an atmosphere, and never opened his
mouth. Here is a proud devil, thought I; here is a limb of Satan
that would rather send us all to destruction than put himself
under obligations to me, because I am not yet one of the salt of
the earth and privileged to snub captains and lord it over
everything dead and alive in a steamboat. I presently climbed
up on the bench; I did not think it was safe to go to sleep while
this lunatic was on watch.

However, I must have gone to sleep in the course of time,
because the next thing I was aware of was the fact that day
was breaking, Mr. W—— gone, and Mr. Bixby at the wheel
again. So it was four o'clock and all well—but me; I felt like a
skinful of dry bones and all of them trying to ache at once.

Mr. Bixby asked me what I had stayed up there for. I confessed that it was to do Mr. W—— a benevolence,—tell him
where he was. It took five minutes for the entire preposterous-
ness of the thing to filter into Mr. Bixby's system, and then I
judge it filled him nearly up to the chin; because he paid me a
compliment—and not much of a one either. He said,—

"Well, taking you by and large, you do seem to be more different kinds of an ass than any creature I ever saw before.
What did you suppose he wanted to know for?"

I said I thought it might be a convenience to him.

"Convenience! D-nation! Didn't I tell you that a man's got
to know the river in the night the same as he'd know his own
front hall?"

"Well, I can follow the front hall in the dark if I know it *is* the front hall; but suppose you set me down in the middle of it in the dark and not tell me which hall it is; how am *I* to know?"

"Well, you've *got* to, on the river!"

"All right. Then I'm glad I never said anything to Mr. W——."

"I should say so! Why, he'd have slammed you through the window and utterly ruined a hundred dollars' worth of window-sash and stuff."

I was glad this damage had been saved, for it would have made me unpopular with the owners. They always hated anybody who had the name of being careless and injuring things.

I went to work now to learn the shape of the river; and of all the eluding and ungraspable objects that ever I tried to get mind or hands on, that was the chief. I would fasten my eyes upon a sharp, wooded point that projected far into the river some miles ahead of me, and go to laboriously photographing its shape upon my brain; and just as I was beginning to succeed to my satisfaction, we would draw up toward it and the exasperating thing would begin to melt away and fold back into the bank! If there had been a conspicuous dead tree standing upon the very point of the cape, I would find that tree inconspicuously merged into the general forest, and occupying the middle of a straight shore, when I got abreast of it! No prominent hill would stick to its shape long enough for me to make up my mind what its form really was, but it was as dissolving and changeful as if it had been a mountain of butter in the hottest corner of the tropics. Nothing ever had the same shape when I was coming down-stream that it had borne when I went up. I mentioned these little difficulties to Mr. Bixby. He said,—

"That's the very main virtue of the thing. If the shapes didn't change every three seconds they wouldn't be of any use. Take this place where we are now, for instance. As long as that hill over yonder is only one hill, I can boom right along the way I'm going; but the moment it splits at the top and forms a V, I know I've got to scratch to starboard in a hurry, or I'll bang this boat's brains out against a rock; and then the moment one of the prongs of the V swings behind the other,

I've got to waltz to larboard again, or I'll have a misunderstanding with a snag that would snatch the keelson out of this steamboat as neatly as if it were a sliver in your hand. If that hill didn't change its shape on bad nights there would be an awful steamboat grave-yard around here inside of a year."

It was plain that I had got to learn the shape of the river in all the different ways that could be thought of,—upside down, wrong end first, inside out, fore-and-aft, and "thort-ships,"—and then know what to do on gray nights when it hadn't any shape at all. So I set about it. In the course of time I began to get the best of this knotty lesson, and my self-complacency moved to the front once more. Mr. Bixby was all fixed, and ready to start it to the rear again. He opened on me after this fashion:—

"How much water did we have in the middle crossing at Hole-in-the-Wall, trip before last?"

I considered this an outrage. I said:—

"Every trip, down and up, the leadsmen are singing through that tangled place for three-quarters of an hour on a stretch. How do you reckon I can remember such a mess as that?"

"My boy, you've got to remember it. You've got to remember the exact spot and the exact marks the boat lay in when we had the shoalest water, in every one of the five hundred shoal places between St. Louis and New Orleans; and you mustn't get the shoal soundings and marks of one trip mixed up with the shoal soundings and marks of another, either, for they're not often twice alike. You must keep them separate."

When I came to myself again, I said,—

"When I get so that I can do that, I'll be able to raise the dead, and then I won't have to pilot a steamboat to make a living. I want to retire from this business. I want a slush-bucket and a brush; I'm only fit for a roustabout. I haven't got brains enough to be a pilot; and if I had I wouldn't have strength enough to carry them around, unless I went on crutches."

"Now drop that! When I say I'll learn* a man the river, I mean it. And you can depend on it, I'll learn him or kill him."

---

* "Teach" is not in the river vocabulary.

CONTINUED PERPLEXITIES

There was no use in arguing with a person like this. I promptly put such a strain on my memory that by and by even the shoal water and the countless crossing-marks began to stay with me. But the result was just the same. I never could more than get one knotty thing learned before another presented itself. Now I had often seen pilots gazing at the water and pretending to read it as if it were a book; but it was a book that told me nothing. A time came at last, however, when Mr. Bixby seemed to think me far enough advanced to bear a lesson on water-reading. So he began:—

"Do you see that long, slanting line on the face of the water? Now, that's a reef. Moreover, it's a bluff reef. There is a solid sand-bar under it that is nearly as straight up and down as the side of a house. There is plenty of water close up to it, but mighty little on top of it. If you were to hit it, you would knock the boat's brains out. Do you see where the line fringes out at the upper end and begins to fade away?"

"Yes, sir."

"Well, that is a low place; that is the head of the reef. You can climb over there, and not hurt anything. Cross over, now, and follow along close under the reef—easy water there—not much current."

I followed the reef along till I approached the fringed end. Then Mr. Bixby said,—

"Now get ready. Wait till I give the word. She won't want to mount the reef; a boat hates shoal water. Stand by—wait—wait—keep her well in hand. *Now* cramp her down! Snatch her! snatch her!"

He seized the other side of the wheel and helped to spin it around until it was hard down, and then we held it so. The boat resisted, and refused to answer for a while, and next she came surging to starboard, mounted the reef, and sent a long, angry ridge of water foaming away from her bows.

"Now watch her; watch her like a cat, or she'll get away from you. When she fights strong and the tiller slips a little, in a jerky, greasy sort of way, let up on her a trifle; it is the way she tells you at night that the water is too shoal; but keep edging her up, little by little, toward the point. You are well up on the bar now; there is a bar under every point, because the water that comes down around it forms an eddy and allows the sediment to sink. Do you see those fine lines on the face of the water that branch out like the ribs of a fan? Well, those are little reefs; you want to just miss the ends of them, but run them pretty close. Now look out—look out! Don't you crowd that slick, greasy-looking place; there ain't nine feet there; she won't stand it. She begins to smell it; look sharp, I tell you! Oh, blazes, there you go! Stop the starboard wheel! Quick! Ship up to back! Set her back!"

The engine bells jingled and the engines answered promptly, shooting white columns of steam far aloft out of the 'scape pipes, but it was too late. The boat had "smelt" the bar in good earnest; the foamy ridges that radiated from her bows suddenly disappeared, a great dead swell came rolling forward and swept ahead of her, she careened far over to larboard, and went tearing away toward the shore as if she were about scared to death. We were a good mile from where we ought to have been, when we finally got the upper hand of her again.

During the afternoon watch the next day, Mr. Bixby asked me if I knew how to run the next few miles. I said:—

"Go inside the first snag above the point, outside the next one, start out from the lower end of Higgins's wood-yard, make a square crossing, and"—

"That's all right. I'll be back before you close up on the next point."

But he wasn't. He was still below when I rounded it and entered upon a piece of river which I had some misgivings about. I did not know that he was hiding behind a chimney to see how I would perform. I went gayly along, getting prouder and prouder, for he had never left the boat in my sole charge such a length of time before. I even got to "setting" her and letting the wheel go, entirely, while I vaingloriously turned my back and inspected the stern marks and hummed a tune, a sort of easy indifference which I had prodigiously admired in Bixby and other great pilots. Once I inspected rather long, and when

I faced to the front again my heart flew into my mouth so suddenly that if I hadn't clapped my teeth together I should have lost it. One of those frightful bluff reefs was stretching its deadly length right across our bows! My head was gone in a moment; I did not know which end I stood on; I gasped and could not get my breath; I spun the wheel down with such rapidity that it wove itself together like a spider's web; the boat answered and turned square away from the reef, but the reef followed her! I fled, but still it followed still it kept—right across my bows! I never looked to see where I was going, I only fled. The awful crash was imminent—why didn't that villain come? If I committed the crime of ringing a bell, I might get thrown overboard. But better that than kill the boat. So in blind desperation I started such a rattling "shivaree" down below as never had astounded an engineer in this world before, I fancy. Amidst the frenzy of the bells the engines began to back and fill in a furious way, and my reason forsook its throne—we were about to crash into the woods on the other side of the river. Just then Mr. Bixby stepped calmly into view on the hurricane deck. My soul went out to him in gratitude. My distress vanished; I would have felt safe on the brink of Niagara, with Mr. Bixby on the hurricane deck. He blandly and sweetly took his tooth-pick out of his mouth between his fingers, as if it were a cigar,—we were just in the act of climbing an overhanging big tree, and the passengers were scudding astern like rats,—and lifted up these commands to me ever so gently:—

"Stop the starboard. Stop the larboard. Set her back on both."

The boat hesitated, halted, pressed her nose among the boughs a critical instant, then reluctantly began to back away.

"Stop the larboard. Come ahead on it. Stop the starboard. Come ahead on it. Point her for the bar."

I sailed away as serenely as a summer's morning. Mr. Bixby came in and said, with mock simplicity,—

"When you have a hail, my boy, you ought to tap the big bell three times before you land, so that the engineers can get ready."

344
AUTOBIOGRAPHICAL WRITINGS

I blushed under the sarcasm, and said I hadn't had any hail.

"Ah! Then it was for wood, I suppose. The officer of the watch will tell you when he wants to wood up."

I went on consuming, and said I wasn't after wood.

"Indeed? Why, what could you want over here in the bend, then? Did you ever know of a boat following a bend up-stream at this stage of the river?"

"No, sir,—and I wasn't trying to follow it. I was getting away from a bluff reef."

"No, it wasn't a bluff reef; there isn't one within three miles of where you were."

"But I saw it. It was as bluff as that one yonder."

"Just about. Run over it!"

"Do you give it as an order?"

"Yes. Run over it!"

"If I don't, I wish I may die."

"All right; I am taking the responsibility."

I was just as anxious to kill the boat, now, as I had been to save her before. I impressed my orders upon my memory, to be used at the inquest, and made a straight break for the reef. As it disappeared under our bows I held my breath; but we slid over it like oil.

"Now, don't you see the difference? It wasn't anything but a *wind* reef. The wind does that."

"So I see. But it is exactly like a bluff reef. How am I ever going to tell them apart?"

"I can't tell you. It is an instinct. By and by you will just naturally *know* one from the other, but you never will be able to explain why or how you know them apart."

It turned out to be true. The face of the water, in time, became a wonderful book—a book that was a dead language to the uneducated passenger, but which told its mind to me without reserve, delivering its most cherished secrets as clearly as if it uttered them with a voice. And it was not a book to be read once and thrown aside, for it had a new story to tell every day. Throughout the long twelve hundred miles there was never a page that was void of interest, never one that you could leave unread without loss, never one that you would want to skip, thinking you could find higher enjoyment in some other thing. There never was so wonderful a book written by man; never one whose interest was so absorbing, so unflagging, so sparklingly renewed with every re-perusal. The passenger who could not read it was charmed with a peculiar sort of faint dimple on its surface (on the rare occasions when he did not overlook it altogether); but to the pilot that was an *italicized* passage; indeed, it was more than that, it was a legend of the largest capitals, with a string of shouting exclamation points at the end of it; for it meant that a wreck or a rock was buried there that could tear the life out of the strongest vessel that ever floated. It is the faintest and simplest expression the water ever makes, and the most hideous to a pilot's eye. In truth, the passenger who could not read this book saw nothing but all manner of pretty pictures in it, painted by the sun and shaded by the clouds, whereas to the trained eye these were not pictures at all, but the grimmest and most dead-earnest of reading-matter.

Now when I had mastered the language of this water, and had come to know every trifling feature that bordered the great river as familiarly as I knew the letters of the alphabet, I had made a valuable acquisition. But I had lost something, too. I had lost something which could never be restored to me while I lived. All the grace, the beauty, the poetry, had gone out of the majestic river! I still kept in mind a certain wonderful sunset which I witnessed when steamboating was new to me. A broad expanse of the river was turned to blood; in the middle distance the red hue brightened into gold, through which a solitary log came floating, black and conspicuous; one place a long, slanting mark lay sparkling upon the water; in another the surface was broken by boiling, tumbling rings, that were as many-tinted as an opal; where the ruddy flush was faintest, was a smooth spot that was covered with graceful circles and radiating lines, ever so delicately traced; the shore on our left was densely wooded, and the sombre shadow that fell from this forest was broken in one place by a long, ruffled trail that shone like silver; and high above the forest wall a clean-stemmed dead tree waved a single leafy bough that glowed like a flame in the unobstructed splendor that was flowing from the sun.

There were graceful curves, reflected images, woody heights, soft distances; and over the whole scene, far and near, the dissolving lights drifted steadily, enriching it, every passing moment with new marvels of coloring.

I stood like one bewitched. I drank it in, in a speechless rapture. The world was new to me, and I had never seen anything like this at home. But as I have said, a day came when I began to cease from noting the glories and the charms which the moon and the sun and the twilight wrought upon the river's face; another day came when I ceased altogether to note them. Then, if that sunset scene had been repeated, I should have looked upon it without rapture, and should have commented upon it, inwardly, after this fashion: This sun means that we are going to have wind to-morrow; that floating log means that the river is rising, small thanks to it; that slanting mark on the water refers to a bluff reef which is going to kill somebody's steamboat one of these nights, if it keeps on stretching out like that; those tumbling "boils" show a dissolving bar and a changing channel there; the lines and circles in the slick water over yonder are a warning that that troublesome place is shoaling up dangerously; that silver streak in the shadow of the forest is the "break" from a new snag, and he has located himself in the very best place he could have found to fish for steamboats; that tall dead tree, with a single living branch, is not going to last long, and then how is a body ever going to get through this blind place at night without the friendly old landmark?

No, the romance and the beauty were all gone from the river. All the value any feature of it had for me now was the amount of usefulness it could furnish toward compassing the safe piloting of a steamboat. Since those days, I have pitied doctors from my heart. What does the lovely flush in a beauty's cheek mean to a doctor but a "break" that ripples above some deadly disease? Are not all her visible charms sown thick with what are to him the signs and symbols of hidden decay? Does he ever see her beauty at all, or doesn't he simply view her professionally, and comment upon her unwholesome condition all to himself? And doesn't he sometimes wonder whether he has gained most or lost most by learning his trade?

COMPLETING MY EDUCATION

Whosoever has done me the courtesy to read my chapters which have preceded this may possibly wonder that I deal so minutely with piloting as a science. It was the prime purpose of those chapters; and I am not quite done yet. I wish to show, in the most patient and painstaking way, what a wonderful science it is. Ship channels are buoyed and lighted, and therefore it is a comparatively easy undertaking to learn to run them; clear-water rivers, with gravel bottoms, change their channels very gradually, and therefore one needs to learn them but once; but piloting becomes another matter when you apply it to vast streams like the Mississippi and the Missouri, whose alluvial banks cave and change constantly, whose snags are always hunting up new quarters, whose sand-bars are never at rest, whose channels are forever dodging and shirking, and whose obstructions must be confronted in all nights and all weathers without the aid of a single light-house or a single buoy; for there is neither light nor buoy to be found anywhere in all this three or four thousand miles of villanous river.* I feel justified in enlarging upon this great science for the reason that I feel sure no one has ever yet written a paragraph about it who had piloted a steamboat himself, and so had a practical knowledge of the subject. If the theme was hackneyed, I should be obliged to deal gently with the reader; but since it is wholly new, I have felt at liberty to take up a considerable degree of room with it.

When I had learned the name and position of every visible feature of the river; when I had so mastered its shape that I could shut my eyes and trace it from St. Louis to New Orleans; when I had learned to read the face of the water as one would cull the news from the morning paper; and finally, when I had trained my dull memory to treasure up an endless array of soundings and crossing-marks, and keep fast hold of them, I judged that my education was complete: so I got to tilting my cap to the side of my head, and wearing a tooth-pick in my

* True at the time referred to: not true now (1882).

mouth at the wheel. Mr. Bixby had his eye on these airs. One day he said:—

"What is the height of that bank yonder, at Burgess's?"

"How can I tell, sir? It is three-quarters of a mile away."

"Very poor eye—very poor. Take the glass."

I took the glass, and presently said:—

"I can't tell. I suppose that that bank is about a foot and a half high."

"Foot and a half! That's a six-foot bank. How high was the bank along here last trip?"

"I don't know; I never noticed."

"You didn't? Well, you must always do it hereafter."

"Why?"

"Because you'll have to know a good many things that it tells you. For one thing, it tells you the stage of the river—tells you whether there's more water or less in the river along here than there was last trip."

"The leads tell me that." I rather thought I had the advantage of him there.

"Yes, but suppose the leads lie? The bank would tell you so, and then you'd stir those leadsmen up a bit. There was a ten-foot bank here last trip, and there is only a six-foot bank now. What does that signify?"

"That the river is four feet higher than it was last trip."

"Very good. Is the river rising or falling?"

"Rising."

"No, it ain't."

"I guess I am right, sir. Yonder is some drift-wood floating down the stream."

"A rise *starts* the drift-wood, but then it keeps on floating a while after the river is done rising. Now the bank will tell you about this. Wait till you come to a place where it shelves a little. Now here: do you see this narrow belt of fine sediment? That was deposited while the water was higher. You see the drift-wood begins to strand, too. The bank helps in other ways. Do you see that stump on the false point?"

"Ay, ay, sir."

"Well, the water is just up to the roots of it. You must make a note of that."

"Why?"

"Because that means that there's seven feet in the chute of 103."

"But 103 is a long way up the river yet."

"That's where the benefit of the bank comes in. There is water enough in 103 *now*, yet there may not be by the time we get there; but the bank will keep us posted all along. You don't run close chutes on a falling river, up-stream, and there are precious few of them that you are allowed to run at all down-stream. There's a law of the United States against it. The river may be rising by the time we get to 103, and in that case we'll run it. We are drawing—how much?"

"Six feet aft—six and a half forward."

"Well, you do seem to know something."

"But what I particularly want to know is, if I have got to keep up an everlasting measuring of the banks of this river, twelve hundred miles, month in and month out?"

"Of course!"

My emotions were too deep for words for a while. Presently I said,—

"And how about these chutes? Are there many of them?"

"I should say so! I fancy we shan't run any of the river this trip as you've ever seen it run before—so to speak. If the river begins to rise again, we'll go up behind bars that you've always seen standing out of the river, high and dry, like the roof of a house; we'll cut across low places that you've never noticed at all, right through the middle of bars that cover three hundred acres of river; we'll creep through cracks where you've always thought was solid land; we'll dart through the woods and leave twenty-five miles of river off to one side; we'll see the hind side of every island between New Orleans and Cairo."

"Then I've got to go to work and learn just as much more river as I already know."

"Just about twice as much more, as near as you can come at it."

"Well, one lives to find out. I think I was a fool when I went into this business."

"Yes, that is true. And you are yet. But you'll not be when you've learned it."

"Ah, I never can learn it!"

"I will see that you *do*."

By and by I ventured again:—

"Have I got to learn all this thing just as I know the rest of the river—shapes and all—and so I can run it at night?"

"Yes. And you've got to have good fair marks from one end of the river to the other, that will help the bank tell you when there is water enough in each of these countless places—like that stump, you know. When the river first begins to rise, you can run half a dozen of the deepest of them; when it rises a foot more you can run another dozen; the next foot will add a couple of dozen, and so on: so you see you have to know your banks and marks to a dead moral certainty, and never get them mixed; for when you start through one of those cracks, there's no backing out again, as there is in the big river; you've got to go through, or stay there six months if you get caught on a falling river. There are about fifty of these cracks which you can't run at all except when the river is brimful and over the banks."

"This new lesson is a cheerful prospect."

"Cheerful enough. And mind what I've just told you; when you start into one of those places you've got to go through. They are too narrow to turn around in, too crooked to back out of, and the shoal water is always *up at the head;* never elsewhere. And the head of them is always likely to be filling up, little by little, so that the marks you reckon their depth by, this season, may not answer for next."

"Learn a new set, then, every year?"

"Exactly. Cramp her up to the bar! What are you standing up through the middle of the river for?"

The next few months showed me strange things. On the same day that we held the conversation above narrated we met a great rise coming down the river. The whole vast face of the stream was black with drifting dead logs, broken boughs, and great trees that had caved in and been washed away. It required the nicest steering to pick one's way through this rushing raft, even in the day-time, when crossing from point to point; and at night the difficulty was mightily increased; every now and then a huge log, lying deep in the water, would suddenly appear right under our bows, coming head-on; no use to try to avoid it then; we could only stop the engines, and one wheel would walk over that log from one end to the other, keeping up a thundering racket and careening the boat in a way that was very uncomfortable to passengers. Now and then we would hit one of these sunken logs a rattling bang, dead in the center, with a full head of steam, and it would stun the boat as if she had hit a continent. Sometimes this log would lodge and stay right across our nose, and back the Mississippi up before it; we would have to do a little crawfishing, then, to get away from the obstruction. We often hit *white* logs in the dark, for we could not see them till we were right on them, but a black log is a pretty distinct object at night. A white snag is an ugly customer when the daylight is gone.

Of course, on the great rise, down came a swarm of prodigious timber-rafts from the head waters of the Mississippi, coal barges from Pittsburgh, little trading scows from everywhere, and broad-horns from "Posey County," Indiana, freighted with "fruit and furniture"—the usual term for describing it, though in plain English the freight thus aggrandized was hoop poles and pumpkins. Pilots bore a mortal hatred to these craft; and it was returned with usury. The law required all such helpless traders to keep a light burning, but it was a law that was often broken. All of a sudden, on a murky night, a light would hop up, right under our bows, almost, and an agonized voice, with the backwoods "whang" to it, would wail out:—

"Whar'n the —— you goin' to! Cain't you see nothin', you dash-dashed aig-suckin', sheep-stealin', one-eyed son of a stuffed monkey!"

Then for an instant, as we whistled by, the red glare from our furnaces would reveal the scow and the form of the gesticulating orator, as if under a lightning-flash, and in that instant our firemen and deck-hands would send and receive a tempest of missiles and profanity, one of our wheels would walk off with the crashing fragments of a steering-oar, and down the dead blackness would shut again. And that flatboatman would be sure to go into New Orleans and sue our boat, swearing stoutly that he had a light burning all the time, when in truth his gang had the lantern down below to sing and lie and drink and gamble by, and no watch on deck. Once, at night, in one of those forest-bordered crevices (behind an island) which steamboatmen intensely describe with the phrase "as dark as the inside of a cow," we should have eaten up a Posey County family, fruit, furniture, and all, but that they happened to be fiddling down below and we just caught the sound of the music in time to sheer off, doing no serious damage, unfortunately, but coming so near it that we had good hopes for a moment. These people brought up their lantern, then, of course; and as we backed and filled to get away, the precious family stood in the light of it—both sexes and various ages—and cursed us till everything turned blue. Once a coalboatman sent a bullet through our pilot-house when we borrowed a steering-oar of him in a very narrow place.

THE RIVER RISES

During this big rise these small-fry craft were an intolerable nuisance. We were running chute after chute,—a new world to me,—and if there was a particularly cramped place in a chute, we would be pretty sure to meet a broad-horn there; and if he failed to be there, we would find him in a still worse locality, namely, the head of the chute, on the shoal water. And then there would be no end of profane cordialities exchanged.

Sometimes, in the big river, when we would be feeling our way cautiously along through a fog, the deep hush would suddenly be broken by yells and a clamor of tin pans, and all in an instant a log raft would appear vaguely through the webby veil, close upon us; and then we did not wait to swap knives, but snatched our engine bells out by the roots and piled on all the steam we had, to scramble out of the way! One doesn't hit a rock or a solid log raft with a steamboat when he can get excused.

You will hardly believe it, but many steamboat clerks always carried a large assortment of religious tracts with them in those old departed steamboating days. Indeed they did. Twenty times a day we would be cramping up around a bar, while a string of these small-fry rascals were drifting down into the head of the bend away above and beyond us a couple of miles. Now a skiff would dart away from one of them, and come fighting its laborious way across the desert of water. It would "ease all" in the shadow of our forecastle, and the panting oarsmen would shout, "Gimme a pa-a-per!" as the skiff drifted swiftly astern. The clerk would throw over a file of New Orleans journals. If these were picked up *without comment*, you might notice that now a dozen other skiffs had been drifting down upon us without saying anything. You understand, they had been waiting to see how No. 1 was going to fare. No. 1 making no comment, all the rest would bend to their oars and come on, now; and as fast as they came the clerk would heave over neat bundles of religious tracts, tied to shingles. The amount of hard swearing which twelve packages of religious literature will command when impartially divided up among twelve raftsmen's crews, who have pulled a heavy skiff two miles on a hot day to get them, is simply incredible.

As I have said, the big rise brought a new world under my vision. By the time the river was over its banks we had forsaken our old paths and were hourly climbing over bars that had stood ten feet out of water before; we were shaving stumpy shores, like that at the foot of Madrid Bend, which I had always seen avoided before; we were clattering through chutes like that of 82, where the opening at the foot was an unbroken wall of timber till our nose was almost at the very spot. Some of these chutes were utter solitudes. The dense, untouched forest overhung both banks of the crooked little crack, and one could believe that human creatures had never intruded there before. The swinging grape-vines, the grassy nooks and vistas glimpsed as we swept by, the flowering creepers waving their red blossoms from the tops of dead trunks, and all the spendthrift richness of the forest foliage, were wasted and thrown away there. The chutes were lovely places to steer in; they were deep, except at the head; the current was gentle; under the "points" the water was absolutely dead, and the invisible banks so bluff that where the tender willow thickets projected you could bury your boat's broadside in them as you tore along, and then you seemed fairly to fly.

Behind other islands we found wretched little farms, and wretcheder little log-cabins; there were crazy rail fences sticking a foot or two above the water, with one or two jeans-clad, chills-racked, yellow-faced male miserables roosting on the top-rail, elbows on knees, jaws in hands, grinding tobacco and discharging the result at floating chips through crevices left by lost teeth; while the rest of the family and the few farm-animals were huddled together in an empty wood-flat riding at her moorings close at hand. In this flatboat the family would have to cook and eat and sleep for a lesser or greater number of days (or possibly weeks), until the river should fall two or three feet and let them get back to their log-cabin and their chills again—chills being a merciful provision of an all-wise Providence to enable them to take exercise without exertion. And this sort of watery camping out was a thing which these people were rather liable to be treated to a couple of times a year: by the December rise out of the Ohio, and the June rise out of the Mississippi. And yet these were kindly dispensations, for they at least enabled the poor things to rise from the dead now and then, and look upon life when a steamboat went by. They appreciated the blessing, too, for they spread their mouths and eyes wide open and made the most of these occasions. Now what *could* these banished creatures find to do to keep from dying of the blues during the low-water season!

Once, in one of these lovely island chutes, we found our course completely bridged by a great fallen tree. This will serve to show how narrow some of the chutes were. The passengers had an hour's recreation in a virgin wilderness, while the boat-hands chopped the bridge away; for there was no such thing as turning back, you comprehend.

From Cairo to Baton Rouge, when the river is over its banks, you have no particular trouble in the night, for the thousand-mile wall of dense forest that guards the two banks all the way is only gapped with a farm or wood-yard opening at intervals, and so you can't "get out of the river" much easier than you could get out of a fenced lane; but from Baton Rouge to New Orleans it is a different matter. The river is more than a mile wide, and very deep—as much as two hundred feet, in places. Both banks, for a good deal over a hundred miles, are shorn of their timber and bordered by continuous sugar plantations, with only here and there a scattering sapling or row of ornamental China-trees. The timber is shorn off clear to the rear of the plantations, from two to four miles. When the first frost threatens to come, the planters snatch off their crops in a hurry. When they have finished grinding the cane, they form the refuse of the stalks (which they call *bagasse*) into great piles and set fire to them, though in other sugar countries the bagasse is used for fuel in the furnaces of the sugar mills. Now the piles of damp bagasse burn slowly, and smoke like Satan's own kitchen.

An embankment ten or fifteen feet high guards both banks of the Mississippi all the way down that lower end of the river, and this embankment is set back from the edge of the shore from ten to perhaps a hundred feet, according to circumstances; say thirty or forty feet, as a general thing. Fill that whole region with an impenetrable gloom of smoke from a hundred miles of burning bagasse piles, when the river is over the banks, and turn a steamboat loose along there at midnight and see how she will feel. And see how you will feel, too! You find yourself away out in the midst of a vague, dim sea that is shoreless, that fades out and loses itself in the murky distances; for you cannot discern the thin rib of embankment, and you are always imagining you see a straggling tree when you don't. The plantations themselves are transformed by the smoke, and look like a part of the sea. All through your watch you are tortured with the exquisite misery of uncertainty. You hope you are keeping in the river, but you do not know. All that you are sure about is that you are likely to be within six feet of the bank *and* destruction, when you think you are a good half-mile from shore. And you are sure, also, that if you chance suddenly to fetch up against the embankment and topple your chimneys overboard, you will have the small comfort of knowing that it is about what you were expecting to do. One of the great Vicksburg packets darted out into a sugar plantation one night, at such a time, and had to stay there a week. But there was no novelty about it; it had often been done before.

I thought I had finished this chapter, but I wish to add a curious thing, while it is in my mind. It is only relevant in that it is connected with piloting. There used to be an excellent pilot on the river, a Mr. X., who was a somnambulist. It was said that if his mind was troubled about a bad piece of river, he was pretty sure to get up and walk in his sleep and do strange things. He was once fellow-pilot for a trip or two with George Ealer, on a great New Orleans passenger packet. During a considerable part of the first trip George was uneasy, but got over it by and by, as X. seemed content to stay in his bed when asleep. Late one night the boat was approaching Helena, Arkansas; the water was low, and the crossing above the town in a very blind and tangled condition. X. had seen the crossing since Ealer had, and as the night was particularly drizzly, sullen, and dark, Ealer was considering whether he had not better have X. called to assist in running the place, when the door opened and X. walked in. Now, on very dark nights, light is a deadly enemy to piloting; you are aware that if you stand in a lighted room, on such a night, you cannot see things in the street to any purpose; but if you put out the lights and stand in the gloom you can make out objects in the street pretty well. So, on very dark nights, pilots do not smoke; they allow no fire in the pilot-house stove, if there is a crack which can allow the least ray to escape; they order the furnaces to be curtained with huge tarpaulins and the sky-lights to be closely blinded. Then no light whatever issues from the boat. The undefinable shape that now entered the pilot-house had Mr. X.'s voice. This said,—

"Let me take her, George; I've seen this place since you have, and it is so crooked that I reckon I can run it myself easier than I could tell you how to do it."

"It is kind of you, and I swear I am willing. I haven't got another drop of perspiration left in me. I have been spinning around and around the wheel like a squirrel. It is so dark I can't tell which way she is swinging till she is coming around like a whirligig."

So Ealer took a seat on the bench, panting and breathless. The black phantom assumed the wheel without saying anything, steadied the waltzing steamer with a turn or two, and then stood at ease, coaxing her a little to this side and then to that, as gently and as sweetly as if the time had been noonday. When Ealer observed this marvel of steering, he wished he had not confessed! He stared, and wondered, and finally said,—

"Well, I thought I knew how to steer a steamboat, but that was another mistake of mine."

X. said nothing, but went serenely on with his work. He rang for the leads; he rang to slow down the steam; he worked the boat carefully and neatly into invisible marks, then stood at the centre of the wheel and peered blandly out into the blackness, fore and aft, to verify his position; as the leads shoaled more and more, he stopped the engines entirely, and the dead silence and suspense of "drifting" followed; when the shoalest water was struck, he cracked on the steam, carried her handsomely over, and then began to work her warily into the next system of shoal marks; the same patient, heedful use of leads and engines followed, the boat slipped through without touching bottom, and entered upon the third and last intricacy of the crossing; imperceptibly she moved through the gloom, crept by inches into her marks, drifted tediously till the shoalest water was cried, and then, under a tremendous head of steam, went swinging over the reef and away into deep water and safety!

Ealer let his long-pent breath pour out in a great, relieving sigh, and said:—

"That's the sweetest piece of piloting that was ever done on the Mississippi River! I wouldn't believed it could be done, if I hadn't seen it."

There was no reply, and he added:

"Just hold her five minutes longer, partner, and let me run down and get a cup of coffee."

A minute later Ealer was biting into a pie, down in the "texas," and comforting himself with coffee. Just then the night watchman happened in, and was about to happen out again, when he noticed Ealer and exclaimed,—

"Who is at the wheel, sir?"

"X."

"Dart for the pilot-house, quicker than lightning!"

The next moment both men were flying up the pilot-house companion-way, three steps at a jump! Nobody there! The great steamer was whistling down the middle of the river at her own sweet will! The watchman shot out of the place again; Ealer seized the wheel, set an engine back with power, and held his breath while the boat reluctantly swung away from a "towhead," which she was about to knock into the middle of the Gulf of Mexico!

By and by the watchman came back and said,—

"Didn't that lunatic tell you he was asleep, when he first came up here?"

"No."

"Well, he was. I found him walking along on top of the railings, just as unconcerned as another man would walk a pavement; and I put him to bed; now just this minute there he was again, away astern, going through that sort of tight-rope deviltry the same as before."

"Well, I think I'll stay by next time he has one of those fits. But I hope he'll have them often. You just ought to have seen him take this boat through Helena crossing. *I* never saw anything so gaudy before. And if he can do such gold-leaf, kid-glove, diamond-breastpin piloting when he is sound asleep, what *couldn't* he do if he was dead!"

SOUNDING

When the river is very low, and one's steamboat is "drawing all the water" there is in the channel,—or a few inches more, as was often the case in the old times,—one must be painfully circumspect in his piloting. We used to have to "sound" a number of particularly bad places almost every trip when the river was at a very low stage.

Sounding is done in this way. The boat ties up at the shore, just above the shoal crossing; the pilot not on watch takes his "cub" or steersman and a picked crew of men (sometimes an officer also), and goes out in the yawl—provided the boat has not that rare and sumptuous luxury, a regularly-devised "sounding-boat"—and proceeds to hunt for the best water, the pilot on duty watching his movements through a spy-glass, meantime, and in some instances assisting by signals of the boat's whistle, signifying "try higher up" or "try lower down"; for the surface of the water, like an oil-painting, is more expressive and intelligible when inspected from a little distance than very close at hand. The whistle signals are seldom necessary, however; never, perhaps, except when the wind confuses the significant ripples upon the water's surface. When the yawl has reached the shoal place, the speed is slackened, the pilot begins to sound the depth with a pole ten or twelve feet long, and the steersman at the tiller obeys the order to "hold her up to starboard"; or "let her fall off to larboard";* or "steady—steady as you go."

When the measurements indicate that the yawl is approaching the shoalest part of the reef, the command is given to "Ease all!" Then the men stop rowing and the yawl drifts with the current. The next order is, "Stand by with the buoy!" The moment the shallowest point is reached, the pilot delivers the order, "Let go the buoy!" and over she goes. If the pilot is not satisfied, he sounds the place again; if he finds better water higher up or lower down, he removes the buoy to that place. Being finally satisfied, he gives the order, and all the men stand their oars straight

---

* The term "larboard" is never used at sea now, to signify the left hand; but was always used on the river in my time.

up in the air, in line; a blast from the boat's whistle indicates that
the signal has been seen; then the men "give way" on their oars
and lay the yawl alongside the buoy; the steamer comes creeping
carefully down, is pointed straight at the buoy, husbands her
power for the coming struggle, and presently, at the critical
moment, turns on all her steam and goes grinding and wallow-
ing over the buoy and the sand, and gains the deep water beyond.
Or maybe she doesn't; maybe she "strikes and swings." Then she
has to while away several hours (or days) sparring herself off.

Sometimes a buoy is not laid at all, but the yawl goes ahead,
hunting the best water, and the steamer follows along in its
wake. Often there is a deal of fun and excitement about sounding, especially if it is a glorious summer day, or a blustering
night. But in winter the cold and the peril take most of the fun
out of it.

A buoy is nothing but a board four or five feet long, with one
end turned up; it is a reversed school-house bench, with one of
the supports left and the other removed. It is anchored on the
shoalest part of the reef by a rope with a heavy stone made fast
to the end of it. But for the resistance of the turned-up end of
the reversed bench, the current would pull the buoy under
water. At night, a paper lantern with a candle in it is fastened
on top of the buoy, and this can be seen a mile or more, a little
glimmering spark in the waste of blackness.

Nothing delights a cub so much as an opportunity to go out
sounding. There is such an air of adventure about it; often
there is danger; it is so gaudy and man-of-war-like to sit up in
the stern-sheets and steer a swift yawl; there is something fine
about the exultant spring of the boat when an experienced old
sailor crew throw their souls into the oars; it is lovely to see
the white foam stream away from the bows; there is music in
the rush of the water; it is deliciously exhilarating, in summer,
to go speeding over the breezy expanses of the river when the
world of wavelets is dancing in the sun. It is such grandeur,
too, to the cub, to get a chance to give an order; for often the
pilot will simply say, "Let her go about!" and leave the rest to
the cub, who instantly cries, in his sternest tone of command,
"Ease, starboard! Strong on the larboard! Starboard, give way!

With a will, men!" The cub enjoys sounding for the further reason that the eyes of the passengers are watching all the yawl's movements with absorbing interest, if the time be daylight; and if it be night, he knows that those same wondering eyes are fastened upon the yawl's lantern as it glides out into the gloom and dims away in the remote distance.

One trip a pretty girl of sixteen spent her time in our pilot-house with her uncle and aunt, every day and all day long. I fell in love with her. So did Mr. Thornburg's cub, Tom G——. Tom and I had been bosom friends until this time; but now a coolness began to arise. I told the girl a good many of my river adventures, and made myself out a good deal of a hero; Tom tried to make himself appear to be a hero, too, and succeeded to some extent, but then he always had a way of embroidering. However, virtue is its own reward, so I was a barely perceptible trifle ahead in the contest. About this time something happened which promised handsomely for me: the pilots decided to sound the crossing at the head of 21. This would occur about nine or ten o'clock at night, when the passengers would be still up; it would be Mr. Thornburg's watch, therefore my chief would have to do the sounding. We had a perfect love of a sounding-boat—long, trim, graceful, and as fleet as a greyhound; her thwarts were cushioned; she carried twelve oarsmen; one of the mates was always sent in her to transmit orders to her crew, for ours was a steamer where no end of "style" was put on.

We tied up at the shore above 21, and got ready. It was a foul night, and the river was so wide, there, that a landsman's uneducated eyes could discern no opposite shore through such a gloom. The passengers were alert and interested; everything was satisfactory. As I hurried through the engine-room, picturesquely gotten up in storm toggery, I met Tom, and could not forbear delivering myself of a mean speech:—

"Ain't you glad *you* don't have to go out sounding?"

Tom was passing on, but he quickly turned, and said,—

"Now just for that, you can go and get the sounding-pole yourself. I was going after it, but I'd see you in Halifax, now, before I'd do it."

"Who wants you to get it? *I* don't. It's in the sounding-boat."

"It ain't, either. It's been new-painted; and it's been up on the ladies' cabin guards two days, drying."

I flew back, and shortly arrived among the crowd of watching and wondering ladies just in time to hear the command:

"Give way, men!"

I looked over, and there was the gallant sounding-boat booming away, the unprincipled Tom presiding at the tiller, and my chief sitting by him with the sounding-pole which I had been sent on a fool's errand to fetch. Then that young girl said to me,—

"Oh, how awful to have to go out in that little boat on such a night! Do you think there is any danger?"

I would rather have been stabbed. I went off, full of venom, to help in the pilot-house. By and by the boat's lantern disappeared, and after an interval a wee spark glimmered upon the face of the water a mile away. Mr. Thornburg blew the whistle in acknowledgment, backed the steamer out, and made for it. We flew along for a while, then slackened steam and went cautiously gliding toward the spark. Presently Mr. Thornburg exclaimed,—

"Hello, the buoy-lantern's out!"

He stopped the engines. A moment or two later he said,—

"Why, there it is again!"

So he came ahead on the engines once more, and rang for the leads. Gradually the water shoaled up, and then began to deepen again! Mr. Thornburg muttered:—

"Well, I don't understand this. I believe that buoy has drifted off the reef. Seems to be a little too far to the left. No matter, it is safest to run over it, anyhow."

So, in that solid world of darkness we went creeping down on the light. Just as our bows were in the act of ploughing over it, Mr. Thornburg seized the bell-ropes, rang a startling peal, and exclaimed,—

"My soul, it's the sounding-boat!"

A sudden chorus of wild alarms burst out far below—a

pause—and then a sound of grinding and crashing followed. Mr. Thornburg exclaimed,—

"There! the paddle-wheel has ground the sounding-boat to lucifer matches! Run! See who is killed!"

I was on the main-deck in the twinkling of an eye. My chief and the third mate and nearly all the men were safe. They had discovered their danger when it was too late to pull out of the way; then, when the great guards overshadowed them a moment later, they were prepared and knew what to do; at my chief's order they sprang at the right instant, seized the guard, and were hauled aboard. The next moment the sounding-yawl swept aft to the wheel and was struck and splintered to atoms. Two of the men and the cub Tom were missing—a fact which spread like wild-fire over the boat. The passengers came flocking to the forward gangway, ladies and all, anxious-eyed, white-faced, and talked in awed voices of the dreadful thing. And often and again I heard them say, "Poor fellows! poor boy, poor boy!"

By this time the boat's yawl was manned and away, to search for the missing. Now a faint call was heard, off to the left. The yawl had disappeared in the other direction. Half the people rushed to one side to encourage the swimmer with their shouts; the other half rushed the other way to shriek to the yawl to turn about. By the callings the swimmer was approaching, but some said the sound showed failing strength. The crowd massed themselves against the boiler-deck railings, leaning over and staring into the gloom; and every faint and fainter cry wrung from them such words as "Ah, poor fellow, poor fellow! is there *no* way to save him?"

But still the cries held out, and drew nearer, and presently the voice said pluckily,—

"I can make it! Stand by with a rope!"

What a rousing cheer they gave him! The chief mate took his stand in the glare of a torch-basket, a coil of rope in his hand, and his men grouped about him. The next moment the swimmer's face appeared in the circle of light, and in another one the owner of it was hauled aboard, limp and drenched, while cheer on cheer went up. It was that devil Tom.

The yawl crew searched everywhere, but found no sign of the two men. They probably failed to catch the guard, tumbled back, and were struck by the wheel and killed. Tom had never jumped for the guard at all, but had plunged head-first into the river and dived under the wheel. It was nothing; I could have done it easy enough, and I said so; but everybody went on just the same, making a wonderful to-do over that ass, as if he had done something great. That girl couldn't seem to have enough of that pitiful "hero" the rest of the trip; but little I cared; I loathed her, any way.

The way we came to mistake the sounding-boat's lantern for the buoy-light was this. My chief said that after laying the buoy he fell away and watched it till it seemed to be secure; then he took up a position a hundred yards below it and a little to one side of the steamer's course, headed the sounding-boat up-stream, and waited. Having to wait some time, he and the officer got to talking; he looked up when he judged that the steamer was about on the reef; saw that the buoy was gone, but supposed that the steamer had already run over it; he went on with his talk; he noticed that the steamer was getting very close down to him, but that was the correct thing; it was her business to shave him closely, for convenience in taking him aboard; he was expecting her to sheer off, until the last moment; then it flashed upon him that she was trying to run him down, mistaking his lantern for the buoy-light; so he sang out, "Stand by to spring for the guard, men!" and the next instant the jump was made.

A PILOT'S NEEDS

But I am wandering from what I was intending to do; that is, make plainer than perhaps appears in the previous chapters some of the peculiar requirements of the science of piloting. First of all, there is one faculty which a pilot must incessantly cultivate until he has brought it to absolute perfection. Nothing short of perfection will do. That faculty is memory. He cannot stop with merely thinking a thing is so and so; he must *know* it; for this is eminently one of the "exact" sciences. With what scorn a pilot was looked upon, in the old times, if he ever ventured to deal in that feeble phrase "I think," instead of the vigorous one "I know!" One cannot easily realize what a tremendous thing it is to know every trivial detail of twelve hundred miles of river and know it with absolute exactness. If you will take the longest street in New York, and travel up and down it, conning its features patiently until you know every house and window and lamp-post and big and little sign by heart, and know them so accurately that you can instantly name the one you are abreast of when you are set down at random in that street in the middle of an inky black night, you will then have a tolerable notion of the amount and the exactness of a pilot's knowledge who carries the Mississippi River in his head. And then, if you will go on until you know every street crossing, the character, size, and position of the crossing-stones, and the varying depth of mud in each of those numberless places, you will have some idea of what the pilot must know in order to keep a Mississippi steamer out of trouble. Next, if you will take half of the signs in that long street, and *change their places* once a month, and still manage to know their new positions accurately on dark nights, and keep up with these repeated changes without making any mistakes, you will understand what is required of a pilot's peerless memory by the fickle Mississippi.

I think a pilot's memory is about the most wonderful thing in the world. To know the Old and New Testaments by heart, and be able to recite them glibly, forward or backward, or begin at random anywhere in the book and recite both ways and never trip or make a mistake, is no extravagant mass of knowledge, and no marvellous facility, compared to a pilot's massed knowledge of the Mississippi and his marvellous facility in the handling of it. I make this comparison deliberately, and believe I am not expanding the truth when I do it. Many will think my figure too strong, but pilots will not.

And how easily and comfortably the pilot's memory does its work; how placidly effortless is its way; how *unconsciously* it lays up its vast stores, hour by hour, day by day, and never loses or mislays a single valuable package of them all! Take an instance. Let a leadsman cry, "Half twain! half twain! half twain! half twain! half twain!" until it becomes as monotonous as the ticking of a clock; let conversation be going on all the time, and the pilot be doing his share of the talking, and no longer consciously listening to the leadsman; and in the midst of this endless string of half twains let a single "quarter twain!" be interjected, without emphasis, and then the half twain cry go on again, just as before: two or three weeks later that pilot can describe with precision the boat's position in the river when that quarter twain was uttered, and give you such a lot of head-marks, stern-marks, and side-marks to guide you, that you ought to be able to take the boat there and put her in that same spot again yourself! The cry of "quarter twain" did not really take his mind from his talk, but his trained faculties instantly photographed the bearings, noted the change of depth, and laid up the important details for future reference without requiring any assistance from *him* in the matter. If you were walking and talking with a friend, and another friend at your side kept up a monotonous repetition of the vowel sound A, for a couple of blocks, and then in the midst interjected an R, thus, A, A, A, A, A, R, A, A, A, etc., and gave the R no emphasis, you would not be able to state, two or three weeks afterward, that the R had been put in, nor be able to tell what objects you were passing at the moment it was done. But you could if your memory had been patiently and laboriously trained to do that sort of thing mechanically.

Give a man a tolerably fair memory to start with, and piloting will develop it into a very colossus of capability. But *only*

in the matters it is daily drilled in. A time would come when
the man's faculties could not help noticing landmarks and
soundings, and his memory could not help holding on to them
with the grip of a vice; but if you asked that same man at noon
what he had had for breakfast, it would be ten chances to one
that he could not tell you. Astonishing things can be done with
the human memory if you will devote it faithfully to one particular line of business.

At the time that wages soared so high on the Missouri River,
my chief, Mr. Bixby, went up there and learned more than a
thousand miles of that stream with an ease and rapidity that
were astonishing. When he had seen each division *once* in the
day-time and *once* at night, his education was so nearly complete that he took out a "daylight" license; a few trips later he
took out a full license, and went to piloting day and night—
and he ranked A 1, too.

Mr. Bixby placed me as steersman for a while under a pilot
whose feats of memory were a constant marvel to me. However, his memory was born in him, I think, not built. For
instance, somebody would mention a name. Instantly Mr.
Brown would break in:—

"Oh, I knew *him*. Sallow-faced, red-headed fellow, with a
little scar on the side of his throat, like a splinter under the
flesh. He was only in the Southern trade six months. That was
thirteen years ago. I made a trip with him. There was five feet
in the upper river then; the 'Henry Blake' grounded at the foot
of Tower Island drawing four and a half; the 'George Elliott'
unshipped her rudder on the wreck of the 'Sunflower'——"

"Why, the 'Sunflower' didn't sink until——"

"*I* know when she sunk; it was three years before that, on
the 2d of December; Asa Hardy was captain of her, and his
brother John was first clerk; and it was his first trip in her, too;
Tom Jones told me these things a week afterward in New
Orleans; he was first mate of the 'Sunflower.' Captain Hardy
stuck a nail in his foot the 6th of July of the next year, and
died of the lockjaw on the 15th. His brother John died two
years after,—3d of March,—erysipelas. I never saw either of the
Hardys,—they were Alleghany River men,—but people who

knew them told me all these things. And they said Captain Hardy wore yarn socks winter and summer just the same, and his first wife's name was Jane Shook,—she was from New England,—and his second one died in a lunatic asylum. It was in the blood. She was from Lexington, Kentucky. Name was Horton before she was married."

And so on, by the hour, the man's tongue would go. He could *not* forget anything. It was simply impossible. The most trivial details remained as distinct and luminous in his head, after they had lain there for years, as the most memorable events. His was not simply a pilot's memory; its grasp was universal. If he were talking about a trifling letter he had received seven years before, he was pretty sure to deliver you the entire screed from memory. And then, without observing that he was departing from the true line of his talk, he was more than likely to hurl in a long-drawn parenthetical biography of the writer of that letter; and you were lucky indeed if he did not take up that writer's relatives, one by one, and give you their biographies, too.

Such a memory as that is a great misfortune. To it, all occurrences are of the same size. Its possessor cannot distinguish an interesting circumstance from an uninteresting one. As a talker, he is bound to clog his narrative with tiresome details and make himself an insufferable bore. Moreover, he cannot stick to his subject. He picks up every little grain of memory he discerns in his way, and so is led aside. Mr. Brown would start out with the honest intention of telling you a vastly funny anecdote about a dog. He would be "so full of laugh" that he could hardly begin; then his memory would start with the dog's breed and personal appearance; drift into a history of his owner; of his owner's family, with descriptions of weddings and burials that had occurred in it, together with recitals of congratulatory verses and obituary poetry provoked by the same; then this memory would recollect that one of these events occurred during the celebrated "hard winter" of such and such a year, and a minute description of that winter would follow, along with the names of people who were frozen to death, and statistics showing the high figures which pork and hay went up to. Pork and hay would suggest corn and fodder; corn and fodder would suggest cows and horses; cows and horses would suggest the circus and certain celebrated bareback riders; the transition from the circus to the menagerie was easy and natural; from the elephant to equatorial Africa was but a step; then of course the heathen savages would suggest religion; and at the end of three or four hours' tedious jaw, the watch would change, and Brown would go out of the pilot-house muttering extracts from sermons he had heard years before about the efficacy of prayer as a means of grace. And the original first mention would be all you had learned about that dog, after all this waiting and hungering.

A pilot must have a memory; but there are two higher qualities which he must also have. He must have good and quick judgment and decision, and a cool, calm courage that no peril can shake. Give a man the merest trifle of pluck to start with, and by the time he has become a pilot he cannot be unmanned by any danger a steamboat can get into; but one cannot quite say the same for judgment. Judgment is a matter of brains, and a man must *start* with a good stock of that article or he will never succeed as a pilot.

The growth of courage in the pilot-house is steady all the time, but it does not reach a high and satisfactory condition until some time after the young pilot has been "standing his own watch" alone and under the staggering weight of all the responsibilities connected with the position. When an apprentice has become pretty thoroughly acquainted with the river, he goes clattering along so fearlessly with his steamboat, night or day, that he presently begins to imagine that it is *his* courage that animates him; but the first time the pilot steps out and leaves him to his own devices he finds out it was the other man's. He discovers that the article has been left out of his own cargo altogether. The whole river is bristling with exigencies in a moment; he is not prepared for them; he does not know how to meet them; all his knowledge forsakes him; and within fifteen minutes he is as white as a sheet and scared almost to death. Therefore pilots wisely train these cubs by various strategic tricks to look danger in the face a little more calmly. A favorite way of theirs is to play a friendly swindle upon the candidate.

Mr. Bixby served me in this fashion once, and for years afterward I used to blush, even in my sleep, when I thought of it. I had become a good steersman; so good, indeed, that I had all the work to do on our watch, night and day. Mr. Bixby seldom made a suggestion to me; all he ever did was to take the wheel on particularly bad nights or in particularly bad crossings, land the boat when she needed to be landed, play gentleman of leisure nine-tenths of the watch, and collect the wages. The lower river was about bank-full, and if anybody had questioned my ability to run any crossing between Cairo and New Orleans without help or instruction, I should have felt irreparably hurt. The idea of being afraid of any crossing in the lot, in the *day-time*, was a thing too preposterous for contemplation. Well, one matchless summer's day I was bowling down the bend above Island 66, brimful of self-conceit and carrying my nose as high as a giraffe's, when Mr. Bixby said—

"I am going below a while. I suppose you know the next crossing?"

This was almost an affront. It was about the plainest and simplest crossing in the whole river. One couldn't come to any harm, whether he ran it right or not; and as for depth, there never had been any bottom there. I knew all this, perfectly well.

"Know how to *run* it? Why, I can run it with my eyes shut."

"How much water is there in it?"

"Well, that is an odd question. I couldn't get bottom there with a church steeple."

"You think so, do you?"

The very tone of the question shook my confidence. That was what Mr. Bixby was expecting. He left, without saying anything more. I began to imagine all sorts of things. Mr. Bixby, unknown to me, of course, sent somebody down to the forecastle with some mysterious instructions to the leadsmen, another messenger was sent to whisper among the officers, and then Mr. Bixby went into hiding behind a smoke-stack where he could observe results. Presently the captain stepped out on the hurricane deck; next the chief mate appeared; then a clerk. Every moment or two a straggler was added to my audience; and before I got to the head of the island I had fifteen or twenty people assembled down there under my nose. I began to wonder what the trouble was. As I started across, the captain glanced aloft at me and said, with a sham uneasiness in his voice,—

"Where is Mr. Bixby?"

"Gone below, sir."

But that did the business for me. My imagination began to construct dangers out of nothing, and they multiplied faster than I could keep the run of them. All at once I imagined I saw shoal water ahead! The wave of coward agony that surged through me then came near dislocating every joint in me. All my confidence in that crossing vanished. I seized the bell-rope; dropped it, ashamed; seized it again; dropped it once more; clutched it tremblingly once again, and pulled it so feebly that I could hardly hear the stroke myself. Captain and mate sang out instantly, and both together,—

"Starboard lead there! and quick about it!"

This was another shock. I began to climb the wheel like a squirrel; but I would hardly get the boat started to port before I would see new dangers on that side, and away I would spin to the other; only to find perils accumulating to starboard, and be crazy to get to port again. Then came the leadsman's sepulchral cry:—

"D-e-e-p four!"

Deep four in a bottomless crossing! The terror of it took my breath away.

"M-a-r-k three! M-a-r-k three! Quarter-*less*-three! Half twain!"

This was frightful! I seized the bell-ropes and stopped the engines.

"Quarter twain! Quarter twain! *Mark* twain!"

I was helpless. I did not know what in the world to do. I was quaking from head to foot, and I could have hung my hat on my eyes, they stuck out so far.

"Quarter *less* twain! Nine and a *half!*"

We were *drawing* nine! My hands were in a nerveless flutter. I could not ring a bell intelligibly with them. I flew to the speaking-tube and shouted to the engineer,—

"Oh, Ben, if you love me, *back* her! Quick, Ben! Oh, back the immortal *soul* out of her!"

I heard the door close gently. I looked around, and there stood Mr. Bixby, smiling a bland, sweet smile. Then the audience on the hurricane deck sent up a thundergust of humiliating laughter. I saw it all, now, and I felt meaner than the meanest man in human history. I laid in the lead, set the boat in her marks, came ahead on the engines, and said:—

"It was a fine trick to play on an orphan, *wasn't* it? I suppose I'll never hear the last of how I was ass enough to heave the lead at the head of 66."

"Well, no, you won't, maybe. In fact I hope you won't; for I want you to learn something by that experience. Didn't you *know* there was no bottom in that crossing?"

"Yes, sir, I did."

"Very well, then. You shouldn't have allowed me or anybody else to shake your confidence in that knowledge. Try to remember that. And another thing: when you get into a dangerous place, don't turn coward. That isn't going to help matters any."

It was a good enough lesson, but pretty hardly learned. Yet about the hardest part of it was that for months I so often had to hear a phrase which I had conceived a particular distaste for. It was, "Oh, Ben, if you love me, back her!"

I TAKE A FEW EXTRA LESSONS

During the two or two and a half years of my apprenticeship, I served under many pilots, and had experience of many kinds of steamboatmen and many varieties of steamboats; for it was not always convenient for Mr. Bixby to have me with him, and in such cases he sent me with somebody else. I am to this day profiting somewhat by that experience; for in that brief, sharp schooling, I got personally and familiarly acquainted with about all the different types of human nature that are to be found in fiction, biography, or history. The fact is daily borne in upon me, that the average shore-employment requires as much as forty years to equip a man with this sort of an education. When I say I am still profiting by this thing, I do not mean that it has constituted me a judge of men—no, it has not done that, for judges of men are born, not made. My profit is various in kind and degree, but the feature of it which I value most is the zest which that early experience has given to my later reading. When I find a well-drawn character in fiction or biography, I generally take a warm personal interest in him, for the reason that I have known him before—met him on the river.

The figure that comes before me oftenest, out of the shadows of that vanished time, is that of Brown, of the steamer "Pennsylvania"—the man referred to in a former chapter, whose memory was so good and tiresome. He was a middle-aged, long, slim, bony, smooth-shaven, horse-faced, ignorant, stingy, malicious, snarling, fault-hunting, mote-magnifying tyrant. I early got the habit of coming on watch with dread at my heart. No matter how good a time I might have been having with the off-watch below, and no matter how high my spirits might be when I started aloft, my soul became lead in my body the moment I approached the pilot-house.

I still remember the first time I ever entered the presence of that man. The boat had backed out from St. Louis and was "straightening down"; I ascended to the pilot-house in high feather, and very proud to be semi-officially a member of the executive family of so fast and famous a boat. Brown was at the wheel. I paused in the middle of the room, all fixed to make my bow, but Brown did not look around. I thought he took a furtive glance at me out of the corner of his eye, but as not even this notice was repeated, I judged I had been mistaken. By this time he was picking his way among some dangerous "breaks" abreast the wood-yards; therefore it would not be proper to interrupt him; so I stepped softly to the high bench and took a seat.

There was silence for ten minutes; then my new boss turned and inspected me deliberately and painstakingly from head to heel for about—as it seemed to me—a quarter of an hour. After which he removed his countenance and I saw it no more for some seconds; then it came around once more, and this question greeted me:—

"Are you Horace Bigsby's cub?"

"Yes, sir."

After this there was a pause and another inspection. Then:

"What's your name?"

I told him. He repeated it after me. It was probably the only thing he ever forgot; for although I was with him many months he never addressed himself to me in any other way than "Here!" and then his command followed.

"Where was you born?"

"In Florida, Missouri."

A pause. Then:—

"Dern sight better stayed there!"

By means of a dozen or so of pretty direct questions, he pumped my family history out of me.

The leads were going now in the first crossing. This interrupted the inquest. When the leads had been laid in he resumed:—

"How long you been on the river?"

I told him. After a pause:—

"Where'd you get them shoes?"

I gave him the information.

"Hold up your foot!"

I did so. He stepped back, examined the shoe minutely and contemptuously, scratching his head thoughtfully, tilting his high sugar-loaf hat well forward to facilitate the operation, then ejaculated, "Well, I'll be dod derned!" and returned to his wheel.

What occasion there was to be dod derned about it is a thing which is still as much of a mystery to me now as it was then. It must have been all of fifteen minutes—fifteen minutes of dull, homesick silence—before that long horse-face swung round upon me again—and then what a change! It was as red as fire, and every muscle in it was working. Now came this shriek:

"Here!—You going to set there all day?"

I lit in the middle of the floor, shot there by the electric suddenness of the surprise. As soon as I could get my voice I said apologetically: "I have had no orders, sir."

"You've had no *orders!* My, what a fine bird we are! We must have *orders!* Our father was a *gentleman*—owned slaves—and *we've* been to *school.* Yes, *we* are a gentleman, *too*, and got to have *orders!* ORDERS, is it? ORDERS is what you want! Dod dern my skin, *I'll* learn you to swell yourself up and blow around *here* about your dod-derned *orders!* G'way from the wheel!" (I had approached it without knowing it.)

I moved back a step or two and stood as in a dream, all my senses stupefied by this frantic assault.

"What you standing there for? Take that ice-pitcher down to the texas-tender—Come, move along, and don't you be all day about it!"

The moment I got back to the pilot-house Brown said:—

"Here! What was you doing down there all this time?"

"I couldn't find the texas-tender; I had to go all the way to the pantry."

"Derned likely story! Fill up the stove."

I proceeded to do so. He watched me like a cat. Presently he shouted:—

"Put down that shovel! Derndest numskull I ever saw—ain't even got sense enough to load up a stove."

All through the watch this sort of thing went on. Yes, and the subsequent watches were much like it during a stretch of months. As I have said, I soon got the habit of coming on duty with dread. The moment I was in the presence, even in the darkest night, I could feel those yellow eyes upon me, and knew their owner was watching for a pretext to spit out some venom on me. Preliminarily he would say:—

"Here! Take the wheel."

Two minutes later:—

"*Where* in the nation you going to? Pull her down! pull her down!"

After another moment:—

"Say! You going to hold her all day? Let her go—meet her! meet her!"

Then he would jump from the bench, snatch the wheel from me, and meet her himself, pouring out wrath upon me all the time.

George Ritchie was the other pilot's cub. He was having good times now; for his boss, George Ealer, was as kind-hearted as Brown wasn't. Ritchie had steered for Brown the season before; consequently, he knew exactly how to entertain himself and plague me, all by the one operation. Whenever I took the wheel for a moment on Ealer's watch, Ritchie would sit back on the bench and play Brown, with continual ejaculations of "Snatch her! snatch her! Derndest mud-cat I ever saw!" "Here! Where are you going *now!* Going to run over that snag?" "Pull her *down!* Don't you hear me? Pull her *down!*" "There she goes! *Just* as I expected! I *told* you not to cramp that reef. G'way from the wheel!"

So I always had a rough time of it, no matter whose watch it was; and sometimes it seemed to me that Ritchie's good-natured badgering was pretty nearly as aggravating as Brown's dead-earnest nagging.

I often wanted to kill Brown, but this would not answer. A cub had to take everything his boss gave, in the way of vigorous comment and criticism; and we all believed that there was a United States law making it a penitentiary offence to strike or threaten a pilot who was on duty. However, I could *imagine* myself killing Brown; there was no law against that; and that was the thing I used always to do the moment I was abed. Instead of going over my river in my mind, as was my duty, I threw business aside for pleasure, and killed Brown. I killed Brown every night for months; not in old, stale, commonplace

ways, but in new and picturesque ones—ways that were sometimes surprising for freshness of design and ghastliness of situation and environment.

Brown was *always* watching for a pretext to find fault; and
if he could find no plausible pretext, he would invent one. He
would scold you for shaving a shore, and for not shaving it; for
hugging a bar, and for not hugging it; for "pulling down" when
not invited, and for *not* pulling down when not invited; for firing up without orders, and for waiting *for* orders. In a word, it
was his invariable rule to find fault with *everything* you did;
and another invariable rule of his was to throw all his remarks
(to you) into the form of an insult.

One day we were approaching New Madrid, bound down
and heavily laden. Brown was at one side of the wheel, steering; I was at the other, standing by to "pull down" or "shove
up." He cast a furtive glance at me every now and then. I had
long ago learned what that meant; viz., he was trying to invent
a trap for me. I wondered what shape it was going to take. By
and by he stepped back from the wheel and said in his usual
snarly way:—

"Here!—See if you've got gumption enough to round her to."

This was simply *bound* to be a success; nothing could prevent it; for he had never allowed me to round the boat to before;
consequently, no matter how I might do the thing, he could
find free fault with it. He stood back there with his greedy eye
on me, and the result was what might have been foreseen: I lost
my head in a quarter of a minute, and didn't know what I was
about; I started too early to bring the boat around, but detected
a green gleam of joy in Brown's eye, and corrected my mistake.
I started around once more while too high up, but corrected
myself again in time. I made other false moves, and still managed to save myself; but at last I grew so confused and anxious
that I tumbled into the very worst blunder of all—I got too far
down before beginning to fetch the boat around. Brown's
chance was come.

His face turned red with passion; he made one bound,
hurled me across the house with a sweep of his arm, spun the
wheel down, and began to pour out a stream of vituperation

upon me which lasted till he was out of breath. In the course of this speech he called me all the different kinds of hard names he could think of, and once or twice I thought he was even going to swear—but he had never done that, and he didn't this time. "Dod dern" was the nearest he ventured to the luxury of swearing, for he had been brought up with a wholesome respect for future fire and brimstone.

That was an uncomfortable hour; for there was a big audience on the hurricane deck. When I went to bed that night, I killed Brown in seventeen different ways—all of them new.

BROWN AND I EXCHANGE
COMPLIMENTS

Two trips later I got into serious trouble. Brown was steering; I was "pulling down." My younger brother appeared on the hurricane deck, and shouted to Brown to stop at some landing or other, a mile or so below. Brown gave no intimation that he had heard anything. But that was his way: he never condescended to take notice of an underclerk. The wind was blowing; Brown was deaf (although he always pretended he wasn't), and I very much doubted if he had heard the order. If I had had two heads, I would have spoken; but as I had only one, it seemed judicious to take care of it; so I kept still.—

Presently, sure enough, we went sailing by that plantation. Captain Klinefelter appeared on the deck, and said:

"Let her come around, sir, let her come around. Didn't Henry tell you to land here?"

"*No*, sir!"

"I sent him up to do it."

"He *did* come up; and that's all the good it done, the dodderned fool. He never said anything."

"Didn't *you* hear him?" asked the captain of me.

Of course I didn't want to be mixed up in this business, but there was no way to avoid it; so I said:—

"Yes, sir."

I knew what Brown's next remark would be, before he uttered it. It was:—

"Shut your mouth! You never heard anything of the kind."

I closed my mouth, according to instructions. An hour later Henry entered the pilot-house, unaware of what had been going on. He was a thoroughly inoffensive boy, and I was sorry to see him come, for I knew Brown would have no pity on him. Brown began, straightway:—

"Here! Why didn't you tell me we'd got to land at that plantation?"

"I did tell you, Mr. Brown."

"It's a lie!"

I said:—

"You lie, yourself. He did tell you."

Brown glared at me in unaffected surprise; and for as much as a moment he was entirely speechless; then he shouted to me:—

"I'll attend to your case in a half a minute!" then to Henry, "And you leave the pilot-house; out with you!"

It was pilot law, and must be obeyed. The boy started out, and even had his foot on the upper step outside the door, when Brown, with a sudden access of fury, picked up a ten-pound lump of coal and sprang after him; but I was between, with a heavy stool, and I hit Brown a good honest blow which stretched him out.

I had committed the crime of crimes,—I had lifted my hand against a pilot on duty! I supposed I was booked for the penitentiary sure, and couldn't be booked any surer if I went on and squared my long account with this person while I had the chance; consequently I stuck to him and pounded him with my fists a considerable time,—I do not know how long, the pleasure of it probably made it seem longer than it really was; but in the end he struggled free and jumped up and sprang to the wheel: a very natural solicitude, for, all this time, here was this steamboat tearing down the river at the rate of fifteen miles an hour and nobody at the helm! However, Eagle Bend was two miles wide at this bank-full stage, and correspondingly long and deep: and the boat was steering herself straight down the middle and taking no chances. Still, that was only luck—a body *might* have found her charging into the woods.

Perceiving at a glance that the "Pennsylvania" was in no danger, Brown gathered up the big spy-glass, war-club fashion, and ordered me out of the pilot-house with more than Comanche bluster. But I was not afraid of him now; so, instead of going, I tarried, and criticised his grammar; I reformed his ferocious speeches for him, and put them into good English, calling his attention to the advantage of pure English over the bastard dialect of the Pennsylvania collieries whence he was extracted. He could have done his part to admiration in a crossfire of mere vituperation, of course; but he was not equipped for this species of controversy; so he presently laid aside his glass and took the wheel, muttering and shaking his head; and

I retired to the bench. The racket had brought everybody to the hurricane deck, and I trembled when I saw the old captain looking up from amid the crowd. I said to myself, "Now I *am* done for!"—For although, as a rule, he was so fatherly and indulgent toward the boat's family, and so patient of minor short-comings, he could be stern enough when the fault was worth it.

I tried to imagine what he *would* do to a cub pilot who had been guilty of such a crime as mine, committed on a boat guard-deep with costly freight and alive with passengers. Our watch was nearly ended. I thought I would go and hide somewhere till I got a chance to slide ashore. So I slipped out of the pilot-house, and down the steps, and around to the texas door,—and was in the act of gliding within, when the captain confronted me! I dropped my head, and he stood over me in silence a moment or two, then said impressively,—

"Follow me."

I dropped into his wake; he led the way to his parlor in the forward end of the texas. We were alone, now. He closed the after door; then moved slowly to the forward one and closed that. He sat down; I stood before him. He looked at me some little time, then said,—

"So you have been fighting Mr. Brown?"

I answered meekly:—

"Yes, sir."

"Do you know that that is a very serious matter?"

"Yes, sir."

"Are you aware that this boat was ploughing down the river fully five minutes with no one at the wheel?"

"Yes sir."

"Did you strike him first?"

"Yes, sir."

"What with?"

"A stool, sir."

"Hard?"

"Middling, sir."

"Did it knock him down?"

"He—he fell, sir."

"Did you follow it up? Did you do anything further?"

"Yes, sir." .

"What did you do?"

"Pounded him, sir."

"Pounded him?"

"Yes, sir."

"Did you pound him much?—that is, severely?"

"One might call it that, sir, maybe."

"I'm deucèd glad of it! Hark ye, never mention that I said that. You have been guilty of a great crime; and don't you ever be guilty of it again, on this boat. *But*—lay for him ashore! Give him a good sound thrashing, do you hear? I'll pay the expenses. Now go—and mind you, not a word of this to anybody. Clear out with you!—you've been guilty of a great crime, you whelp!"

I slid out, happy with the sense of a close shave and a mighty deliverance; and I heard him laughing to himself and slapping his fat thighs after I had closed his door.

When Brown came off watch he went straight to the captain, who was talking with some passengers on the boiler deck, and demanded that I be put ashore in New Orleans—and added:—

"I'll never turn a wheel on this boat again while that cub stays."

The captain said:—

"But he needn't come round when you are on watch, Mr. Brown."

"I won't even stay on the same boat with him. *One* of us has got to go ashore."

"Very well," said the captain, "let it be yourself," and resumed his talk with the passengers.

During the brief remainder of the trip I knew how an emancipated slave feels; for I was an emancipated slave myself. While we lay at landings I listened to George Ealer's flute, or to his readings from his two Bibles, that is to say, Goldsmith and Shakspeare, or I played chess with him—and would have beaten him sometimes, only he always took back his last move and ran the game out differently.

A CATASTROPHE

We lay three days in New Orleans, but the captain did not succeed in finding another pilot; so he proposed that I should stand a daylight watch, and leave the night watches to George Ealer. But I was afraid; I had never stood a watch of any sort by myself, and I believed I should be sure to get into trouble in the head of some chute, or ground the boat in a near cut through some bar or other. Brown remained in his place; but he would not travel with me. So the captain gave me an order on the captain of the "A. T. Lacey" for a passage to St. Louis, and said he would find a new pilot there and my steersman's berth could then be resumed. The "Lacey" was to leave a couple of days after the "Pennsylvania."

The night before the "Pennsylvania" left, Henry and I sat chatting on a freight pile on the levee till midnight. The subject of the chat, mainly, was one which I think we had not exploited before—steamboat disasters. One was then on its way to us, little as we suspected it; the water which was to make the steam which should cause it was washing past some point fifteen hundred miles up the river while we talked—but it would arrive at the right time and the right place. We doubted if persons not clothed with authority were of much use in cases of disaster and attendant panic, still they might be of *some* use; so we decided that if a disaster ever fell within our experience we would at least stick to the boat, and give such minor service as chance might throw in the way. Henry remembered this, afterward, when the disaster came, and acted accordingly.

The "Lacey" started up the river two days behind the "Pennsylvania." We touched at Greenville, Miss., a couple of days out, and somebody shouted:

"The "Pennsylvania" is blown up at Ship Island, and a hundred and fifty lives lost!"

At Napoleon, Arkansas, the same evening, we got an extra, issued by a Memphis paper, which gave some particulars. It mentioned my brother, and said he was not hurt.

Further up the river we got a later extra. My brother was

again mentioned, but this time as being hurt beyond help. We did not get full details of the catastrophe until we reached Memphis. This is the sorrowful story:—

It was six o'clock on a hot summer morning. The "Pennsylvania" was creeping along, north of Ship Island, about sixty miles below Memphis, on a half-head of steam, towing a wood-flat which was fast being emptied. George Ealer was in the pilot-house—alone, I think; the second engineer and a striker had the watch in the engine-room; the second mate had the watch on deck; George Black, Mr. Wood, and my brother, clerks, were asleep, as were also Brown and the head engineer, the carpenter, the chief mate, and one striker; Capt. Klinefelter was in the barber's chair, and the barber was preparing to shave him. There were a good many cabin passengers aboard, and three or four hundred deck passengers—so it was said at the time—and not very many of them were astir. The wood being nearly all out of the flat now, Ealer rang to "come ahead" full steam, and the next moment four of the eight boilers exploded with a thunderous crash, and the whole forward third of the boat was hoisted toward the sky! The main part of the mass, with the chimneys, dropped upon the boat again, a mountain of riddled and chaotic rubbish—and then, after a little, fire broke out.

Many people were flung to considerable distances and fell in the river; among these were Mr. Wood and my brother, and the carpenter. The carpenter was still stretched upon his mattress when he struck the water seventy-five feet from the boat. Brown, the pilot, and George Black, chief clerk, were never seen or heard of after the explosion. The barber's chair, with Captain Klinefelter in it and unhurt, was left with its back overhanging vacancy—everything forward of it, floor and all, had disappeared; and the stupefied barber, who was also unhurt, stood with one toe projecting over space, still stirring his lather unconsciously and saying not a word.

When George Ealer saw the chimneys plunging aloft in front of him, he knew what the matter was; so he muffled his face in the lapels of his coat, and pressed both hands there tightly to keep this protection in its place so that no steam could get to his nose or mouth. He had ample time to attend to these details while he was going up and returning. He presently landed on top of the unexploded boilers, forty feet below the former pilot-house, accompanied by his wheel and a rain of other stuff, and enveloped in a cloud of scalding steam. All of the many who breathed that steam died; none escaped. But Ealer breathed none of it. He made his way to the free air as quickly as he could; and when the steam cleared away he returned and climbed up on the boilers again, and patiently hunted out each and every one of his chessmen and the several joints of his flute.

By this time the fire was beginning to threaten. Shrieks and groans filled the air. A great many persons had been scalded, a great many crippled; the explosion had driven an iron crowbar through one man's body—I think they said he was a priest. He did not die at once, and his sufferings were very dreadful. A young French naval cadet, of fifteen, son of a French admiral, was fearfully scalded, but bore his tortures manfully. Both mates were badly scalded, but they stood to their posts, nevertheless. They drew the wood-boat aft, and they and the captain fought back the frantic herd of frightened immigrants till the wounded could be brought there and placed in safety first.

When Mr. Wood and Henry fell in the water, they struck out for shore, which was only a few hundred yards away; but Henry presently said he believed he was not hurt (what an unaccountable error!) and therefore would swim back to the boat and help save the wounded. So they parted, and Henry returned.

By this time the fire was making fierce headway, and several persons who were imprisoned under the ruins were begging piteously for help. All efforts to conquer the fire proved fruitless; so the buckets were presently thrown aside and the officers fell to with axes and tried to cut the prisoners out. A striker was one of the captives; he said he was not injured, but could not free himself, and when he saw that the fire was likely to drive away the workers, he begged that some one would shoot him, and thus save him from the more dreadful death. The fire did drive the axemen away, and they had to listen, helpless, to this poor fellow's supplications till the flames ended his miseries.

The fire drove all into the wood-flat that could be accommodated there; it was cut adrift then, and it and the burning steamer floated down the river toward Ship Island. They moored the flat at the head of the island, and there, unsheltered from the blazing sun, the half-naked occupants had to remain, without food or stimulants, or help for their hurts, during the rest of the day. A steamer came along, finally, and carried the unfortunates to Memphis, and there the most lavish assistance was at once forthcoming. By this time Henry was insensible. The physicians examined his injuries and saw that they were fatal, and naturally turned their main attention to patients who could be saved.

Forty of the wounded were placed upon pallets on the floor of a great public hall, and among these was Henry. There the ladies of Memphis came every day, with flowers, fruits, and dainties and delicacies of all kinds, and there they remained and nursed the wounded. All the physicians stood watches there, and all the medical students; and the rest of the town furnished money, or whatever else was wanted. And Memphis knew how to do all these things well; for many a disaster like the "Pennsylvanias"'s had happened near her doors, and she was experienced, above all other cities on the river, in the gracious office of the Good Samaritan.

The sight I saw when I entered that large hall was new and strange to me. Two long rows of prostrate forms—more than forty, in all—and every face and head a shapeless wad of loose raw cotton. It was a grewsome spectacle. I watched there six days and nights, and a very melancholy experience it was. There was one daily incident which was peculiarly depressing: this was the removal of the doomed to a chamber apart. It was done in order that the *morale* of the other patients might not be injuriously affected by seeing one of their number in the death-agony. The fated one was always carried out with as little stir as possible, and the stretcher was always hidden from sight by a wall of assistants; but no matter: everybody knew what that cluster of bent forms, with its muffled step and its slow movement, meant; and all eyes watched it wistfully, and a shudder went abreast of it like a wave.

I saw many poor fellows removed to the "death-room," and saw them no more afterward. But I saw our chief mate carried thither more than once. His hurts were frightful, especially his scalds. He was clothed in linseed oil and raw cotton to his waist, and resembled nothing human. He was often out of his mind; and then his pains would make him rave and shout and sometimes shriek. Then, after a period of dumb exhaustion, his disordered imagination would suddenly transform the great apartment into a forecastle, and the hurrying throng of nurses into the crew; and he would come to a sitting posture and shout, "Hump yourselves, *hump* yourselves, you petrifactions, snail-bellies, pall-bearers! going to be all *day* getting that hatful of freight out?" and supplement this explosion with a firmament-obliterating irruption of profanity which nothing could stay or stop till his crater was empty. And now and then while these frenzies possessed him, he would tear off handfuls of the cotton and expose his cooked flesh to view. It was horrible. It was bad for the others, of course—this noise and these exhibitions; so the doctors tried to give him morphine to quiet him. But, in his mind or out of it, he would not take it. He said his wife had been killed by that treacherous drug, and he would die before he would take it. He suspected that the doctors were concealing it in his ordinary medicines and in his water—so he ceased from putting either to his lips. Once, when he had been without water during two sweltering days, he took the dipper in his hand, and the sight of the limpid fluid, and the misery of his thirst, tempted him almost beyond his strength; but he mastered himself and threw it away, and after that he allowed no more to be brought near him. Three times I saw him carried to the death-room, insensible and supposed to be dying; but each time he revived, cursed his attendants, and demanded to be taken back. He lived to be mate of a steamboat again.

But he was the only one who went to the death-room and returned alive. Dr. Peyton, a principal physician, and rich in all the attributes that go to constitute high and flawless character, did all that educated judgment and trained skill could do for Henry; but, as the newspapers had said in the beginning, his hurts were past help. On the evening of the sixth day his wandering mind busied itself with matters far away, and his nerveless fingers "picked at his coverlet." His hour had struck; we bore him to the death-room, poor boy.

A SECTION IN MY BIOGRAPHY

In due course I got my license. I was a pilot now full fledged. I dropped into casual employments; no misfortunes resulting, intermittent work gave place to steady and protracted engagements. Time drifted smoothly and prosperously on, and I supposed—and hoped—that I was going to follow the river the rest of my days, and die at the wheel when my mission was ended. But by and by the war came, commerce was suspended, my occupation was gone.

I had to seek another livelihood. So I became a silver miner in Nevada; next, a newspaper reporter; next, a gold miner, in California; next, a reporter in San Francisco; next, a special correspondent in the Sandwich Islands; next, a roving correspondent in Europe and the East; next, an instructional torchbearer on the lecture platform; and, finally, I became a scribbler of books, and an immovable fixture among the other rocks of New England.

In so few words have I disposed of the twenty-one slow-drifting years that have come and gone since I last looked from the windows of a pilot-house.

Let us resume, now.

EARLY YEARS IN FLORIDA, MISSOURI

I was born the 30th of November, 1835, in the almost invisible village of Florida, Monroe County, Missouri. I suppose Florida had less than three hundred inhabitants. It had two streets, each a couple of hundred yards long; the rest of the avenues mere lanes, with rail fences and corn fields on either side. Both the streets and the lanes were paved with the same material— tough black mud, in wet times, deep dust in dry.

Most of the houses were of logs—all of them, indeed, except three or four; these latter were frame ones. There were none of brick, and none of stone. There was a log church, with a puncheon floor and slab benches. A puncheon floor is made of logs whose upper surfaces have been chipped flat with the adze. The cracks between the logs were not filled; there was no carpet; consequently, if you dropped anything smaller than a peach it was likely to go through. The church was perched upon short sections of logs, which elevated it two or three feet from the ground. Hogs slept under there, and whenever the dogs got after them during services the minister had to wait till the disturbance was over. In winter there was always a refreshing breeze up through the puncheon floor; in summer there were fleas enough for all.

A slab bench is made of the outside cut of a saw-log, with the bark side down; it is supported on four sticks driven into auger holes at the ends; it has no back, and no cushions. The church was twilighted with yellow tallow candles in tined sconces hung against the walls. Week days, the church was a schoolhouse.

There were two stores in the village. My uncle John A.

Quarles was proprietor of one of them. It was a very small establishment, with a few rolls of "bit" calicoes on half a dozen shelves, a few barrels of salt mackerel, coffee, and New Orleans sugar behind the counter, stacks of brooms, shovels, axes, hoes, rakes, and such things, here and there, a lot of cheap hats, bonnets, and tinware strung on strings and suspended from the walls; and at the other end of the room was another counter with bags of shot on it, a cheese or two, and a keg of powder; in front of it a row of nail kegs and a few pigs of lead; and behind it a barrel or two of New Orleans molasses and native corn whisky on tap. If a boy bought five or ten cents' worth of anything he was entitled to half a handful of sugar from the barrel; if a woman bought a few yards of calico she was entitled to a spool of thread in addition to the usual gratis "trimmin's"; if a man bought a trifle he was at liberty to draw and swallow as big a drink of whisky as he wanted.

Everything was cheap—apples, peaches, sweet potatoes, Irish potatoes, and corn, ten cents a bushel; chickens ten cents apiece, butter six cents a pound, eggs three cents a dozen, coffee and sugar five cents a pound, whisky ten cents a gallon. I do not know how prices are out there in interior Missouri now (1877), but I know what they are here in Hartford, Connecticut. To wit: apples, three dollars a bushel; peaches five dollars; Irish potatoes (choice Bermudas) five dollars; chickens a dollar to a dollar and a half apiece, according to weight; butter forty-five to sixty cents a pound, eggs fifty to sixty cents a dozen; coffee forty-five cents a pound, native whisky four or five dollars a gallon, I believe; but I can be certain only concerning the sort which I use myself, which is Scotch and costs ten dollars a gallon when you take two gallons—more when you take less.

Thirty to forty years ago, out yonder in Missouri, the ordinary cigar cost thirty cents a hundred, but most people did not try to afford them, since smoking a pipe cost nothing in that tobacco-growing country. Connecticut is also given up to tobacco raising to-day, yet we pay ten dollars a hundred for Connecticut cigars and fifteen to twenty-five dollars a hundred for the imported article.

At first my father owned slaves, but by and by he sold them, and hired others by the year from the farmers. For a girl of fifteen he paid twelve dollars a year and gave her two linsey-woolsey frocks and a pair of "stogy" shoes—cost, a modification of nothing; for a negro woman of twenty-five, as general house servant, he paid twenty-five dollars a year and gave her shoes and the aforementioned linsey-woolsey frocks; for a strong negro woman of forty, as cook, washer, etc., he paid forty dollars a year and the customary two suits of clothes; and for an able-bodied man he paid from seventy-five to a hundred dollars a year and gave him two suits of jeans and two pairs of "stogy" shoes—an outfit that cost about three dollars. But times have changed. We pay our German nursemaid $155 a year; Irish housemaid, $150; Irish laundress, $150; negro woman, as cook, $240; young negro man, to wait on door and table, $360; Irish coachman, $600 a year, with gas, hot and cold water, and dwelling consisting of parlor, kitchen, and two bedrooms, connected with the stable, free.

(Written in 1877)

A MISSISSIPPI RIVER STORY

One evening on board a Mississippi steamboat, a boy of ten years lay asleep in a berth,—a long, slim-legged boy, he was, encased in quite a short shirt; it was the first time he had ever made a trip on a steamboat, and so he was troubled, and scared, and had gone to bed with his head filled with impending snaggings, and explosions, and conflagrations, and sudden death. About ten o'clock some twenty ladies were sitting around about the ladies' saloon, quietly reading, sewing, embroidering, and so on, and among them sat a sweet, benignant old dame with round spectacles on her nose and her busy knitting-needles in her hands. Now all of a sudden, into the midst of this peaceful scene burst that slim-shanked boy in the brief shirt, wild-eyed, erect-haired, and shouting, "Fire, fire! *jump and run, the boat's afire and there ain't a minute to lose!*" All those ladies looked sweetly up and smiled, nobody stirred, the old lady pulled her spectacles down, looked over them, and said, gently,—

"But you mustn't catch cold, child. Run and put on your breast-pin, and then come and tell us all about it."

It was a cruel chill to give to a poor little devil's gushing vehemence. He was expecting to be a sort of hero—the creator of a wild panic—and here everybody sat and smiled a mocking smile, and an old woman made fun of his bugbear. I turned and crept humbly away—for I was that boy—and never even cared to discover whether I had dreamed the fire or actually seen it.

MY BOYHOOD'S HOME

MY BOYHOOD'S HOME

[*1882*] We took passage in one of the fast boats of the St. Louis and St. Paul Packet Company, and started up the river.

When I, as a boy, first saw the mouth of the Missouri River, it was twenty-two or twenty-three miles above St. Louis, according to the estimate of pilots; the wear and tear of the banks has moved it down eight miles since then; and the pilots say that within five years the river will cut through and move the mouth down five miles more, which will bring it within ten miles of St. Louis.

About nightfall we passed the large and flourishing town of Alton, Illinois, and before daylight next morning the town of Louisiana, Missouri, a sleepy village in my day, but a brisk railway centre now; however, all the towns out there are railway centres now. I could not clearly recognize the place. This seemed odd to me, for when I retired from the rebel army in '61 I retired upon Louisiana in good order; at least in good enough order for a person who had not yet learned how to retreat according to the rules of war, and had to trust to native genius. It seemed to me that for a first attempt at a retreat it was not badly done. I had done no advancing in all that campaign that was at all equal to it.

There was a railway bridge across the river here well sprinkled with glowing lights, and a very beautiful sight it was.

At seven in the morning we reached Hannibal, Missouri, where my boyhood was spent. I had had a glimpse of it fifteen years ago, and another glimpse six years earlier, but both were so brief that they hardly counted. The only notion of the town that remained in my mind was the memory of it as I had known it when I first quitted it twenty-nine years ago. That picture of it was still as clear and vivid to me as a photograph. I stepped ashore with the feeling of one who returns out of a dead-and-gone generation. I had a sort of realizing sense of what the Bastille prisoners must have felt when they used to come out and look upon Paris after years of captivity, and note how curiously the familiar and the strange were mixed together before them. I saw the new houses—saw them plainly enough—but they did not affect the older picture in my mind, for through their solid bricks and mortar I saw the vanished houses, which had formerly stood there, with perfect distinctness.

It was Sunday morning, and everybody was abed yet. So I passed through the vacant streets, still seeing the town as it was, and not as it is, and recognizing and metaphorically shaking hands with a hundred familiar objects which no longer exist; and finally climbed Holliday's Hill to get a comprehensive view. The whole town lay spread out below me then, and I could mark and fix every locality, every detail. Naturally, I was a good deal moved. I said, "Many of the people I once knew in this tranquil refuge of my childhood are now in heaven; some, I trust, are in the other place."

The things about me and before me made me feel like a boy again—convinced me that I was a boy again, and that I had simply been dreaming an unusually long dream; but my reflections spoiled all that; for they forced me to say, "I see fifty old houses down yonder, into each of which I could enter and find either a man or a woman who was a baby or unborn when I noticed those houses last, or a grandmother who was a plump young bride at that time."

From this vantage ground the extensive view up and down the river, and wide over the wooded expanses of Illinois, is very beautiful—one of the most beautiful on the Mississippi, I think; which is a hazardous remark to make, for the eight hundred miles of river between St. Louis and St. Paul afford an unbroken succession of lovely pictures. It may be that my affection for the one in question biases my judgment in its favor; I cannot say as to that. No matter, it was satisfyingly beautiful to me, and it had this advantage over all the other friends whom I was about to greet again: it had suffered no change; it was as young and fresh and comely and gracious as ever it had been; whereas, the faces of the others would be old, and scarred with the campaigns of life, and marked with their griefs and defeats, and would give me no upliftings of spirit.

An old gentleman, out on an early morning walk, came along, and we discussed the weather, and then drifted into other matters. I could not remember his face. He said he had been living here twenty-eight years. So he had come after my time, and I had never seen him before. I asked him various questions; first about a mate of mine in Sunday-school—what became of him?

"He graduated with honor in an Eastern college, wandered off into the world somewhere, succeeded at nothing, passed out of knowledge and memory years ago, and is supposed to have gone to the dogs."

"He was bright, and promised well when he was a boy."

"Yes, but the thing that happened is what became of it all."

I asked after another lad, altogether the brightest in our village school when I was a boy.

"He, too, was graduated with honors, from an Eastern college; but life whipped him in every battle, straight along, and he died in one of the Territories, years ago, a defeated man."

I asked after another of the bright boys.

"He is a success, always has been, always will be, I think."

I enquired after a young fellow who came to the town to study for one of the professions when I was a boy.

"He went at something else before he got through—went from medicine to law, or from law to medicine—then to some other new thing; went away for a year, came back with a young wife; fell to drinking, then to gambling behind the door; finally took his wife and two children to her father's, and went off to Mexico; went from bad to worse, and finally died there, without a cent to buy a shroud, and without a friend to attend the funeral."

"Pity, for he was the best-natured and most cheery and hopeful young fellow that ever was."

I named another boy.

"Oh, he is all right. Lives here yet; has a wife and children, and is prospering."

Same verdict concerning other boys.

I named three school-girls.

"The first two live here, are married and have children; the other is long ago dead—never married."

I named, with emotion, one of my early sweethearts.

"She is all right. Been married three times; buried two husbands, divorced from the third, and I hear she is getting ready to marry an old fellow out in Colorado somewhere. She's got children scattered around here and there, most everywheres."

The answer to several other enquiries was brief and simple—

"Killed in the war."

I named another boy.

"Well, now, his case *is* curious! There wasn't a human being in this town but knew that that boy was a perfect chucklehead; perfect dummy; just a stupid ass, as you may say. Everybody knew it, and everybody said it. Well, if that very boy isn't the first lawyer in the State of Missouri to-day, I'm a Democrat!"

"Is that so?"

"It's actually so. I'm telling you the truth."

"How do you account for it?"

"Account for it? There ain't any accounting for it, except that if you send a damned fool to St. Louis, and you don't tell them he's a damned fool, *they'll* never find it out. There's one thing sure—if I had a damned fool I should know what to do with him: ship him to St. Louis—it's the noblest market in the world for that kind of property. Well, when you come to look at it all around, and chew at it and think it over, *don't* it just bang anything you ever heard of?"

"Well, yes; it does seem to. But don't you think maybe it was the Hannibal people who were mistaken about the boy, and not the St. Louis people?"

"Oh, nonsense! The people here have known him from the very cradle—they knew him a hundred times better than the St. Louis idiots *could* have known him. No, if you have got any damned fools that you want to realize on, take my advice—send them to St. Louis."

I mentioned a great number of people whom I had formerly known. Some were dead, some were gone away, some had prospered, some had come to naught; but as regarded a dozen or so of the lot, the answer was comforting:

"Prosperous—live here yet—town littered with their children."

I asked about Miss ——.

"Died in the insane asylum three or four years ago—never was out of it from the time she went in; and was always suffering too; never got a shred of her mind back."

If he spoke the truth, here was a heavy tragedy, indeed. Thirty-six years in a mad-house, that some young fools might have some fun! I was a small boy at the time; and I saw those giddy young ladies come tiptoeing into the room where Miss —— sat reading at midnight by a lamp. The girl at the head of the file wore a shroud and a doughface; she crept behind the victim, touched her on the shoulder, and she looked up and screamed, and then fell into convulsions. She did not recover from the fright, but went mad. In these days it seems incredible that people believed in ghosts so short a time ago. But they did.

After asking after such other folk as I could call to mind, I finally enquired about *myself*:

"Oh, he succeeded well enough—another case of damned fool. If they'd sent him to St. Louis, he'd have succeeded sooner."

It was with much satisfaction that I recognized the wisdom of having told this candid gentleman, in the beginning, that my name was Smith.

PAST AND PRESENT

Being left to myself, up there, I went on picking out old houses in the distant town, and calling back their former inmates out of the mouldy past. Among them I presently recognized the house of the father of Lem Hackett (fictitious name). It carried me back more than a generation in a moment, and landed me in the midst of a time when the happenings of life were not the natural and logical results of great general laws, but of special orders, and were freighted with very precise and distinct purposes—partly punitive in intent, partly admonitory; and usually local in application.

When I was a small boy, Lem Hackett was drowned—on a Sunday. He fell out of an empty flat-boat, where he was play-ing. Being loaded with sin, he went to the bottom like an anvil. He was the only boy in the village who slept that night. We others all lay awake, repenting. We had not needed the infor-mation, delivered from the pulpit that evening, that Lem's was a case of special judgment—we knew that, already. There was a ferocious thunder-storm that night, and it raged continu-ously until near dawn. The winds blew, the windows rattled, the rain swept along the roof in pelting sheets, and at the brief-est of intervals the inky blackness of the night vanished, the houses over the way glared out white and blinding for a quiv-ering instant, then the solid darkness shut down again and a splitting peal of thunder followed which seemed to rend every-thing in the neighborhood to shreds and splinters. I sat up in bed quaking and shuddering, waiting for the destruction of the world, and expecting it. To me there was nothing strange or incongruous in Heaven's making such an uproar about Lem Hackett. Apparently it was the right and proper thing to do. Not a doubt entered my mind that all the angels were grouped together, discussing this boy's case and observing the awful bombardment of our beggarly little village with satisfaction and approval. There was one thing which disturbed me in the most serious way: that was the thought that this centring of the celestial interest on our village could not fail to attract the attention of the observers to people among us who might otherwise have escaped notice for years. I felt that I was not only one of those people, but the very one most likely to be discovered. That discovery could have but one result: I should be in the fire with Lem before the chill of the river had been fairly warmed out of him. I knew that this would be only just and fair. I was increasing the chances against myself all the time, by feeling a secret bitterness against Lem for having attracted this fatal attention to me, but I could not help it—this sinful thought persisted in infesting my breast in spite of me. Every time the lightning glared I caught my breath, and judged I was gone. In my terror and misery, I meanly began to suggest other boys, and mention acts of theirs which were wickeder than mine, and peculiarly needed punishment—and I tried to pretend to myself that I was simply doing this in a casual way, and without intent to divert the heavenly attention to them for the purpose of getting rid of it myself. With deep sagacity I put these mentions into the form of sorrowing recollections and left-handed sham-supplications that the sins of those boys might be allowed to pass unnoticed—"Possibly they may repent." "It is true that Jim Smith broke a window and lied about it—but maybe he did not mean any harm. And although Tom Holmes says more bad words than any other boy in the village, he probably intends to repent—though he has never said he would. And whilst it is a fact that John Jones did fish a little on Sunday, once, he didn't really catch anything but only just one small useless mud-cat; and maybe that wouldn't have been so awful if he had thrown it back—as he says he did, but he didn't. Pity but they would repent of these dreadful things—and maybe they will yet."

But while I was shamefully trying to draw attention to these poor chaps—who were doubtless directing the celestial attention to me at the same moment, though I never once suspected that—I had heedlessly left my candle burning. It was not a time to neglect even trifling precautions. There was no occasion to add anything to the facilities for attracting notice to me—so I put the light out.

It was a long night to me, and perhaps the most distressful one I ever spent. I endured agonies of remorse for sins which I knew I had committed, and for others which I was not certain about, yet was sure that they had been set down against me in a book by an angel who was wiser than I and did not trust such important matters to memory. It struck me, by and by, that I had been making a most foolish and calamitous mistake, in one respect: doubtless I had not only made my own destruction sure by directing attention to those other boys, but had already accomplished theirs!—Doubtless the lightning had stretched them all dead in their beds by this time! The anguish and the fright which this thought gave me made my previous sufferings seem trifling by comparison.

Things had become truly serious. I resolved to turn over a new leaf instantly; I also resolved to connect myself with the church the next day, if I survived to see its sun appear. I resolved to cease from sin in all its forms, and to lead a high and blameless life forever after. I would be punctual at church and Sunday-school; visit the sick; carry baskets of victuals to the poor (simply to fulfil the regulation conditions, although I knew we had none among us so poor but they would smash the basket over my head for my pains); I would instruct other boys in right ways, and take the resulting trouncings meekly; I would subsist entirely on tracts; I would invade the rum shop and warn the drunkard—and finally, if I escaped the fate of those who early become too good to live, I would go for a missionary.

The storm subsided toward daybreak, and I dozed gradually to sleep with a sense of obligation to Lem Hackett for going to eternal suffering in that abrupt way, and thus preventing a far more dreadful disaster—my own loss.

But when I rose refreshed, by and by, and found that those other boys were still alive, I had a dim sense that perhaps the whole thing was a false alarm; that the entire turmoil had been on Lem's account and nobody's else. The world looked so bright and safe that there did not seem to be any real occasion to turn over a new leaf. I was a little subdued, during that day, and perhaps the next; after that, my purpose of reforming slowly dropped out of my mind, and I had a peaceful, comfortable time again, until the next storm.

That storm came about three weeks later; and it was the most unaccountable one, to me, that I had ever experienced; for on the afternoon of that day, "Dutchy" was drowned. Dutchy belonged to our Sunday-school. He was a German lad who did not know enough to come in out of the rain; but he was exasperatingly good, and had a prodigious memory. One Sunday he made himself the envy of all the youth and the talk of all the admiring village, by reciting three thousand verses of Scripture without missing a word; then he went off the very next day and got drowned.

Circumstances gave to his death a peculiar impressiveness. We were all bathing in a muddy creek which had a deep hole in it, and in this hole the coopers had sunk a pile of green hickory hoop poles to soak, some twelve feet under water. We were diving and "seeing who could stay under longest." We managed to remain down by holding on to the hoop poles. Dutchy made such a poor success of it that he was hailed with laughter and derision every time his head appeared above water. At last he seemed hurt with the taunts, and begged us to stand still on the bank and be fair with him and give him an honest count— "be friendly and kind just this once, and not miscount for the sake of having the fun of laughing at him." Treacherous winks were exchanged, and all said, "All right, Dutchy—go ahead, we'll play fair."

Dutchy plunged in, but the boys, instead of beginning to count, followed the lead of one of their number and scampered to a range of blackberry bushes close by and hid behind it. They imagined Dutchy's humiliation, when he should rise after a superhuman effort and find the place silent and vacant, nobody there to applaud. They were "so full of laugh" with the idea that they were continually exploding into muffled cackles. Time swept on, and presently one who was peeping through the briers, said, with surprise:—

"Why, he hasn't come up yet!"

The laughing stopped.

"Boys, it's a splendid dive," said one.

"Never mind that," said another, "the joke on him is all the better for it."

There was a remark or two more, and then a pause. Talking ceased, and all began to peer through the vines. Before long, the boys' faces began to look uneasy, then anxious, then terrified. Still there was no movement of the placid water. Hearts began to beat fast, and faces to turn pale. We all glided out, silently, and stood on the bank, our horrified eyes wandering back and forth from each other's countenances to the water.

"Somebody must go down and see!"

Yes, that was plain; but nobody wanted that grisly task.

"Draw straws!"

So we did—with hands which shook so that we hardly knew what we were about. The lot fell to me, and I went down. The water was so muddy I could not see anything, but I felt around among the hoop poles, and presently grasped a limp wrist which gave me no response—and if it had I should not have known it, I let it go with such a frightened suddenness.

The boy had been caught among the hoop poles and entangled there, helplessly. I fled to the surface and told the awful news. Some of us knew that if the boy were dragged out at once he might possibly be resuscitated, but we never thought of that. We did not think of anything; we did not know what to do, so we did nothing—except that the smaller lads cried, piteously, and we all struggled frantically into our clothes, putting on anybody's that came handy, and getting them wrong-side-out and upside-down, as a rule. Then we scurried away and gave the alarm, but none of us went back to see the end of the tragedy. We had a more important thing to attend to: we all flew home, and lost not a moment in getting ready to lead a better life.

The night presently closed down. Then came on that tremendous and utterly unaccountable storm. I was perfectly dazed; I could not understand it. It seemed to me that there must be some mistake. The elements were turned loose, and they rattled and banged and blazed away in the most blind and frantic manner. All heart and hope went out of me, and the dismal thought kept floating through my brain, "If a boy who knows three thousand verses by heart is not satisfactory, what chance is there for anybody else?"

Of course I never questioned for a moment that the storm was on Dutchy's account, or that he or any other inconsequential animal was worthy of such a majestic demonstration from on high; the lesson of it was the only thing that troubled me; for it convinced me that if Dutchy, with all his perfections, was not a delight, it would be vain for me to turn over a new leaf, for I must infallibly fall hopelessly short of that boy, no matter how hard I might try. Nevertheless I did turn it over—a highly educated fear compelled me to do that—but succeeding days of cheerfulness and sunshine came bothering around, and within a month I had so drifted backward that again I was as lost and comfortable as ever.

Breakfast time approached while I mused these musings and called these ancient happenings back to mind; so I got me back into the present and went down the hill.

On my way through town to the hotel, I saw the house which was my home when I was a boy. At present rates, the people who now occupy it are of no more value than I am; but in my time they would have been worth not less than five hundred dollars apiece. They are colored folk.

After breakfast I went out alone again, intending to hunt up some of the Sunday-schools and see how this generation of pupils might compare with their progenitors who had sat with me in those places and had probably taken me as a model— though I do not remember as to that now. By the public square there had been in my day a shabby little brick church called the "Old Ship of Zion," which I had attended as a Sunday-school scholar; and I found the locality easily enough, but not the old church; it was gone, and a trig and rather hilarious new edifice was in its place. The pupils were better dressed and better looking than were those of my time; consequently they did not resemble their ancestors; and consequently there was nothing familiar to me in their faces. Still, I contemplated them with a deep interest and a yearning wistfulness, and if I had been a girl I would have cried; for they were the offspring, and represented, and occupied the places, of boys and girls some of whom I had loved to love, and some of whom I had loved to hate, but all of whom were dear to me for the one reason or the other, so many years gone by—and, Lord, where be they now!

I was mightily stirred, and would have been grateful to be allowed to remain unmolested and look my fill; but a bald-summited superintendent who had been a tow-headed Sunday-school mate of mine on that spot in the early ages, recognized me, and I talked a flutter of wild nonsense to those children to hide the thoughts which were in me, and which could not have been spoken without a betrayal of feeling that would have been recognized as out of character with me.

Making speeches without preparation is no gift of mine; and I was resolved to shirk any new opportunity, but in the next and larger Sunday-school I found myself in the rear of the assemblage; so I was very willing to go on the platform a moment for the sake of getting a good look at the scholars. On the spur of the moment I could not recall any of the old idiotic talks which visitors used to insult me with when I was a pupil there; and I was sorry for this, since it would have given me time and excuse to dawdle there and take a long and satisfying look at what I feel at liberty to say was an array of fresh young comeliness not matchable in another Sunday-school of the same size. As I talked merely to get a chance to inspect; and as I strung out the random rubbish solely to prolong the inspection, I judged it but decent to confess these low motives, and I did so.

If the Model Boy was in either of these Sunday-schools, I did not see him. The Model Boy of my time—we never had but the one—was perfect: perfect in manners, perfect in dress, perfect in conduct, perfect in filial piety, perfect in exterior godliness; but at bottom he was a prig; and as for the contents of his skull, they could have changed place with the contents of a pie, and nobody would have been the worse off for it but the pie. This fellow's reproachlessness was a standing reproach to every lad in the village. He was the admiration of all the mothers, and the detestation of all their sons. I was told what became of him, but as it was a disappointment to me, I will not enter into details. He succeeded in life.

A VENDETTA AND OTHER THINGS

During my three days' stay in the town, I woke up every morning with the impression that I was a boy—for in my dreams the faces were all young again, and looked as they had looked in the old times—but I went to bed a hundred years old, every night—for meantime I had been seeing those faces as they are now.

Of course I suffered some surprises, along at first, before I had become adjusted to the changed state of things. I met young ladies who did not seem to have changed at all; but they turned out to be the daughters of the young ladies I had in mind—sometimes their granddaughters. When you are told that a stranger of fifty is a grandmother, there is nothing surprising about it; but if, on the contrary, she is a person whom you knew as a little girl, it seems impossible. You say to yourself, "How can a little girl be a grandmother?" It takes some little time to accept and realize the fact that while you have been growing old, your friends have not been standing still, in that matter.

I noticed that the greatest changes observable were with the women, not the men. I saw men whom thirty years had changed but slightly; but their wives had grown old. These were good women; it is very wearing to be good.

There was a saddler whom I wished to see; but he was gone. Dead, these many years, they said. Once or twice a day, the saddler used to go tearing down the street, putting on his coat as he went; and then everybody knew a steamboat was coming. Everybody knew, also, that John Stavely was not expecting anybody by the boat—or any freight, either; and Stavely must have known that everybody knew this, still it made no difference to him; he liked to seem to himself to be expecting a hundred thousand tons of saddles by this boat, and so he went on all his life, enjoying being faithfully on hand to receive and receipt for those saddles, in case by any miracle they should come. A malicious Quincy paper used always to refer to this town, in derision, as "Stavely's Landing." Stavely was one of my earliest admirations; I envied him his rush of imaginary business, and the display he was able to make of it, before strangers, as he went flying down the street, struggling with his fluttering coat.

But there was a carpenter who was my chiefest hero. He was a mighty liar, but I did not know that; I believed everything he said. He was a romantic, sentimental, melodramatic fraud, and his bearing impressed me with awe. I vividly remember the first time he took me into his confidence. He was planing a board, and every now and then he would pause and heave a deep sigh; and occasionally mutter broken sentences—confused and not intelligible—but out of their midst an ejaculation sometimes escaped which made me shiver and did me good: one was, "O God, it is his blood!" I sat on the tool-chest and humbly and shudderingly admired him; for I judged he was full of crime. At last he said in a low voice:—

"My little friend, can you keep a secret?"

I eagerly said I could.

"A dark and dreadful one?"

I satisfied him on that point.

"Then I will tell you some passages in my history; for oh, I *must* relieve my burdened soul, or I shall die!"

He cautioned me once more to be "as silent as the grave"; then he told me he was a "red-handed murderer." He put down his plane, held his hands out before him, contemplated them sadly, and said:

"Look—with these hands I have taken the lives of thirty human beings!"

The effect which this had upon me was an inspiration to him, and he turned himself loose upon his subject with interest and energy. He left generalizing, and went into details— began with his first murder; described it, told what measures he had taken to avert suspicion; then passed to his second homicide, his third, his fourth, and so on. He had always done his murders with a bowie-knife, and he made all my hairs rise by suddenly snatching it out and showing it to me.

At the end of this first *séance* I went home with six of his fearful secrets among my freightage, and found them a great help to my dreams, which had been sluggish for a while back.

I sought him again and again, on my Saturday holidays; in fact I spent the summer with him—all of it which was valuable to me. His fascinations never diminished, for he threw something fresh and stirring, in the way of horror, into each successive murder. He always gave names, dates, places—everything. This by and by enabled me to note two things: that he had killed his victims in every quarter of the globe, and that these victims were always named Lynch. The destruction of the Lynches went serenely on, Saturday after Saturday, until the original thirty had multiplied to sixty,—and more to be heard from yet; then my curiosity got the better of my timidity, and I asked how it happened that these justly punished persons all bore the same name.

My hero said he had never divulged that dark secret to any living being; but felt that he could trust me, and therefore he would lay bare before me the story of his sad and blighted life. He had loved one "too fair for earth," and she had reciprocated "with all the sweet affection of her pure and noble nature." But he had a rival, a "base hireling" named Archibald Lynch, who said the girl should be his, or he would "dye his hands in her heart's best blood." The carpenter, "innocent and happy in love's young dream," gave no weight to the threat, but led his "golden-haired darling to the altar," and there the two were made one; there also, just as the minister's hands were stretched in blessing over their heads, the fell deed was done—with a knife—and the bride fell a corpse at her husband's feet. And what did the husband do? He plucked forth that knife, and, kneeling by the body of his lost one, swore to "consecrate his life to the extermination of all the human scum that bear the hated name of Lynch."

That was it. He had been hunting down the Lynches and slaughtering them, from that day to this—twenty years. He had always used that same consecrated knife; with it he had murdered his long array of Lynches, and with it he had left upon the forehead of each victim a peculiar mark—a cross, deeply incised. Said he:—

"The cross of the Mysterious Avenger is known in Europe, in America, in China, in Siam, in the Tropics, in the Polar

Seas, in the deserts of Asia, in all the earth. Wherever in the uttermost parts of the globe a Lynch has penetrated, there has the Mysterious Cross been seen, and those who have seen it have shuddered and said, 'It is his mark; he has been here!' You have heard of the Mysterious Avenger—look upon him, for before you stands no less a person! But beware—breathe not a word to any soul. Be silent, and wait. Some morning this town will flock aghast to view a gory corpse; on its brow will be seen the awful sign, and men will tremble and whisper, 'He has been here—it is the Mysterious Avenger's mark!' You will come here, but I shall have vanished; you will see me no more."

This ass had been reading the "Jibbenainosay," no doubt, and had had his poor romantic head turned by it; but as I had not yet seen the book then, I took his inventions for truth, and did not suspect that he was a plagiarist.

However, we had a Lynch living in the town; and the more I reflected upon his impending doom, the more I could not sleep. It seemed my plain duty to save him, and a still plainer and more important duty to get some sleep for myself, so at last I ventured to go to Mr. Lynch and tell him what was about to happen to him—under strict secrecy. I advised him to "fly," and certainly expected him to do it. But he laughed at me; and he did not stop there; he led me down to the carpenter's shop, gave the carpenter a jeering and scornful lecture upon his silly pretensions, slapped his face, made him get down on his knees and beg—then went off and left me to contemplate the cheap and pitiful ruin of what, in my eyes, had so lately been a majestic and incomparable hero. The carpenter blustered, flourished his knife, and doomed this Lynch in his usual volcanic style, the size of his fateful words undiminished; but it was all wasted upon me; he was a hero to me no longer, but only a poor, foolish, exposed humbug. I was ashamed of him, and ashamed of myself; I took no further interest in him, and never went to his shop any more. He was a heavy loss to me, for he was the greatest hero I had ever known. The fellow must have had some talent; for some of his imaginary murders were so vividly and dramatically described that I remember all their details yet.

The people of Hannibal are not more changed than is the town. It is no longer a village; it is a city, with a mayor, and a council, and water-works, and probably a debt. It has fifteen thousand people, is a thriving and energetic place, and is paved like the rest of the west and south—where a well-paved street and a good sidewalk are things so seldom seen, that one doubts them when he does see them. The customary half-dozen railways centre in Hannibal now, and there is a new depot, which cost a hundred thousand dollars. In my time the town had no specialty, and no commercial grandeur; the daily packet usually landed a passenger and bought a catfish, and took away another passenger and a hatful of freight; but now a huge commerce in lumber has grown up and a large miscellaneous commerce is one of the results. A deal of money changes hands there now.

Bear Creek—so called, perhaps, because it was always so particularly bare of bears—is hidden out of sight now, under islands and continents of piled lumber, and nobody but an expert can find it. I used to get drowned in it every summer regularly, and be drained out, and inflated and set going again by some chance enemy; but not enough of it is unoccupied now to drown a person in. It was a famous breeder of chills and fever in its day. I remember one summer when everybody in town had this disease at once. Many chimneys were shaken down, and all the houses were so racked that the town had to be rebuilt. The chasm or gorge between Lover's Leap and the hill west of it is supposed by scientists to have been caused by glacial action. This is a mistake.

There is an interesting cave a mile or two below Hannibal, among the bluffs. I would have liked to revisit it, but had not time. In my time the person who then owned it turned it into a mausoleum for his daughter, aged fourteen. The body of this poor child was put into a copper cylinder filled with alcohol, and this was suspended in one of the dismal avenues of the cave. The top of the cylinder was removable; and it was said to be a common thing for the baser order of tourists to drag the dead face into view and examine it and comment upon it.

A QUESTION OF LAW

The slaughter-house is gone from the mouth of Bear Creek and so is the small jail (or "calaboose") which once stood in its neighborhood. A citizen asked, "Do you remember when Jimmy Finn, the town drunkard, was burned to death in the calaboose?"

Observe, now, how history becomes defiled, through lapse of time and the help of the bad memories of men. Jimmy Finn was not burned in the calaboose, but died a natural death in a tan vat, of a combination of delirium tremens and spontaneous combustion. When I say natural death, I mean it was a natural death for Jimmy Finn to die. The calaboose victim was not a citizen; he was a poor stranger, a harmless, whiskey-sodden tramp. I know more about his case than anybody else; I knew too much of it, in that by-gone day, to relish speaking of it. That tramp was wandering about the streets one chilly evening, with a pipe in his mouth, and begging for a match; he got neither matches nor courtesy; on the contrary, a troop of bad little boys followed him around and amused themselves with nagging and annoying him. I assisted; but at last, some appeal which the wayfarer made for forbearance, accompanying it with a pathetic reference to his forlorn and friendless condition, touched such sense of shame and remnant of right feeling as were left in me, and I went away and got him some matches, and then hied me home and to bed, heavily weighted as to conscience, and unbuoyant in spirit. An hour or two afterward, the man was arrested and locked up in the calaboose by the marshal—large name for a constable, but that was his title. At two in the morning, the church-bells rang for fire, and everybody turned out, of course—I with the rest. The tramp had used his matches disastrously: he had set his straw bed on fire, and the oaken sheathing of the room had caught. When I reached the ground, two hundred men, women, and children stood massed together, transfixed with horror, and staring at the grated windows of the jail. Behind the iron bars, and tugging frantically at them, and screaming for help, stood the tramp; he seemed like a black object set against a sun, so white and intense was the light at his back. That marshal could not be found, and he had the only key. A battering-ram was quickly improvised, and the thunder of its blows upon the door had so encouraging a sound that the spectators broke into wild cheering, and believed the merciful battle won. But it was not so. The timbers were too strong; they did not yield. It was said that the man's death-grip still held fast to the bars after he was dead; and that in this position the fires wrapped him about and consumed him. As to this, I do not know. What was seen, after I recognized the face that was pleading through the bars, was seen by others, not by me.

I saw that face, so situated, every night for a long time afterward; and I believed myself as guilty of the man's death as if I had given him the matches purposely that he might burn himself up with them. I had not a doubt that I should be hanged if my connection with this tragedy were found out. The happenings and the impressions of that time are burned into my memory, and the study of them entertains me as much now as they themselves distressed me then. If anybody spoke of that grisly matter, I was all ears in a moment, and alert to hear what might be said, for I was always dreading and expecting to find out that I was suspected; and so fine and so delicate was the perception of my guilty conscience that it often detected suspicion in the most purposeless remarks, and in looks, gestures, glances of the eye, which had no significance, but which sent me shivering away in a panic of fright, just the same. And how sick it made me when somebody dropped, howsoever carelessly and barren of intent, the remark that "murder will out!" For a boy of ten years, I was carrying a pretty weighty cargo.

All this time I was blessedly forgetting one thing—the fact that I was an inveterate talker in my sleep. But one night I awoke and found my bed-mate—my younger brother—sitting up in bed and contemplating me by the light of the moon. I said:—

"What is the matter?"

"You talk so much I can't sleep."

I came to a sitting posture in an instant, with my kidneys in my throat and my hair on end.

"What did I say? Quick—out with it—what did I say?"

"Nothing much."

"It's a lie—you know everything!"

"Everything about what?"

"You know well enough. About *that*."

"About *what*? I don't know what you are talking about. I think you are sick or crazy or something. But anyway, you're awake, and I'll get to sleep while I've got a chance."

He fell asleep and I lay there in a cold sweat, turning this new terror over in the whirling chaos which did duty as my mind. The burden of my thought was, How much did I divulge? How much does he know?—what a distress is this uncertainty! But by and by I evolved an idea—I would wake my brother and probe him with a supposititious case. I shook him up, and said—

"Suppose a man should come to you drunk—"

"This is foolish—I never get drunk."

"I don't mean you, idiot—I mean the man. Suppose a *man* should come to you drunk, and borrow a knife, or a tomahawk, or a pistol, and you forgot to tell him it was loaded, and—"

"How could you load a tomahawk?"

"I don't mean the tomahawk, and I didn't *say* the tomahawk; I said the pistol. Now, don't you keep breaking in that way, because this is serious. There's been a man killed."

"What! In this town?"

"Yes, in this town."

"Well, go on—I won't say a single word."

"Well, then, suppose you forgot to tell him to be careful with it, because it was loaded, and he went off and shot himself with that pistol—fooling with it, you know, and probably doing it by accident, being drunk. Well, would it be murder?"

"No—suicide."

"No, no! I don't mean *his* act, I mean yours. Would you be a murderer for letting him have that pistol?"

After deep thought came this answer,—

"Well, I should think I was guilty of something—maybe murder—yes, probably murder, but I don't quite know."

This made me very uncomfortable. However, it was not a

decisive verdict. I should have to set out the real case—there seemed to be no other way. But I would do it cautiously, and keep a watch out for suspicious effects. I said:—

"I was supposing a case, but I am coming to the real one now. Do you know how the man came to be burned up in the calaboose?"

"No."

"Haven't you the least idea?"

"Not the least."

"Wish you may die in your tracks if you have?"

"Yes, wish I may die in my tracks."

"Well, the way of it was this. The man wanted some matches to light his pipe. A boy got him some. The man set fire to the calaboose with those very matches, and burnt himself up."

"Is that so?"

"Yes, it is. Now, is that boy a murderer, do you think?"

"Let me see. The man was drunk?"

"Yes, he was drunk."

"Very drunk?"

"Yes."

"And the boy knew it?"

"Yes, he knew it."

There was a long pause. Then came this heavy verdict:—

"If the man was drunk, and the boy knew it, the boy murdered that man. This is certain."

Faint, sickening sensations crept along all the fibres of my body, and I seemed to know how a person feels who hears his death sentence pronounced from the bench. I waited to hear what my brother would say next. I believed I knew what it would be, and I was right. He said,—

"I know the boy."

I had nothing to say; so I said nothing. I simply shuddered. Then he added,—

"Yes, before you got half through telling about the thing, I knew perfectly well who the boy was; it was Ben Coontz!"

I came out of my collapse as one who rises from the dead. I said, with admiration:—

"Why, how in the world did you ever guess it?"

"You told me in your sleep."

I said to myself, "How splendid that is! This is a habit which must be cultivated."

My brother rattled innocently on:—

"When you were talking in your sleep, you kept mumbling something about 'matches,' which I couldn't make anything out of; but just now, when you began to tell me about the man and the calaboose and the matches, I remembered that in your sleep you mentioned Ben Coontz two or three times; so I put this and that together, you see, and right away I knew it was Ben that burnt that man up."

I praised his sagacity effusively. Presently he asked,—

"Are you going to give him up to the law?"

"No," I said; "I believe that this will be a lesson to him. I shall keep an eye on him, of course, for that is but right; but if he stops where he is and reforms, it shall never be said that I betrayed him."

"How good you are!"

"Well, I try to be. It is all a person can do in a world like this."

And now, my burden being shifted to other shoulders, my terrors soon faded away.

The day before we left Hannibal, a curious thing fell under my notice,—the surprising spread which longitudinal time undergoes there. I learned it from one of the most unostentatious of men,—the colored coachman of a friend of mine, who lives three miles from town. He was to call for me at the Park Hotel at 7.30 P.M., and drive me out. But he missed it considerably,—did not arrive till ten. He excused himself by saying:—

"De time is mos' an hour en a half slower in de country en what it is in de town; you'll be in plenty time, boss. Sometimes we shoves out early for church, Sunday, en fetches up dah right plum in de middle er de sermon. Diffunce in de time. A body can't make no calculations 'bout it."

I had lost two hours and a half; but I had learned a fact worth four.

JANE LAMPTON CLEMENS

This was my mother. When she died, in October, 1890, she was well along in her eighty-eighth year; a mighty age, a well contested fight for life for one who at forty was so delicate of body as to be accounted a confirmed invalid and destined to pass soon away. I knew her well during the first twenty-five years of my life; but after that I saw her only at wide intervals, for we lived many days' journey apart. I am not proposing to write about her, but merely to talk about her; not give her formal history, but merely make illustrative extracts from it, so to speak; furnish flashlight glimpses of her character, not a processional view of her career. Technically speaking, she had no career; but she had a character, and it was of a fine and striking and lovable sort.

What becomes of the multitudinous photographs which one's mind takes of people? Out of the million which my mental camera must have taken of this first and closest friend, only one clear and strongly defined one of early date remains. It dates back forty-seven years; she was forty years old, then, and I was eight. She held me by the hand, and we were kneeling by the bedside of my brother, two years older than I, who lay dead, and the tears were flowing down her cheeks unchecked. And she was moaning. That dumb sign of anguish was perhaps new to me, since it made upon me a very strong impression—an impression which holds its place still with the picture which it helped to intensify and make memorable.

She had a slender, small body, but a large heart—a heart so large that everybody's griefs and everybody's joys found welcome in it and hospitable accommodation. The greatest difference which I find between her and the rest of the people whom I have known is this, and it is a remarkable one: those others felt a strong interest in a few things, whereas, to the very day of her death, she felt a strong interest in the whole world and everything and everybody in it. In all her life she never knew such a thing as a half-hearted interest in affairs and people, or an interest which drew a line and left out certain affairs and was indifferent to certain people. The invalid who takes a strenuous and indestructible interest in everything and everybody but himself, and to whom a dull moment is an unknown thing and an impossibility, is a formidable adversary for disease and a hard invalid to vanquish. I am certain that it was this feature of my mother's makeup that carried her so far toward ninety.

Her interest in people and dumb animals was warm, personal, friendly. She always found something to excuse, and as a rule to love, in the toughest of them—even if she had to put it there herself. She was the natural ally and friend of the friendless. It was believed that, Presbyterian as she was, she could be beguiled into saying a soft word for the devil himself; and so the experiment was tried. The abuse of Satan began; one conspirator after another added his bitter word, his malign reproach, his pitiless censure, till at last, sure enough, the unsuspecting subject of the trick walked into the trap. She admitted that the indictment was sound: that Satan was utterly wicked and abandoned, just as these people had said; *but*, would any claim that he had been treated fairly? A sinner was but a sinner; Satan was just that, like the rest. What saves the rest—their own efforts alone? No—or none might ever be saved. To their feeble efforts is added the mighty help of pathetic, appealing, imploring prayers that go up daily out of all the churches in Christendom and out of myriads upon myriads of pitying hearts. But who prays for Satan? Who, in eighteen centuries, has had the common humanity to pray for the one sinner that needed it most, our one fellow and brother who most needed a friend yet had not a single one, the one sinner among us all who had the highest and clearest *right* to every Christian's daily and nightly prayers for the plain and unassailable reason that his was the first and greatest need, he being among sinners the supremest?

This Friend of Satan was a most gentle spirit, and an unstudied and unconscious pathos was her native speech. When her pity or her indignation was stirred by hurt or shame inflicted upon some defenseless person or creature, she was the most eloquent person I have heard speak. It was seldom eloquence of a fiery or violent sort, but gentle, pitying, persuasive, appealing; and so genuine and so nobly and simply worded and so touchingly uttered, that many times I have seen it win the reluctant and splendid applause of tears. Whenever anybody or any creature was being oppressed, the fears that belonged to her sex and her small stature retired to the rear, and her soldierly qualities came promptly to the front. One day in our village I saw a vicious devil of a Corsican, a common terror in the town, chasing his grown daughter past cautious male citizens with a heavy rope in his hand, and declaring he would wear it out on her. My mother spread her door wide to the refugee, and then, instead of closing and locking it after her, stood in it and stretched her arms across it, barring the way. The man swore, cursed, threatened her with his rope, but she did not flinch or show any sign of fear; she only stood straight and fine, and lashed him, shamed him, derided him, defied him, in tones not audible to the middle of the street, but audible to the man's conscience and dormant manhood; and he asked her pardon, and gave her his rope, and said, with a most great and blasphemous oath that she was the bravest woman he ever saw; and so went his way without another word, and troubled her no more. He and she were always good friends after that, for in her he had found a long-felt want—somebody who was not afraid of him.

One day in St. Louis she walked out into the street and greatly surprised a burly cartman who was beating his horse over the head with the butt of his heavy whip; for she took the whip away from him and then made such a persuasive appeal in behalf of the ignorantly offending horse that he was tripped into saying he was to blame, and also into volunteering a promise which of course he couldn't keep, for he was not built that way—a promise that he wouldn't ever abuse a horse again.

That sort of interference in behalf of abused animals was a common thing with her all her life; and her manner must have been without offense and her good intent transparent, for she always carried her point, and also won the courtesy, and often the friendly applause, of the adversary. All the race of dumb animals had a friend in her. By some subtle sign the homeless, hunted, bedraggled and disreputable cat recognized her at a glance as the born refuge and champion of his sort—and followed her home. His instinct was right, he was as welcome as the prodigal son. We had nineteen cats at one time, in 1845. And there wasn't one in the lot that had any character; not one that had any merit, except the cheap and tawdry merit of being unfortunate. They were a vast burden to us all—including my mother—but they were out of luck, and that was enough; they had to stay. However, better these pets than no pets at all; children must have pets, and we were not allowed to have caged ones. An imprisoned creature was out of the question— my mother would not have allowed a rat to be restrained of its liberty.

In the small town of Hannibal, Missouri, when I was a boy, everybody was poor but didn't know it; and everybody was comfortable, and did know it. And there were grades of society, people of good family, people of unclassified family, people of no family. Everybody knew everybody, and was affable to everybody, and nobody put on any visible airs; yet the class lines were quite clearly drawn, and the familiar social life of each class was restricted to that class. It was a little democracy which was full of Liberty, Equality, and Fourth of July, and sincerely so, too; yet you perceive that the aristocratic taint was there. It was there, and nobody found fault with the fact, or ever stopped to reflect that its presence was an inconsistency.

I suppose that this state of things was mainly due to the circumstance that the town's population had come from slave states and still had the institution of slavery with them in their new home. My mother, with her large nature and liberal sympathies, was not intended for an aristocrat, yet through her breeding she was one. Few people knew it, perhaps, for it was an instinct, I think, rather than a principle. So its outward manifestation was likely to be accidental, not intentional; and also not frequent. But I knew of that weak spot. I knew that privately she was proud of the Lambtons, now Earls of Durham, who had occupied the family lands for nine hundred years; that they were feudal lords of Lambton Castle and holding the high position of ancestors of hers when the Norman Conqueror came over to divert the Englishry. I argued—cautiously, and with mollifying circumlocutions, for one had to be careful when he was on that holy ground, and mustn't cavort—that there was no particular merit in occupying a piece of land for nine hundred years, with the friendly assistance of an entail; anybody could do it, with intellect or without; therefore the entail was the thing to be proud of, just the entail and nothing else; consequently she was merely descended from a mortgage. Whereas my own ancestry was quite a different and superior thing, because it had the addition of an ancestor—one Clement—who *did* something; something which was very creditable to him and satisfactory to me, in that he was a member of the court that tried Charles I and delivered him over to the executioner. Ostensibly this was chaff, but at the bottom it was not. I had a very real respect for that ancestor, and this respect has increased with the years, not diminished. He did what he could toward reducing the list of crowned shams of his day. However, I can say this for my mother, that I never heard her refer in any way to her gilded ancestry when any person not a member of the family was present, for she had good American sense. But with other Lamptons whom I have known it was different.

"Col. Sellers" was a Lampton,* and a tolerably near relative of my mother's; and when he was alive, poor old airy soul, one of the earliest things a stranger was likely to hear from his lips was some reference to the "head of our line," flung off with a painful casualness that was wholly beneath criticism as a work

* James Lampton, a cousin of Mark Twain's mother.

of art. It compelled inquiry, of course; it was intended to compel it. Then followed the whole disastrous history of how the Lambton heir came to this country a hundred and fifty years or so ago, disgusted with that foolish fraud, hereditary aristocracy; and married, and shut himself away from the world in the remotenesses of the wilderness, and went to breeding ancestors of future American Claimants, while at home in England he was given up as dead and his titles and estates turned over to his younger brother, usurper and personally responsible for the perverse and unseatable usurpers of our day. And the Colonel always spoke with studied and courtly deference of the Claimant of his day—a second cousin of his—and referred to him with entire seriousness as "the Earl." "The Earl" was a man of parts, and might have accomplished something for himself but for the calamitous accident of his birth. He was a Kentuckian, and a well-meaning man; but he had no money and no time to earn any; for all his time was taken up in trying to get me, and others of his tribe, to furnish him capital to fight his claim through the House of Lords with. He had all the documents, all the proofs; he knew he could win. And so he dreamed his life away, always in poverty, sometimes in actual want, and died at last, far from home, and was buried from a hospital by strangers who did not know he was an earl, for he did not look it. That poor fellow used to sign his letters "Durham," and he would find fault with me for voting the Republican ticket, for the reason that it was unaristocratic, and by consequence un-Lamptonian. And presently along would come a letter from some red-hot Virginian son of my other branch and abuse me bitterly for the same vote—on the ground that the Republican was an aristocratic party and it was not becoming in the descendant of a regicide to train with that kind of animals. And so I used to almost wish I hadn't had any ancestors, they were so much trouble to me.

As I have said, we lived in a slave-holding community; indeed, when slavery perished my mother had been in daily touch with it for sixty years. Yet, kind-hearted and compassionate as she was, I think she was not conscious that slavery was a bald, grotesque, and unwarrantable usurpation. She had never heard it assailed in any pulpit, but had heard it defended and sanctified in a thousand; her ears were familiar with Bible texts that approved it, but if there were any that disapproved it they had not been quoted by her pastors; as far as her experience went, the wise and the good and the holy were unanimous in the conviction that slavery was right, righteous, sacred, the peculiar pet of the Deity, and a condition which the slave himself ought to be daily and nightly thankful for. Manifestly, training and association can accomplish strange miracles. As a rule our slaves were convinced and content.

There was nothing about the slavery of the Hannibal region to rouse one's dozing humane instincts to activity. It was the mild domestic slavery, not the brutal plantation article. Cruelties were very rare, and exceedingly and wholesomely unpopular. To separate and sell the members of a slave family to different masters was a thing not well liked by the people, and so it was not often done, except in the settling of estates. I have no recollection of ever seeing a slave auction in that town; but I am suspicious that that is because the thing was a common and commonplace spectacle, not an uncommon and impressive one. I vividly remember seeing a dozen black men and women chained to each other, once, and lying in a group on the pavement, awaiting shipment to the southern slave market. Those were the saddest faces I ever saw. Chained slaves could not have been a common sight, or this picture would not have taken so strong and lasting a hold upon me.

The "nigger trader" was loathed by everybody. He was regarded as a sort of human devil who bought and conveyed poor helpless creatures to hell—for to our whites and blacks alike the Southern plantation was simply hell; no milder name could describe it. If the threat to sell an incorrigible slave "down the river" would not reform him, nothing would—his case was past cure.

It is commonly believed that an infallible effect of slavery was to make such as lived in its midst hard-hearted. I think it had no such effect—speaking in general terms. I think it stupefied everybody's humanity, as regarded the slave, but stopped there. There were no hard-hearted people in our town or I mean there were no more than would be found in any other town of the same size in any other country; and in my experience hard-hearted people are very rare everywhere.

(*Written in 1890–91*)

THE SPACE-ANNIHILATING
POWER OF THOUGHT

[*A Bombay hotel, 1896*] There was a vast glazed door which opened upon the balcony. It needed closing, or cleaning, or something, and a native got down on his knees and went to work at it. He seemed to be doing it well enough, but perhaps he wasn't, for the burly German put on a look that betrayed dissatisfaction, then without *explaining* what was wrong, gave the native a brisk cuff on the jaw and *then* told him where the defect was. It seemed such a shame to do that before us all. The native took it with meekness, saying nothing, and not showing in his face or manner any resentment. I had not seen the like of this for fifty years. It carried me back to my boyhood, and flashed upon me the forgotten fact that this was the *usual* way of explaining one's desires to a slave. I was able to remember that the method seemed right and natural to me in those days, I being born to it and unaware that elsewhere there were other methods; but I was also able to remember that those unresented cuffings made me sorry for the victim and ashamed for the punisher. My father was a refined and kindly gentleman, very grave, rather austere, of rigid probity, a sternly just and upright man, albeit he attended no church and never spoke of religious matters, and had no part nor lot in the pious joys of his Presbyterian family, nor ever seemed to suffer from this deprivation. He laid his hand upon me in punishment only twice in his life, and then not heavily; once for telling him a lie— which surprised me, and showed me how unsuspicious he was, for that was not my maiden effort. He punished me those two times only, and never any other member of the family at all; yet every now and then he cuffed our harmless slave boy,

Lewis, for trifling little blunders and awkwardnesses. My father had passed his life among the slaves from his cradle up, and his cuffings proceeded from the custom of the time, not from his nature. When I was ten years old I saw a man fling a lump of iron-ore at a slave-man in anger, for merely doing something awkwardly—as if that were a crime. It bounded from the man's skull, and the man fell and never spoke again. He was dead in an hour. I knew the man had a right to kill his slave if he wanted to, and yet it seemed a pitiful thing and somehow wrong, though why wrong I was not deep enough to explain if I had been asked to do it. Nobody in the village approved of that murder, but of course no one said much about it.

It is curious—the space-annihilating power of thought. For just one second, all that goes to make the *me* in me was in a Missourian village, on the other side of the globe, vividly seeing again these forgotten pictures of fifty years ago, and wholly unconscious of all things but just those; and in the next second I was back in Bombay, and that kneeling native's smitten cheek was not done tingling yet! Back to boyhood—fifty years; back to age again, another fifty; and a flight equal to the circumference of the globe—all in two seconds by the watch!

HUNTING THE DECEITFUL TURKEY

When I was a boy my uncle and his big boys hunted with the rifle, the youngest boy Fred and I with a shotgun—a small single-barrelled shotgun which was properly suited to our size and strength; it was not much heavier than a broom. We carried it turn about, half an hour at a time. I was not able to hit anything with it, but I liked to try. Fred and I hunted feathered small game, the others hunted deer, squirrels, wild turkeys, and such things. My uncle and the big boys were good shots. They killed hawks and wild geese and such like on the wing; and they didn't wound or kill squirrels, they *stunned* them. When the dogs treed a squirrel, the squirrel would scamper aloft and run out on a limb and flatten himself along it, hoping to make himself invisible in that way—and not quite succeeding. You could see his wee little ears sticking up. You couldn't see his nose, but you knew where it was. Then the hunter, despising a "rest" for his rifle, stood up and took offhand aim at the limb and sent a bullet into it immediately under the squirrel's nose, and down tumbled the animal, unwounded but unconscious; the dogs gave him a shake and he was dead. Sometimes when the distance was great and the wind not accurately allowed for, the bullet would hit the squirrel's head; the dogs could do as they pleased with that one—the hunter's pride was hurt, and he wouldn't allow it to go into the game-bag.

In the first faint gray of the dawn the stately wild turkeys would be stalking around in great flocks, and ready to be sociable and answer invitations to come and converse with other excursionists of their kind. The hunter concealed himself and imitated the turkey-call by sucking the air through the

legbone of a turkey which had previously answered a call like
that and lived only just long enough to regret it. There is nothing that furnishes a perfect turkey-call except that bone.
Another of Nature's treacheries, you see. She is full of them;
half the time she doesn't know which she likes best—to betray
her child or protect it. In the case of the turkey she is badly
mixed: she gives it a bone to be used in getting it into trouble,
and she also furnishes it with a trick for getting itself out of
the trouble again. When a mamma-turkey answers an invitation and finds she has made a mistake in accepting it, she does
as the mamma-partridge does—remembers a previous engagement and goes limping and scrambling away, pretending to be
very lame; and at the same time she is saying to her not-visible
children, "Lie low, keep still, don't expose yourselves; I shall
be back as soon as I have beguiled this shabby swindler out of
the country."

When a person is ignorant and confiding, this immoral
device can have tiresome results. I followed an ostensibly lame
turkey over a considerable part of the United States one morning, because I believed in her and could not think she would
deceive a mere boy, and one who was trusting her and considering her honest. I had the single-barrelled shotgun, but my
idea was to catch her alive. I often got within rushing distance
of her, and then made my rush; but always, just as I made my
final plunge and put my hand down where her back had been,
it wasn't there; it was only two or three inches from there and
I brushed the tail-feathers as I landed on my stomach—a very
close call, but still not quite close enough; that is, not close
enough for success, but just close enough to convince me that I
could do it next time. She always waited for me, a little piece
away, and let on to be resting and greatly fatigued; which was
a lie, but I believed it, for I still thought her honest long after I
ought to have begun to doubt her, suspecting that this was no
way for a high-minded bird to be acting. I followed, and followed, and followed, making my periodical rushes, and getting up and brushing the dust off, and resuming the voyage
with patient confidence; indeed, with a confidence which grew,
for I could see by the change of climate and vegetation that we

were getting up into the high latitudes, and as she always looked a little tireder and a little more discouraged after each rush, I judged that I was safe to win, in the end, the competition being purely a matter of staying power and the advantage lying with me from the start because she was lame.

Along in the afternoon I began to feel fatigued myself. Neither of us had had any rest since we first started on the excursion, which was upwards of ten hours before, though latterly we had paused awhile after rushes, I letting on to be thinking about something else; but neither of us sincere, and both of us waiting for the other to call game but in no real hurry about it, for indeed those little evanescent snatches of rest were very grateful to the feelings of us both; it would naturally be so, skirmishing along like that ever since dawn and not a bite in the mean time; at least for me, though sometimes as she lay on her side fanning herself with a wing and praying for strength to get out of this difficulty a grasshopper happened along whose time had come, and that was well for her, and fortunate, but I had nothing—nothing the whole day.

More than once, after I was very tired, I gave up taking her alive, and was going to shoot her, but I never did it, although it was my right, for I did not believe I could hit her; and besides, she always stopped and posed, when I raised the gun, and this made me suspicious that she knew about me and my marksmanship, and so I did not care to expose myself to remarks.

I did not get her, at all. When she got tired of the game at last, she rose from almost under my hand and flew aloft with the rush and whir of a shell and lit on the highest limb of a great tree and sat down and crossed her legs and smiled down at me, and seemed gratified to see me so astonished.

I was ashamed, and also lost; and it was while wandering the woods hunting for myself that I found a deserted log cabin and had one of the best meals there that in my life-days I have eaten. The weed-grown garden was full of ripe tomatoes, and I ate them ravenously, though I had never liked them before. Not more than two or three times since have I tasted anything that was so delicious as those tomatoes. I surfeited myself with them, and did not taste another one until I was in middle life.

I can eat them now, but I do not like the look of them. I suppose we have all experienced a surfeit at one time or another. Once, in stress of circumstances, I ate part of a barrel of sardines, there being nothing else at hand, but since then I have always been able to get along without sardines.

ESSAYS

MY BOYHOOD DREAMS

The dreams of my boyhood? No, they have not been realized. For all who are old, there is something infinitely pathetic about the subject which you have chosen, for in no gray-head's case can it suggest any but one thing—disappointment. Disappointment is its own reason for its pain: the quality or dignity of the hope that failed is a matter aside. The dreamer's valuation of the thing lost—not another man's—is the only standard to measure it by, and his grief for it makes it large and great and fine, and is worthy of our reverence in all cases. We should carefully remember that. There are sixteen hundred million people in the world. Of these there is but a trifling number—in fact, only thirty-eight millions—who can understand why a person should have an ambition to belong to the French army; and why, belonging to it, he should be proud of that; and why, having got down that far, he should want to go on down, down, down till he struck bottom and got on the General Staff; and why, being stripped of his livery, or set free and reinvested with his self-respect by any other quick and thorough process, let it be what it might, he should wish to return to his strange serfage. But no matter: the estimate put upon these things by the fifteen hundred and sixty millions is no proper measure of their value: the proper measure, the just measure, is that which is put upon them by Dreyfus, and is cipherable merely upon the littleness or the vastness of the *disappointment* which their loss cost him.

There you have it: the measure of the magnitude of a dream-failure is the measure of the disappointment the failure cost the dreamer; the value, in others' eyes, of the thing lost, has nothing to do with the matter. With this straightening-out and classification of the dreamer's position to help us, perhaps we can put ourselves in his place and respect his dream—Dreyfus's, and the dreams our friends have cherished and reveal to us. Some that I call to mind, some that have been revealed to me, are curious enough; but we may not smile at them, for they were precious to the dreamers, and their failure has left scars which give them dignity and pathos. With this theme in my mind, dear heads that were brown when they and mine were young together rise old and white before me now, beseeching me to speak for them, and most lovingly will I do it.

Howells, Hay, Aldrich, Matthews, Stockton, Cable, Remus—how their young hopes and ambitions come flooding back to my memory now, out of the vague far past, the beautiful past, the lamented past! I remember it so well—that night we met together—it was in Boston, and Mr. Fields was there, and Mr. Osgood, and Ralph Keeler, and Boyle O'Reilly, lost to us now these many years—and under the seal of confidence revealed to each other what our boyhood dreams had been: dreams which had not as yet been blighted, but over which was stealing the gray of the night that was to come—a night which we prophetically *felt*, and this feeling oppressed us and made us sad. I remember that Howells's voice broke twice, and it was only with great difficulty that he was able to go on; in the end he wept. For he had hoped to be an auctioneer. He told of his early struggles to climb to his goal, and how at last he attained to within a single step of the coveted summit. But there misfortune after misfortune assailed him, and he went down, and down, and down, until now at last, weary and disheartened, he had for the present given up the struggle and become editor of the *Atlantic Monthly*. This was in 1830. Seventy years are gone since, and where now is his dream? It will never be fulfilled. And it is best so; he is no longer fitted for the position; no one would take him now; even if he got it, he would not be able to do himself credit in it, on account of his deliberateness of speech and lack of trained professional vivacity; he would be put on real estate, and would have the pain of seeing younger and abler men intrusted with the furniture and other such goods—goods which draw a mixed and intellectually low order of customers, who must be beguiled of their bids by a vulgar and specialized humor and sparkle, accompanied with antics.

But it is not the thing lost that counts, but only the *disappointment* the loss brings to the dreamer that had coveted that thing and had set his heart of hearts upon it, and when we remember this, a great wave of sorrow for Howells rises in our breasts, and we wish for his sake that his fate could have been different.

At that time Hay's boyhood dream was not yet past hope of realization, but it was fading, dimming, wasting away, and the wind of a growing apprehension was blowing cold over the perishing summer of his life. In the pride of his young ambition he had aspired to be a steamboat mate; and in fancy saw himself dominating a forecastle some day on the Mississippi and dictating terms to roustabouts in high and wounding tones. I look back now, from this far distance of seventy years, and note with sorrow the stages of that dream's destruction. Hay's history is but Howells's, with differences of detail. Hay climbed high toward his ideal; when success seemed almost sure, his foot upon the very gang-plank, his eye upon the capstan, misfortune came and his fall began. Down—down—down—ever down: Private Secretary to the President; Colonel in the field; Chargé d'Affaires in Paris; Chargé d'Affaires in Vienna; Poet; Editor of the *Tribune;* Biographer of Lincoln; Ambassador to England; and now at last there he lies—Secretary of State, Head of Foreign Affairs. And he has fallen like Lucifer, never to rise again. And his dream—where now is his dream? Gone down in blood and tears with the dream of the auctioneer.

And the young dream of Aldrich—where is that? I remember yet how he sat there that night fondling it, petting it; seeing it recede and ever recede; trying to be reconciled and give it up, but not able yet to bear the thought; for it had been his hope to be a horse-doctor. He also climbed high, but, like the others, fell; then fell again, and yet again, and again and again. And now at last he can fall no further. He is old now, he has ceased to struggle, and is only a poet. No one would risk a horse with him now. His dream is over.

Has *any* boyhood dream ever been fulfilled? I must doubt it. Look at Brander Matthews. He wanted to be a cowboy. What is he to-day? Nothing but a professor in a university. Will he ever be a cowboy? It is hardly conceivable.

Look at Stockton. What was Stockton's young dream? He hoped to be a barkeeper. See where *he* has landed.

Is it better with Cable? What was Cable's young dream? To be ring-master in the circus, and swell around and crack the whip. What is he to-day? Nothing but a theologian and novelist.

And Uncle Remus—what was his young dream? To be a buccaneer. Look at him now.

Ah, the dreams of our youth, how beautiful they are, and how perishable! The ruins of these might-have-beens, how pathetic! The heart-secrets that were revealed that night now so long vanished, how they touch me as I give them voice! Those sweet privacies, how they endeared us to each other! We were under oath never to tell any of these things, and I have always kept that oath inviolate when speaking with persons whom I thought not worthy to hear them.

Oh, our lost Youth—God keep its memory green in our hearts! for Age is upon us, with the indignity of its infirmities, and Death beckons!

TO THE ABOVE OLD PEOPLE

Sleep! for the Sun that scores another Day
Against the Tale allotted You to stay,
   Reminding You, is Risen, and now
Serves Notice—ah, ignore it while You may!

The chill Wind blew, and those who stood before
The Tavern murmured, "Having drunk his Score,
   Why tarries He with empty Cup? Behold,
The Wine of Youth once poured, is poured no more.

"Come, leave the Cup, and on the Winter's Snow
Your Summer Garment of Enjoyment throw:
   Your Tide of Life is ebbing fast, and it,
Exhausted once, for You no more shall flow."

While yet the Phantom of false Youth was mine,
I heard a Voice from out the Darkness whine,
   "O Youth, O whither gone? Return,
And bathe my Age in thy reviving Wine."

In this subduing Draught of tender green
And kindly Absinth, with its wimpling Sheen
   Of dusky half-lights, let me drown
The haunting Pathos of the Might-Have-Been.

For every nickeled Joy, marred and brief,
We pay some day its Weight in golden Grief
   Mined from our Hearts. Ah, murmur not—
From this one-sided Bargain dream of no Relief!

The Joy of Life, that streaming through their Veins
Tumultuous swept, falls slack—and wanes
   The Glory in the Eye—and one by one
Life's Pleasures perish and make place for Pains.

Whether one hide in some secluded Nook—
Whether at Liverpool or Sandy Hook—
   'Tis one. Old Age will search him out—and He—
He—He—when ready will know where to look.

From Cradle unto Grave I keep a House
Of Entertainment where may drowse
   Bacilli and kindred Germs—or feed—or breed
Their festering Species in a deep Carouse.

Think—in this battered Caravanserai,
Whose Portals open stand all Night and Day,

How Microbe after Microbe with his Pomp
Arrives unasked, and comes to stay.

Our ivory Teeth, confessing to the Lust
Of masticating, once, now own Disgust
   Of Clay-plug'd Cavities—full soon our Snags
Are emptied, and our Mouths are filled with Dust.

Our Gums forsake the Teeth and tender grow,
And fat, like over-ripened Figs—we know
   The Sign—the Riggs Disease is ours, and we
Must list this Sorrow, add another Woe:

Our Lungs begin to fail and soon we Cough,
And chilly Streaks play up our Backs, and off
   Our fever'd Foreheads drips an icy Sweat—
We scoffed before, but now we may not scoff.

Some for the Bunions that afflict us prate
Of Plasters unsurpassable, and hate
   To cut a Corn—ah cut, and let the Plaster go,
Nor murmur if the Solace come too late.

Some for the Honors of Old Age, and some
Long for its Respite from the Hum
   And Clash of sordid Strife—O Fools,
The Past should teach them what's to Come:

Lo, for the Honors, cold Neglect instead!
For Respite, disputations Heirs a Bed
   Of Thorns for them will furnish. Go,
Seek not Here for Peace—but Yonder—with the Dead.

For whether Zal and Rustam heed this Sign,
And even smitten thus, will not repine,
   Let Zal and Rustam shuffle as they may,
The Fine once levied they must Cash the Fine.

O Voices of the Long Ago that were so dear!
Fall'n Silent, now, for many a Mould'ring Year,
   O whither are ye flown? Come back,
And break my Heart, but bless my grieving ear.

Some happy Day my Voice will Silent fall,
And answer not when some that love it call:
   Be glad for Me when this you note—and think
I've found the Voices lost, beyond the Pall.

So let me grateful drain the Magic Bowl
That medicines hurt Minds and on the Soul
   The Healing of its Peace doth lay—if then
Death claim me—Welcome be his Dole!

              SANNA, SWEDEN, *September 15th*.

Private.—If you don't know what Riggs's Disease of the Teeth
is, the dentist will tell you. I've had it—and it is more than interesting.   S. L. C.

EDITORIAL NOTE

Fearing that there might be some mistake, we submitted a
proof of this article to the (American) gentlemen named in it,
and asked them to correct any errors of detail that might have
crept in among the facts. They reply with some asperity that
errors cannot creep in among facts where there are no facts for
them to creep in among; and that none are discoverable in this
article, but only baseless aberrations of a disordered mind.
They have no recollection of any such night in Boston, nor
elsewhere; and in their opinion there was never any such night.
They have *met* Mr. Twain, but have had the prudence not to
intrust any privacies to him—particularly under oath; and
they think they now see that this prudence was justified, since
he has been untrustworthy enough to even betray privacies
which had no existence. Further, they think it a strange thing

that Mr. Twain, who was never invited to meddle with any-body's boyhood dreams but his own, has been so gratuitously anxious to see that other peoples are placed before the world that he has quite lost his head in his zeal and forgotten to make any mention of his own at all. Provided we insert this explanation, they are willing to let his article pass; otherwise they must require its suppression in the interest of truth.

P.S.—These replies having left us in some perplexity, and also in some fear lest they might distress Mr. Twain if published without his privity, we judged it but fair to submit them to him and give him an opportunity to defend himself. But he does not seem to be troubled, or even aware that he is in a delicate situation. He merely says:

"Do not worry about those former young people. They can write good literature, but when it comes to speaking the truth, they have not had my training.—MARK TWAIN."

The last sentence seems obscure, and liable to an unfortunate construction. It plainly needs refashioning, but we cannot take the responsibility of doing it.—EDITOR.

IS SHAKESPEARE DEAD?

VI

When Shakespeare died, in 1616, great literary productions attributed to him as author had been before the London world and in high favor for twenty-four years. Yet his death was not an event. It made no stir, it attracted no attention. Apparently his eminent literary contemporaries did not realize that a celebrated poet had passed from their midst. Perhaps they knew a play-actor of minor rank had disappeared, but did not regard him as the author of his Works. "We are justified in assuming" this.

His death was not even an event in the little town of Stratford. Does this mean that in Stratford he was not regarded as a celebrity of *any* kind?

"We are privileged to assume"—no, we are indeed *obliged* to assume—that such was the case. He had spent the first twenty-two or twenty-three years of his life there, and of course knew everybody and was known by everybody of that day in the town, including the dogs and the cats and the horses. He had spent the last five or six years of his life there, diligently trading in every big and little thing that had money in it; so we are compelled to assume that many of the folk there in those said latter days knew him personally, and the rest by sight and hearsay. But not as a *celebrity?* Apparently not. For everybody soon forgot to remember any contact with him or any incident connected with him. The dozens of townspeople, still alive, who had known of him or known about him in the first twenty-three years of his life were in the same unremembering condition: if they knew of any incident connected with that period of his life they didn't tell about it. Would they if they had been asked? It is most likely. Were they asked? It is pretty apparent that they were not. Why weren't they? It is a very plausible guess that nobody there or elsewhere was interested to know.

For seven years after Shakespeare's death nobody seems to have been interested in him. Then the quarto was published, and Ben Jonson awoke out of his long indifference and sang a song of praise and put it in the front of the book. Then silence fell *again*.

For sixty years. Then inquiries into Shakespeare's Stratford life began to be made, of Stratfordians. Of Stratfordians who had known Shakespeare or had seen him? No. Then of Stratfordians who had seen people who had known or seen people who had seen Shakespeare? No. Apparently the inquiries were only made of Stratfordians who were not Stratfordians of Shakespeare's day, but later comers; and what they had learned had come to them from persons who had not seen Shakespeare; and what they had learned was not claimed as *fact*, but only as legend—dim and fading and indefinite legend; legend of the calf-slaughtering rank, and not worth remembering either as history or fiction.

Has it ever happened before—or since—that a celebrated person who had spent exactly half of a fairly long life in the village where he was born and reared, was able to slip out of this world and leave that village voiceless and gossipless behind him—utterly voiceless, utterly gossipless? And permanently so? I don't believe it has happened in any case except Shakespeare's. And couldn't and wouldn't have happened in his case if he had been regarded as a celebrity at the time of his death.

When I examine my own case—but let us do that, and see if it will not be recognizable as exhibiting a condition of things quite likely to result, most likely to result, indeed substantially *sure* to result in the case of a celebrated person, a benefactor of the human race. Like me.

My parents brought me to the village of Hannibal, Missouri, on the banks of the Mississippi, when I was two and a half years old. I entered school at five years of age, and drifted from one school to another in the village during nine and a half years. Then my father died, leaving his family in exceed-ingly straitened circumstances; wherefore my book-education came to a standstill forever, and I became a printer's appren-tice, on board and clothes, and when the clothes failed I got a hymn-book in place of them. This for summer wear, probably. I lived in Hannibal fifteen and a half years, altogether, then ran away, according to the custom of persons who are intend-ing to become celebrated. I never lived there afterward. Four years later I became a "cub" on a Mississippi steamboat in the St. Louis and New Orleans trade, and after a year and a half of hard study and hard work the U. S. inspectors rigorously exam-ined me through a couple of long sittings and decided that I knew every inch of the Mississippi—thirteen hundred miles—in the dark and in the day—as well as a baby knows the way to its mother's paps day or night. So they licensed me as a pilot—knighted me, so to speak—and I rose up clothed with author-ity, a responsible servant of the United States government.

Now then. Shakespeare died young—he was only fifty-two. He had lived in his native village twenty-six years, or about that. He died celebrated (if you believe everything you read in the books). Yet when he died nobody there or elsewhere took any notice of it; and for sixty years afterward no townsman remembered to say anything about him or about his life in Stratford. When the inquirer came at last he got but one fact—no, *legend*—and got that one at second hand, from a person who had only heard it as a rumor, and didn't claim copyright in it as a production of his own. He couldn't, very well, for its date antedated his own birth-date. But necessarily a number of persons were still alive in Stratford who, in the days of their youth, had seen Shakespeare nearly every day in the last five years of his life, and they would have been able to tell that inquirer some first-hand things about him if he had in those last days been a celebrity and therefore a person of interest to the villagers. Why did not the inquirer hunt them up and inter-view them? Wasn't it worth while? Wasn't the matter of suffi-cient consequence? Had the inquirer an engagement to see a dog-fight and couldn't spare the time?

It all seems to mean that he never had any literary celebrity, there or elsewhere, and no considerable repute as actor and manager.

Now then, I am away along in life—my seventy-third year being already well behind me—yet *sixteen* of my Hannibal schoolmates are still alive to-day, and can tell—and do tell—inquirers dozens and dozens of incidents of their young lives and mine together; things that happened to us in the morning of life, in the blossom of our youth, in the good days, the dear days, "the days when we went gipsying, a long time ago." Most of them creditable to me, too. One child to whom I paid court when she was five years old and I eight still lives in Hannibal, and she visited me last summer, traversing the necessary ten or twelve hundred miles of railroad without damage to her patience or to her old-young vigor. Another little lassie to whom I paid attention in Hannibal when she was nine years old and I the same, is still alive—in London—and hale and hearty, just as I am. And on the few surviving steamboats—those lingering ghosts and remembrancers of great fleets that plied the big river in the beginning of my water-career—which is exactly as long ago as the whole invoice of the life-years of Shakespeare number—there are still findable two or three river-pilots who saw me do creditable things in those ancient days; and several white-headed engineers; and several roustabouts and mates; and several deck-hands who used to heave the lead for me and send up on the still night air the "six—feet—*scant!*" that made me shudder, and the "M-a-r-k—*twain!*" that took the shudder away, and presently the darling "By the d-e-e-p—*four!*" that lifted me to heaven for joy.* They know about me, and can tell. And so do printers, from St. Louis to New York; and so do newspaper reporters, from Nevada to San Francisco. And so do the police. If Shakespeare had really been celebrated, like me, Stratford could have told things about him; and if my experience goes for anything, they'd have done it.

* Four fathoms—twenty-four feet.

VII

If I had under my superintendence a controversy appointed to decide whether Shakespeare wrote Shakespeare or not, I believe I would place before the debaters only the one question, *Was Shakespeare ever a practicing lawyer?* and leave everything else out.

It is maintained that the man who wrote the plays was not merely myriad-minded, but also myriad-accomplished: that he not only knew some thousands of things about human life in all its shades and grades, and about the hundred arts and trades and crafts and professions which men busy themselves in, but that he could *talk* about the men and their grades and trades accurately, making no mistakes. Maybe it is so, but have the experts spoken, or is it only Tom, Dick, and Harry? Does the exhibit stand upon wide, and loose, and eloquent generalizing—which is not evidence, and not proof—or upon details, particulars, statistics, illustrations, demonstrations?

Experts of unchallengeable authority have testified definitely as to only one of Shakespeare's multifarious craft-equipments, so far as my recollections of Shakespeare-Bacon talk abide with me—his law-equipment. I do not remember that Wellington or Napoleon ever examined Shakespeare's battles and sieges and strategies, and then decided and established for good and all, that they were militarily flawless; I do not remember that any Nelson, or Drake or Cook ever examined his seamanship and said it showed profound and accurate familiarity with that art; I don't remember that any king or prince or duke has ever testified that Shakespeare was letter-perfect in his handling of royal court-manners and the talk and manners of aristocracies; I don't remember that any illustrious Latinist or Grecian or Frenchman or Spaniard or Italian has proclaimed him a past-master in those languages; I don't remember—well, I don't remember that there is *testimony*—great testimony—imposing testimony—unanswerable and unattackable testimony as to any of Shakespeare's hundred specialties, except one—the law.

Other things change, with time, and the student cannot

trace back with certainty the changes that various trades and their processes and technicalities have undergone in the long stretch of a century or two and find out what their processes and technicalities were in those early days, but with the law it is different: it is mile-stoned and documented all the way back, and the master of that wonderful trade, that complex and intricate trade, that awe-compelling trade, has competent ways of knowing whether Shakespeare-law is good law or not; and whether his law-court procedure is correct or not, and whether his legal shop-talk is the shop-talk of a veteran practitioner or only a machine-made counterfeit of it gathered from books and from occasional loiterings in Westminster.

Richard H. Dana served two years before the mast, and had every experience that falls to the lot of the sailor before the mast of our day. His sailor-talk flows from his pen with the sure touch and the ease and confidence of a person who has *lived* what he is talking about, not gathered it from books and random listenings. Hear him:

> Having hove short, cast off the gaskets, and made the bunt of each sail fast by the jigger, with a man on each yard, at the word the whole canvas of the ship was loosed, and with the greatest rapidity possible everything was sheeted home and hoisted up, the anchor tripped and cat-headed, and the ship under headway.

Again:

> The royal yards were all crossed at once, and royals and sky-sails set, and, as we had the wind free, the booms were run out, and all were aloft, active as cats, laying out on the yards and booms, reeving the studding-sail gear; and sail after sail the captain piled upon her, until she was covered with canvas, her sails looking like a great white cloud resting upon a black speck.

Once more. A race in the Pacific:

> Our antagonist was in her best trim. Being clear of the point, the breeze became stiff, and the royal-masts bent under our

sails, but we would not take them in until we saw three boys spring into the rigging of the *California;* then they were all furled at once, but with orders to our boys to stay aloft at the top-gallant mast-heads and loose them again at the word. It was my duty to furl the fore-royal; and while standing by to loose it again, I had a fine view of the scene. From where I stood, the two vessels seemed nothing but spars and sails, while their narrow decks, far below, slanting over by the force of the wind aloft, appeared hardly capable of supporting the great fabrics raised upon them. The *California* was to windward of us, and had every advantage; yet, while the breeze was stiff we held our own. As soon as it began to slacken she ranged a little ahead, and the order was given to loose the royals. In an instant the gaskets were off and the bunt dropped. "Sheet home the fore-royal!"—"Weather sheet's home!"—"Lee sheet's home!"— "Hoist away, sir!" is bawled from aloft. "Overhaul your clewlines!" shouts the mate. "Aye-aye, sir, all clear!"—"Taut leech! belay! Well the lee brace; haul taut to windward!" and the royals are set.

What would the captain of any sailing-vessel of our time say to that? He would say, "The man that wrote that didn't learn his trade out of a book, he has *been* there!" But would this same captain be competent to sit in judgment upon Shakespeare's seamanship—considering the changes in ships and ship-talk that have necessarily taken place, unrecorded, unremembered, and lost to history in the last three hundred years? It is my conviction that Shakespeare's sailor-talk would be Choctaw to him. For instance—from *The Tempest:*

Master. Boatswain!

Boatswain. Here, master; what cheer?

Master. Good, speak to the mariners: fall to't, yarely, or we run ourselves to ground; bestir, bestir!

(Enter mariners.)

Boatswain. Heigh, my hearts! cheerly, cheerly, my hearts! yare, yare! Take in the topsail. Tend to the master's whistle. . . . Down with the topmast! yare! lower, lower! Bring her to

try wi' the main course. . . . Lay her a-hold, a-hold! Set her two
courses. Off to sea again; lay her off.

That will do, for the present; let us yare a little, now, for a
change.

If a man should write a book and in it make one of his characters say, "Here, devil, empty the quoins into the standing
galley and the imposing stone into the hell-box; assemble the
comps around the frisket and let them jeff for takes and be
quick about it," I should recognize a mistake or two in the
phrasing, and would know that the writer was only a printer
theoretically, not practically.

I have been a quartz miner in the silver regions—a pretty
hard life; I know all the palaver of that business: I know all
about discovery claims and the subordinate claims; I know
all about lodes, ledges, outcroppings, dips, spurs, angles, shafts,
drifts, inclines, levels, tunnels, air-shafts, "horses," clay casings,
granite casings; quartz mills and their batteries; arastras, and
how to charge them with quicksilver and sulphate of copper;
and how to clean them up, and how to reduce the resulting
amalgam in the retorts, and how to cast the bullion into pigs;
and finally I know how to screen tailings, and also how to hunt
for something less robust to do, and find it. I know the *argot* of
the quartz-mining and milling industry familiarly; and so
whenever Bret Harte introduces that industry into a story, the
first time one of his miners opens his mouth I recognize from
his phrasing that Harte got the phrasing by listening—like
Shakespeare—I mean the Stratford one—not by experience.
No one can talk the quartz dialect correctly without learning it
with pick and shovel and drill and fuse.

I have been a surface-miner—gold—and I know all its mysteries, and the dialect that belongs with them; and whenever
Harte introduces that industry into a story I know by the
phrasing of his characters that neither he nor they have ever
served that trade.

I have been a "pocket" miner—a sort of gold mining not
findable in any but one little spot in the world, so far as I
know. I know how, with horn and water, to find the trail of a

pocket and trace it step by step and stage by stage up the mountain to its source, and find the compact little nest of yellow metal reposing in its secret home under the ground. I know the language of that trade, that capricious trade, that fascinating buried-treasure trade, and can catch any writer who tries to use it without having learned it by the sweat of his brow and the labor of his hands.

I know several other trades and the *argot* that goes with them; and whenever a person tries to talk the talk peculiar to any of them without having learned it at its source I can trap him always before he gets far on his road.

And so, as I have already remarked, if I were required to superintend a Bacon-Shakespeare controversy, I would narrow the matter down to a single question—the only one, so far as the previous controversies have informed me, concerning which illustrious experts of unimpeachable competency have testified: *Was the author of Shakespeare's Works a lawyer?*— a lawyer deeply read and of limitless experience? I would put aside the guesses, and surmises, and perhapses, and might-have-beens, and could-have beens, and must-have-beens, and we-are justified-in-presumings, and the rest of those vague spectres and shadows and indefiniteness, and stand or fall, win or lose, by the verdict rendered by the jury upon that single question. If the verdict was Yes, I should feel quite convinced that the Stratford Shakespeare, the actor, manager, and trader who died so obscure, so forgotten, so destitute of even village consequence that sixty years afterward no fellow-citizen and friend of his later days remembered to tell anything about him, did not write the Works.

Chapter XIII of *The Shakespeare Problem Restated* bears the heading "Shakespeare as a Lawyer," and comprises some fifty pages of expert testimony, with comments thereon, and I will copy the first nine, as being sufficient all by themselves, as it seems to me, to settle the question which I have conceived to be the master-key to the Shakespeare-Bacon puzzle.

THE TURNING-POINT
OF MY LIFE

I

If I understand the idea, the *Bazar* invites several of us to write upon the above text. It means the change in my life's course which introduced what must be regarded by me as the most *important* condition of my career. But it also implies—without intention, perhaps—that that turning-point *itself* was the creator of the new condition. This gives it too much distinction, too much prominence, too much credit. It is only the *last* link in a very long chain of turning-points commissioned to produce the cardinal result; it is not any more important than the humblest of its ten thousand predecessors. Each of the ten thousand did its appointed share, on its appointed date, in forwarding the scheme, and they were all necessary; to have left out any one of them would have defeated the scheme and brought about *some other* result. I know we have a fashion of saying "such and such an event was the turning-point in my life," but we shouldn't say it. We should merely grant that its place as *last* link in the chain makes it the most *conspicuous* link; in real importance it has no advantage over any one of its predecessors.

Perhaps the most celebrated turning-point recorded in history was the crossing of the Rubicon. Suetonius says:

> Coming up with his troops on the banks of the Rubicon, he halted for a while, and, revolving in his mind the importance of the step he was on the point of taking, he turned to those about him and said, "We may still retreat; but if we pass this little bridge, nothing is left for us but to fight it out in arms."

This was a stupendously important moment. And all the incidents, big and little, of Cæsar's previous life had been leading up to it, stage by stage, link by link. This was the *last* link—merely the last one, and no bigger than the others; but as we gaze back at it through the inflating mists of our imagination, it looks as big as the orbit of Neptune.

You, the reader, have a *personal* interest in that link, and so have I; so has the rest of the human race. It was one of the links in your life-chain, and it was one of the links in mine. We may wait, now, with bated breath, while Cæsar reflects. Your fate and mine are involved in his decision.

While he was thus hesitating, the following incident occurred. A person remarked for his noble mien and graceful aspect appeared close at hand, sitting and playing upon a pipe. When not only the shepherds, but a number of soldiers also, flocked to listen to him, and some trumpeters among them, he snatched a trumpet from one of them, ran to the river with it, and, sounding the advance with a piercing blast, crossed to the other side. Upon this, Cæsar exclaimed: "Let us go whither the omens of the gods and the iniquity of our enemies call us. *The die is cast.*"

So he crossed—and changed the future of the whole human race, for all time. But that stranger was a link in Cæsar's life-chain, too; and a necessary one. We don't know his name, we never hear of him again; he was very casual; he acts like an accident; but he was no accident, he was there by compulsion of *his* life-chain, to blow the electrifying blast that was to make up Cæsar's mind for him, and thence go piping down the aisles of history forever.

If the stranger hadn't been there! But he *was*. And Cæsar crossed. With such results! Such vast events—each a link in the *human race's* life-chain; each event producing the next one, and that one the next one, and so on: the destruction of the republic; the founding of the empire; the breaking up of the empire; the rise of Christianity upon its ruins; the spread of the religion to other lands—and so on: link by link took its appointed place at its appointed time, the discovery of America being one of them; our Revolution another; the inflow of

English and other immigrants another; their drift westward (my ancestors among them) another; the settlement of certain of them in Missouri, which resulted in *me*. For I was one of the unavoidable results of the crossing of the Rubicon. If the stranger, with his trumpet blast, had stayed away (which he *couldn't*, for he was an appointed link) Cæsar would not have crossed. What would have happened, in that case, we can never guess. We only know that the things that did happen would not have happened. They might have been replaced by equally prodigious things, of course, but their nature and results are beyond our guessing. But the matter that interests me personally is that I would not be *here* now, but somewhere else; and probably black—there is no telling. Very well, I am glad he crossed. And very really and thankfully glad, too, though I never cared anything about it before.

II

To me, the most important feature of my life is its literary feature. I have been professionally literary something more than forty years. There have been many turning-points in my life, but the one that was the last link in the chain appointed to conduct me to the literary guild is the most *conspicuous* link in that chain. *Because* it was the last one. It was not any more important than its predecessors. All the other links have an inconspicuous look, except the crossing of the Rubicon; but as factors in making me literary they are all of the one size, the crossing of the Rubicon included.

I know how I came to be literary, and I will tell the steps that led up to it and brought it about.

The crossing of the Rubicon was not the first one, it was hardly even a recent one; I should have to go back ages before Cæsar's day to find the first one. To save space I will go back only a couple of generations and start with an incident of my boyhood. When I was twelve and a half years old, my father died. It was in the spring. The summer came, and brought with it an epidemic of measles. For a time, a child died almost every day. The village was paralyzed with fright, distress, despair. Children that were not smitten with the disease were imprisoned in their homes to save them from the infection. In the homes there were no cheerful faces, there was no music, there was no singing but of solemn hymns, no voice but of prayer, no romping was allowed, no noise, no laughter, the family moved spectrally about on tiptoe, in a ghostly hush. I was a prisoner. My soul was steeped in this awful dreariness— and in fear. At some time or other every day and every night a sudden shiver shook me to the marrow, and I said to myself, "There, I've got it! and I shall die." Life on these miserable terms was not worth living, and at last I made up my mind to get the disease and have it over, one way or the other. I escaped from the house and went to the house of a neighbor where a playmate of mine was very ill with the malady. When the chance offered I crept into his room and got into bed with him. I was discovered by his mother and sent back into captivity. But I had the disease; they could not take that from me. I came near to dying. The whole village was interested, and anxious, and sent for news of me every day; and not only once a day, but several times. Everybody believed I would die; but on the four-teenth day a change came for the worse and they were disap-pointed.

This was a turning-point of my life. (Link number one.) For when I got well my mother closed my school career and apprenticed me to a printer. She was tired of trying to keep me out of mischief, and the adventure of the measles decided her to put me into more masterful hands than hers.

I became a printer, and began to add one link after another to the chain which was to lead me into the literary profession. A long road, but I could not know that; and as I did not know what its goal was, or even that it had one, I was indifferent. Also contented.

A young printer wanders around a good deal, seeking and finding work; and seeking again, when necessity commands. N. B. Necessity is a *Circumstance*; Circumstance is man's master—and when Circumstance commands, he must obey; he may argue the matter—that is his privilege, just as it is the honorable privilege of a falling body to argue with the attraction of gravitation—but it won't do any good, he must *obey*. I wandered for ten years, under the guidance and dictatorship of Circumstance, and finally arrived in a city of Iowa, where I worked several months. Among the books that interested me in those days was one about the Amazon. The traveler told an alluring tale of his long voyage up the great river from Para to the sources of the Madeira, through the heart of an enchanted land, a land wastefully rich in tropical wonders, a romantic land where all the birds and flowers and animals were of the museum varieties, and where the alligator and the crocodile and the monkey seemed as much at home as if they were in the Zoo. Also, he told an astonishing tale about *coca*, a vegetable product of miraculous powers, asserting that it was so nourishing and so strength-giving that the native of the mountains of the Madeira region would tramp up hill and down all day on a pinch of powdered coca and require no other sustenance.

I was fired with a longing to ascend the Amazon. Also with a longing to open up a trade in coca with all the world. During months I dreamed that dream, and tried to contrive ways to get to Para and spring that splendid enterprise upon an unsuspecting planet. But all in vain. A person may *plan* as much as he wants to, but nothing of consequence is likely to come of it until the magician *Circumstance* steps in and takes the matter off his hands. At last Circumstance came to my help. It was in this way. Circumstance, to help or hurt another man, made him lose a fifty-dollar bill in the street; and to help or hurt me, made me find it. I advertised the find, and left for the Amazon the same day. This was another turning-point, another link.

Could Circumstance have ordered another dweller in that town to go to the Amazon and open up a world-trade in coca on a fifty-dollar basis and been obeyed? No, I was the only one. There were other fools there—shoals and shoals of them—but they were not of my kind. I was the only one of my kind.

Circumstance is powerful, but it cannot work alone; it has to have a partner. Its partner is man's *temperament*—his natural disposition. His temperament is not his invention, it is *born* in him, and he has no authority over it, neither is he responsible for its acts. He cannot change it, nothing can change it, nothing can modify it—except temporarily. But it won't stay modified. It is permanent, like the color of the man's eyes and the shape of his ears. Blue eyes are gray in certain unusual lights; but they resume their natural color when that stress is removed.

A Circumstance that will coerce one man will have no effect upon a man of a different temperament. If Circumstance had thrown the bank-note in Cæsar's way, his temperament would not have made him start for the Amazon. His temperament would have compelled him to do something with the money, but not that. It might have made him advertise the note—and *wait*. We can't tell. Also, it might have made him go to New York and buy into the Government, with results that would leave Tweed nothing to learn when it came his turn.

Very well, Circumstance furnished the capital, and my temperament told me what to do with it. Sometimes a temperament is an ass. When that is the case the owner of it is an ass, too, and is going to remain one. Training, experience, association, can temporarily so polish him, improve him, exalt him that people will think he is a mule, but they will be mistaken. Artificially he *is* a mule, for the time being, but at bottom he is an ass yet, and will remain one.

By temperament I was the kind of person that *does* things. Does them, and reflects afterward. So I started for the Amazon without reflecting and without asking any questions. That was more than fifty years ago. In all that time my temperament has not changed, by even a shade. I have been punished many and many a time, and bitterly, for doing things and reflecting afterward, but these tortures have been of no value to me: I still do the thing commanded by Circumstance and Temperament, and reflect afterward. Always violently. When I am reflecting, on those occasions, even deaf persons can hear me think.

I went by the way of Cincinnati, and down the Ohio and Mississippi. My idea was to take ship, at New Orleans, for Para. In New Orleans I inquired, and found there was no ship leaving for Para. Also, that there never had *been* one leaving for Para. I reflected. A policeman came and asked me what I was doing, and I told him. He made me move on, and said if he caught me reflecting in the public street again he would run me in.

After a few days I was out of money. Then Circumstance arrived, with another turning-point of my life—a new link. On my way down, I had made the acquaintance of a pilot. I begged him to teach me the river, and he consented. I became a pilot.

By and by Circumstance came again—introducing the Civil War, this time, in order to push me ahead another stage or two toward the literary profession. The boats stopped running, my livelihood was gone.

Circumstance came to the rescue with a new turning-point and a fresh link. My brother was appointed secretary to the new Territory of Nevada, and he invited me to go with him and help him in his office. I accepted.

In Nevada, Circumstance furnished me the silver fever and I went into the mines to make a fortune, as I supposed; but that was not the idea. The idea was to advance me another step toward literature. For amusement I scribbled things for the Virginia City *Enterprise*. One isn't a printer ten years without setting up acres of good and bad literature, and learning— unconsciously at first, consciously later—to discriminate between the two, within his mental limitations; and meantime he is unconsciously acquiring what is called a "style." One of my efforts attracted attention, and the *Enterprise* sent for me and put me on its staff.

And so I became a journalist—another link. By and by Circumstance and the Sacramento *Union* sent me to the Sandwich Islands for five or six months, to write up sugar. I did it; and threw in a good deal of extraneous matter that hadn't anything to do with sugar. But it was this extraneous matter that helped me to another link.

It made me notorious, and San Francisco invited me to lecture. Which I did. And profitably. I had long had a desire to travel and see the world, and now Circumstance had most kindly and unexpectedly hurled me upon the platform and furnished me the means. So I joined the "Quaker City Excursion."

When I returned to America, Circumstance was waiting on the pier—with the *last* link—the conspicuous, the consummating, the victorious link: I was asked to *write a book*, and I did it, and called it *The Innocents Abroad*. Thus I became at last a member of the literary guild. That was forty-two years ago, and I have been a member ever since. Leaving the Rubicon incident away back where it belongs, I can say with truth that the reason I am in the literary profession is because I had the measles when I was twelve years old.

III

Now what interests me, as regards these details, is not the details themselves, but the fact that none of them was foreseen by me, none of them was planned by me, I was the author of none of them. Circumstance, working in harness with my temperament, created them all and compelled them all. I often offered help, and with the best intentions, but it was rejected—as a rule, uncourteously. I could never plan a thing and get it to come out the way I planned it. It came out some other way—some way I had not counted upon.

And so I do not admire the human being—as an intellectual marvel—as much as I did when I was young, and got him out of books, and did not know him personally. When I used to read that such and such a general did a certain brilliant thing, I believed it. Whereas it was not so. Circumstance did it by help of his temperament. The circumstance would have failed of effect with a general of another temperament: he might see the chance, but lose the advantage by being by nature too slow or too quick or too doubtful. Once General Grant was asked a question about a matter which had been much debated by the public and the newspapers; he answered the question without any hesitancy. "General, who planned the march through Georgia?" "The enemy!" He added that the enemy usually makes your plans for you. He meant that the enemy by neglect or through force of circumstances leaves an opening for you, and you see your chance and take advantage of it.

Circumstances do the planning for us all, no doubt, by help of our temperaments. I see no great difference between a man and a watch, except that the man is conscious and the watch isn't, and the man *tries* to plan things and the watch doesn't. The watch doesn't wind itself and doesn't regulate itself— these things are done exteriorly. Outside influences, outside circumstances, wind the *man* and regulate him. Left to himself, he wouldn't get regulated at all, and the sort of time he would keep would not be valuable. Some rare men are wonderful watches, with gold case, compensation balance, and all those things, and some men are only simple and sweet and humble Waterburys. I am a Waterbury. A Waterbury of that kind, some say.

A nation is only an individual multiplied. It makes plans and Circumstance comes and upsets them—or enlarges them. Some patriots throw the tea overboard; some other patriots destroy a Bastille. The *plans* stop there; then Circumstance comes in, quite unexpectedly, and turns these modest riots into a revolution.

And there was poor Columbus. He elaborated a deep plan to find a new route to an old country. Circumstance revised his plan for him, and he found a new *world*. And *he* gets the credit of it to this day. He hadn't anything to do with it.

Necessarily the scene of the real turning-point of my life (and of yours) was the Garden of Eden. It was there that the first link was forged of the chain that was ultimately to lead to the emptying of me into the literary guild. Adam's *temperament* was the first command the Deity ever issued to a human being on this planet. And it was the only command Adam would *never* be able to disobey. It said, "Be weak, be water, be characterless, be cheaply persuadable." The later command, to let the fruit alone, was certain to be disobeyed. Not by Adam himself, but by his *temperament*—which he did not create and had no authority over. For the *temperament* is the man; the thing tricked out with clothes and named Man is merely its

Shadow, nothing more. The law of the tiger's temperament is, Thou shalt kill; the law of the sheep's temperament is, Thou shalt not kill. To issue later commands requiring the tiger to let the fat stranger alone, and requiring the sheep to imbue its hands in the blood of the lion is not worth while, for those commands *can't* be obeyed. They would invite to violations of the law of *temperament*, which is supreme, and takes precedence of all other authorities. I cannot help feeling disappointed in Adam and Eve. That is, in their temperaments. Not in *them*, poor helpless young creatures—afflicted with temperaments made out of butter; which butter was commanded to get into contact with fire and *be melted*. What I cannot help wishing is, that Adam and Eve had been postponed, and Martin Luther and Joan of Arc put in their place—that splendid pair equipped with temperaments not made of butter, but of asbestos. By neither sugary persuasions nor by hell fire could Satan have beguiled *them* to eat the apple.

There would have been results! Indeed, yes. The apple would be intact to-day; there would be no human race; there would be no *you;* there would be no *me*. And the old, old creation-dawn scheme of ultimately launching me into the literary guild would have been defeated.

Glossary

Aldrich, Thomas Bailey (1836–1907). Massachusetts writer whom Clemens befriended during the 1870s. Through the 1880s, Aldrich edited the *Atlantic Monthly*.

"Alfred T. Lacey." STEAMBOAT on which Clemens traveled to Memphis after leaving the PENNSYLVANIA in June 1858. The *Lacey* may also have been the first boat on which he served as a licensed pilot in May 1859.

Alta California. See SAN FRANCISCO ALTA CALIFORNIA.

American Publishing Company. HARTFORD firm specializing in subscription books sold throughout the United States by door-to-door canvassers. The company published *The Innocents Abroad* (1869), *Roughing It* (1872), *The Gilded Age* (1873), *Mark Twain's Sketches New & Old* (1875), *Tom Sawyer* (1876), *A Tramp Abroad* (1880), *Pudd'nhead Wilson* (1894), and *Following the Equator* (1897).

Atlantic Monthly. Boston literary magazine with a national readership in which Clemens published "OLD TIMES ON THE MISSISSIPPI" and more than a dozen stories and sketches between 1875 and 1880, while his friend W. D. HOWELLS was editor.

bar. Underwater ridge of sand or gravel formed by river currents.

Bates, Edward (1793–1869). Missouri lawyer who served as President Abraham Lincoln's attorney general. Bates got Sam Clemens's brother Orion CLEMENS appointed secretary of the new NEVADA territorial government in 1861.

Bear Creek. Stream running through HANNIBAL, about one-half mile south of Clemens's boyhood home. Children often swam in the stream. By Clemens's own account, two of his friends drowned in the creek, and he nearly drowned in it several times himself.

Beckwith, James Carroll (1852–1917). HANNIBAL-born portrait artist who painted a picture of Clemens smoking a corncob pipe when both men were vacationing in the Catskill Mountains in 1890.

Bixby, Horace E. (1826–1912). Veteran STEAMBOAT pilot who trained Clemens on the Lower Mississippi. Identified as "Mr. B." in the original "OLD TIMES ON THE MISSISSIPPI" articles, Bixby had a long career as a pilot and captain on the river and enjoyed some celebrity as Mark Twain's "lightning pilot."

Blankenship, Tom (born c. 1831). HANNIBAL boy of Clemens's time who was the primary model for Huck Finn. Like Huck, he was the son of a disreputable town drunk but differed in growing up in a large family.

Bliss, Elisha (1822–1880). Officer of the AMERICAN PUBLISH-ING COMPANY. who signed Clemens to write THE INNOCENTS ABROAD and other books. Clemens suspected Bliss of cheating him and severed his connections with Bliss's company in 1880—the year Bliss died. However, he published two more books with the company during the mid-1890s, when Bliss's son, Frank Bliss (1843–1915), was managing it.

boiler deck. STEAMBOAT deck directly above the main deck. Despite its name, the deck has passenger cabins, not boilers.

Bowen, Sam (c. 1838–1878). A younger brother of Will BOWEN, Sam Bowen grew up with Clemens in HANNIBAL and preceded him as a Mississippi STEAMBOAT pilot.

Bowen, Will (1836–1893). One of Clemens's friends during his boyhood, Bowen also became a Mississippi STEAMBOAT pilot and worked with Clemens on several boats. He left the river in 1868 and apparently saw Clemens for the last time, in HARTFORD, in 1888.

Briggs, John B. (1837–1907). Another of Clemens's closest childhood friends, Briggs was the model for Tom Sawyer's pal Ben Rogers. He spent the rest of his life in HANNIBAL, where Clemens last saw him in 1902.

Brown, William (c. 1810s–1858). Unpleasant pilot under whom Clemens trained on the STEAMBOAT "PENNSYLVANIA" while Horace BIXBY was on the Missouri River in 1858. Brown died when the "Pennsylvania" blew up near Memphis.

Buffalo. Upstate New York city in which Clemens lived from August 1869 to March 1871, while editing the *Buffalo Express*, of which he was part owner. After marrying Olivia Langdon on February 2, 1870, he began his married life in a large house at 472 Delaware Avenue purchased by his father-in-law. In early 1871, he sold the house and his interest in the newspaper at a loss and moved to HARTFORD.

Cable, George Washington (1844–1925). Southern writer known for stories set in Louisiana, such as *Old Creole Days* (1879) and *The Grandissimes* (1880). Clemens met Cable in New Orleans in 1882 and went on a long lecture tour with him in late 1884. Afterward, the men had little contact.

Cairo. Illinois town located at the confluence of the Ohio and Mississippi rivers—the location generally regarded as the dividing point between the Upper and Lower Mississippi. Pronounced kay-ROH.

Calaveras County. California county in the Sierra Nevada foothills east of SAN FRANCISCO where Clemens briefly prospected for gold in early 1865. Clemens immortalized the county by making it the setting for his JUMPING FROG STORY.

Caprivi, Leo von (1831–1899). Chancellor of Germany when Clemens was in Berlin in late 1891. Otto von Bismarck's successor, Caprivi held the post from 1890 to 1894.

Cardiff Hill. Known as Holliday's Hill during Clemens's time, the southern tip of a long escarpment rising about three hundred feet above the north end of HANNIBAL, alongside the MISSISSIPPI RIVER. The hill now takes its modern name from the fictional hill in *Tom Sawyer* for which it was the model.

Carleton, George Washington (1832–1901). New York publisher who excluded Clemens's JUMPING FROG STORY from a book edited by Artemus WARD in 1865 and two years later rejected Clemens's first collection of sketches (later published by C. H. WEBB). Carleton admitted his blunder when he saw Clemens in Switzerland in 1898.

Carson City. Capital of NEVADA in which Orion CLEMENS built a house while serving as secretary of the territorial government. Sam Clemens often visited the town while reporting for the VIRGINIA CITY TERRITORIAL ENTERPRISE. He first used the pen name "Mark Twain" in a newspaper story he wrote here.

Cave, Hannibal. Large limestone cave two miles south of HANNIBAL in which Clemens played as a boy. The cave served as the model for the cave near St. Petersburg in *Tom Sawyer* and *Huckleberry Finn*. It has been transformed into a tourist attraction.

chutes. Narrow river channels cutting across sections of land around which the main channels wrap. As the chutes deepen and widen, they eventually become CUT-OFFS.

Cincinnati. Ohio city in which Clemens worked as a printer from late October 1856 through mid-February 1857.

Civil War (1861–1865). Conflict that halted STEAMBOAT traffic on the Lower Mississippi in April 1861, ending Clemens's career as a pilot. After returning to HANNIBAL, Clemens served briefly in a militia unit called up by the state's pro-Confederacy governor. In mid-1861, he went to the Far West with his brother and did not return to the East until more than a year after the war ended.

Clapp, Henry. See SATURDAY PRESS.

Clara, Aunt. See SPAULDING, CLARA.

Clemens, Benjamin (1832–1842). Brother of Clemens who died in HANNIBAL when Clemens was only six years old.

Clemens, Clara (1874–1962). Second of Clemens's three daughters and the only child to outlive him. As sole heir of Clemens's estate, Clara played a strong role in determining which of his unpublished works—including his autobiographical dictations—could be published. Her efforts to suppress his more controversial and darker writings long helped to preserve the image of Mark Twain as a genial humorist.

Clemens, Henry (1838–1858). Clemens's youngest sibling and the one to whom he was closest during his youth. Sam and Henry did printing work for their brother Orion in Iowa. In early 1858, Sam got Henry an unpaid position as a "MUD CLERK" aboard the STEAMBOAT "PENNSYLVANIA," on which he was a cub pilot. Henry died from injuries sustained in the explosion of the boat's boiler in June. Sam afterward blamed himself for his brother's death. He later modeled Tom Sawyer's half-brother, Sid, on Henry.

Clemens, Jane Lampton (1803–1890). Clemens's mother, who outlived all but three of her seven children—Orion, Pamela, and

Sam. After being widowed in 1847, she lived alternately with Orion and Pamela and spent her last years living with Orion in KEOKUK, Iowa. Sam corresponded with her regularly but saw her infrequently. A cheerful, fun-loving person and superior storyteller, Jane Clemens had a seminal influence on Sam's life and writing career and was the model for Tom Sawyer's Aunt Polly.

Clemens, Jean (1880–1909). Clemens's youngest daughter. Jean had delicate health from her infancy, when she contracted scarlet fever. During the 1890s, she began having epileptic seizures and was in and out of sanitariums after her mother died in 1904. Most of her last year she lived with her father in Redding, Conn., where she succumbed to a heart attack during a seizure on Christmas Eve, 1909. Clemens then wrote "The Death of Jean" and called it the final chapter of his autobiography.

Clemens, John Marshall (1798–1847). Clemens's father. Born in Virginia, John M. Clemens studied law and later held government legal positions but never established his own law practice. He failed in several business ventures and left his family impoverished when he died. His son used him as a model for several characters, including Judge Driscoll in *Pudd'nhead Wilson*.

Clemens, Langdon (1870–1872). Clemens's first child and only son. Frail from the moment of his premature birth, Langdon died from diphtheria at the age of twenty-two months. Clemens blamed himself for his son's death because he had allowed the boy's blanket to slip off him during an outing in severely cold weather.

Clemens, Livy (Olivia) (1845–1904). Clemens's wife. A member of the genteel and prosperous Langdon family in ELMIRA, Livy married Clemens on February 2, 1870. After contracting Pott's disease as a teenager, she never enjoyed vigorous health but nevertheless bore four children. She was essentially an invalid during her last years.

Clemens, Margaret L. (1830–1839). Sister of Clemens whose death in FLORIDA, Mo., helped prompt the family's move to HANNIBAL in 1839.

Clemens, Orion (1825–1897). Clemens's oldest sibling and only brother, of four, to live past 1858. Orion (pronounced or'REE-on) was intelligent and capable but was also inclined to vacillate in his opinions and to pursue unrealistic dreams. Consequently, he failed at almost everything he attempted. His greatest achievement occurred during the early 1860s, when he was secretary to the government of NEVADA. Afterward, his life slid downward and he became dependent on his brother's financial support. Sam's feelings toward Orion were a mixture of love and exasperation; he used his brother as a model for some of his most eccentric fictional characters.

Clemens, Pamela. See MOFFETT, Pamela Clemens.

Clemens, Susy (1872–1896). Clemens's oldest daughter and favorite child. At thirteen, she began composing a book about her father, much of which he later incorporated into his autobiographical dictations. When Clemens undertook his round-the-world lecture tour in 1895–1896, Susy and her sister Jean stayed behind in ELMIRA. They were to rejoin the family in London after the tour ended, but Susy died from spinal meningitis on August 18, 1896, while staying in the family's HARTFORD home. Her death was a blow from which neither parent ever fully recovered, and it ensured the family would never again live in Hartford.

Cleveland, Grover (1837–1908). President of the United States (1885–1889, 1893–1897) whose 1884 election Clemens supported as a MUGWUMP. Clemens met Cleveland when the latter was governor of New York in 1884 and later conferred with him in the White House about copyright law.

corn-dodger. Small baked or fried cornmeal cake.

Crane, Susan Langdon (1836–1924). Clemens's sister-in-law, the "Aunt Susy" of Susy CLEMENS's manuscript. The adopted daughter of Olivia and Jervis LANGDON, Crane inherited QUARRY FARM, where Clemens's family spent most of their summers between 1871 and 1889. Her husband, Theodore Crane (1831–1889), had been her father's business manager.

crossing. Location on river where STEAMBOATS shifted from one side to the other to take advantage of different currents.

cub pilot. Unlicensed STEAMBOAT apprentice PILOT.

Cutler, William K. Husband of Ellen Cutler, head of the CARSON CITY Sanitary Ball committee, whom Clemens offended in 1864 by publishing an article in the VIRGINIA CITY TERRITORIAL ENTERPRISE jokingly suggesting that her charity was raising money for an eastern miscegenation society. Cutler's angry response to Clemens led to one of the men challenging the other to a duel. Shortly thereafter, Clemens left NEVADA for SAN FRANCISCO.

cut-off. Place where a river cuts a channel through a neck of land that eventually replaces a bend in the river.

Daggett, Rollin Mallory (1831–1901). NEVADA journalist whom Clemens befriended when both worked for the VIRGINIA CITY TERRITORIAL ENTERPRISE. Daggett later represented NEVADA in the U.S. Congress (1879–1881) and was U.S. minister to the HAWAIIAN ISLANDS (1882–1885).

Daniel (Dan'l), Uncle (born c. 1805). Slave on John QUARLES's FLORIDA, Mo., farm whom Clemens knew as a boy and later used as the model for Jim in *Huckleberry Finn*.

Dawson, John D. (born c. 1812). Clemens's last schoolteacher. A native Scot, Dawson started his HANNIBAL school in 1847 but left for California to prospect for gold two years later.

Dodge, Mary Mapes (1831–1905). Author of *Hans Brinker, or the Silver Skates* (1865) and editor of *St. Nicholas Magazine*, which serialized *Tom Sawyer Abroad* in 1894. She and Clemens had been cordial friends since 1890, but her censorious editing of his story greatly angered him.

Dolby, George (died 1900). English lecture agent who organized two lecture tours in England for Clemens during the early 1870s.

Dutchy. Unidentified HANNIBAL boy who LIFE ON THE MISSISSIPPI says drowned about three weeks after Lem HACKETT—which would have been around September 1847.

Ealer, George (fl. 1850s). Pilot on the STEAMBOAT "PENNSYLVANIA" when Clemens was a CUB PILOT on the boat in 1857–1858. Ealer helped broaden Clemens's literary education and interested him in the Baconian theory of Shakespearean authorship. Ealer was unhurt when the "Pennsylvania" blew up in 1858.

easy water. Slow-moving part of a river near its banks in which STEAMBOATS could navigate upstream more rapidly.

Elmira. New York city near the state's Pennsylvania border in which Clemens's in-laws lived. Clemens married Livy Langdon there in 1870, and he and his family spent most of their summers at his sister-in-law Susan CRANE's nearby QUARRY FARM from 1871 through 1889. He and all the members of his family are buried in the town's Woodlawn Cemetery.

Emerson, Ralph Waldo (1803–1882). New England Transcendental philosopher and poet whom Clemens burlesqued in a speech at WHITTIER's seventieth birthday dinner in 1877. Emerson's hearing was too poor for him to be offended by what Clemens said.

Emperor of Germany. See WILHELM II.

Finn, Jimmy (died 1845). HANNIBAL town drunk during Clemens's youth who was one of the models for Huckleberry Finn's alcoholic father, Pap Finn.

Florida. Missouri village, about forty miles southwest of HANNIBAL, in which Clemens was born in 1835. In 1839, his family relocated to Hannibal, but he spent most of his boyhood summers at his uncle John QUARLES's Florida farm. The house in which he was born is now preserved inside a modern museum near Mark Twain Lake, which was created by the damming of the Salt River in 1983.

G., Dr. See MEREDITH, Dr. Hugh.

Garth, John H. (1837–1899). Childhood friend of Clemens. After graduating from the University of Missouri and living in New York City during the 1860s, Garth returned to HANNIBAL, where he ran the family tobacco business and built up a large estate.

George ("colored butler"). See GRIFFIN, George.

Gilded Age: A Tale of To-day, The (1873). Novel coauthored by Clemens and his HARTFORD neighbor C. D. WARNER. The first eleven chapters of the book are a fictionalized account of how Clemens's family came from eastern Tennessee to Missouri.

Gillis, Jim (c. 1830–1907). Brother of William and Steve GILLIS who began prospecting in California's Tuolumne County in 1849. From December 1864 through February 1865, Clemens stayed with Gillis and a man named Dick Stoker at Tuolumne's JACKASS HILL and dabbled in prospecting. Gillis was a masterful storyteller whose yarns influenced Clemens's later writings.

Gillis, Steve (1838–1918). Printer who befriended Clemens while both worked for the VIRGINIA CITY TERRITORIAL

ENTERPRISE in NEVADA. In 1864, he roomed with Clemens in SAN FRANCISCO. When Clemens went to the mining camp of Gillis's brothers in Tuolumne County in December, Gillis returned to newspaper work in VIRGINIA CITY. Three decades later, he left NEVADA and spent his last years quartz-mining in Tuolumne.

Goodman, Joe (1838–1917). Editor and coproprietor of the VIRGINIA CITY TERRITORIAL ENTERPRISE while Clemens reported for the paper during the early 1860s. By encouraging lively and imaginative writing that need not adhere strictly to facts, Goodman was an important influence in Clemens's development as a writer. After Clemens left the paper in 1864, he and Goodman remained lifelong friends.

Grant, Ulysses S. (1822–1885). Union Army commander at the close of the Civil War and later president of the United States (1869–1877). Clemens first met Grant in 1867 and spoke at an army reunion for Grant in 1879. After he formed his publishing firm, Charles L. Webster & Co., in 1884, he offered Grant a generous royalty agreement to publish his memoirs at a moment when Grant's business failures had left him impoverished.

Gridley, Reuel (1829–1870). Native HANNIBAL resident whom Clemens encountered in NEVADA, where he ran a general store. During the CIVIL WAR, Gridley raised more than $150,000 for a Union soldier relief fund by repeatedly auctioning off the same sack of flour throughout NEVADA, California, and the East Coast.

Griffin, George (died 1897). African-American butler who worked for the Clemens family from 1875 until 1891, when the family went to Europe.

Hackett, Lem. Pseudonym used in LIFE ON THE MISSISSIPPI for Clemens's boyhood friend Clint Levering, who drowned on August 13, 1847 (a *Friday*, not a Sunday, as the book states).

Hannibal. Mississippi River town in northeastern Missouri in which Clemens lived from ages four through seventeen. By 1853, he and everyone in his family had left the town, but he revisited it at least seven times. In May 1882, he spent several days there—a visit described at length in Life on the Mississippi. His last visit occurred twenty years later, when he returned to Missouri to accept an honorary degree at the state university. His family lived in several different houses in Hannibal, always near the river, around Main and Hill streets. The family's two-story house at 206 Hill Street is now preserved as the Mark Twain Boyhood Home. It is maintained by a foundation that also oversees several other historic buildings and two first-class museums honoring Mark Twain's memory. Clemens's Hannibal years left a deep imprint on his consciousness that can be read in his autobiography and his fictional works, especially in *Tom Sawyer* and *Huckleberry Finn*, whose village of St. Petersburg is closely modeled on Hannibal.

Hannibal Courier. Newspaper for which Clemens set type as a boy until around 1851, when he began working for his brother Orion's newspaper.

Hannibal Journal. Newspaper purchased around 1850 by Orion Clemens, who merged it with the *Western Union*, which he already owned. Sam Clemens set type for the paper and occasionally wrote sketches for it until he left Hannibal in mid-1853. His autobiography mistakenly alludes to the paper's being owned by an uncle.

Harris, Joel Chandler (1848–1908). Southern writer famous for his Uncle Remus folk tales written in an African-American dialect that Clemens regarded as masterful. Clemens first met Harris in New Orleans in 1882. He hoped to go on a lecture tour with Harris but found him too bashful to speak in public.

Harte, Bret (1836–1902). Western writer who befriended Clemens in San Francisco during the mid-1860s and helped him develop his writing skills while he was editing the *Overland Monthly*, in which he published some of his own stories, such as "The Luck of Roaring Camp." Clemens credited Harte with making him a professional writer and later collaborated with him on a play, *Ah Sin*, but eventually came to despise him.

Hartford. Capital of Connecticut in which Clemens lived from 1871 until 1891, when he took his family to Europe. Hartford was also home to the AMERICAN PUBLISHING COMPANY, which published Clemens's first major books, and the Colt Arms Factory, in which the protagonist of *A Connecticut Yankee in King Arthur's Court* worked before being transported to sixth-century England. In 1874, Clemens and his wife had a magnificent home built on Hartford's Farmington Avenue. The family never returned to the house after 1891, but it was later restored to its original appearance and is now a public museum honoring Mark Twain.

Hawaiian Islands. Pacific island chain known by outsiders as the Sandwich Islands during Clemens's time. In mid-1866, Clemens spent four months there and wrote twenty-five travel letters to the SACRAMENTO UNION. He later revised portions of them to make up chapters 62–77 of *Roughing It*. After he returned to SAN FRANCISCO from the islands, he discovered his letters had been widely reprinted and there was great public interest in Hawaii. On October 2, 1866, he launched his professional lecturing career with a speech titled "Our Fellow Savages of the Sandwich Islands."

Hay, John (1838–1905). American statesman, diplomat, journalist, and writer who was the U.S. secretary of state during his last years. Hay met Clemens in 1871 and remained his friend through the rest of his life.

Holliday's Hill. See CARDIFF HILL.

Holmes, Oliver Wendell (1809–1894). New England physician and writer whom Clemens burlesqued in a speech at

WHITTIER's seventieth birthday dinner in December 1877. Despite Clemens's embarrassment afterward, Holmes evidently was not offended.

Howells, William Dean (1837–1920). Novelist, critic, and editor who was Clemens's intimate friend and literary adviser. From the time they met in 1869, Howells and Clemens frequently shared ideas about their writing, and Howells used his position as editor of the ATLANTIC MONTHLY to publish Clemens's work and elevate his literary reputation.

hurricane deck. Deck immediately above the boiler deck on a STEAMBOAT.

Innocents Abroad, The (1869). Clemens's first major book, an embellished account of the 1867 QUAKER CITY cruise to Europe and the Holy Land. Adapted from travel letters he wrote to newspapers, the book was his best-selling work during his lifetime and likely the best-selling travel book of the nineteenth century. Its success elevated his national reputation and moved him to abandon journalism in favor of book authorship. Its large sales also set a standard against which he judged the success of his later books.

Is Shakespeare Dead? (1909). The last book Clemens published during his lifetime, this brief volume argues that William SHAKESPEARE could not have written all the plays credited to him and contrasts what is known about Shakespeare's life with what is known about Clemens's own life.

Italy. European country to which Clemens paid extended visits in 1867, 1878, 1892–1893, and 1903–1904. His wife, Livy, died near Florence on June 5, 1904, after being taken there in the hope her fragile health would improve.

Jackass Hill. Also known as Jackass Gulch, a mining camp in California's Tuolumne County where Clemens prospected several months in 1864–1865 with Jim GILLIS and Dick Stoker. A replica of the cabin in which he stayed has been a tourist attraction on the site since 1922.

Jamestown. Eastern Tennessee town in which Clemens's family lived from about 1827 to about 1831. Three of his siblings were born there, but his autobiography errs in including among them his oldest brother, Orion CLEMENS, who was born in Gainesboro, Tenn. The sibling whom Clemens omitted was Pleasant Clemens, who died a few months after being born in 1828 or 1829.

jumping frog story. Sketch about a mining camp gambler that Clemens published in the SATURDAY PRESS in 1865. After first appearing as "Jim Smiley and His Jumping Frog," it was later republished as "The Notorious Jumping Frog of Calaveras County," and then as "The Celebrated Jumping Frog of Calaveras County."

Keokuk. Southeastern Iowa town in which Clemens and other members of his family lived after leaving HANNIBAL. During the mid-1850s, Clemens worked in his brother Orion CLEMENS's Keokuk printing shop. According to his autobiography, he found a fifty-dollar bill blowing through the town during the winter of 1856–1857 and used the money to go to CINCINNATI, where he began a brief career as an itinerant printer. In 1872, Orion settled permanently in Keokuk, which was his wife's hometown. During the mid-1880s, Orion and Sam's mother settled there, too.

Klinefelter, John S. (1810–1885). Captain of the STEAMBOAT "PENNSYLVANIA" when Clemens served aboard the boat as an apprentice pilot. Klinefelter was unhurt when the boat's boilers blew up in June 1858.

"Lacey" (steamboat). See "ALFRED T. LACEY."

Lampton, James J. (1817–1887). Cousin of Clemens's mother, Jane Lampton CLEMENS. An irrepressible optimist who constantly planned grandiose business schemes, Lampton was the model for Colonel SELLERS in THE GILDED AGE.

Langdon, Jervis (1809–1870). Clemens's father-in-law, a prosperous ELMIRA businessman. Langdon lent Clemens money enabling him to buy an interest in the *Buffalo Express* in 1869, and he gave Clemens and his daughter a fine house in BUFFALO when they married the following year. Afterward, his health rapidly declined, and he died of stomach cancer on August 6, 1870. His widow, Olivia L. Langdon, lived until 1890.

Langdon, Olivia. See CLEMENS, Livy.

larboard. Left, or port, side of a vessel when facing forward, toward the bow.

lead line. Sounding line cast from vessels to measure the depth of rivers and inland waterways.

leadsman. Steamboatman who casts the LEAD LINE and calls out water depths.

Leary, Katy (1856–1934). Servant who worked for Clemens's family from 1880 until 1910 and was present at almost every major event in their lives.

Life on the Mississippi **(1883).** Travel book comprising three distinct parts: Three chapters on the history of the MISSISSIPPI RIVER; eighteen chapters on Clemens's cub piloting experiences expanding on the "OLD TIMES ON THE MISSISSIPPI" articles he published in the ATLANTIC MONTHLY in 1875; and thirty-eight chapters chronicling his return visit to the river in 1882.

Longfellow, Henry Wadsworth (1807–1882). New England poet whom Clemens burlesqued in a speech at WHITTIER's seventieth birthday dinner in December 1877. Clemens afterward apologized to Longfellow, who assured him he had not been offended.

McAleer, Patrick (1846–1906). Coachman who worked for Clemens from 1870 to 1891 and again in 1905. Clemens remembered him as a perfect employee and unfailing gentleman.

"Mark Twain." Pen name Clemens adopted on February 3, 1863, while writing for the VIRGINIA CITY TERRITORIAL ENTERPRISE and later signed on all his published work. The name comes from a nautical expression indicating a depth of two fathoms (twelve feet) that LEADSMEN call out while sounding rivers.

Mayo, Frank (1839–1896). Stage name of Frank McGuire, an actor noted for playing robust characters. During the 1890s, he played the lead role in a touring production of *Pudd'nhead Wilson*, which he dramatized himself.

Meredith, Dr. Hugh (1806–1864). "Dr. G." in the autobiography, the Clemens family physician in both FLORIDA and HANNIBAL, MO., and a close friend and business associate of John M. CLEMENS.

minstrel show. See NIGGER-SHOW.

Mississippi River. Clemens spent most of his early years near the Mississippi River. During his seventeen years in HANNIBAL, his family resided within a few hundred yards of the river. He later resided in other river towns—ST. LOUIS, KEOKUK, and MUSCATINE, Iowa. From 1857 through early 1861, he piloted STEAMBOATS between St. Louis and New Orleans. After going west in 1861, he revisited the Mississippi River several times, including a prolonged trip on the river in 1882. In addition to LIFE ON THE MISSISSIPPI, the river figures prominently in THE GILDED AGE (1873), TOM SAWYER (1876), *Huckleberry Finn* (1884), *Pudd'nhead Wilson* (1894), and *Tom Sawyer, Detective* (1896).

Moffett, Pamela Clemens (1827–1904). Clemens's sister and the model for Tom Sawyer's cousin Mary. Pamela (pronounced pah-MEE-lah) married William A. Moffett, a merchant, and settled in ST. LOUIS in 1851. After her husband died in 1865, she lived with her mother, Jane Lampton CLEMENS, in ST. LOUIS and later in Fredonia, N.Y. She corresponded regularly with Sam throughout her life. She is the only child of Jane and John M. CLEMENS with direct descendants still living in the twenty-first century.

Moffett, Samuel Erasmus (1860–1908). Clemens's nephew, the son of Pamela Clemens MOFFETT. Clemens greatly admired Moffett's character and intellect and was deeply shocked when Moffett drowned in a swimming accident in 1908.

Monday Evening Club. Twenty-member discussion group formed in HARTFORD in 1869. After becoming a member in 1873, Clemens presented about one paper per year through the 1880s.

mud-cat. Type of MISSISSIPPI RIVER catfish held in low esteem for eating because of its muddy flavor.

mud clerk. Unpaid apprentice clerk, or assistant purser, on a STEAMBOAT.

mugwumps. Nickname for disaffected Republican Party members who supported reform candidates in the 1884, 1888, and 1892 presidential elections.

Muscatine. Southeastern Iowa town in which Clemens briefly resided in 1854, while his brother Orion CLEMENS published a local newspaper there.

Nasby, Petroleum V. (1833–1888). Pseudonym of political satirist David Ross Locke, a popular lecturer whom Clemens admired. The two men met in HARTFORD around 1868 or 1869 and remained casual friends through later years.

Nash, Thomas S. (born c. 1835). Boyhood friend of Clemens, whose autobiography recalls how Nash contracted scarlet fever after falling into the icy MISSISSIPPI RIVER. Clemens fictionalized the incident in *No. 44, The Mysterious Stranger*, an unfinished story that was posthumously published in 1982.

Nast, Thomas (1840–1902). Editorial cartoonist famous for his *Harper's Weekly* cartoons pillorying Boss Tweed's New York City political machine during the 1870s. Clemens and Nast met during the 1860s and made several unsuccessful efforts to mount a joint lecture tour. Meanwhile, Nast playfully lampooned Clemens in several cartoons.

Nevada. Western state in which it may be said that "MARK TWAIN" was born. When the federal government separated Nevada from Utah to make it an autonomous territory in 1861, Orion CLEMENS became the new government's secretary, and Sam Clemens went west with him to serve in mid-1861. About a month after reaching CARSON CITY, Sam turned to prospecting for silver and accumulating mining claims. After those enterprises failed, he began reporting for the VIRGINIA CITY TERRITORIAL ENTERPRISE in September 1862. He started signing "MARK TWAIN" to articles the following February and remained in VIRGINIA CITY until May 1864. His autobiography touches on this period of his life, which he more fully describes—and embellishes—in *Roughing It* (1872).

nigger-show. Clemens's term for African-American minstrel shows, which were among his favorite forms of entertainment.

North American Review. Weekly New York magazine that published "Chapters from My Autobiography" in twenty-five installments from September 1906 through December 1907. George Harvey (1864–1928) edited the magazine from 1899 to 1926 and personally selected most of the autobiographical material used in the magazine. Between 1894 and 1905, Clemens also published a dozen other pieces in the magazine, including some of his strongest anti-imperialist essays.

Nye, James Warren (1815–1876). New York government official who served as the first governor of Nevada Territory (1861–1864) and, along with William M. Stewart (1827–1909), was elected to represent NEVADA in the U.S. Senate after it became a state in late 1864. During Nye's frequent and long absences from NEVADA, Orion CLEMENS served as acting governor.

"Old Times on the Mississippi." Seven-article series published in the January–June and August 1875 issues of the ATLANTIC MONTHLY and later expanded in LIFE ON THE MISSISSIPPI (1883). Clemens's autobiographical dictations repeatedly confuse the titles of the magazine series with his book's title— possibly because of a pirated book edition. His articles were widely reprinted in American newspapers and were also collected in an unauthorized book titled *Old Times on the Mississippi* (1876), issued by a pirate Canadian firm. When Clemens wrote LIFE ON THE MISSISSIPPI, he lightly revised the original magazine articles, making them chapters 4–17 of his book, and added five more chapters, including one covering his two years as a licensed pilot in a single terse paragraph. Textual differences between the "Old Times" articles and the LIFE ON THE MISSISSIPPI chapters are minor. In addition to rewording several dozen sentences, Clemens spelled out names he had originally rendered as initials, such as "Mr. Bixby" for "Mr. B." and "George Ealer" for "George E." Initials he did not spell out include "Mr. W." (Strother WILEY), "Tom G.," "Mr. X.," and "Captain Y." (possibly Captain Patrick Yore), none of whom has been confidently identified.

Oxford University. Venerable English institution that awarded Clemens an honorary doctor of laws degree on June 26, 1907 (his autobiographical dictation gives an incorrect date). Other 1907 honorees included British author Rudyard Kipling, English physicist Joseph Norman Lockyer, English art and literary critic Sidney Colvin, French sculptor Auguste Rodin, French composer Camille Saint-Saëns, and William Booth, the English founder of the Salvation Army.

packet. STEAMBOAT that moves passengers, freight, and mail on the same regularly scheduled route.

"Paul Jones." STEAMBOAT on which Clemens traveled from CINCINNATI, Ohio, to New Orleans in February 1857. He met the pilot Horace BIXBY on this boat but returned upriver with Bixby on the "Colonel Crossman"—in contrast to his account in LIFE ON THE MISSISSIPPI. Clemens described the "Paul Jones" as "an ancient tub," but it was actually only two years old when he boarded it.

Peake, Dr. William Humphrey (born 1775?). Intimate friend of Clemens's father, John M. CLEMENS, and one of HANNIBAL's leading citizens during Clemens's youth.

"Pennsylvania." Four-year-old STEAMBOAT on which Clemens was an apprentice pilot in late 1857 and again in early 1858. After an altercation with PILOT William BROWN, Clemens left the boat, whose boilers exploded near Memphis on June 13. His brother Henry CLEMENS died from injuries received in that accident.

Phelps, William Walter (1839–1894). U.S. ambassador to Germany (1889–1893) with whom Clemens frequently socialized while he was staying in Berlin during late 1891 and early 1892.

Philadelphia. Pennsylvania city in which Clemens spent a total of almost five months in late 1853 and in early 1854. During each stay, he set type for newspapers, including the *Pennsylvania Inquirer and National Gazette*.

"Pier No. 70." Term in headnotes to "Chapters from My Autobiography" alluding to Clemens's age. He saw seventy as the "scriptural age" because of the phrase "The days of our years are threescore years and ten" in Psalms 90:10.

pilot-house. Glass-enclosed structure on the top deck of a STEAMBOAT from which PILOTS steer the vessel.

pilots. STEAMBOAT crew members responsible for steering boats through rivers. Clemens himself was a licensed pilot on the Lower Mississippi during the late 1850s. During his time, piloting was a highly skilled profession that required strong nerves, excellent judgment, and intimate knowledge of the constantly changing conditions along river courses. Such was the importance of pilots that in matters of navigation, their authority was greater than that of their captains. Clemens provided a rich account of what pilots needed to learn in "OLD TIMES ON THE MISSISSIPPI" and in LIFE ON THE MISSISSIPPI.

Plasmon. Powdered food supplement derived from skim milk in which Clemens began investing heavily around 1900. By 1909, the venture collapsed and Clemens lost his entire investment.

Pond, James B. (1838–1903). Lecture agent who managed Clemens's 1884–1885 tour with G. W. CABLE and the first leg of Clemens's around-the-world lecture tour, on which he accompanied Clemens across North America in 1895.

Prince and the Pauper, The (1881). Historical novel in which a pauper boy and Crown Prince Edward of England accidentally change places, and the pauper becomes king when Henry VIII dies. Clemens's daughters loved the story and staged dramatic adaptations of it in their home.

Quaker City. Steamship on which Clemens toured the Mediterranean Sea in an organized excursion in late 1867. With his passage paid by the SAN FRANCISCO ALTA CALIFORNIA, he earned his keep by writing a series of travel letters for the newspaper during the voyage. Those letters and a few he wrote to other newspapers were widely reprinted throughout North America, and he returned home to discover he was a national celebrity. He enhanced his reputation by lecturing on his trip and later adapted his letters to his first major book, THE INNOCENTS ABROAD.

Quarles, John Adams (1802–1876). Brother-in-law of Clemens's mother, Jane Lampton CLEMENS, whose sister Patsy

Lampton he married. After achieving modest prosperity as a farmer and shopkeeper in FLORIDA, Mo., during the mid-1830s, Quarles persuaded John M. CLEMENS to bring his family there. The Clemens family moved to HANNIBAL in 1839 but continued to spend their summers on the Quarles farm, where Sam Clemens became intimately acquainted with his uncle's African-American slaves. Clemens later used the Quarles farm in his fiction—most notably as the Phelps farm in *Huckleberry Finn*. He also modeled that novel's Jim on Quarles's slave Uncle DANIEL. In 2011, a project to reconstruct the buildings of the farm on their original sites was well under way.

Quarry Farm. Property overlooking ELMIRA owned by Clemens's sister-in-law Susan Langdon CRANE. Between 1871 and 1889, Clemens's family spent most of their summers at the farm, and Clemens did much of his most important writing there in a study Crane had built for him. The study now stands on the campus of Elmira College, which also owns the farmhouse.

Raymond, John T. (1836–1887). Stage name of comic actor John O'Brien, who began playing Colonel SELLERS in the first dramatic adaptation of THE GILDED AGE in 1874. After Clemens had Raymond's unauthorized production stopped, he adapted its script to a new play titled *Colonel Sellers*, with which Raymond toured for twelve years.

Redpath, James (1833–1891). Lecture promoter who founded the Boston Lyceum Bureau in 1869 to put lecture touring on a more professional basis. He signed Clemens to two several-month tours, in 1869–1870 and in 1871–1872. He later sold his company to James B. POND.

Reid, Whitelaw (1837–1912). Journalist who succeeded Horace Greeley as editor of the *New York Tribune* in 1872 and held that post until 1905. Reid was U.S. ambassador to Great Britain when Clemens visited England in 1907 to accept an honorary OXFORD UNIVERSITY degree and used the occasion to host a dinner in Clemens's honor in London. The following year, Clemens spoke at a dinner in Reid's honor in New York.

Remus, Uncle. See HARRIS, Joel Chandler.

Ritchie, George. STEAMBOAT pilot with whom Clemens apprenticed on the PENNSYLVANIA, whose 1858 explosion Ritchie survived. Ritchie later survived another steamboat explosion in which he was badly injured.

Robards, John Lewis (1838–1925). Boyhood friend of Clemens who later earned a law degree and became a civic leader in HANNIBAL. Clemens saw Robards each time he revisited Hannibal and corresponded with him until at least 1908. After Clemens died, Robards helped arrange for the erection of a monumental statue of Clemens in HANNIBAL.

roustabout. Unskilled deckhand who performed a wide variety of duties on a STEAMBOAT.

Sacramento Union. Influential newspaper published in California's state capital that commissioned Clemens to write twenty-five travel letters from the HAWAIIAN ISLANDS in 1866.

St. Louis. Missouri's biggest city during the nineteenth century and a major MISSISSIPPI RIVER port. Clemens first visited the city when he was about ten and later returned many times. His brother Orion CLEMENS worked as a printer in St. Louis during the 1840s and later made his connection with Edward BATES there. His sister Pamela Clemens MOFFETT lived there during the 1850s and early 1860s, and Sam often stayed with her while working as a printer in the city and while he was piloting STEAMBOATS on the river.

San Francisco. California city in which Clemens lived during the mid-1860s. He first visited San Francisco in May 1863, while vacationing from his newspaper reporting job in VIRGINIA CITY, Nev. During that visit, he got involved in the local literary scene. A year later, he and Steve GILLIS relocated to San Francisco and worked for the SAN FRANCISCO MORNING CALL while rooming together. Clemens left San Francisco at the end of 1866 but returned in April 1868 and spent several months there working on the manuscript of THE INNOCENTS ABROAD with the help of Bret HARTE. After again leaving the city on July 6, he never returned to California.

San Francisco Alta California. Daily newspaper that commissioned Clemens as a roving reporter in 1866 and paid his fare on the following year's QUAKER CITY excursion, in return for travel letters Clemens wrote during the voyage. Before adapting the *Alta* letters to THE INNOCENTS ABROAD (1869), Clemens had to settle a dispute with Noah Brooks (1830–1903) and other *Alta* editors who wanted to publish their own book from the letters. When he returned to SAN FRANCISCO in 1868, he persuaded the editors to waive their interest in his letters. The dispute embittered him toward the newspaper, but he afterward wrote another dozen travel letters for the paper from the eastern United States.

San Francisco Morning Call. Newspaper for which Clemens worked as a reporter from June to October 1864. In contrast to his previous experience with the VIRGINIA CITY TERRITORIAL ENTERPRISE, the *Call* made no use of his creative writing talent, and his experience with the paper was mostly unpleasant.

Sandwich Islands. See HAWAIIAN ISLANDS.

Saturday Press. Weekly New York magazine edited by Henry Clapp (1814–1875) that published Clemens's JUMPING FROG STORY in its November 18, 1865, issue after book publisher George CARLETON rejected it for a collection of sketches edited by Artemus WARD. The story was a great success, but the magazine itself never published another issue, and Clemens later credited his story with having killed the magazine.

Sellers, Colonel. Flamboyant character in THE GILDED AGE whose chief traits are generosity and unbridled confidence in grandiose schemes, although they usually come to nothing. His most characteristic remark is "There's millions in it!" Clemens modeled Sellers closely on his mother's cousin James LAMPTON. He later made Sellers the central character in *The American Claimant* (1892), in which Sellers—like Lampton—claims to be the rightful holder of an English earldom. After *The Gilded Age* came out, actor John T. RAYMOND portrayed Sellers in a dramatic adaptation of the novel that he soon renamed *Colonel Sellers*.

Shakespeare, William (1564–1616). English playwright with whose work Clemens was familiar from an early age. Clemens's writings are filled with references and allusions to Shakespeare. The last book he published during his lifetime was IS SHAKESPEARE DEAD?

shoal water. Shallow water.

slack water. Slowest-moving river water.

Smarr, Samuel (c. 1788–1845). Missouri cattleman who was murdered in HANNIBAL by a local merchant. Clemens saw Smarr die inside a drugstore and later fictionalized the man's death in *Huckleberry Finn*, in which a man named Boggs is murdered.

sounding. Measuring the depth of water in a river.

Spaulding, Clara (1849–1936). Native of ELMIRA who was a lifelong friend of Livy CLEMENS. Known to the Clemens children as "Aunt Clara," she accompanied the Clemens family to Europe in 1878–1879. In 1886, she married ELMIRA's mayor, John B. Stanchfield (1855–1921).

Stanchfield, Mrs. John B. See SPAULDING, CLARA.

starboard. Right side of a vessel when looking toward the bow.

steamboats. Between February 1857 and May 1861, Clemens piloted at least eighteen different steamboats, only a few of which he mentions by name in his autobiographical writings. Steamboats appear in many of his fictional works but usually only briefly. The lengthiest descriptions of them in his novels occur in THE GILDED AGE, a deleted passage in *Pudd'nhead Wilson*, and *Huckleberry Finn*'s passage about the wrecked *Walter Scott*.

Stevenson, Robert Louis (1850–1894). Scottish author of *Treasure Island* (1883), *Kidnapped* (1886), and *The Strange Case of Dr. Jekyll and Mr. Hyde* (1886)—which fascinated Clemens. Stevenson and Clemens met in a New York City park in April 1888.

stile. Steps built over rural fences in place of gates.

Stockton, Frank R. (1834–1902). Prolific fiction writer and an editor of Mary Mapes DODGE's *St. Nicholas Magazine*.

Stoddard, Charles Warren (1843–1909). Poet and travel writer whom Clemens met in SAN FRANCISCO during the mid-1860s. Afterward, they remained friends and went to England together in late 1873.

Stowe, Harriet Beecher (1811–1896). Author of *Uncle Tom's Cabin* (1852), who was Clemens's next-door neighbor in HARTFORD.

Tennessee land. During the 1820s and 1830s, John M. CLEMENS bought large tracts of land in eastern Tennessee's Fentress County that he bequeathed to his family to guarantee their future prosperity. However, thanks to his son Orion CLEMENS's poor management, the land brought only what Sam Clemens called the "curse" of beginning life prospectively rich. Clemens did make profitable use of the land in THE GILDED AGE, in which the lives of family members modeled on his own are ruined by their frustrated hopes of profiting from the "Tennessee land" left by their father. Clemens's estimates that the land covered more than seventy thousand acres appear to be wildly exaggerated. The actual total may have been fewer than twenty thousand acres.

Territorial Enterprise. See VIRGINIA CITY TERRITORIAL ENTERPRISE.

texas deck. Part of a STEAMBOAT housing the officers' cabins—typically directly below the PILOT-HOUSE.

Tichborne Claimant. Subject of a highly publicized legal case in England in which an Australian named Thomas Castro claimed to be the missing heir of an aristocratic family. His claim was denied in a long trial that ended in early 1872. A year later, Castro was tried for perjury in another long trial. He was sentenced to prison after he was proven to be an Englishman named Arthur Orton. Clemens attended Castro/Orton's trial in June 1873 and had C. W. STODDARD clip newspaper accounts of the case. Years later, Orton confessed his imposture. Clemens discusses him in *Following the Equator* (1897) and *Is Shakespeare Dead?* (1909).

Tom Sawyer, The Adventures of (1876). First novel Clemens wrote on his own and arguably his most autobiographical work of long fiction. Set in a town closely modeled on HANNIBAL, the novel integrates incidents from Clemens's boyhood into the story of an ordinary boy living in Missouri during the 1840s.

Tom Sawyer, Detective (1896). Novella that returns Tom and Huck to the Phelps farm in Arkansas that they had visited in *Huckleberry Finn*.

towhead. Low-lying river island.

Tramp Abroad, A (1880). Clemens's account of the first part of his 1878–1879 visit to Europe. The book focuses mostly on

Germany and Switzerland, with briefer attention to France and northern Italy.

Twichell, Joseph Hopkins (1838–1918). Congregationalist minister who spent his entire career in HARTFORD's Asylum Hill church. He and Clemens met in 1868 and became life-long friends. Although Clemens never formally joined Twichell's church, he attended its services regularly. Twichell officiated at Clemens's wedding and at the funerals of most members of Clemens's family, including Clemens himself. Twichell played an influential role in Clemens's writing work, including "OLD TIMES ON THE MISSISSIPPI," which he encouraged Clemens to write.

Vassar College. Women's college in Poughkeepsie, N.Y., at which Clemens spoke on the college's Founders' Day on May 1, 1885. The college became coeducational in 1969.

Vienna. Capital of Austria, in which Clemens and his family resided from late September 1897 through May 1899.

Virginia City. Western NEVADA boom town in which Clemens worked as a reporter during the early 1860s. *Roughing It* (1872) offers a vivid and highly embellished account of his experiences there during the mining town's "flush times." Clemens left Virginia City for SAN FRANCISCO in mid-1864 but returned there to lecture in October 1866 and May 1868. Modern Virginia City is primarily a tourist destination.

Virginia City Territorial Enterprise. Daily newspaper for which Clemens reported from September 1862 to May 1864. After relocating to SAN FRANCISCO, he served as the *Enterprise*'s Pacific coast correspondent for another year. Writing for the paper was an important phase in his development as a writer. Under Joe GOODMAN's tutelage, he developed a lively and fearless style. In February 1863, he used the pen name "MARK TWAIN" for the first time, in a report on the territorial legislature he wrote for the *Enterprise*. The *Territorial*

Enterprise office building now standing in VIRGINIA CITY houses a Mark Twain museum containing relics said to be from Clemens's days as a reporter. However, the museum's claim that Clemens worked in that building is misleading. The present building was erected in 1876—eight years after Clemens left Virginia City for the last time.

W., Mr. See WILEY, Strother.

Ward, Artemus (1834–1867). Pseudonym of humorist Charles Farrar Browne, whom Clemens befriended in NEVADA in late 1863. Although their acquaintance was brief, Ward played an important role in encouraging Clemens's writing, and his great success as a lecturer helped motivate Clemens later to take up lecturing himself.

Warner, Charles Dudley (1829–1900). Journalist, author, and HARTFORD neighbor of Clemens. Responding to their wives' challenge to write a novel better than those currently being published, Warner and Clemens coauthored THE GILDED AGE (1873), which was the first novel for both of them.

Washington, D.C. National capital, which Clemens first visited in 1854. In late 1867, he returned to the city as private secretary to NEVADA senator William M. Stewart. Repelled by the political corruption he observed, he left Washington early the following year and afterward often wrote disparagingly about the city, most notably in THE GILDED AGE.

Webb, Charles Henry (1834–1905). Writer and editor whom Clemens first met in NEVADA in 1863 before Webb began editing SAN FRANCISCO literary magazines that published some of Clemens's sketches. Webb later returned to New York, where he published Clemens's first book, *The Celebrated Jumping Frog of Calaveras County and Other Sketches*, in 1867, after G. W. CARLETON turned it down. Clemens later soured on Webb.

Whitmore, Franklin Gray (1846–1926). Clemens's business agent in HARTFORD from around 1887 until 1903.

Whittier, John Greenleaf (1807–1892). New England journalist and poet at whose seventieth birthday dinner in December 1877 Clemens delivered a speech burlesquing EMERSON, LONGFELLOW, and HOLMES that afterward caused him considerable embarrassment.

Wiley, Strother. The "Mr. W." of LIFE ON THE MISSISSIPPI, Wiley was a STEAMBOAT pilot whom Clemens knew on two boats during the late 1850s.

Wilhelm II (1859–1941). Emperor of Germany to whom Clemens's autobiography alludes. On February 20, 1892, Clemens attended a private banquet in Berlin at which he met Wilhelm, who told him LIFE ON THE MISSISSIPPI was his favorite American book.

Wolfe, Jim (born c. 1833). Young print shop assistant who lodged with Clemens's family in HANNIBAL during the early 1850s.

yawl. Small rowboat attached to a STEAMBOAT. Often used for SOUNDING a river.

Youth. Affectionate nickname that Clemens's wife, Livy, often used for him.

THE STORY OF PENGUIN CLASSICS

Before 1946 . . . "Classics" are mainly the domain of academics and students; readable editions for everyone else are almost unheard of. This all changes when a little-known classicist, E. V. Rieu, presents Penguin founder Allen Lane with the translation of Homer's *Odyssey* that he has been working on in his spare time.

1946 Penguin Classics debuts with *The Odyssey,* which promptly sells three million copies. Suddenly, classics are no longer for the privileged few.

1950s Rieu, now series editor, turns to professional writers for the best modern, readable translations, including Dorothy L. Sayers's *Inferno* and Robert Graves's unexpurgated *Twelve Caesars.*

1960s The Classics are given the distinctive black covers that have remained a constant throughout the life of the series. Rieu retires in 1964, hailing the Penguin Classics list as "the greatest educative force of the twentieth century."

1970s A new generation of translators swells the Penguin Classics ranks, introducing readers of English to classics of world literature from more than twenty languages. The list grows to encompass more history, philosophy, science, religion, and politics.

1980s The Penguin American Library launches with titles such as *Uncle Tom's Cabin* and joins forces with Penguin Classics to provide the most comprehensive library of world literature available from any paperback publisher.

1990s The launch of Penguin Audiobooks brings the classics to a listening audience for the first time, and in 1999 the worldwide launch of the Penguin Classics Web site extends their reach to the global online community.

The 21st Century Penguin Classics are completely redesigned for the first time in nearly twenty years. This world-famous series now consists of more than 1,300 titles, making the widest range of the best books ever written available to millions—and constantly redefining what makes a "classic."

The Odyssey continues . . .

The best books ever written

PENGUIN CLASSICS

SINCE 1946

CLICK ON A CLASSIC
www.penguinclassics.com

The world's greatest literature at your fingertips

Constantly updated information on more than a thousand titles,
from Icelandic sagas to ancient Indian epics, Russian drama to
Italian romance, American greats to African masterpieces

•

The latest news on recent additions to the list, updated
editions, and specially commissioned translations

•

Original essays by leading writers

•

A wealth of background material, including biographies
of every classic author from Aristotle to Zamyatin, plot
synopses, readers' and teachers' guides, useful Web links

•

Online desk and examination copy assistance for academics

•

Trivia quizzes, competitions, giveaways, news on
forthcoming screen adaptations